East Asian Security

International Security Readers

Strategy and Nuclear Deterrence (1984)

Military Strategy and the Origins of the First World War (1985)

Conventional Forces and American Defense Policy (1986)

The Star Wars Controversy (1986)

Naval Strategy and National Security (1988)

Military Strategy and the Origins of the First World War, revised and expanded edition (1991)

—published by Princeton University Press

Soviet Military Policy (1989)

Conventional Forces and American Defense Policy, revised edition (1989)

Nuclear Diplomacy and Crisis Management (1990)

The Cold War and After: Prospects for Peace (1991)

America's Strategy in a Changing World (1992)

The Cold War and After: Prospects for Peace, expanded edition (1993)

Global Dangers: Changing Dimensions of International Security (1995)

The Perils of Anarchy: Contemporary Realism and International Security (1995)

Debating the Democratic Peace (1996)

East Asian Security (1996)

—published by The MIT Press

East Asian Security

AN *International Security* READER

EDITED BY
Michael E. Brown
Sean M. Lynn-Jones
and Steven E. Miller

THE MIT PRESS
CAMBRIDGE, MASSACHUSETTS
LONDON, ENGLAND

The contents of this book were first published in International Security (ISSN 0162-2889), a publication of The MIT Press under the sponsorship of the Center for Science and International Affairs at Harvard University.

Aaron L. Friedberg, "Ripe for Rivalry: Prospects for Peace in a Multipolar Asia," 18:3 (Winter 1993/94); Richard K. Betts, "Wealth, Power, and Instability: East Asia and the United States after the Cold War," 18:3 (Winter 1993/94); Desmond Ball, "Arms and Affluence: Military Acquisitions in the Asia-Pacific Region," 18:3 (Winter 1993/94); Denny Roy, "Hegemon on the Horizon? China's Threat to East Asian Security" 19:1 (Summer 1994); Michael G. Gallagher, "China's Illusory Threat to the South China Sea," 19:1 (Summer 1994); Gerald Segal, "East Asia and the 'Constrainment' of China," 20:4 (Spring 1996); Alastair Iain Johnston, "China's New 'Old Thinking': The Concept of Limited Deterrence," 20:3 (Winter 1995/96); Banning N. Garrett and Bonnie S. Glaser, "Chinese Perspectives on Nuclear Arms Control," 20:3 (Winter 1995/96); Peter J. Katzenstein and Nobuo Okawara, "Japan's National Security: Structures, Norms, and Policies," 17:4 (Spring 1993); Thomas U. Berger, "From Sword to Chrysanthemum: Japan's Culture of Anti-Militarism," 17:4 (Spring 1993); Saburo Ienaga, "The Glorification of War in Japanese Education," 18:3 (Winter 1993/94).

Library of Congress Cataloging-in-Publication Data
East Asian security / edited by Michael E. Brown, Sean M. Lynn-Jones, and Steven E. Miller.
p. cm.
An international security reader
Includes bibliographical references.
ISBN 0-262-52220-9 (pbk. : alk. paper)
1. National security—East Asia. 2. Political stability—East Asia. 3. East Asia—Economic conditions I. Brown, Michael E. (Michael Edward), 1954– . II. Lynn-Jones, Sean M. III. Miller, Steven E. IV. Series.
UA832.5.E36 1996
355'.03305—dc20 96-6329
CIP

Contents

The Contributors

MICHAEL E. BROWN is Managing Editor of *International Security* and Associate Director of the International Security Program at the Center for Science and International Affairs, Harvard University.

SEAN M. LYNN-JONES is Editor of *International Security* and Research Associate at the Center for Science and International Affairs, Harvard University.

STEVEN E. MILLER is Editor-in-Chief of *International Security* and Director of the International Security Program at the Center for Science and International Affairs, Harvard University.

AARON L. FRIEDBERG is Associate Professor of Politics and International Affairs at Princeton University and Director of the Research Program in International Security at Princeton's Center of International Studies.

RICHARD K. BETTS is Professor of Political Science, Director of International Security Policy Studies in the School of International and Public Affairs, and member of the Institute of War and Peace Studies at Columbia University.

DESMOND BALL is a Professor in the Strategic and Defence Studies Centre, Australian National University, Canberra.

DENNY ROY is Research Fellow in North-East Asian Security Studies at the Strategic and Defence Studies Centre, Australian National University, Canberra.

MICHAEL G. GALLAGHER taught in Miami at the University of Miami and Florida International University. He currently resides in San Diego, California.

GERALD SEGAL is Senior Fellow at the International Institute for Strategic Studies, London.

ALASTAIR IAIN JOHNSTON is Assistant Professor of Government at Harvard University.

BANNING N. GARRETT is a Washington-based consultant on Asian affairs.

BONNIE S. GLASER is a Washington-based consultant on Asian affairs.

PETER J. KATZENSTEIN is the Walter S. Carpenter, Jr., Professor of International Studies at Cornell University.

NOBUO OKAWARA is Associate Professor at Kyushu University.

THOMAS U. BERGER is Assistant Professor of Political Science at the Johns Hopkins University.

SABURO IENAGA was Professor Emeritus of Education at Tokyo University of Education.

Acknowledgments

The editors gratefully acknowledge the assistance that has made this book possible. A deep debt is owed to all those at the Center for Science and International Affairs (CSIA), Harvard University, who have played an editorial role at *International Security*. We are grateful for support from the Carnegie Corporation of New York. Special thanks go to Bridgett Neely, Spring 1996 intern, and Meara E. Keegan at CSIA as well as Katy Stenhouse at the MIT Press for their invaluable help in preparing this volume for publication.

Preface | Sean M. Lynn-Jones

Dramatic changes in East Asia have put the region at the head of the world's strategic agenda.[1] Many analysts claim that the region will be plagued by increasing insecurity; even those who disagree concede that East Asia's security problems have changed. Virtually all observers from the region and outside agree that the rapid economic growth of many East Asian economies has increased the strategic importance of the region. Old foreign and security policies are being reconsidered by Asian and non-Asian countries. The trajectory of change in the region's strategic circumstances and security policies remains unclear.

The changes in the Asia-Pacific region are partly attributable to the end of the Cold War. Even before the collapse of the Soviet Union, Moscow had begun a broad strategic retrenchment in East Asia. Soviet military deployments in the region were scaled back. With the demise of the Soviet Union, the United States became the only superpower with a substantial military presence in the Pacific region. The demise of the Soviet threat, coupled with America's apparent desire to turn inward, soon raised questions about the scope and longevity of the U.S. military commitment in East Asia

More important, however, have been the economic and political changes in East Asia itself. Despite recent setbacks, Japan's five decades of economic growth since World War II have made it the world's second-largest economy. Fluctuations in exchange rates often come close to making it number one. China's sustained double-digit economic growth of the last decade has catapulted it into third place in the global economic standings, behind the United States and Japan. Observers now debate whether China remains a "developing" country. The economic achievements of South Korea, Taiwan, Hong Kong, and Singapore have been at least as spectacular as China's. And Thailand, Indonesia, and Malaysia have seen their economies accelerate in recent years. Not all East Asian countries have joined in this economic boom, but the region as a whole now produces a much larger share of global output.

At the same time that East Asia has boomed economically, there have been gradual political changes in the region. Many countries, especially in Southeast Asia, are no longer plagued by internal conflicts. Some states, such as Burma

1. There is some disagreement over whether the term "East Asian" should be abandoned in favor of "Asia-Pacific." The editors recognize that this is a complicated debate, but choose to use "East Asia" here because this volume focuses on China and Japan, states that clearly can be described as "East Asian." Had this book included more extensive discussions of the roles of Australia, New Zealand, Canada, the United States, and the micro-state of Oceania, it might have been called "Asia-Pacific Security."

(Myanmar), still suffer from domestic instability, but civil wars and insurgences are no longer prevalent. In addition, East Asian countries have become more conscious of their unique Asian identity. Many leaders in the region now emphasize that there is a distinctive Asian approach to political and economic issues. Efforts to promote cooperation among East Asian countries have increased.

The first three essays in this volume present overviews of strategic developments in the Asia-Pacific region. Aaron Friedberg's "Ripe for Rivalry: Prospects for Peace in a Multipolar Asia," argues that Asia is likely to see more international conflict than Europe. Ethnic and civil wars may occasionally flare up in Europe, but "in the long run it is Asia that seems far more likely to be the cockpit of great power conflict."

Friedberg rests his case on the claim that the factors that contribute to international stability in Europe are absent in Asia. First, Asia lacks stable democratic states with relatively equitable internal distributions of wealth and income. Most European states are stable democracies with relatively low social and economic stratification. These factors seem to reduce international conflicts. In Asia, however, there remains a diverse range of types of states, including Stalinist North Korea, Southeast Asia's mix of modernizing and authoritarian governments, the liberal democracies of Australasia, and China's evolving mixture of communism and capitalism. Many Asian states face domestic political and social instability caused by rapid economic changes.

Second, Asian states are less interconnected than their European counterparts. Asia's economies are far less interdependent with one another than are Europe's; much of Asia's trade is with non-Asian countries. There are few strong regional institutions that provide a basis for pan-Asian cooperation. If neo-liberal theorists are right in their claim that international institutions can facilitate international cooperation, Asia's prospects for peace seem bleaker than Europe's.

Third, war may seem to offer more benefits and fewer costs in Asia than in Europe. Nuclear weapons have helped to deter war in Europe, but they are unevenly distributed in Asia. Aggression may still promise economic benefits in Asia. Even if conquest does not pay, motives such as prestige may lead Asian states to use force.

Friedberg concludes by noting that Asia is entering a transitional period of rapid change. This new era may lead to an accelerating arms race and recurrent crises, but Asia's future is by no means certain. Friedberg argues that a continuing U.S. strategic presence in Asia would probably reduce the incentives for regional conflict. He sees no assurance that the United States will follow such a course.

In "Wealth, Power, and Instability: East Asia and the United States after the Cold War," Richard Betts assesses competing liberal and realist visions of East Asia's future. He agrees with Friedberg's assessment that East Asia is becoming less stable. The future distribution of international power in Asia is uncertain and potentially dangerously fluid. Economic liberalization without political democratization may be destabilizing. China, not Japan, threatens to overturn the region's equilibrium. The United States will have to pay a high price to remain the dominant military power in East Asia. Americans may not be willing to pay that price. A trend toward ambiguous U.S. commitments to Taiwan and other Asian allies invites dangerous miscalculations.

Betts puts his analysis in the context of the continuing debate between realist and liberal schools of thought in international relations theory. He notes that each school is itself divided into several variants. Realists argue over whether multipolar, bipolar, or unipolar international systems are the most war-prone. Liberals differ on whether economic liberty (free trade), political liberty (democracy), or international institutions are most important in preventing war. Despite these ambiguities and contradictions, liberalism and realism seem to offer opposite prescriptions for post-Cold War U.S. policy toward East Asia. Realists worry about the rise of new economic powers in East Asia, whereas liberals would remain sanguine if these new great powers were to become liberal democracies. Realists thus call for using U.S. power to, for example, balance against Chinese military power, regardless of China's ideological orientation and domestic politics. Liberals, on the other hand, argue for U.S. efforts to promote liberalization in China.

Betts's analysis of the potential configurations of power in East Asia leads him to make the following recommendations for U.S. policy. First, the United States should prevent any power (other than the United States) from becoming dominant in Asia. Second, this policy should be restrained if a likely Asian hegemon is a liberal democracy. Third, the United States should encourage the growth of international and regional institutions in East Asia. They may help preserve peace; they almost certainly wouldn't hurt. Fourth, the United States should rank the various potential configurations of power in East Asia as follows: (1) a concert of great powers; (2) regional bipolarity pitting Russia against the United States; (3) a multipolar balance that includes the U.S.-Japan alliance; (4) regional dominance by a democratic China, Russia, or Japan;

(5) bipolarity of some combination of local powers; (6) a global coalition to contain a non-democratic Asian hegemon.

Regardless of which scenario emerges, the United States should maintain its military presence in Northeast Asia, improve relations with Vietnam, and plan to provide arms—but not troops—to Taiwan if there is a clash between Taipei and Beijing.

It has become commonplace to claim that the Asia-Pacific region is in the throes of a new arms race. Desmond Ball takes exception to this conventional wisdom. In "Arms and Affluence: Military Acquisitions in the Asia-Pacific Region," he presents a comprehensive overview of the region's military buildup. He argues that there is not yet an arms race, but regional confidence-building measures need to be adopted to head off potential dangers of current weapons acquisition programs.

Ball argues that many of Asia's military acquisitions cannot be explained by military and geostrategic factors. Instead, weapons are purchased and built because economic growth generates more resources for defense, because of the potential for bribes and other forms of corruption in the defense procurement process, because advanced weapons are a source of technology with potential civilian applications, and because arms exporters ply their wares more aggressively now that the end of the Cold War has eliminated some of their lucrative traditional markets. Some countries buy advanced weapons simply for their prestige value. It is also true, however, that many Asian countries prefer to pursue policies of self-reliance, partly because they fear that the drawdown of U.S. forces will increase regional instability and uncertainty.

Most of the military acquisitions in East Asia fall into the following categories: national command, control, and communication systems; national technical intelligence systems; multi-role fighter aircraft; maritime reconnaissance aircraft; modern surface combatants; anti-ship missiles; submarines; electronic warfare capabilities; and rapid deployment forces.

Ball argues that several aspects of East Asia's military build-up are disturbing. Many countries are buying arms in an atmosphere of uncertainty and lack of trust. Some of the weapons (e.g., maritime strike aircraft, warships, anti-ship missiles, and submarines) pose significant offensive threats. Many of them raise the risks of crisis instability. Because there is little prospect of formal arms control agreements that will constrain military acquisition programs, Ball recommends that East Asian countries pursue confidence and security building measures to increase transparency and to institutionalize a regional security dialogue.

The next section of essays examines the future of China's role in the Asia-Pacific region. Many analysts, particularly in the United States, have argued that China's growing power threatens to destabilize the entire region. Some U.S. strategists point to China as the next great threat to American security interests. Denny Roy, in "Hegemon on the Horizon? China's Threat to East Asian Security," argues that China's rising economic strength poses the greatest security challenge in East Asia. China's economy may eclipse Japan's, and China faces fewer constraints on its ability to acquire a massive military arsenal. Beijing's new-found strength will make it more assertive. China may use force to achieve its goals.

According to Roy, China is more likely than Japan to become an Asian hegemon, for two reasons. First, Japan suffers from inherent economic vulnerabilities. It lacks natural resources, its labor force is aging and shrinking, its savings rate is declining, and its corporate capital-to-debt ratio is dangerously unfavorable. Second, Japan is unlikely to become a military superpower. Economic worries will prevent higher defense spending. And most Japanese continue to oppose expanding Japan's armed forces. Japan's "peace constitution" and lingering concerns of Japan's World War II victims in Asia pose large political obstacles to any attempt at remilitarization.

Unlike Japan, China has enormous latent human and natural resources that could be tapped to fuel a bid for Asian hegemony. Its economy, which has enjoyed double-digit growth in recent years, is now the world's third largest. China also may be able to capitalize on economic relations with the entrepreneurial overseas Chinese of Southeast Asia, an advantage not shared by Japan. To realize its potential, China will have to avoid regional fractionalization, privatize state-owned enterprises, control inflation, crack down on rampant corruption, and curb its population growth rate. These obstacles may be surmountable.

China faces fewer barriers to becoming a military superpower than does Japan. China's military potential worries its neighbors less because it has not engaged in aggression on Japan's scale during the twentieth century. China has attempted to reassure its neighbors of its benign intentions. Some, including Malaysia, apparently have been persuaded, although others remain concerned about China's military modernization. However worrisome, China's growing military power seems less threatening than a fully rearmed Japan.

Beijing's rise to power threatens East Asian security in two ways. First, China may be tempted to seek Asian hegemony, resuming its historical role as the "Middle Kingdom." A more prosperous China will not necessarily be a more peaceful China. Because China's government is authoritarian and unstable, it is more likely to use force regardless of public opinion. It may be tempted to embark on hostile overseas adventures to divert attention from domestic problems. In addition, China is a revisionist state—dissatisfied with its position in the existing international system that may use force to right past injustices and to recover former Chinese territory. And no domestic culture of antimilitarism restrains Beijing's leaders.

Second, China's growing power may provoke a Japanese response, leading to a bipolar security competition in Asia. Both countries remember the Pacific War, and view each other's military activities with suspicion. Japan and China continue to compete for influence in Southeast Asia. China's increasing naval presence in that region poses a threat to the sea lanes that are Japan's economic jugular vein.

Roy considers three potential responses that the United States and other Asia-Pacific powers might make to China's challenge. First, they might attempt to isolate China economically and choke off its growth. Such an embargo is politically impossible, however, because many countries would circumvent it. Moreover, economic woes in China might cause a massive refugee exodus and internal instability.

Second, other powers might seek to reduce Beijing's control over China's various regions. China's business partners could seek to enhance the economies and autonomy of China's most dynamic regions. But such a policy would provoke a backlash from Beijing, coupled with a rising tide of Chinese nationalism. Links between Beijing and China's regions might even grow stronger in the face of external attempts to divide China.

Third, policy toward China might rest on continuing attempts to encourage Chinese economic development, combined with incentives for political liberalization. The United States would seek to organize an anti-China coalition only if China engages in threatening behavior.

Michael Gallagher takes a more sanguine view of China's existing military capabilities. In "China's Illusory Threat to the South China Sea" he argues that Chinese defense forces are not yet capable of challenging Beijing's rivals in the South China Sea. The military balance in this area does not clearly favor China.

Gallagher focuses on the dispute between China and several members of the Association of Southeast Asian Nations (ASEAN) over the Spratly Islands in the South China Sea. China, Taiwan, Malaysia, Brunei, Vietnam, and the Philippines have laid claim to some or all of these islands, which are significant because they straddle vital sea lanes and are surrounded by potentially vast oil reserves and fish stocks.

China can deploy much larger forces than its Southeast Asian neighbors, but most ASEAN members have modernized their armed forces in recent years. Singapore, Malaysia, and Indonesia all have acquired sophisticated aircraft and naval vessels. Their main military bases are close to the Spratlys, whereas China's are far away. China lacks the modern aircraft to provide air cover for military operations in the Spratlys. Without air cover, its naval vessels would be vulnerable to the modern anti-ship missiles deployed by several ASEAN states.

China also faces international political constraints on its behavior in the Spratlys. Any aggressive Chinese actions would provoke an anti-Chinese reaction in ASEAN and closer ties between ASEAN members and the United States. ASEAN's growing economic ties with China also may give its members some leverage over Beijing's behavior.

Domestic constraints further reduce the likelihood of aggressive Chinese actions in the South China Sea. Many of China's soldiers may be employed in controlling domestic unrest instead of engaging in international aggression. Fears of internal instability may constrain Beijing's appetite for foreign adventures. Since 1949, China has shown that it prefers to put its "domestic house in order" before going to war.

Gerald Segal's "East Asia and the 'Constrainment' of China" analyzes how East Asia should respond to China's growing power. So far, the debate on this issue has been between proponents of "engagement" and "containment." Segal argues that these categories are inadequate. He suggests that engagement with China is a necessary, but insufficient, first step. China's neighbors and other powers also must defend their interests by constraining China. The question is whether they have the will to adopt such a policy of "constrainment."

Segal contends that China is weaker than it appears at a first glance. Statistics on its territory, population, and economic growth conceal its massive social problems and weak leadership. China's economy depends on continued access to foreign markets and technology. Other East Asian states, particularly Japan, may be able to manage a growing China.

Whatever the objective prospects, Segal sees little evidence that East Asian states have the will to balance against China. East Asia is fragmented. Some countries may tend to lean toward China because they have substantial ethnic Chinese populations. The Koreas view their relations with China through the narrow prism of the issue of their unification. In Northeast Asia, the issue of North Korean nuclear weapons is intimately related to policy toward China. In Southeast Asia, this issue is not salient at all. There are no strong East Asian regional security institutions that might serve as a basis for common policies against China.

Proponents of engagement with China claim that balancing China is unnecessary because China will be restrained by economic interdependence. This school of thought suggests that China's dependence on the international economy will prevent it from becoming too assertive or aggressive toward its neighbors. Segal points out that ASEAN's engagement with China has not prevented Chinese military actions against the Philippines in the Spratly Islands. He suggests that the lesson of these events is that engagement is not sufficient to restrain China. At least some states in East Asia seem to share this conclusion. China did moderate its behavior in the South China Sea in late 1995 after it became clear that other states might begin to balance against it.

Segal concludes that China will pursue a complex and uncertain foreign policy, plagued by internal divisions and invocations of intense nationalism to forge domestic unity. It is not very constrained by economic interdependence, but its behavior probably can be moderated by concerted external pressure. Other states, in East Asia and beyond, will have to maintain such pressure in order for it to be effective.

Despite China's growing military and strategic importance, few analysts have examined contemporary Chinese views on military doctrine. In China's New 'Old Thinking': The Concept of Limited Deterrence, Alastair Iain Johnston attempts to fill this void. He argues that Chinese strategists adhere to a set of concepts called "limited deterrence." This strategy requires tactical theater, and strategic nuclear forces sufficient to deter escalation of conventional or nuclear war. It also requires capabilities to control escalation and compel the enemy to back down should deterrence fail. This nuclear doctrine forms the basis for planned Chinese nuclear forces.

Johnston recounts the history of Chinese attitudes toward nuclear weapons, arguing that since the 1950s Beijing has seen a nuclear arsenal as its ticket to international power and prestige. Recent Chinese thinking, which has produced the concept of "limited deterrence," rests on two assumptions: (1) nuclear weapons have not changed the fundamental nature of war; and (2) deterrence depends on having operationally usable nuclear weapons. Chinese strategists appear uncomfortable with the notion of mutual assured destruction as the basis of nuclear deterrence. Instead, they seem to regard deterrence as the product of robust nuclear war-fighting capabilities.

According to Johnston, Chinese strategists reject both minimum deterrence and what they call "maximum deterrence." They reject minimum deterrence's exclusive emphasis on second-strike capabilities intended to inflict unacceptable damage for two reasons. First, such minimum capabilities might be vulnerable to a disarming first strike. Second, a nuclear arsenal configured for minimum deterrence cannot be used for intrawar deterrence or to prevail in any escalatory competition. Chinese strategists associate "maximum deterrence" with the nuclear doctrines of the United States and the Soviet Union. In their view, the superpowers' doctrines were designed to achieve a first-strike advantage and to support hegemonistic foreign policies. China rejects this approach because of its commitment to a No First Use doctrine and because it lacks the economic and technological capabilities to build this kind of arsenal.

Limited deterrence occupies a middle ground between minimum and maximum deterrence. It calls for striking a wide range of tactical, theater, and strategic military and industrial targets, not just the population centers that would be targeted in a minimum deterrence strategy. These targeting requirements create a need for a large and diverse nuclear arsenal and command and control capabilities.

Johnston notes that the strategy of limited deterrence seems to contradict China's No First Use pledge. China's nuclear strategists appear to be developing a nuclear doctrine that would ultimately lead to the violation or abandonment of that pledge. Some strategists have hinted interest in launch-on-warning or launch-under-attack policies, while others seem to favor preemptive strikes.

Johnston details the military capabilities that China would have to acquire in order to pursue a limited nuclear deterrence strategy. These include space-based early warning capabilities, anti-satellite weapons, ballistic missile defenses, theater and tactical nuclear weapons, and civil defense. China currently lacks these capabilities. Moreover, its ballistic missiles are inaccurate and take two hours to fuel. China's doctrine of limited nuclear deterrence apparently serves as a guide to future military acquisitions.

China's future policies on nuclear weapons may be influenced by Beijing's interactions with the rest of the world. Johnston suggests that intergovernmental and nongovernmental contacts could persuade Chinese strategists to reconsider minimum deterrence. He notes that similar discussions with Soviet scientists and policy analysts may have contributed to Gorbachev's new thinking and the revolution in Soviet military thinking that preceded the end of the

Cold War. This type of engagement might persuade China to embrace the global trend toward delegitimizing the utility of nuclear weapons, instead of heading in the opposite direction.

In "Chinese Perspectives on Nuclear Arms Control," Banning Garrett and Bonnie Glaser examine contemporary Chinese thinking on nuclear arms control. Drawing on interviews that they conducted with the growing community of Chinese civilian analysts and officials, Garrett and Glaser argue that China in the 1980s recognized the benefits of participating in negotiations on arms control. Nevertheless, China has continued to improve its own nuclear arsenal.

China has traditionally held a realpolitik view of the world, believing that all states must pursue their interests through self-help policies. Garrett and Glaser suggest that this traditional view is now being challenged by a nascent perspective of "security interdependence." Some Chinese analysts now recognize that states, including China, can sometimes improve their security through multilateral agreements to reduce mutual threats. This type of thinking has influenced China to support the Nuclear Non-Proliferation Treaty (NPT) after years of opposing it, and to participate in negotiations on a Comprehensive Test Ban Treaty (CTBT). China continues to seek No-First-Use pledges from the other nuclear powers, as well as assurances that they will not use nuclear weapons against non-nuclear states.

Despite the signs of some new thinking and new policies, Garrett and Glaser point out that China has yet to engage in talks on strategic nuclear arms reductions. Beijing has indicated that it will participate in such negotiations in the future, but has neither set any timetable nor specified the conditions necessary for Chinese participation. If the United States and Russia continue to reduce their nuclear arsenals, international pressure may compel China to join in strategic arms talks. China may decide not to participate if other countries deploy missile defenses that would reduce the effectiveness of China's nuclear weapons.

Garrett and Glaser conclude that only a minority of Chinese analysts and officials accept the proposition that security must be mutual; most believe that China need not adjust its military capabilities to reassure other states. China's slow moves toward participation in nuclear arms control regimes reflect its sensitivity to the political costs of potential isolation. Nevertheless, the idea of security interdependence is beginning to play a role in Chinese security policy. Like Johnston, Garrett and Glaser call for an expanded official and unofficial dialogue between U.S. and Chinese strategists and arms controllers.

The final section of essays in this volume considers the likely future security behavior of Japan. Since the end of the Cold War, American impressions of Japan have included many divergent views. Some writers have predicted a second Pacific War between the United States and Japan. Others have declared that Japan already has beaten the United States in a peaceful struggle for power; while the United States exhausted itself competing with the Soviet Union, Japan "won" the Cold War. Some foreign observers have questioned Japan's commitment to democratic values and predicted that Japanese militarism and nationalism will emerge again. In general, the most alarmist views of Japan emerged shortly after the end of the Cold War. More recent interpretations have been more moderate, reflecting increased awareness of Japan's domestic economic and political problems, as well as recognition that China seems more likely to undermine the equilibrium in East Asia. The essays included here reflect these views, but still consider the conditions under which Japan might become a remilitarized or aggressive state.

In "Japan's National Security: Structures, Norms, and Policies," Peter Katzenstein and Nobuo Okawara argue that pessimists are wrong in their belief that Japan is destined to become a nuclear-armed military superpower. They contend that such a security policy is precluded by Japan's domestic structure and social and legal norms. The structure of the Japanese state ensures that civilian leaders will maintain control over the Japanese military.

Katzenstein and Okawara contrast their explanation of Japanese security with the leading contending explanations, and find the alternatives lacking. They argue that explanations that focus on the international distribution of power and the Hobbesian nature of international politics are inferior to their emphasis on domestic structures and norms. These international explanations look solely at the nature of the international system. They lead to inconsistent predictions. Some analysts claim that the regional distribution of power in East Asia has not changed much since the end of the Cold War; thus Japan's security policy will change only incrementally. Others say that a clash between the United States and Japan is now inevitable, because the two countries are destined to be geostrategic rivals. Adding international regimes to the list of important international factors may provide better explanatory power, but this approach still must take into account domestic norms and structures. The international order and international regimes did not change much between the 1920s and 1930s, but Japan's security policy became much more aggressive because of domestic changes within Japan.

Katzenstein and Okawara conclude that there will be no major changes in Japan's security policy. Japan's political structures and anti-militarism will remain in place. Despite an emerging debate, few Japanese want their country to acquire nuclear weapons, to send troops abroad, or to invest in larger military forces. Japan will continue to hold a comprehensive definition of security, with an emphasis on economic as well as military threats. In addition, Japan will maintain a close, if evolving, security relationship with the United States.

Thomas Berger's "From Sword to Chrysanthemum: Japan's Culture of Anti-militarism" argues that Japan will retain its pacifist stance despite the upheaval in the international system during the 1990s. Like Katzenstein and Okawara, Berger rejects arguments that Japan will become a more aggressive military power. He notes that some realist scholars and analysts claim that Japan will inevitably be compelled by systemic imperatives to seek international hegemony. Berger also recognizes that other scholars believe that Japan's nationalistic culture and failure to express guilt over its atrocities during World War II suggest that Japan will return to a militarist policy.

According to Berger, neither school of thought's claims about Japan are supported by the evidence. Japan is not rearming for a new round of military expansion. Japan has a high defense budget, but its high manpower and equipment costs mean that its forces remain relatively small. Its Self Defense Forces are designed to complement and cooperate with U.S. forces in the region. Rising defense spending in the 1980s was intended to reassure the United States that Japan would share military burdens; Japanese defense spending actually declined after the end of the Cold War. Moreover, attempts to increase nationalistic feeling in Japan have encountered sharp domestic opposition. Japanese public opinion has been skeptical of any attempts to send Japanese troops overseas.

Japan's future security policy will remain rooted in Japan's culture of anti-militarism. In the aftermath of Japan's defeat in World War Two, the Japanese people blamed their military for leading the country into disaster. Ruling elites helped to spread this belief to divert attention from their own complicity in Japan's strategic blunders. Although not all Japanese shared exactly the same culture of anti-militarism, there was and is a centrist consensus that favors keeping the Japanese military small and under firm civilian control, maintaining the U.S.-Japan Mutual Security Treaty, and avoiding international military involvements.

Berger calls for some adjustments in Japan's security policy. Japanese anti-militarism should not be allowed to prevent Japan from playing a more active multilateral security role. Instead of relying almost entirely on the United States for its security, Japan should develop a broader network of security ties. Such a policy would reduce American resentment over Japan's perceived unwillingness to share the burden of its own defense, as well as providing Japan additional allies if the United States decides to reduce its commitments in East Asia. In the long run, it might contribute to the emergence of effective regional security institutions in East Asia.

Saburo Ienaga's "The Glorification of War in Japanese Education" reminds us that Japan's previous descent into militarism was fueled by teaching nationalistic history in its schools. Professor Ienaga writes with an authority that comes from his involvement in several landmark lawsuits that challenged Japanese government censorship of his textbooks. Government officials requested that passages critical of Japan's aggressive acts in the Pacific War be removed from textbooks written by Ienaga. He filed suit on the grounds that such actions were violations of constitutional guarantees of free speech and academic freedom.

Ienaga argues that Japan became an aggressor state in the late nineteenth century and continued to be so until 1945. The Japanese educational system inculcated students with chauvinist myths that glorified war and death in battle. This pattern intensified during the 1930s, although earlier textbooks also had taught martial virtues and encouraged students to die for Emperor and country.

Japan's school textbooks and curricula were revamped during the American occupation. But signs of the prewar militarism began to re-emerge during the "reverse course" of the early 1950s, when U.S. policy shifted in an effort to ensure that Japan would become a staunch anti-communist ally. Ienaga optimistically sees "scant possibility of a revival of the militarism that overwhelmed prewar Japan," but he worries over the "increasing promilitary slant in education." This trend, along with Japan's increased defense spending, more public support for overseas military deployments, greater veneration for the Emperor, and other signs of intense patriotism, calls into question Japan's post-1945 commitment to the ideals of peace and democracy.

The essays in this volume do not address every item on the Asia-Pacific security agenda. This book, for example, does not present a detailed analysis of the conflict on the Korean peninsula. No articles herein focus exclusively on the future of the U.S. role in East Asia, which remains a hotly-debated subject.[2]

---

2. See for example, Joseph S. Nye, Jr., "The Case for Deep Engagement," *Foreign Affairs*, Vol. 74, No. 4 (July/August 1995), pp. 90–102; and Chalmers Johnson and E.B. Keehn, "The Pentagon's Ossified Strategy," in ibid., pp. 103–114. See also Robert A. Scalapino, "The US Commitment to Asia," *Journal of Strategic Studies*, Vol. 18, No. 3 (September 1995), pp. 68–83.

And this volume does not examine the important political and economic changes taking place within and between the members of the Association of South-East Asian Nations: Brunei, Indonesia, Malaysia, the Philippines, Thailand, Singapore, and Vietnam.[3] Finally, this book scarcely touches on the potential emergence of regional Asia-Pacific security institutions. At present, attempts to build security regimes for the entire Asia-Pacific region remain embryonic, but such institutions might fundamentally change existing approaches to security in East Asia. Additional articles and books will be necessary to address these topics, as well as the many complex internal security challenges that confront many states in East Asia. Nevertheless, by focusing on East Asia's changing strategic circumstances and, in particular, the possible security policies of China and Japan, the editors of this volume hope to contribute to further analysis and debate on what are certain to be some of the most challenging security issues of the first decades of the twenty-first century.

---

3. See Amitav Acharya, *A New Regional Order in Southeast Asia: ASEAN in the Post-Cold War Era*, Adelphi Paper No. 279 (London: International Institute for Strategic Studies, 1993).

Part I:
East Asian Security After the Cold War

Ripe for Rivalry

Prospects for Peace in a Multipolar Asia

Aaron L. Friedberg

Recent rhetoric notwithstanding, the dominant trend in world politics today is toward regionalization rather than globalization, toward fragmentation rather than unification. The weakening of the liberal economic order and the apparent emergence of embryonic trading blocs is only one indication of this larger tendency. The acceleration of technological progress and the intensification of international economic competition among the most advanced states are rendering large portions of the less developed "periphery" even more peripheral and isolated than they have been in the past. With the end of the Cold War, conflicts in areas where outside powers might once have felt their vital interests to be engaged are now left to proceed uninterrupted.

In strategic terms, bipolarity is giving way, not to unipolarity (with the United States bestriding the world like a colossus) nor yet to simple multipolarity (with a group of roughly equal, globally engaged "great powers"), but to a set of regional subsystems in which clusters of contiguous states interact mainly with one another. This is nothing new. Despite advances in weapons and communications technology, most states have historically been concerned primarily with the capabilities and intentions of their neighbors. Those that could afford to worry about far-flung enemies and to inject themselves into distant conflicts have been the exception rather than the rule. With the end of the superpower rivalry, the collapse of the Soviet empire and, as seems likely, a substantial retraction of American power, these more traditional patterns of strategic interaction (always present, even during the Cold War) will again become dominant.[1]

Aaron L. Friedberg is Associate Professor of Politics and International Affairs at Princeton University and Director of the Research Program in International Security at Princeton's Center of International Studies.

The author wishes to thank Desaix Anderson, Henry Bienen, Thomas Christensen, and Min Xin Pei for their comments and Geoffrey Herrera for research assistance.

1. One recent study concludes similarly that "regional multipolar processes are likely to become a more and more important feature of international politics." Thomas J. Christensen and Jack Snyder, "Predicting Alliance Patterns," *International Organization*, Vol. 44, No. 2 (Spring 1990), p. 168. For another analysis that also foresees a movement toward regionalization see Joseph A. Camilleri, "Alliances in the Emerging Post–Cold War Security System" (unpublished manuscript), March 11, 1992.

International Security, Vol. 18, No. 3 (Winter 1993/94), pp. 5–33

The movement toward "multi-multipolarity" is being propelled by political developments as much as by shifts in the underlying distribution of material resources. In this new and more fragmented world, the United States will still be the single richest and strongest nation (although the size of its economic and military leads will diminish as others grow faster and as the United States reduces its armed forces), but it will be less inclined to project its power into every corner of the globe. Meanwhile, other nations will become more capable of acting independently in pursuit of their own interests and, whether out of ambition or necessity, more inclined to do so.

What are the likely implications of these developments and, in particular, what will they mean for the chances of war and peace? In western academic circles, and especially among American experts on issues of international security, discussion of the impending return to regional multipolarity has thus far centered almost exclusively on Europe. Here, predictably enough, adherents of the two main contending schools of international relations theory come to strikingly different conclusions about what the future will hold. Neo-realists believe, first, that the structure of an international system (i.e., the distribution of power among states) will determine its destiny and, second, that multipolar systems are more prone to instability than those that are bipolar. The end of the Cold War, in their view, means a return to multipolarity and therefore the beginning of a new era of conflict among the major European powers.[2]

Neo-liberals, by contrast, maintain that the structure of a system may be less important in determining its functioning than a range of other factors, including the domestic regimes of the nations of which it is composed and the level and character of their economic and institutional interconnections. Based on an assessment of the non-structural factors at work there, most neo-liberals foresee rising levels of integration and harmony in Western Europe and, ultimately, in central and eastern Europe as well.[3]

---

2. See John Mearsheimer,"Back to the Future: Instability in Europe After the Cold War," *International Security*, Vol. 15, No. 1 (Summer 1990), pp. 5–56.

3. For explications of these views see: Stephen Van Evera, "Primed for Peace: Europe After the Cold War," *International Security*, Vol. 15, No. 3 (Winter 1990/91), pp. 7–57; Robert Jervis, "The Future of World Politics: Will It Resemble the Past?" *International Security*, Vol. 16, No. 3 (Winter 1991/92), pp. 39–73; Jack Snyder, "Averting Anarchy in the New Europe," *International Security*, Vol. 14, No. 4 (Spring 1990), pp. 5–41; James M. Goldgeier and Michael McFaul, "Core and Periphery in the Post–Cold War Era," *International Organization*, Vol. 46, No. 2 (Spring 1992), pp. 467–491; Richard H. Ullman, *Securing Europe* (Princeton: Princeton University Press, 1991); and letters by Stanley Hoffmann and Robert Keohane in "Correspondence: Back to the Future, Part II: International Relations Theory and Post–Cold War Europe," *International Security*, Vol.

The fate of Europe is certainly an issue of great concern. But Europe is not the world's only concentration of wealth and power and, indeed, by early in the next century, it may no longer even be the most important one.[4] Moreover, generalizations about the future of relations among the "great" or "major" powers that simply extrapolate from the conditions expected to obtain in one regional sub-system should be regarded with considerable suspicion. What is true of Europe may not be true for other parts of the world.

On the eastern half of the Eurasian landmass, as on its western wing, a new multipolar sub-system is beginning to emerge out of the wreckage of the Cold War. While firm predictions are impossible (or, in any case, imprudent), the workings of this new Asian system could turn out to be far different from those of its European counterpart. In Europe, as the neo-liberal optimists suggest, there appears to be an abundance of factors at work that should serve to mitigate the troubling tendencies to which multipolar systems have often been prone in the past. In Asia, by contrast, many of these same soothing forces are either absent or of dubious strength and permanence.[5] While civil wars and ethnic strife will continue for some time to smolder along Europe's peripheries, in the long run it is Asia that seems far more likely to be the cockpit of great power conflict. The half millennium during which Europe was the world's primary generator of war (as well as of wealth and knowledge) is coming to a close. But, for better and for worse, Europe's past could be Asia's future.

The Dynamics of Multipolarity

Neo-realist pessimism about the prospects for a multipolar peace rests largely on the assertion that, "for the sake of stability," "smaller is better . . . [and]

15, No. 2 (Fall 1990), pp. 191–194. Jervis and Goldgeier and McFaul make the same arguments more generally about the relations among the nations of the "developed world," i.e., Western Europe, the United States and Japan (Jervis), or the "great powers" of the advanced industrial "core" (Goldgeier and McFaul).

4. By the second decade of the twenty-first century, East Asia's economic output is likely to exceed that of both North America and the European Community. See Urban C. Lehner, "Belief in an Imminent Asian Century Is Gaining Sway," *Wall Street Journal*, May 17, 1993, p. A12.

5. Throughout this essay I use the term "Asia" to refer to the region extending from Southwest Asia, across China to Northeast Asia and including the offlying islands at the western edge of the Pacific rim. (See map, p. 33.) The list of "poles" or "major powers" around which a new Asian sub-system will take shape includes, by virtue of their location and their actual and potential military capabilities, China, Japan, Russia, and perhaps India. Whether the United States remains an Asian power will depend on its willingness to continue to project some fraction of its military might into the region.

two is best of all."[6] The validity of this claim is by no means self-evident and, indeed, it has been the object of a prolonged, heated, and ultimately inconclusive scholarly debate.[7] Disagreement on the comparative merits of systems with two or more dominant powers is unresolvable on either deductive grounds (clever arguments can be made on both sides of the question) or, because of the relative rarity of bipolar systems, on the basis of historical evidence. In any case, with the sudden collapse of the old bipolar order, a new and more pressing issue has begun to assert itself: What may account for differences in the functioning of systems of similar structure? And, specifically, why is it that some multipolar systems have proven more stable (in terms both of their duration and of the level of conflict within them) than others?

The answer to these questions comes in two parts. First, at the level of structure, multipolar systems *do* seem prone to certain pathologies. Systems in which power is distributed at the outset more or less evenly among a substantial number of states do not remain indefinitely in peaceful equilibrium. As, inevitably, the distribution of power among states shifts, wars tend to break out. The history of the European state system before 1945 is a story of multipolarity; it is also a story of war, and not only small wars for limited ends, but big, system-shattering struggles. The mere existence of an assortment of potential alliance partners has not always guaranteed the prompt formation of countervailing coalitions, as advocates of multipolarity suggest

6. Kenneth N. Waltz, *Theory of International Politics* (Reading, Mass: Addison-Wesley, 1979), p. 161.
7. For the first round in this debate see Karl W. Deutsch and J. David Singer, "Multipolar Power Systems and International Stability," *World Politics*, Vol. 16, No. 3 (April 1964), pp. 390–406; Kenneth N. Waltz, "The Stability of a Bipolar World," *Daedalus*, Vol. 93, No. 9 (Summer 1964), pp. 881–909. Waltz elaborates his position in *Theory of International Politics*, pp. 129–193. Similar views are expressed in Mearsheimer, "Back to the Future," pp. 13–18. For elaborations of the deductive arguments on all sides see Van Evera, "Primed for Peace," pp. 33–40; Richard Rosecrance, "Bipolarity, Multipolarity, and the Future," *Journal of Conflict Resolution*, Vol. 10, No. 3 (September 1966), pp. 314–327; Patrick James and Michael Brecher, "Stability and Polarity: New Paths for Inquiry," *Journal of Peace Research*, Vol. 25, No. 1 (1988), pp. 31–42; Alvin M. Saperstein, "The 'Long Peace'—Result of a Bipolar Competitive World?" *Journal of Conflict Resolution*, Vol. 35, No. 1 (March 1991), pp. 68–79. For efforts to resolve the question empirically see Michael Haas, "International Subsystems: Stability and Polarity," *American Political Science Review*, Vol. 64, No. 1 (1970), pp. 98–123; and Jack S. Levy, "The Polarity of the System and International Stability: An Empirical Analysis," in Alan Ned Sabrosky, ed., *Polarity and War: The Changing Structure of International Conflict* (Boulder, Colo.: Westview, 1985), pp. 41–66. Regarding the impact of bipolarity (and other factors) on the course of the Cold War, see John Lewis Gaddis, "The Long Peace: Elements of Stability in the Postwar International System," *International Security*, Vol. 10, No. 4 (Spring 1986), pp. 99–142.

that it should.[8] In other words, the balance has not always balanced, or balanced quickly enough to deter an aggressive state or alliance.

A variety of non-structural factors may impede efficient balancing, but the frequent failure of multipolar systems to equilibrate promptly is also directly related to the complexity of their structures. Traditional enthusiasts for multipolarity like Hans Morgenthau argued that the complexity of a world with more rather than fewer centers of power would induce caution in decision-makers.[9] Instead, and with some regularity, complexity seems to have contributed to miscalculation (both on the part of potential aggressors, who underestimate the size, power and resolve of the coalitions that ultimately form to oppose them, and on the part of their victims, who are often slow to cooperate in confronting a shared threat), and miscalculation has contributed to war.[10]

Whether or not they are correct about the comparative virtues of bipolarity, the neo-realists are probably right that, all other things being equal, multipolar systems are intrinsically unstable. In the real world, however, everything else is not equal, and non-structural factors can serve either to exacerbate or to mitigate the tendencies that are inherent in a system's structure. A variety of such factors have been identified by students of past instances of multipolarity. Wise leaders, blessed with superior powers of calculation and an exceptional grasp of the dynamics of international politics, are sometimes able to keep a complex system in balance, even during periods of dramatic change. Their departure from the scene may be the prelude to breakdown and war.[11] An understanding by statesmen of the true implications of shifts in military technology can lead to appropriate alliance policies,

---

8. This argument is summarized in Van Evera, "Primed for Peace," pp. 36–37.
9. Thus, according to Hans Morgenthau, "the greater the number of active players, the greater the number of possible combinations and the greater also the uncertainty as to the combinations that will actually oppose each other. . . . the extreme flexibility of the balance of power resulting from the utter unreliability of alliances made it imperative for all players to be cautious in their moves . . . and, since risks were hard to calculate, compelled them to take as small risks as possible." Hans Morgenthau, *Politics Among Nations: The Struggle for Peace and Power* (New York: Knopf, 1973), pp. 339–340.
10. See the discussions in Mearsheimer, "Back to the Future," pp. 16–17; Van Evera, "Primed for Peace," p. 35.
11. This claim is sometimes made for Bismarck. For various accounts of his role in keeping the European peace see Gordon A. Craig and Alexander L. George, *Force and Statecraft: Diplomatic Problems of Our Time* (New York: Oxford University Press, 1983), pp. 35–40; George Kennan, *The Decline of Bismarck's European Order: Franco-Russian Relations, 1875–1890* (Princeton: Princeton University Press, 1979), pp. 331–424; Edward Crankshaw, *Bismarck* (New York: Penguin Books, 1983), pp. 388–414.

while a misunderstanding will increase the odds of miscalculation and failure.[12] The shared memory of a recent, devastating war can help to dampen the competitive dynamics to which a multipolar system might otherwise be prone.[13] The "restraining influence of a moral consensus,"[14] or the absence of "ideological impediments,"[15] can contribute to coordination and cooperation, as can homogeneity in domestic structures and the existence of recognized rules of international conduct.[16] When powerful states pursue moderate goals, equilibrium is easier to preserve; when one or more is "revolutionary" in its aims, the task will be more difficult.[17]

Anticipating the dynamics of the post–Cold War world will require gaining a better understanding of the ways in which non-structural factors have influenced the workings of past multipolar systems.[18] Robert Jervis's observation about the functioning of the Concert of Europe applies more generally to such systems: "We still know too little about the conditions that are most propitious" for the maintenance of their stability.[19]

EUROPE

Students of world politics have identified a wide assortment of mitigating factors which, they predict, will dampen the potentially worrisome consequences of a return to multipolarity in Europe. These factors may be grouped into three categories: the changed character of the European states, the nature of the linkages among them, and the shifting costs and benefits of war.

STATES. Comparing the end of the twentieth century to its beginning, Stephen Van Evera concludes that "the domestic orders of most European

---

12. See Christensen and Snyder, "Predicting Alliance Patterns."
13. See Robert Jervis's discussion of the establishment and demise of the Concert of Europe in Stephen D. Krasner, ed., *International Regimes* (Ithaca: Cornell University Press, 1983), pp. 178–184.
14. See the discussion of the seventeenth, eighteenth, and nineteenth centuries in Morgenthau, *Politics Among Nations*, pp. 214–217.
15. Inis L. Claude, Jr., *Power and International Relations* (New York: Random House, 1962), p. 91.
16. Stanley Hoffmann, *Gulliver's Troubles; Or, the Setting of American Foreign Policy* (New York: McGraw Hill, 1968), p. 13.
17. Ibid., p. 12.
18. For recent efforts to combine structural and non-structural factors to explain alliance behavior see Christensen and Snyder, "Predicting Alliance Patterns"; and Randall Schweller, "Tripolarity and the Second World War," *International Studies Quarterly*, Vol. 37 (1993), pp. 73–103. On the role of polarity and ideological polarization in explaining great power cooperation, see Benjamin Miller, "Explaining Great Power Cooperation in Conflict Management," *World Politics*, Vol. 45, No. 1 (October 1992), pp. 1–46.
19. Robert Jervis, "A Political Science Perspective on the Balance of Power and the Concert," *American Historical Review*, Vol. 97, No. 3 (June 1992), p. 724.

states have changed in ways that make renewed aggression unlikely."[20] The internal changes to which Van Evera and others point are political, socio-economic and cultural.

First, and most important, the nations of Western Europe are unquestionably more democratic than they were earlier in this century. Van Evera regards the rapid spread of democracy from west to east as a trend that is "bound to continue, because key pre-conditions for democracy . . . are now far more widespread in Europe than they were eighty years ago."[21] Assuming the continued spread and consolidation of democracy, and assuming that what has been true in the past will be true in the future (i.e., that democracies do not fight one another), there is therefore good reason to expect that Europe will be peaceful.[22]

A second set of changes that distinguishes the nations of the "new Europe" from those of the old, Van Evera argues, has to do with their economic and social structures. Not only are today's European states wealthier than their predecessors, but wealth and incomes are distributed far more equally among their populations than has ever been true in the past. Increased equality and material well-being contribute directly to the stability of democratic societies. Moreover, the socio-economic "leveling" that the nations of both Eastern and Western Europe have experienced during the twentieth century has made them less subject to the evils of militarism, hyper-nationalism, and social imperialism and to the aggressive external policies that so often accompanied these domestic disorders. Such policies, Van Evera argues, were largely the product of efforts by elites to "bolster their domestic position by distracting publics with foreign confrontations, or by seeking successful foreign wars."[23]

---

20. Van Evera, "Primed for Peace," p. 9.
21. Ibid., p. 26.
22. Ibid., pp. 26–28; Jervis, "The Future of World Politics," p. 53; Goldgeier and McFaul, "Core and Periphery," pp. 485–486; Ullman, *Securing Europe*, pp. 41–42. Although the historical reality of a democratic "zone of peace" is by now almost universally accepted, there is still considerable disagreement as to its causes and, therefore, its future prospects. See Michael W. Doyle, "Kant, Liberal Legacies, and Foreign Affairs, Part 1," *Philosophy and Public Affairs*, Vol. 12, No. 3 (Summer 1983), pp. 205–235; and Doyle, "Kant, Liberal Legacies, and Foreign Affairs, Part 2," ibid., No. 4 (Fall 1983), pp. 323–353. For discussion of the various alternative explanations for the existence of the zone of peace see T. Clifton Morgan and Sally Howard Campbell, "Domestic Structure, Decisional Constraints, and War," *Journal of Conflict Resolution*, Vol. 35, No. 2 (June 1991), pp. 187–211; Carol R. Ember, Melvin Ember, and Bruce Russett, "Peace Among Participatory Polities," *World Politics*, Vol. 44, No. 4 (July 1992), pp. 573–599; Spencer R. Weart, "The History of Peace Among Republics" (unpublished manuscript, October 1992).
23. Van Evera, "Primed for Peace," p. 25.

Changes in politics, economics, and the structure of society have also been accompanied by shifts in culture. At least among the developed countries (again, with special reference to the nations of Western Europe), Jervis concludes, "we may now be seeing . . . the triumph of interests over passions." West Europeans today are less bellicose and chauvinistic than their ancestors. They are less likely to believe that "war is . . . good, or even . . . honorable," and less inclined to rely on attachment to their nation "as a source of identity and personal satisfaction."[24] Such shifts in culture are both reflected and reinforced in a variety of ways. Jervis cites "the absence of territorial disputes" among the West European states as one important piece of evidence of a "change in values."[25] Van Evera notes the "dramatic decline of nationalist propaganda, especially in European schools" and the accompanying emergence in the postwar period of "a single shared version of European history."[26]

LINKAGES. It is not only the changing nature of the European states themselves that is expected to offset the effects of a return to multipolarity, but also the evolving character of the economic, institutional, and cultural interconnections among them.

The nations of the "developed world" are distinguished by their capitalist economic systems and by their high degree of mutual economic exchange. This is especially true in Western Europe, where barriers to the free movement of people, goods, capital, and technology have now been drastically lowered. Rising levels of economic interdependence may not create peace, but, through their impact on national welfare, they can increase its benefits and diminish the appeal of war. While they will inevitably give rise to some dislocations, trans-national flows of trade and investment also help to create domestic groups with a strong interest in preserving free exchange and therefore in maintaining peace.[27]

In addition to their economic ties, since the end of the Second World War the nations of Western Europe have become enmeshed in a dense web of institutions, what Richard Ullman has described as "a thick alphabet soup of international agencies."[28] International institutions help to promote peace

24. Jervis, "The Future of World Politics," p. 52.
25. Ibid., p. 53.
26. Van Evera, "Primed for Peace," p. 24.
27. For a concise summary of these views see Jervis, "The Future of World Politics," pp. 48–52. See also Goldgeier and McFaul, "Core and Periphery," pp. 482–486.
28. Ullman, *Securing Europe*, p. 145.

by assisting in the resolution of disputes and by easing all forms of mutually beneficial interstate cooperation. Over time the very act of participation can itself be a cause of peace. "Insofar as states regularly follow the rules and standards of international institutions," writes Robert Keohane, "they signal their willingness to continue patterns of cooperation, and therefore reinforce expectations of stability."[29]

Joint participation in international institutions can breed mutual understanding and an important measure of trust. This effect is evident in the relative ease with which the nations of Western Europe accepted the reunification of Germany. Had these countries not spent the preceding four decades in a form of institutional "family therapy" with their former archenemy, they would undoubtedly have been more suspicious of its motives and more fearful of its expanded power.

The final form of interconnection that links the nations of Europe is cultural. The obverse of the waning of national identification to which Jervis and others refer is the growth of "ties of mutual . . . identification" and the development of an "altered psychology, whereby individuals identify less deeply with their nations and more with broader entities, values, and causes."[30] At least in the established democracies of the west, over the course of the postwar period individuals have become less inclined to take greatest pride in their nationality and more disposed to think of themselves as "Europeans" than as "Germans" or "Frenchmen."[31]

At the level of international relations, a feeling of collective identity is essential to the formation of what Hedley Bull has described as a society of states. In the eighteenth and nineteenth centuries, Bull claims, Europeans shared a sense of solidarity and "cultural differentiation" from other regions and peoples. Although insufficient in themselves to prevent war, these feelings of commonality and uniqueness made it easier for the European powers to formulate rules of behavior and to create and sustain international institutions.[32] In today's Europe too, a measure of common culture and shared history has arguably helped to ease institution-building, and institutions, in turn, have promoted cooperation and peace.

---

29. Keohane, "Back to the Future: Part II," p. 193.
30. Jervis, "The Future of World Politics," p. 55.
31. For evidence, see Ronald Inglehart, *Culture Shift in Advanced Industrial Society* (Princeton: Princeton University Press, 1990), pp. 410–412. Whether these tendencies will continue to grow stronger is, of course, uncertain.
32. See Hedley Bull, *The Anarchical Society* (New York: Columbia University Press, 1977), pp. 33–38.

COSTS AND BENEFITS. Much of the maneuvering and anxiety that characterized the multipolar worlds of the past was a reflection of the ever-present threat of war. If, for reasons having nothing to do with the structure of the international system, that threat has now sharply diminished, there may be less cause to fear a return to multipolarity.

Theorists of international relations cite two sets of reasons for believing that, at least among the most developed nations, the probability of war has indeed fallen sharply. First and most obvious, the Industrial Revolution brought with it tremendous increases in the destructiveness of weaponry and warfare, culminating in the advent of nuclear explosives. By raising the costs of war between nations that possess them, these terrible implements of destruction have helped to reduce its likelihood.[33] Because they divert so many resources from more productive endeavors, modern armed forces also have substantial costs in peacetime. As they turn their attention increasingly to economic competition, the most advanced nations will have good reason to avoid extensive preparations for war, to say nothing of war itself.[34]

While the costs of war have risen rapidly over the last two hundred years, its benefits have fallen markedly. The shift from agriculture to industry as the primary source of wealth has diminished the value of land and the appeal of territorial conquest.[35] Growing nationalist sentiment and the increased availability and effectiveness of defensive weapons have made it more difficult for invaders to take territory, subdue populations, and extract gains.[36] Noting that these long-term trends were insufficient to prevent the First and Second World Wars, Stephen Van Evera argues more specifically that it is "the shift toward knowledge-based forms of production in advanced industrial economies since 1945 [that] has reduced the ability of conquerors to extract resources," and thereby diminished "the risk of war in Europe by making conquest more difficult and less rewarding."[37]

---

33. Jervis, "The Future of World Politics," pp. 47–48. For the argument that technological advance had made war "a major anachronism" even before the advent of nuclear weapons, see John Mueller, *Retreat From Doomsday: The Obsolescence of Major War* (New York: Basic Books, 1989).
34. Goldgeier and McFaul, "Core and Periphery," p. 479. This argument is developed most fully in Richard Rosecrance, *The Rise of the Trading State: Commerce and Conquest in the Modern World* (New York: Basic Books, 1986).
35. Carl Kaysen, "Is War Obsolete?" *International Security*, Vol. 14, No. 4 (Spring 1990), pp. 42–64.
36. Klaus Knorr, *The Power of Nations: The Political Economy of International Relations* (New York: Basic Books, 1975), pp. 124–125.
37. Van Evera, "Primed For Peace," p. 14–15.

The movement toward democracy, equality, and cosmopolitanism in each of the states of Europe, the increasingly dense and diverse linkages between them and the mounting costs and declining benefits of war among them have mutually reinforcing effects. Even if, taken separately, no one of these "forces for peace" was sufficiently powerful to transform the character of international relations, taken as a whole their impact will be "overwhelming." By comparison, Robert Jervis concludes, "the influence of the polarity of the international system is slight. Even if multipolar systems are less stable than bipolar ones and even if the future world will be multipolar, it is hard to see how the overall result could be dangerous."[38] At least in Western Europe or, more generally, among the "developed states," an increasingly equal distribution of power need not imply an increased risk of instability and war.

ASIA

But what of Asia? Assuming for the moment that the optimists are right about Europe, will their arguments apply with equal force on the other side of Eurasia? Will the same array of mitigating factors be at work there and, if not, what are the likely implications?

STATES. If, as is alleged of Europe, the states of Asia are also converging toward a norm of democracy, prosperity, socio-economic equity, and post-nationalist political culture, that process is still in its very earliest stages. For some time to come the region is likely to be marked more by a diversity of governmental and societal forms than by any obvious unity. Thus, while at best two of the four largest powers in Asia may be considered securely democratic (Japan and India, with the future of the latter open to doubt), one (China) is not, and the fate of the other (Russia) hangs in the balance. Among the region's less powerful states there are a handful of stable European-style liberal democracies (Australia and New Zealand), several totalitarian regimes (Burma, North Korea, and Vietnam), and a large number that display varying mixes of democracy and authoritarianism (the Philippines, South Korea, Thailand, the new nations of Central Asia, Malaysia, Singapore, Taiwan, and Pakistan).[39] Whatever happens in the center of Europe, in Asia there will continue to be numerous interactions between democratic and

38. Jervis, "The Future of World Politics," p. 54.
39. For one assessment of the degree of political rights and civil liberties in the countries of the region, see Freedom House Survey Team, *Freedom in the World: Political Rights and Civil Liberties, 1989–1990* (New York: Freedom House, 1990).

non-democratic states (and, what may prove to be more interesting from a theoretical point of view, between states with varying degrees and institutional forms of democracy). These will involve dealings not only between big and small powers or among lesser powers, but among big powers as well. The collapse of the Soviet empire does not mean that all the world's most powerful states will soon reside in the democratic zone of peace.

Just as the nations of Asia display an assortment of domestic political structures, so too there are wide variations in their present levels of economic output and per capita incomes. Despite these differences, most of the countries along the western side of the Pacific rim share two common features; first, a relatively low level of income inequality and, second, an extraordinarily high rate of overall national economic growth.[40] The absence of steep socio-economic stratification may eliminate one possible motivation for the sorts of diversionary external policies that Van Evera points to as a major cause of war in nineteenth and early twentieth century Europe. On the other hand, rapid national economic growth, and the shared feelings of power and entitlement that tend to go with it, may be at least as important a cause of expansionism as the efforts of embattled elites to maintain their domestic power. As Samuel Huntington has suggested: "The external expansion of the UK and France, Germany and Japan, the Soviet Union and the United States coincided with phases of intense industrialization and economic development."[41] Beginning in the late 1970s China entered into precisely such a phase. Between 1978 and 1994 the Chinese economy will have quadrupled in size and it could double again by 2002. By 2010 China will probably have gone in twenty years from being the world's fourth largest economy to its biggest.[42] If the historical correlation between extraordinarily rapid internal growth and external expansion holds, the implications for Asian stability will be troubling indeed.

In the case of China, aggregate measures of growth and income distribution also conceal striking regional differences. As the country's coastal provinces grow richer faster, and as they become more closely linked to the economies

---

40. For useful recent surveys see "Special Report/Pacific Rim," *Fortune*, October 5, 1992, pp. 111–132; Pacific Economic Cooperation Council, *Pacific Economic Outlook, 1992–1993* (Washington, D.C.: U.S. National Committee for Pacific Economic Cooperation, 1992); "Asia's Emerging Economies," *The Economist*, November 16, 1991, pp. 3–16.
41. Samuel P. Huntington, "America's Changing Strategic Interests," *Survival*, Vol. 33, No. 1 (January/February 1991), p. 12. On the American experience see Ernest R. May, *Imperial Democracy: The Emergence of America as a Great Power* (New York: Harcourt Brace and World, 1961).
42. "When China Wakes," *The Economist*, November 28, 1992, pp. 3–4.

and societies of Hong Kong and Taiwan, mainland China may tend to become divided into a poorer and more conservative interior and a wealthier and more liberal seaboard. These divisions could have far-reaching political consequences. Certainly the events of 1989 suggest that China's domestic stability and even its continued existence in its present geographical form cannot simply be taken for granted. Nor can the possibility that elites might manufacture foreign threats, in an attempt to overcome growing regional divisions, be entirely ruled out.[43]

Recent developments demonstrate the continuing presence and power of nationalism, at least in the eastern and southern portions of Europe. Thus far the resurgence of European nationalism has tended to promote disputes and splits within pre-existing nations rather than between them; in Asia it could have both kinds of consequences. Ethnic and religious divisions already threaten the cohesion of India, and the presence of newly independent, predominantly Islamic republics in formerly Soviet Central Asia could arouse the ambitions of their co-religionists in western China.

Elsewhere, despite some recent efforts to minimize national differences, there does not appear to be much evidence that feelings of national identification have faded significantly, even among the populations of the most highly developed Asian countries. The day when Japanese and Koreans think of themselves as more similar than different is not yet at hand.[44] The persistence of Asian nationalism is in part a reflection of the region's diversity, its geographic dispersal, its troubled past and its lack to date of the kinds of soothing interconnections that have existed for some time in Western Europe. But such sentiments could also prove to be a more lasting manifestation of the fact that, in many parts of Asia, nationalism is rooted firmly in ethnic and racial differences.[45]

At present, the hopeful indications of an evolution away from national chauvinism to which some scholars point in Western Europe are largely

---

43. For an overview of the uneven pattern of Chinese regional development see Sheryl WuDunn, "As China Leaps Ahead, The Poor Slip Behind," *New York Times*, May 23, 1993, p. 3. My thinking on the possible political implications of these economic changes has been influenced by discussions with my colleague Min Xin Pei of Princeton University and Arthur Waldron of the U.S. Naval War College and Brown University.

44. The words of a recent popular song, performed by an ethnic Chinese from Singapore, declares that, "Our separate lands/Are one from now on. We are Asians/And we'll sing one song"; this is clearly more an expression of hope than a statement of fact. See Teresa Watanabe, "Toward a New Asian Order," *Los Angeles Times*, May 19, 1992, p. 2.

45. John Gray, "No Nation Is Indivisible," *New York Times Book Review*, December 27, 1992, p. 7.

lacking in Asia. Territorial disputes are rampant in the region and involve big as well as small powers. The list of states that have outstanding differences over the delineation of their land frontiers or maritime boundaries is extremely long and includes: Japan and Russia, Russia and China, China and India, Japan and China, Japan and South Korea, Laos and China, China and Burma, India and Pakistan, Cambodia and Vietnam, China and Vietnam, China and Taiwan, Indonesia and Timor, Malaysia and the Philippines, and—in the case of the Spratly Islands—China, Vietnam, the Philippines, Malaysia, and Taiwan together.[46] In some cases, as where control over newly discovered natural resources is at stake, the mere existence of territorial disputes may not reveal much about the intensity of national feelings (although their persistence could help to strengthen nationalist sentiment). In others, however, the issues are almost entirely symbolic and have everything to do with national pride. Germans may, as Robert Jervis observes, "no longer seem to care that Alsaçe and Lorraine are French."[47] But, regardless of their comparative lack of material value, the Japanese still care intensely that the Northern Territories are Russian.

History too is a subject of disagreement in Asia and, as with territory, controversies over it both reflect and reinforce feelings of national identity and difference. Far from converging on a single, shared interpretation of their recent past, the Asian powers show signs of divergence, each constructing a history that serves its own national purposes. Nor are debates over historical interpretation a merely academic matter. Since the early 1980s, Japan has been embroiled in a series of disputes with China and South Korea over the content of history textbooks officially approved for use in its secondary schools. Chinese and Koreans accuse the Japanese of backing away from their responsibility for the Second World War and of minimizing the brutality of their conduct during that conflict.[48] Although the official Japanese

---

46. See Douglas M. Johnston, "Anticipating Instability in the Asia-Pacific Region," *Washington Quarterly*, Vol. 15, No. 3 (Summer 1992), pp. 104–105. See also Chi-kin Lo, *China's Policy Towards Territorial Disputes: The Case of the South China Sea Islands* (New York: Routledge, 1989). A useful discussion of the background to such disputes is Alexander B. Murphy, "Historical Justification for Territorial Claims," *Annals of the Association of American Geographers*, Vol. 80, No. 4 (1990), pp. 531–548.
47. Jervis, "The Future of World Politics," p. 53.
48. Changes proposed in 1982, for example, would have substituted the phrase "all-around advance into north China" for the more pointed "all-out aggression against China." Arif Dirlik, "'Past Experience, If Not Forgotten, Is a Guide to the Future': or, What Is In a Text? The Politics of History in Chinese-Japanese Relations," *Boundary 2*, Vol. 8, No. 3 (*Japan in the World*, Special Issue, Duke University Press, 1991), p. 34. A textbook in use until 1992 refered to the "incon-

response has generally been conciliatory, the extreme sensitivity on these matters reveals the depth of old wounds and the extent to which they remain unhealed, even between countries that were nominal allies during the Cold War. And what others perceive to be the continuing Japanese effort to rewrite history cannot help but intensify contemporary concerns about their motives and intentions.

LINKAGES. The nations of Western Europe are already joined together by a dense network of interconnections that make it much less likely that they will ever come into conflict with one another. Slowly and with some difficulty, that web has begun to extend from Western to Eastern Europe. The ties among Asian states are, by comparison, much less fully developed, the basis for their establishment is, in some instances, less obvious, and the possible obstacles to their growth more readily apparent.

Long separated by politics and by their differing developmental strategies, the economies of most of the present or potential Asian great powers remain substantially independent of one another. Trade between China and Russia, Russia and Japan, Japan and India, and India and China is still extremely limited, both in absolute terms and as a portion of the imports and exports of each country.[49] The flows of trade and investment between Japan and China have grown rapidly since the end of the 1970s, but they begin from a very low level and remain fresh and potentially fragile. The web of economic interdependence, with all its presumed pacifying effects, has yet to extend fully across Asia.

Trade among a core group of East Asian market economies has expanded markedly in recent years. Nevertheless, intra-Asian commerce is still a significantly smaller fraction of the total trade of all countries in the region than

---

venience" Japan had caused its Asian neighbors "in the past." See David E. Sanger, "Molding Textbooks to Mold Consensus," *New York Times*, November 22, 1992, p. 5. Official Japanese reluctance to admit culpability in the wartime enslavement of Korean "comfort women" has also helped to increase tensions between those two countries. "Japan Apologizes on Korea Sex Issue," *New York Times*, January 18, 1992, p. 2. And see in this issue Saburo Ienaga, "The Glorification of War in Japanese Education," *International Security*, Vol. 18, No. 3 (Winter 1993/94), pp. 113–133.

49. In 1990, for example, Russia accounted for less than 1 percent of Japan's exports and close to 1.5 percent of its imports. The comparable figures for India were 0.6 percent and 0.89 percent. Trade with India accounted for 0.27 percent of China's exports and .18 percent of her imports. Russia absorbed 3.6 percent of Chinese exports and supplied 4 percent of her imports. Figures derived from *Japan Statistical Yearbook* (Tokyo: Sorifu, Tokeikyoku, 1991); and State Statistical Bureau of the People's Republic of China, *China Statistical Yearbook* (Hong Kong: International Centre for the Advancement of Science and Technology, 1990).

is the case for Europe.[50] A substantial portion of the growth captured in recent trade statistics is also the result of the establishment by Japanese firms of production facilities in Southeast Asia. These subsidiaries often import components from Japan and export finished products to other countries both within Asia and beyond. Because it is likely to yield fewer benefits for the host economy, such intra-firm trade may have fewer positive political effects than the more traditional forms of international exchange between indigenous companies. Meanwhile the most advanced Asian economies (Japan and the "four tigers," South Korea, Taiwan, Singapore, and Hong Kong) continue to look outside Asia for export markets and to regard one another as bitter competitors across a range of manufacturing sectors.[51]

Compared to Europe, the process of Asian economic integration was late in getting started and it remains limited in its breadth; its future is also far from assured. Rising trade barriers in Europe and North America could speed the consolidation of an Asian economic zone, but they might also pit Japan against its fast-rising regional rivals in a desperate scramble for shares of a diminishing export market.[52] Whether or not it takes the form of a preferential trading bloc, further regional economic integration may also depend on Japan's willingness and ability to increase markedly its imports of manufactured goods from its Asian trading partners. As the American experience in attempting to gain access to the Japanese market suggests, such changes may be slow in coming. In their absence, notes one economist, "a trading bloc made up of Japan, Taiwan, Korea, Singapore and some of the other developing nations of Southeast Asia would look more like the old Japanese

---

50. In 1989, trade among Japan, Hong Kong, South Korea, the five ASEAN countries, Australia, and New Zealand accounted for 37 percent of their total imports and exports, as compared to 59 percent for the nations of the European Community. "Unblocking the Yen," *The Economist*, November 16, 1991, p. 83.

51. For helpful overviews of the evolving East Asian economy see Richard P. Cronin, *Japan, the United States, and Prospects for the Asia-Pacific Century: Three Scenarios for the Future* (New York: St. Martin's Press, 1992), pp. 8–56; Richard Stubbs, "Reluctant leader, expectant followers: Japan and Southeast Asia," *International Journal*, Vol. 46 (Autumn 1991), pp. 649–667; Dwight H. Perkins, "Prospects for Continued Rapid Growth in East Asia," in Chong-Sik Lee, ed., *In Search of a New Order in East Asia* (Berkeley: Institute of East Asian Studies, 1991), pp. 79–95; Edward J. Lincoln, "Japan's Role in Asia-Pacific Cooperation," in John P. Hardt and Young C. Kim, eds., *Economic Cooperation in the Asia-Pacific Region* (Boulder, Colo.: Westview Press, 1990), pp. 21–45. On the pattern of Japanese investment in Asia and its implications see Dennis Encarnation, *Rivals Beyond Trade: America versus Japan in Global Competition* (Ithaca: Cornell University Press, 1992), pp. 147–182.

52. For a discussion of both possibilities see Cronin, *Japan, the United States, and Prospects for the Asia-Pacific Century*, pp. 111–118.

Co-Prosperity Sphere than it would like a common market of equals," with the lesser partners relegated to performing "low-wage Japanese manufacturing tasks."[53] In the words of one Japanese businessman: "If there were a free-trade zone in Asia tomorrow, Southeast Asian countries would end up economically as Japan's colonies again. That's the best reason to think it won't happen."[54]

Even if it continues to go forward, regional economic integration is no guarantee of harmony and peace among the participants. Higher levels of interdependence can, as has often been pointed out, produce political friction as well as amity.[55] This tendency is certainly evident in the recent course of relations between the United States and Japan. Patterns of exchange that are perceived by one party as grossly unequal and unfair are especially likely to breed dissatisfaction and political conflict. Korea and Taiwan resent the fact that, while they continue to depend heavily on Japan for imports of capital equipment and machinery, their own exports of manufactured goods are being edged out of the Japanese market by Japanese products made in Southeast Asia. As in the U.S.-Japan relationship, the resulting trade imbalances have political as well as economic consequences.[56]

In Southeast Asia the recent recipients of Japanese investment could come to see themselves as having gained little more than the opportunity to provide low-cost labor in foreign-owned factories. Where this is the case, local governments may be more inclined to impose conditions on Japanese firms and less willing to accept such investment in the future. China's history may also make that country's leaders and people sensitive to "unequal treaties" that seem to give special economic privileges to foreigners. Aware of the possibilities for a backlash, Japanese officials have described themselves privately as "very afraid of the political problems created by the over-dominance of Japanese business in some Asian markets."[57] As elsewhere in the relations

53. Lester Thurow, *Head to Head: The Coming Economic Battle Among Japan, Europe and America* (New York: Morrow, 1992), p. 84.
54. "Special Report/Pacific Rim," p. 132.
55. See the discussion in Waltz, *Theory of International Politics*, pp. 151–160; and Robert Gilpin, "The Economic Dimension of International Security," in Henry Bienen, ed., *Power, Economics, and Security: The United States and Japan in Focus* (Boulder, Colo.: Westview Press, 1992), pp. 60–63.
56. John Ridding and Peter Wickenden, "Asian tigers discover Japan is still king of the jungle," *Financial Times*, March 15, 1991, p. 6. Also James Sterngold, "New Asian Anger at Tokyo's Trade," *New York Times*, April 13, 1993, p. D1.
57. These are the words of an unnamed senior MITI planner as reported in "Asia's Emerging Economies," p. 5.

between North and South, perceived inequalities could give rise to conflicts over expropriation, and even to interventions by the rich and powerful in the domestic politics of the poor and weak.

In the long run, the full development of regional economic ties will depend on the evolution of the political relationships among the major Asian powers. If these relationships turn sour and suspicious, the movement toward wider and deeper economic integration will falter and could collapse. As Robert Jervis has pointed out, "expectations of peaceful relations were a necessary condition for the formation of the European Common Market . . . Had the Europeans thought there was a significant chance that they would come to blows, they would not have permitted their economies to grow so interdependent."[58] In Asia, in the aftermath of the Cold War, it is far from certain that today's friend will not be tomorrow's enemy. China's rapid economic growth could transform it into a more democratic, peaceful, and satisfied power, or into a more potent threat to the security of its neighbors. Japan is presently betting on the first path, but, as time passes, its willingness to continue assisting in Chinese development will depend critically on whether such a reassuring outcome continues to seem the most likely.

Next to Europe, Asia appears strikingly under-institutionalized. The rich "alphabet soup" of international agencies that has helped to nurture peaceful relations among the European powers is, in Asia, a very thin gruel indeed. Even when the Cold War was at its lowest depths (and American authority at its peak), the United States was unable to build a set of political and military institutions capable of containing its diverse Asian allies.[59] The one American-led effort to create an Asian counterpart to NATO (SEATO, the South East Asian Treaty Organization) was most notable for its failure. In projecting power into the Pacific during the Cold War, the United States relied instead primarily on a series of bilateral arrangements with its various friends, many of whom did not (and still do not) like or trust one another. While several independent sub-groupings have formed, the most important among them, ASEAN (the Association of South East Asian Nations), has never been much more than a loose collection of the region's less powerful states.[60] With the post–Cold War era already well underway, some movement

58. Jervis, "The Future of World Politics," p. 51.
59. Peter Polomka, "Towards a 'Pacific House'," *Survival*, Vol. 33, No. 2 (March/April 1991), p. 173.
60. In part because of the considerable political differences and lingering mistrust even among its members, ASEAN's power and the scope of its responsibilities remained limited during the

towards the creation of a regional security forum did become evident in the second half of 1993.[61]

In the economic realm, Asia has been described as lagging "behind every other world area in constructing explicit, cooperative arrangements." As in the political-military sphere, this fact reflects the region's cultural, economic, and political diversity.[62] Institutions designed to promote economic cooperation among the nations of Western Europe and between Europe and North America date back to the immediate aftermath of the Second World War. In Asia, despite repeated efforts, the first region-wide inter-governmental organization intended to fulfill a similar function (APEC, Asia-Pacific Economic Cooperation) was finally launched only in November 1989.[63]

A late start in institution-building does not guarantee failure, but it may be both a symptom of underlying problems and a factor contributing to future complications. The deep differences in political structure and economic development that hindered past progress have not simply been swept away by the events of the last several years. Indeed, as the previous discussion suggests, the perceived divergence of interests among some of the region's most important states on economic issues, and perhaps also on matters of security, may actually be growing. It is one thing to suggest constructing new institutions to bridge those gaps, quite another actually to do it.[64]

Although the presence of old structures may inhibit innovation, they can also provide a valuable foundation for future construction. Europe's pre-

---

Cold War. See Gerald Segal, *Rethinking the Pacific* (New York: Oxford University Press, 1991), pp. 357–360.

61. In July 1993 the members of ASEAN agreed to hold regular meetings on security issues and to invite representatives of the United States, Japan, China, Russia, Australia, and Vietnam. It remains to be seen whether this grouping will become an inclusive, regionwide "talking shop" like the Conference on Security and Cooperation in Europe, an anti-Chinese coalition, or an alliance of smaller states dedicated to blocking expansion by any larger power. See David E. Sanger, "Asian Countries, in Shift, Weigh Defense Forum," *New York Times*, May 23, 1993, p. 14; Philip Shenon, "South Asians Seek a Security Forum," *New York Times*, July 24, 1993, p. 2.

62. Donald Crone, "The Politics of Emerging Pacific Cooperation," *Pacific Affairs*, Vol. 65, No. 1 (Spring 1992), p. 68.

63. Ibid., p. 71.

64. As Robert Keohane acknowledges, "insecure states, seeking relative gains, find it extremely difficult to cooperate sufficiently to build significant international institutions." Keohane, "Back to the Future, Part II," p. 193. This caution applies even more strongly in the security arena than in the area of economic cooperation. As in Europe, proposals for an Asian collective security regime essentially assume the problem of insecurity out of existence rather than actually doing anything to solve it. Regarding Europe, see the penetrating analysis by Richard Betts, "Systems for Peace or Causes of War?" *International Security*, Vol. 17, No. 1 (Summer 1992), pp. 5–43.

existing institutional apparatus could yet be torn apart by forces unleashed at the end of the Cold War. The chances that it will survive, however, are increased by the considerable investments that the European states have already made in its establishment and maintenance. Building powerful new institutions from the ground up in the midst of rapid and radical change would be much more difficult, yet this is precisely the task that now faces the nations of Asia.

Aside from questions of timing and interests, the process of institution-building will be further complicated by the lack of a common culture and a "useable" Asian past. This difficulty extends deeper than disputes over recent history. Even in those cases where modern nations share distant roots, as in Northeast Asia, centuries of independent development have led to wide contemporary variations. Taking the region as a whole, the differences in origins and evolution remain more salient than the commonalities. Compared to Europe where "political similarities are supported by rough cultural unity," writes Gerald Segal, "in the Pacific the similarities are barely skin deep."[65] Only if the borders of "Europe" were extended to include North Africa and the Middle East would it contain a similar variety of races, cultures, and religions. Such differences do not make communication and cooperation impossible, but they certainly render it more difficult.

Finally, despite efforts to construct a sense of shared identity, the nations of Asia also lack both a recent memory of cooperation and a tradition of thinking of themselves as members of a distinct political entity.[66] While societal myths are inevitably distortions, at both the domestic and international levels they are also "major structuring principles of reality."[67] However indirectly, the myth of a peaceful, harmonious, and unified Europe has contributed to the progress that has been made toward its own realization. An appropriate Asian myth has yet to be constructed.

COSTS AND BENEFITS. If the prospective costs of war appear unduly high and the benefits sufficiently low, the nations of Asia could remain at peace,

---

65. Segal, "Rethinking the Pacific," pp. 179 and 181.
66. On the competing Japanese and Chinese efforts to construct such a myth by reinterpreting the events of the twentieth century, see Dirlik, "Past Experience," pp. 57–58. The current emphasis on Japan's "Asianness" can also be seen as an attempt to construct a myth of Asia in order to ease the way, both at home and in neighboring countries, for an increased Japanese economic and political role in the region. See Bruce Stokes, "Tilting Toward Asia," *The National Journal*, Vol. 24, No. 28 (July 11, 1992), pp. 1624–1628; and Yotaro Kobayashi, "Re-Asianization Does Not Mean Isolation," *Los Angeles Times*, December 3, 1991, p. 7.
67. Adda B. Bozeman, *Politics and Culture in International History* (Princeton: Princeton University Press, 1960), p. 10.

regardless of the differences in their domestic structures and the weakness of some of the linkages between them. In Asia, however, even these elemental forces for caution and restraint may prove to be insufficient.

To begin with, while nuclear weapons already serve to dampen the dangers of war between Russia and China or China and India, they are not yet evenly distributed across the region. Not all the states that feel themselves threatened by hostile nuclear forces have thus far been either able or willing to acquire matching capabilities of their own. In several cases this is not for any lack of trying; after many years of arduous effort Pakistan and North Korea may soon have operational nuclear forces. For the time being, Japan and South Korea have chosen to continue their Cold War policies of taking shelter beneath the U.S. nuclear umbrella, although their willingness to continue doing so will depend on the intensity of the threats they perceive and their faith in American security guarantees. In the foreseeable future Taiwan could also have both the means and the motivation to acquire nuclear weapons.

Assuming for the moment that an Asia with more nuclear powers would be more stable than one with fewer, there would still be serious difficulties involved in negotiating the transition to such a world. As in other regions, small, nascent nuclear forces will be especially vulnerable to preemption. In Japan the prevailing "nuclear allergy" could lead first to delays in acquiring deterrent forces and then to a desperate and dangerous scramble for nuclear weapons.[68] In Asia the prospects for a peaceful transition may be further complicated by the fact that the present and potential nuclear powers are both numerous and strategically intertwined. The nuclearization of Korea (North, South or, whether through reunification or competitive arms programs, both together) could lead to a similar development in Japan, which might cause China to accelerate and expand its nuclear programs, which could then have an impact on the defense policies of Taiwan, India (and through it, Pakistan) and Russia (which would also be affected by events in Japan and Korea). All of this would influence the behavior of the United States. Similar shockwaves could also travel through the system in different directions (for example, from India to China to Japan to Korea). A rapid, multifaceted expansion in nuclear capabilities could increase the dangers of misperception, miscalculation, and war.

---

68. For the argument that this could happen in Germany, see Snyder, "Averting Anarchy in the New Europe," p. 15.

Even a successful transition to a many-sided nuclear balance would not necessarily guarantee peace. As during the Cold War, nuclear armed states would, of course, remain free to use force against lesser opponents, although by doing so they might run the risk of colliding with one another. As to the possibility of war among the nuclear powers, it is not obvious that nuclear multipolarity will necessarily be as stable as nuclear bipolarity. Forces adequate for deterring a single opponent (by appearing capable of absorbing its first strike and then hitting back against it with overwhelming destructive power) might not be sufficient to deter two or more opponents acting together. The members of such a nuclear alliance might be more inclined to believe that, if they teamed up to attack their common enemy, they could diminish its forces to the point where each could afford to absorb a fraction of the resulting retaliatory blow. These calculations could prove to be mistaken, with disastrous consequences all around but, as Stanley Hoffmann pointed out almost thirty years ago: "The more nuclear powers there are, the more uneven . . . their stage of nuclear development, the more complicated calculations will be [and] the more dangerous yet likely misperceptions will become."[69]

Proliferation would also not eliminate the possibility that nuclear states might use conventional force against one another. During the Cold War, military strategists in both the United States and the Soviet Union worried that the emergence of a nuclear stalemate might increase the danger of a less-than-all-out war between them. The fact that these fears proved empty does not mean that all hostile nuclear powers will necessarily behave with similar restraint in the future. The superpowers avoided fighting both because they knew that there was some chance that even the smallest confrontation could blossom into total war and, equally important, because nothing that they might have considered fighting for seemed worth the risk of escalation. Other leaders, facing different stakes (and with varying degrees of risk-aversion) could make different decisions.[70]

This last point raises the issue of the possible benefits of armed conflict. Much of the case for the declining utility of war turns on the assertion that, for the most developed states, conquest is no longer profitable. Even those

69. Stanley Hoffmann, "Nuclear Proliferation and World Politics," in Alastair Buchan, ed., *A World of Nuclear Powers?* (Englewood Cliffs, N.J.: Prentice-Hall, 1966), p. 107.
70. For a discussion of the so-called "stability/instability paradox" in the context of the superpower confrontation, see Robert Jervis, *The Meaning of the Nuclear Revolution: Statecraft and the Prospect of Armageddon* (Ithaca: Cornell University Press, 1989), pp. 19–22.

who advance this claim acknowledge, however, that it remains open to dispute.[71] Some recent research suggests that, at least during the first half of the twentieth century and under certain conditions, conquerors were in fact able to extract significant net gains from defeated industrial societies.[72] The benefits of controlling territory that contains scarce natural resources (like oil) remain high and, compared to the difficulties involved administering an advanced industrial or post-industrial economy, relatively easy to obtain through conquest.

The view that war must always have an economic motivation is in any case far too narrow. States may fight over territory, not for the returns they expect it to yield, but because they believe it to have symbolic or strategic value. Egypt's initiation of war with Israel in 1973 and Argentina's occupation of the Falkland Islands in 1982 were both motivated by considerations of prestige (and domestic politics) rather than any expectation of direct material benefit. Territorial conquest is also not the only, nor necessarily the most important, motivation for modern warfare. States occasionally use force (as China did against Vietnam in 1979 or the United States did on a much smaller scale in Libya in 1986) to punish a weaker opponent for what they consider to be its unacceptable behavior. As in the case of Israel's 1967 Six-Day War, nations sometimes strike even their most powerful enemies out of fear that they are about to be struck first. Preventive wars (like the one that Japan launched against the United States in 1941) are driven by concerns over long-term shifts in the balance of power, rather than by the anticipation of short-term economic gains.

While the balance of costs and benefits may be shifting, it is simply too early to conclude that war has lost all its appeal, especially in a region as diverse, fast changing, and full of antagonisms and suspicions as Asia will be in the next century.

Conclusions

What is unfolding in Asia is a race between the accelerating dynamics of multipolarity, which could increase the chances of conflict, and the growth

71. Kaysen, "Is War Obsolete?" p. 56.
72. Peter J. Liberman, "Does Conquest Pay?" *Breakthroughs*, Vol. 2, No. 2 (Winter 1992/93), pp. 6–11; and Liberman, "The Spoils of Conquest," *International Security*, Vol. 18, No. 2 (Fall 1993), pp. 125–153.

of mitigating factors that should tend to dampen them and to improve the prospects for a continuing peace. This race is in its early stages and it is still too soon to pick a winner. As underdeveloped as they currently are, the forces conducive to greater stability are probably in the lead, but this is due largely to an early, if slow, start. Which set of forces will gain strength more rapidly?

Most of the mitigating factors discussed here are likely, by their very nature, to evolve at a modest pace. Even nations that have experienced revolutions do not always change their characters overnight. The maturation of democracy in Russia and Korea and its birth in China will take time, as will the fading of decades-old national grievances and the resolution of the disputes that have helped keep them alive. The development of powerful international institutions in Europe took many years. A similar achievement will not be accomplished in Asia, under less auspicious circumstances, with the mere wave of a hand. Economic interdependence is advancing at a rapid pace, but its geographic scope is still limited, its political effects mixed, and its future course uncertain. Nuclear weapons could spread quite quickly across Asia and, by fundamentally altering the balance between the perceived costs and benefits of war, their proliferation could conceivably promote more stability than insecurity. Needless to say, however, this scenario is fraught with uncertainties and dangers.

While they may only just be beginning to do so, the competitive interactions conducive to greater instability could gain strength quite rapidly. The security dilemma is, in essence, an amplifier of anxieties, in which the defensive exertions of the participants stimulate each other and feed back upon themselves. Once initiated, a multi-sided security scramble could accelerate quickly to high levels of competitive military and diplomatic activity. Among its other consequences, this turn of events would likely disrupt the further evolution of whatever mitigating tendencies are presently developing in Asia. Mounting insecurity could intensify feelings of nationalism, slow the construction of sturdy economic and institutional ties, and weaken or reverse any trend toward increasing democratization. If they did not actually promote it, these developments, in turn, would certainly do nothing to discourage further competitive behavior. The anticipation of war, like the expectation of peace, can be a self-fulfilling prophecy. Virtuous upward spirals can become vicious downward ones.

Key Asian states are several years into a process of re-examining their relationships and recalibrating their policies. Because so much remains uncertain, this transitional phase could go on for some time and it may yet lead in a variety of different directions. Initial indications are not encouraging. Since the late 1980s, there has been an increase in arms expenditures across the region and an intensified effort on the part of many Asian states to acquire advanced air and naval systems. Some of this activity reflects the sudden availability of sophisticated weaponry at end-of-the-Cold-War clearance-sale prices, but there is also evidence that a new, multi-sided competition in high technology power-projection capabilities is getting underway.[73]

China has begun to abandon its traditional emphasis on large low-technology ground forces and is seeking to buy or beginning to build the kinds of weapons that it would need to assert claims against its neighbors. Taiwan and several of the ASEAN countries have taken similar steps, presumably to better enable themselves to cope with China and, in the case of a number of Southeast Asian states, one another.[74] South Korea has recently started to reorient its military effort away from exclusive concentration on the familiar northern land threat, and towards the danger of air and sea attack from directions that are, as yet, unspecified.[75] In addition to their more immediate concerns, all of the countries of the region are also looking nervously toward Japan and, at the very least, hedging against the possibility that the Japanese too will begin to expand their capacity for projecting military power.[76]

If it were to begin in earnest, a many-sided arms race could prove extremely difficult to control through negotiations. Past attempts at multilateral arms control certainly give little cause for optimism on this score. Because of the high level of technical competence of several of the likely participants, by

---

73. For an overview see Michael T. Klare, "The Next Great Arms Race," *Foreign Affairs*, Vol. 72, No. 3 (Summer 1993), pp. 136–152. And see, in this issue, Desmond Ball, "Arms and Affluence: Military Acquisitions in the Asia-Pacific Region," *International Security*, Vol. 18, No. 3 (Winter 1993/94), pp. 78–112.
74. On these developments see Gerald Segal, "Managing New Arms Races in the Asia/Pacific," *The Washington Quarterly*, Vol. 15, No. 3 (Summer 1992), pp. 83–101; Peter Goodspeed, "Asian Arms Binge," *Toronto Star*, April 2, 1992, p. A1; James Clad and Patrick Marshall, "Southeast Asia's Quiet Arms Race," *Chicago Tribune*, May 23, 1992, p. 21; Nicholas Kristof, "China Builds Its Military Muscle, Making Some Neighbors Nervous," *New York Times*, January 11, 1993, p. A1.
75. Paul Bracken, "The Korean State and Northeast Asia," *Strategic Review*, Vol. 20, No. 3 (Summer 1992), p. 44.
76. Chinese military planners are clearly concerned about this possibility. Robert Delfs, "A Two-Front Threat," *Far Eastern Economic Review*, December 13, 1990, pp. 29–30. Perhaps more surprising, South Korea's 1991–92 National Defense White Paper openly accuses Japan of moving to expand its offensive capabilities. Sheldon W. Simon, "Regional Security Structures in Asia: The Question of Relevance," in Inis L. Claude, ed., *Collective Security in Europe and Asia* (Carlisle Barracks, Penn.: U.S. Army War College, 1992), p. 36.

early in the next century a full-blown Asian arms competition could also replace the now defunct U.S.-Soviet rivalry as the driving force in the world-wide evolution of military technology.

In taking their first steps into a new and uncertain world, the nations of Asia have chosen thus far to concentrate on stepping up their own military preparations rather than seeking new alliance partners. There is little reason to expect, however, that present patterns of diplomatic alignment will persist indefinitely. Growing concerns about one of their large neighbors could drive the smaller states into more overt alliances with each other and perhaps into choosing between contending regional powers.[77]

Even the larger diplomatic constellations could shift with the passage of time. The continuing resilience of the U.S.-Japan alliance is open to question, as is the likely longevity of the present entente between China and Japan. Some American observers have speculated that "the prospect of a militarily ascendant Japan might conceivably lead to a PRC-Korean mainland coalition to balance Japan's maritime position."[78] More obliquely, Chinese planners have also begun to discuss a range of alternative futures. Analyzing the emerging situation in Europe, a Chinese strategist reports that:

> We can visualise several different scenarios . . . One is that Germany and [Russia] will move closer together . . . On the one hand, the U.S. might ally with Germany to control Europe. Alternately, the U.S. and Britain might combine to balance Germany's influence. *In Asia, the range of possibilities is similar.*[79]

Substituting Japan for Germany, Korea for Britain, and Asia for Europe, this statement suggests that the Chinese have already begun to consider a wide array of possible relationships, including a continuation of the U.S.-Japan alliance, a new Russo-Japanese entente, and an anti-Japanese grouping consisting of the United States and Korea. Where China would fit into any of these pictures is unclear.

---

77. The possibility that Japan and a number of its Southeast Asian neighbors could eventually combine to contain Chinese expansion has already been mentioned (note 60). There is also some evidence that the smaller nations are considering closer military ties with India, perhaps as a way of coping better with both China and Japan. See Makito Ohashi and Joji Takanosu, "Southeast Asians Eye Western Frontier," *Nikkei Weekly*, May 17, 1993, p. 24.
78. Simon, "Regional Security Structures in Asia," pp. 33–34.
79. Delfs, "A Two-Front Threat," p. 28 (emphasis added).

An Asia in which alignments were more fluid, more complex, and less certain might be more likely to see crises escalate into wars. One study of crisis behavior concludes that, in a world with more than two major powers: "Negotiating positions and threat postures will be heavily affected by expectations about the interests and intentions of allies and other third parties. Since such interests and intentions are typically unclear in a multipolar system, there is considerable scope for miscalculation, and the consequences of miscalculation may be serious."[80] It is not obvious that possession of nuclear weapons on all sides would reduce the likelihood of miscalculation in a future multipolar confrontation sufficiently to offset the considerable increase in its probable costs.[81]

Asia will not lack for crises, whether they are handled well or poorly, in the years just ahead. To the south, disputes over borders and resources (especially oil and natural gas) could engage the interests of Japan, China, and India, as well as the members of ASEAN. The relationship between China and Taiwan may yet be resolved through the use of force. To the north, the future shape of Korea and the manner in which it is determined will be matters of intense concern to Japan, China, Russia, and perhaps the United States, to say nothing of the Korean people themselves.

The character of the emerging Asian order could well be determined for some time to come by the events of the next several years. Ironically, for all the uncertainty over its future position, the single most important player in the present drama is undoubtedly the United States. A precipitous withdrawal of U.S. forces in Asia or a marked worsening of U.S.-Japan tensions on economic issues would have broad ramifications. Either development separately, or both together, would tend to confirm the calculations of those who have already begun to discount the future American role in Asia and to anticipate a rapid growth in all forms of Japanese power. One result would be an acceleration in the present East Asian arms buildup; another might be the coalescence of a regional coalition aimed at containing Japan. Faced with an increasingly hostile environment and unable or unwilling to continue to

80. Glenn H. Snyder and Paul Diesing, *Conflict Among Nations: Bargaining, Decision-Making, and System Structure in International Crises* (Princeton: Princeton University Press, 1977), pp. 430–431.
81. For efforts to think through the implications of nuclear multipolarity for crisis behavior see ibid., pp. 450–470. See also Robert E. Osgood and Robert W. Tucker, *Force, Order, and Justice* (Baltimore: Johns Hopkins Press, 1967), pp. 169–179; and Hoffmann, "Nuclear Proliferation and World Politics," pp. 102–118.

rely for its security on the United States, Japan would be forced to seek diplomatic reassurance and military self-reliance. These steps, in turn, could finalize its estrangement from the United States and further fuel the anxieties of its neighbors.

American power is the linchpin that holds Japan in place. By so doing, it delays the full transition to an independent Asian sub-system and allows time for forces that can mitigate the effects of multipolarity to gain in strength. U.S. pique over unresolved economic issues with Japan, a domestic desire for even deeper defense cuts, and the more obvious immediacy of post-Communist crises in eastern Europe could combine to cause the United States to pull back more sharply from Asia than it is currently doing. The fact that such a course of action would be mistaken and dangerous affords no guarantee that it will not be followed.

Asia

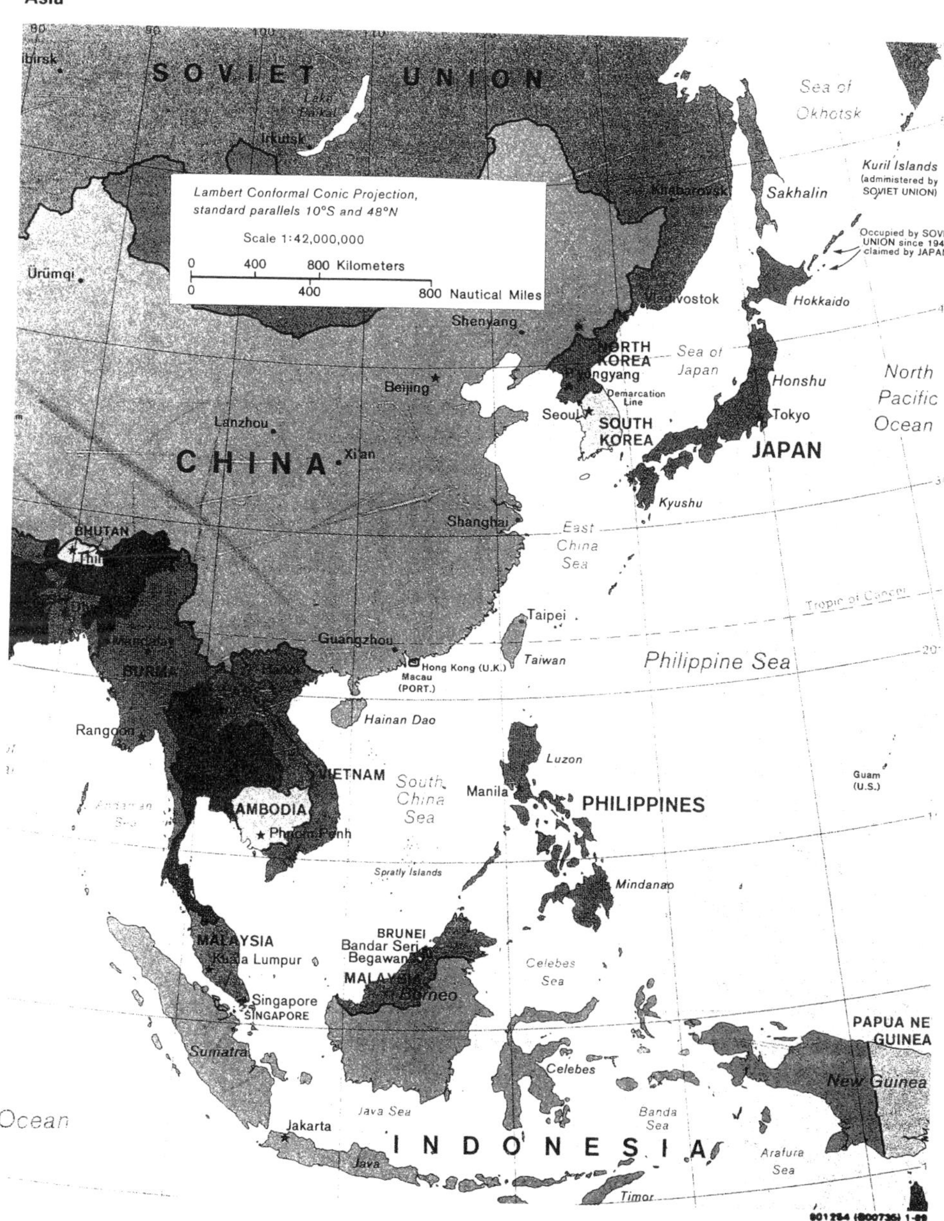

SOURCE: Department of State Bulletin.

Wealth, Power, and Instability

East Asia and the United States after the Cold War

Richard K. Betts

East Asia is becoming a more important interest to the United States at the same time that it is becoming less stable as an arena of great power interaction.[1] This is a bad combination, precisely the opposite of that in Western Europe. It is also not entirely obvious. Superficially, the region appears fairly peaceful at present, but the security order that will replace the Cold War framework is not yet clear.[2]

Richard K. Betts is Professor of Political Science, Director of International Security Policy Studies in the School of International and Public Affairs, and member of the Institute of War and Peace Studies at Columbia University.

This paper was written for the Conference on Asia in Transition sponsored by the MacArthur Foundation at the East-West Center, Honolulu, in January 1993, and was also presented in seminars at the University of Chicago Program on International Politics, Economics, and Security; MIT Center for International Studies; Columbia East Asian Institute; and Harvard Olin Institute for Strategic Studies. The author is grateful to discussants in those sessions, especially Allen Whiting, Robert Ross, Andrew Wallace, and Charles Lipson. For criticisms of various drafts he also thanks Thomas Bernstein, Frederick Brown, Evelyn Colbert, Joseph Collins, Michael Chambers, Thomas Christensen, Gerald Curtis, Francis Fukuyama, Germaine Hoston, Robert Jervis, Chalmers Johnson, Thomas McNaugher, Masashi Nishihara, William Odom, Michel Oksenberg, Jonathan Pollack, Alan Romberg, Randall Schweller, David Shambaugh, Jack Snyder, Yoshihide Soeya, Arthur Waldron, Kenneth Waltz, and Ren Yue. Another version will appear in a volume edited by Robert Ross.

1. This article considers the area from Japan to Burma. South Asia is not discussed, although India may come to figure more in the East Asian balance of power. India has always been underestimated and too often ignored in U.S. strategic studies, but since it is still peripheral to East Asian strategic interactions, it is excluded in order to keep the analytical scope manageable.
2. Ambivalence about how the security situation in Asia should be assessed can be found even among seasoned experts. For example: "The United States and Russia have a growing community of interests. . . . China is fully preoccupied with its domestic problems. Japan, an economic superpower, is only beginning to apply that power for political purposes. . . . In sum the risk of a major power conflict in Asia is at its lowest point in this century"; but, "On the political front one worrisome fact emerges. For the first time in the twentieth century, U.S. relations with China and Japan are troubled simultaneously;" and, "given the likely power relationships in East Asia, U.S. policy can proceed with minimal concern about new hostile coalitions," yet "the current leaders of the People's Republic of China are telling both Russia and Japan that there must be closer cooperation to block a hegemonic America." Robert Scalapino, "The United States and Asia: Future Prospects," *Foreign Affairs*, Vol. 70, No. 5 (Winter 1991/92), pp. 26, 32, 36.

International Security, Vol. 18, No. 3 (Winter 1993/94), pp. 34–77

In the Cold War, U.S. strategy in East Asia was driven by the titanic global struggle with Moscow.[3] The Soviet collapse makes the answers to some basic questions less obvious than they once seemed. Is it now in the interest of the United States for China to succeed in economic liberalization and become prosperous? or for Japan to become a normal state, developing a ratio of military to economic power comparable to that of other large, rich countries? or for Korea to unify? or for Taiwan to democratize? or for Vietnam to remain poor? The answers depend on more fundamental questions. How will the distribution of power in the region evolve, and does it matter? Is it important to have a balance of power in East Asia—a distribution of national capabilities that is not obviously hierarchical[4]—or do booming economies and liberalizing polities make traditional strategic calculations obsolete?

Far more than in the Cold War, when strategic debate became routinized and focused on a familiar menu of issues, these questions force analysis back to first principles about the causes of war and peace. Two broad traditions dominate thinking on this subject: realism and liberalism.[5] Realism has been dominant in academic theory, liberalism in American politics, and both are entangled in all debates about foreign affairs. Assumptions about cause and effect in most arguments derive, often unconsciously, from these philosophies. Unless the underlying logic is examined rather than assumed, policy

---

3. In the 1960s, Beijing was seen as an independent threat, but otherwise its role in U.S. strategy depended on its relation to Soviet power and trans-national Leninism. Washington opposed China in the 1950s largely because of its alliance with the USSR, and courted it in the 1970s and 1980s because of its enmity against the USSR.

4. This is the sense in which I use "balance of power" unless otherwise indicated. The term is notoriously ambiguous in common usage, referring variously to any distribution of power, a roughly equal (usually multipolar) distribution, international stability or equilibrium, deliberate policies to create or maintain equilibrium, automatic equilibrating tendencies in the international system, and other things. See Ernst Haas, "The Balance of Power: Prescription, Concept, or Propaganda?" *World Politics*, Vol. 5, No. 4 (July 1953); Inis L. Claude, Jr., *Power and International Relations* (New York: Random House, 1962), chap. 2; and Martin Wight, "The Balance of Power," in Herbert Butterfield and Martin Wight, eds., *Diplomatic Investigations: Essays in the Theory of International Politics* (Cambridge: Harvard University Press, 1968).

5. All choices cannot be lumped under this dichotomy, which does not subsume serious alternatives such as Marxism-Leninism; however, since Marxism-Leninism never influenced American policymaking, and now exerts scant influence in other countries, that alternative is ignored here. For thinking about international conflict, moreover, Marx and Lenin shared many assumptions with the other schools. If classes are substituted for states, their view of conflict as natural and inevitable is quite similar to realism. Leninist regimes that twisted doctrine to support nationalism had quite realist foreign policies. Pure Marxism, though, believes in progress. When class conflict resolves with the arrival of communism (the stage of development after socialism), the Marxist view resembles the liberal in its assumption that peace and harmony become natural.

proposals often argue past each other because proponents take their premises for granted.

As with the relation between any general theory and specific cases, hardly anyone's views fit snugly within either paradigm. Policymakers also have no interest in endless scholastic debates about them. Making theoretical distinctions explicit, however, is the first step in clarifying the competition of logical frameworks that should replace the Cold War frame of reference.[6] The implications of realist and liberal assumptions are not simple, because there are contradictions within the schools, as well as consistencies between them. This essay outlines how different combinations of assumptions about causes of war and peace produce different conclusions about which economic, political, and military developments in East Asia should be desirable or dangerous. My own position tilts toward realism but is syncretic in significant ways reflected in the recommendations at the end of the article. My main arguments are:

- The balance of power does remain important, and it is up for grabs. Economic, political, and military developments could vary and combine in so many ways that almost all significant possibilities are left open for the number of major power centers contending in the region and the identity of dominant states or coalitions.
- A truncated End of History in East Asia could be destabilizing rather than pacifying. If economic liberalization is decoupled from political democratization, it may underwrite conflict rather than cooperation.
- Although more attention has focused on the potential of Japanese power, the state most likely over time to disturb equilibrium in the region—and the world—is China.
- The United States will not be able to dominate East Asia militarily without paying costs that have been made unthinkable by the end of the Cold War.

6. Officials typically disdain as a naive academic conceit the notion that theory can inform policy. This view is rooted in practitioners' respect for their own experience; in the misconception that a general argument that does not fit all cases well, or any case perfectly, is self-evidently faulty; and in encounters with foolish academics spouting silly or unintelligible theories. Policymakers usually regard themselves as pragmatists operating case-by-case, without theoretical blinders. In reality, experience cannot predict what will happen unless either the future case is absolutely identical to one experienced (which never happens), or the policymaker filters experience through a theory. The difference between academics and officials is not reliance on theory, but whether the theory relied on is explicit or unconscious. For a promising effort to link theory and policy see Alexander George, *Bridging the Gap: Theory and Practice in Foreign Policy* (Washington, D.C.: U.S. Institute of Peace, 1993).

Realist diagnoses may be correct, yet may have to fall back on liberal prescriptions because the price of dominance is too high.

- The specific nature of U.S. strategic commitments in the region—especially in regard to Taiwan—is dangerously vague, and invites miscalculation by Asian adversaries and allies, and by our own leaders, in a prospective crisis.

Assumptions: Power, Values, and Peace

Realists believe that wars are awful but natural, and that states are subject to natural selection. Wars happen because there is nothing to prevent them when countries would rather defend conflicting claims than relinquish them. Without any supranational enforcer, states are the ultimate judges of their own rights and enforcers of their interests, material or moral, as they see them. Power determines whose claims prevail, so peace must flow from a distribution of power that convinces states that the costs of enforcing or resisting claims exceed the gains.[7]

Realist view

Classic liberalism sees wars as unnatural, occurring because states fail to recognize their common interests in efficient market exchange, or because glory-seeking rulers are unconstrained by the will of their subjects, who bear the costs of combat. Peace can emerge from the spread of understanding that liberal norms make the potential for material gain greater from cooperation than from wasteful conflict. Ideas, once properly recognized and buttressed by law, enlightened custom, and institutions to foster cooperation, exert a power of their own.[8]

Liberal

7. Exemplary realists include Thucydides, Niccolò Machiavelli, and Thomas Hobbes, and in the twentieth century, E.H. Carr, Hans Morgenthau, Reinhold Niebuhr, Arnold Wolfers, Kenneth Waltz, and Robert Gilpin. For a representative selection of arguments see Part 2 of Richard K. Betts, ed., *Conflict After the Cold War* (New York: Macmillan, 1994).

8. Examples in this tradition include Immanuel Kant, Hugo Grotius, Adam Smith, and Richard Cobden, and in the twentieth century, Woodrow Wilson, Joseph Schumpeter, Norman Angell, Hedley Bull, and Robert Keohane. See selections in Parts 3–5 of Betts, ed., *Conflict After the Cold War.* For comparative examinations from varying perspectives see Charles Beitz, *Political Theory and International Relations* (Princeton: Princeton University Press, 1979); Joseph S. Nye, Jr., "Neorealism and Neoliberalism," *World Politics,* Vol. 40, No. 2 (January 1988); Robert Gilpin with the assistance of Jean M. Gilpin, *The Political Economy of International Relations* (Princeton: Princeton University Press, 1987), chap. 2.

Within the realist school, all agree that the distribution of national power is the most important concern of policy,[9] but not about *which* distribution is most stable. There are three structural alternatives: multipolarity, bipolarity, or unipolarity. Classical balance of power theorists tend to favor the first,[10] "neorealists" the second,[11] and some others the third.[12] This lack of consensus, as well as the various ambiguities about which strategies produce certain results, make realism quite indeterminate; it is much clearer about what the general problem is than about what the particular solutions should be.

Within the liberal school, there are three main variants. One emphasizes that economic liberty—free markets and trade, division of labor according to comparative advantage, and interdependence—makes countries avoid war in order to maximize material gain.[13] Another sees political liberty as the source of states' confidence in each other's benign intentions; in the past two centuries constitutional democracies have virtually never fought each other.[14] The third, "neoliberal institutionalism," focuses on the role of international organization, informal as well as formal, for cultivating the norms of coop-

9. The latest wave, known as neorealism, focuses entirely on the international structure of power. Old realists consider domestic political and psychological factors as important in explaining decisions for war, but they too emphasize the external distribution of state power as the prime concern for policy.

10. The reasoning is that primacy of one state deprives too many others of independence, or is impossible in the absence of a universal empire; bipolarity is unstable because it invites struggle for primacy, miscalculation, and preventive war; and multipolarity (preferably with five or more great powers) allows flexible alignments to redress developing imbalances. See Edward Vose Gulick, *Europe's Classical Balance of Power: A Case History of the Theory and Practice of One of the Great Concepts of European Statecraft* (New York: Norton, 1967); F.H. Hinsley, *Power and the Pursuit of Peace: Theory and Practice in the History of Relations between States* (New York: Cambridge University Press, 1963); Albert Sorel, *Europe Under the Old Regime,* Francis H. Herrick, trans. (New York: Harper Torchbooks, 1964); Ludwig Dehio, *The Precarious Balance,* 2d ed. (London: Chatto and Windus, 1962).

11. This view derives inductively from the stability of the U.S.-Soviet balance in the Cold War and deductively from the argument that multipolarity makes alliance solidarity too important, and allows crises to escalate too easily when states drag their allies into confrontation. Kenneth N. Waltz, *Theory of International Politics* (Reading: Addison-Wesley, 1979), chap. 8.

12. Geoffrey Blainey, *The Causes of War,* 3d ed. (New York: Free Press, 1988), pp. 109, 112–114; Samuel P. Huntington, "Why International Primacy Matters," *International Security,* Vol. 17, No. 4 (Spring 1993).

13. Early expositors of this view were Richard Cobden and the "Manchester School" in the nineteenth century. For a critique see Blainey, *Causes of War,* chap. 2. For a balanced recent version of the argument see Richard Rosecrance, *The Rise of the Trading State: Commerce and Conquest in the Modern World* (New York: Basic Books, 1986).

14. Michael Doyle, "Liberalism and World Politics," *American Political Science Review,* Vol. 80, No. 4 (December 1986); and Doyle, "Kant, Liberal Legacies, and Foreign Affairs," Parts I and II, *Philosophy and Public Affairs,* Vol. 12, No. 3 (Summer 1984), and ibid. No. 4 (Fall 1983).

erative behavior.[15] Whereas realism is inadequate as a guide to policy because it is indeterminate, the distinction between the first variant of the liberal paradigm and the second and third poses a potential problem. Whatever its impact on inclinations to war or peace may be, *economic* liberalism generates *power,* by virtue of its dynamic impact on national development. Therefore, if political liberalism or neoliberal institutional liberalism turn out to be stronger sources of peaceful behavior than is economic liberalism, economic liberalism might promote realists' worst nightmares about the dangers of imbalance of power if it is decoupled from the other two variants of liberalism—as it could well be in East Asia.

All these variations within the contending schools complicate the prescriptions we might infer. There is no simple correlation between any of the paradigms and the propensity to use force.[16] But on one vital point—the relative importance of national power and ideological values—the basic dichotomy remains relevant to strategy. Realists part company with liberals on the priority of maintaining for its own sake a favorable material power position, conceived in terms of military and economic capability relative to other countries.[17] Liberals, in turn, are more reluctant to subordinate international law, political justice, or absolute prosperity to strategic competition and economic autonomy. Nurturing national power is unobjectionable only as long as it does not impair international cooperation. On the use of force beyond the direct defense of one's own homeland, realists are most inclined to it when the balance of power is at stake, liberals when moral values are at stake. These differences should be highlighted for two reasons.

First, the question of for what objectives and on whose behalf a state should shed blood is the most essential aspect of security policy. In the United States, that issue was contentious enough during the second half of the Cold War, after it fought two hot wars in East Asia. Now, with the passing of the global threats of Soviet national power and transnational

---

15. See, for example, Robert Keohane, *International Institutions and State Power: Essays in International Relations Theory* (Boulder, Colo.: Westview Press, 1989); and Stephen D. Krasner, ed., *International Regimes* (Ithaca: Cornell University Press, 1983). The institutionalist variant of the liberal approach incorporates significant elements of realist logic.

16. For example, realists Henry Kissinger and Hans Morgenthau split on the Vietnam War, as did liberals Henry Jackson and George McGovern. More recently, proponents of intervention in Bosnia, Somalia, and Haiti have more often been found among liberals than realists.

17. Space constraints preclude full discussion of ambiguities and qualifications in definitions of power, especially non-realist definitions. See David Baldwin, *Paradoxes of Power* (New York: Blackwell, 1989), and Joseph S. Nye, Jr., *Bound to Lead: The Changing Nature of American Power* (New York: Basic Books, 1990).

communist ideology, there is no consensus whatever on this question, especially in regard to Asia.

Second, if realism is relevant, it faces an uphill battle in the policy arena because its logic is not automatically compelling to Americans. The Cold War was won without proving which of the two general paradigms was correct, since victory correlated with *both* the assertion of U.S. power and the adversary's acceptance of western ideals. Realism can explain why Gorbachev and his crew decided that glasnost and perestroika were necessary, but not why they gave away the Soviet empire in 1989 without a murmur. Liberal logic is deeply rooted in American society (which is why laissez-faire liberals in the United States are called conservatives).[18] Realism is not; it is an acquired taste, offensive to many Americans when stated baldly, uncloaked in righteousness.

This was not a problem in the Cold War because at many points throughout that period Americans *did not have to choose* between the imperatives of power and of values. The communist threat, like the fascist threat before it, combined military power with anti-liberal ideology, allowing conservative realism's focus on might and liberal idealism's focus on right to converge in a militant policy. It would not otherwise have been as easy for the United States to play power politics so enthusiastically in the half-century after Pearl Harbor.[19]

Winning the Cold War could not help but confirm liberal optimism about the natural progress of history toward peace. An axiomatic liberal consensus is riskier now, however, because without a clear adversary like the USSR it will not complement concern with military power and strategic activism as easily as before. Now the conceptual choices associated with the two main

---

18. Louis Hartz, *The Liberal Tradition in America: An Interpretation of American Political Thought Since the Revolution* (New York: Harcourt, Brace, 1955), argues that liberalism so infuses American political culture that it is taken for granted, and allows politically significant debates to take place only among schools within liberalism.

19. The exception to the consensus was the decade after the 1968 Tet Offensive, when liberals became disillusioned with intervention and argued that interdependence and negotiation rather than military muscle would best serve peace and stability. The debate crested in the Carter administration with the split between the dovish Cyrus Vance and the hawkish Zbigniew Brzezinski. The split was resolved in the hawks' favor after the invasion of Afghanistan, and the reborn consensus was confirmed with Reagan's election. In 1993, however, the Vance school got its revenge, as Warren Christopher and Anthony Lake, his old lieutenants, took charge of foreign policy. Lake described himself and President Clinton as "neo-Wilsonian," opposed to the "classic balance of power" perspective. Steven A. Holmes, "Choice for National Security Adviser Has a Long-Awaited Chance to Lead," *New York Times*, January 3, 1993, p. 16.

paradigms point more often in divergent directions. Nowhere is this more true than in Asia.

World Power, Regional Power, and Strategic Interests

The worldwide structure of power no longer governs the regional structure of power, as it did in the Cold War. Global unipolarity[20] now coincides with regional multipolarity. No country but the United States can project large amounts of military force at all points in the world, but this unique capacity is fractionated by multiple commitments in different regions. Although the United States is in a military class by itself, it cannot act independently in many cases but needs the cooperation of allies to provide bases (such as Saudi Arabia for the Gulf War, or Japan and South Korea in East Asia). Moreover, without the challenge of another superpower to contend with, U.S. military forces are shrinking and likely to level off well below the baseline of the Cold War.[21]

The divergence in U.S. and local trends illustrates the self-liquidating character of unipolarity. In East Asia, in contrast to the United States, militaries are growing. China especially has boosted its defense budget since the late 1980s. It is buying and selling weapons at a fast clip, seeking naval facilities closer to the Malacca Straits, and developing rapid-deployment battalions.[22] This activity is not in itself evidence of malign intent, since China's defense spending was depressed in the 1980s, and most countries increase defense spending as their economies grow. As for Japan, it "alone among

---

20. Other terms used in place of unipolarity include hegemony, hierarchy, and primacy. These connote more about the amount of control that goes with a dominant power position than I wish to assume at most points in this essay. For an activist view of the implications of global unipolarity for U.S. policy, see Charles Krauthammer, "The Unipolar Moment," *Foreign Affairs*, Vol. 70, No. 1 (Winter 1990/91).
21. For a related view of current power structures see the discussion of the "uni-multipolar" world in Samuel P. Huntington, "America's Changing Strategic Interests," *Survival*, Vol. 33, No. 1 (January/February 1991), p. 6.
22. David Shambaugh, "In Shanghai's Busy Shipyards, A Warning About Chinese Might," *International Herald Tribune*, January 15, 1993, p. 8; Nicholas Kristof, "China Raises Military Budget Despite Deficit," *New York Times*, March 17, 1993, p. A9. By some accounts the nominal increase was over half, but Chinese sources claim that it was only 17.2 percent in 1988–91 when discounted for inflation. Qimao Chen, "New Approaches in China's Foreign Policy," *Asian Survey*, Vol. 33, No. 3 (March 1993), p. 245.

the rich countries . . . is still increasing its defense spending in real terms."[23] (See Table 1.)

The situation is similarly mixed in other dimensions of power. Globally, no other country approaches the United States in economic leverage, but this is not true within East Asia. Being Number One in the world in terms of gross national product (GNP), domestic markets, or other indices does not translate into local dominance. Politically, the demise of Marxism-Len-

Table 1. Recent Defense Budget Trends: Great Powers and Middle Powers in East Asia.

	1990	1991	1992	1993	% change 1990–93
U.S.A.	291.4	272.95	270.9	258.87	−11.2
USSR	116.7	--	--	--	--
Russia		52.51	39.68	29.12	−44.5[a]
Japan	28.73	32.68	35.94	39.71	+38.2
China (PRC)[b]	6.06	6.11	6.71	7.31	+20.6
Taiwan	8.69	9.29	10.29[c]	10.45	+20.3
S. Korea	10.62	10.77	11.19	12.06	+13.6
N. Korea[c]	5.23	2.36	2.06	2.19	−58.1
Vietnam[c]	N.A.	1.87	1.75	N.A.	N.A.
Indonesia	1.45	1.55	1.77	1.95	+34.5
Australia	7.01	7.06	6.94	6.96	−0.7

NOTES: Figures in U.S. $ billions. Figures are for defense budgets, which indicate intended level of effort and for which more recent data are available, rather than defense expenditures. NB: Data do not correct for exchange rate fluctuations, hence exaggerate some changes; e.g., change for Japan calculated in yen is only 11.6%

a. 1991–93

b. Estimated actual *expenditures* much higher: $18.79 billion for 1991, $21.76 billion for 1992.

c. Estimates.

SOURCES: *The Military Balance 1990–1991* (London: International Institute for Strategic Studies [IISS], 1990), p. 17; *The Military Balance 1991–1992* (London: IISS, 1991), pp. 19, 150, 157, 164, 169, 180; *The Military Balance 1992–1993* (London: IISS, 1992), pp. 18, 141, 145, 148, 150, 152, 153, 161, 164; *The Military Balance 1993–1994* (London: IISS, 1993), pp. 20, 98, 152, 156, 157, 159, 161, 168, 171.

23. "Asia's Arms Race," *The Economist*, February 20, 1993, p. 19.

inism leaves the United States (and western liberalism in general) without any powerful transnational ideological competition.[24] However, democracy has not surged as far in East Asia as it has in some other regions.[25]

The change from worldwide bipolarity to *unipolarity makes the global dimension of strategic competition irrelevant.* U.S. strategy no longer contends with the prospect of a multi-front global war or an epochal struggle over which of two universalist value systems will dominate the world. If the United States intervenes somewhere now, it cannot be because of a derivative interest in the place as it affects the worldwide balance sheet with another superpower, but because of an intrinsic interest in the place itself.[26]

Where should East Asia rank among American regional strategic priorities? This depends on the relation between stakes and threats. In Cold War military planning, Asia always came second, behind Europe. The wars in Korea and Vietnam (undertaken in large part because of perceived linkage to European security) forced Asia higher on the foreign policy agenda than Presidents Truman, Kennedy, or Johnson wanted. Eisenhower flirted with an "Asia First" policy, to propitiate the Taft-Knowland wing of the Republican Party, but never quite followed through in practice.[27] With the oil embargo and the Iranian Revolution in the 1970s, the Middle East and Persian Gulf began to overtake Asia for second place in the attention of the Pentagon. The 1991 war against Iraq confirmed the new preoccupation.

---

24. In contrast to most realists, I count ideology as an element of power, rather than just a matter of values, when it contributes to social mobilization, willingness to bear high costs for strategic rivalry, and incentives for alliance between countries. The only candidate to replace Marxism-Leninism as a competing global ideology is radical Islam, which hypothetically could coordinate movements in areas as diverse as the Middle East and North Africa, Nigeria, Pakistan, Indonesia, and some of the former Soviet republics of Central Asia, to team up with the regime in Iran. Nothing indicates the probability that coordination would be successful, however, and such a coalition would also lack the industrial power or geographic cohesion to stand up to Western military force.

25. See Charles E. Morrison, "The Future of Democracy in the Asia-Pacific Region: The Security Implications," in Dora Alves, ed., *Evolving Pacific Basin Strategies* (Washington, D.C.: National Defense University Press, 1990).

26. On derivative and intrinsic interests, see Richard K. Betts, "Southeast Asia and U.S. Global Strategy," *Orbis*, Vol. 29, No. 2 (Summer 1985), pp. 354–362. The difference was related to the domino theory. One way of putting it would be to say that the United States committed itself militarily to NATO and the Mutual Security Treaty with Tokyo because it cared (intrinsically) about Western Europe and Japan, while it committed itself militarily in Korea and Vietnam because it cared (derivatively) about Western Europe and Japan.

27. Richard K. Betts, *Soldiers, Statesmen, and Cold War Crises*, 2d ed. (New York: Columbia University Press, 1991), pp. 81–84, and p. 271 note 18. The U.S. Navy promoted a reorientation to Asia during the Reagan administration, to rationalize its maritime strategy, but no U.S. administration ever demoted the NATO commitment from first place.

Reduced attention to Asia as a military problem in the second half of the Cold War followed from U.S. withdrawal from Vietnam and reconciliation with China. (It is ironic how seldom anyone ever notes that the United States spent almost sixty thousand American lives, hundreds of thousands of Indochinese lives, and several hundred billion of today's dollars fighting the Vietnam War in no small part to contain China regionally,[28] only to turn on a dime and embrace China in order to contain the USSR globally.) At the same time as the downshift in military activism, economic stakes were moving in the opposite direction: Asia was outstripping Europe as a U.S. trade partner. By now, two-way trade with East Asia is well over $300 billion, a third more than with Europe.[29] (For U.S. trade with Asia as a whole, the difference is even greater.)

The galloping pace at which East Asia has been closing the gap in power potential can be seen even in the 1980s, after most Asian economies had taken off. (See Table 2.) In terms of the material stakes of most interest to hardheaded strategic realists, the population and growing wealth of East Asia should have boosted it over Europe on the list of priorities some time ago. That did not happen for several reasons, including inertia and, perhaps, a whiff of unconscious racism. Another reason was political affinity. Western Europe was a set of fraternal, stable democracies. In East Asia these have been rare.

Other explanations for the lower military priority of Asia were less inconsistent with balance of power criteria. Material stakes do not automatically dictate levels of military effort. Geographic conditions made the cost of deterrence much higher in Europe than in Asia, in terms of treasure, though it proved much lower in terms of blood. At least half of cumulative U.S. peacetime defense expenditures (including most of the strategic nuclear force) could be fairly attributed to the European commitment,[30] although it was in

28. For example, in 1964–66, when the move to large-scale intervention occurred, China was the focus of official statements on Vietnam between three and five times as often as the Soviet Union was. F.M. Kail, *What Washington Said: Administration Rhetoric and the Vietnam War* (New York: Harper Torchbooks, 1973), Appendix.

29. Secretary of Defense Dick Cheney, *Defense Strategy for the 1990s: The Regional Defense Strategy* (Washington, D.C.: Department of Defense, January 1993), p. 21.

30. Fungibility of forces makes any nominal allocation of expenditures to specific regional commitments contentious, but internal U.S. planning generated force requirements largely for war in Europe. In the early 1960s planners were directed to develop capabilities for a so-called "2½ War" scenario, in which Europe would be only one of the total. The results still allocated about 60 percent of ground force divisions and fighter-attack wings to NATO. William W. Kaufmann, *Planning Conventional Forces, 1950–1980* (Washington, D.C.: Brookings Institution),

Table 2. One Decade of Shifting Power Potential.

	NATO Europe	East Asia	All Europe	All Asia
GNP[a]				
1979	3,728	2,516	7,427	2,716
1989	4,610	4,117	9,032	4,454
% change	23.7	63.6	21.6	64.0
Per Capita GNP[b]				
1979	11,480	1,656	9,400	1,128
1989	13,410	2,349	10,720	1,557
% change	16.8	41.8	14.0	38.0
Population[c]				
1979	324.7	1,519.0	790.2	2,406.2
1989	343.8	1,752.4	842.8	2,859.0
% change	5.9	15.4	6.7	18.8

NOTES:
a. $ U.S. billions, constant 1989 dollars.
b. $ U.S. constant 1989 dollars.
c. Millions.
SOURCE: ACDA, *World Military Expenditures and Arms Transfers 1990* (Washington, D.C.: U.S. GPO, November 1991), pp. 48, 50. "All Asia" is East and South Asia.

Asia that we fought two long, nasty wars after 1945. The conventional Soviet military threat was more manageable in Asia than it was in Europe. In Europe, the challenge was to block an armored advance over land to the English Channel that could extend Communist control over Germany, France, and the rest of the continent, taking a large portion of the world's industrial power into Moscow's ambit. In Asia, Japan was the only modern industrial power for most of the Cold War, and it was protected, as England had been against Napoleon and Hitler, by a buffer of water. China was the sole major state directly threatened by Soviet invasion. The People's Republic was only an ally of convenience for the United States, and just a tacit one at that. The country's strategic depth also made its complete conquest less likely.

For whatever reasons, Asia's importance as an objective strategic interest, as stakes on the global board, seldom paralleled its profile in American

1982), Tables 1 and 2, pp. 6–7. Later, the Nixon Doctrine reduced the criterion to "1½ Wars," of which Europe was the one. It was also an open secret that the United States had a "swing" strategy, by which military forces in the Pacific would move to Europe in the event of war there.

military policy after 1945. More military effort was invested in the region in the first half of the Cold War, when it was less important than Europe, than in the second half, when it was becoming more important. Except for the 1960s, however, when the military commitment was excessive (the Vietnam War), the levels of effort were not out of line with the threats to the stakes. Will this remain true if, as argued at the outset, U.S. interests in East Asia are rising while the region's stability is declining?

The higher stakes are matters of arithmetic. East Asia has about a third of the world's population, a growing share of total world economic product, and the largest portion of American trade outside the Western hemisphere. If policymakers continue to place a higher value on Europe, despite the retreat of the Soviet military threat, it will be for reasons of cultural affinity or something else, but not because of material interest. If the rationale behind U.S. interventions and peacetime presence in Europe in this century was to prevent a hostile power from dominating a vital center of the world's wealth, productivity, and markets, the same logic should apply in East Asia.

But what is the hostile power that should imply a military corollary to the economic stakes? Is there now a natural balance in the region, so that no local state can dominate even if the United States does not act to maintain equilibrium? The evidence of instability is less straightforward than are the stakes. In one sense, stability in the region has never been so good. For more than a century East Asia has been an international subsystem where up to five great powers have interacted, and at the moment they all have decent relations with each other. But of the six dyadic relationships among the current four great powers (U.S.-Japan, U.S.-China, U.S.-Russia, Japan-China, Japan-Russia, Russia-China), *none* has been consistently stable and friendly, and *all* have eventuated in combat at some point in this century. Today there is only one scene of contention where all the great powers' interests intersect—Korea; elsewhere they cooperate or compete in various combinations. Moreover, the regional countries have become actors on the world scene and are no longer just acted upon. This reduces the leverage of the outside great powers. Finally, as the end of the Cold War takes rising middle powers such as South Korea and Taiwan out of the arena of superpower competition, they develop the capacity to maneuver, and thus more countries can complicate international relations.[31]

31. I owe much of this paragraph to discussions with Michel Oksenberg.

The most important local countries remain the great powers: China, Japan, and Russia. When the Cold War subsumed strategic competition in Asia we did not worry about China and Japan as independent actors (except for the decade between the Sino-Soviet split and Sino-American rapprochement); without the Soviet threat, it is hard to see why either China or Japan should not become more independent. This does not mean that the great powers cannot avoid direct conflict and feel content to secure defense of their interests with minimal military means, even if economic nationalism prevails. As James Kurth suggested in the waning days of the Cold War:

> If a Pacific Basin international system based upon the concepts of international mercantilism and finite deterrence were to come into being . . . the United States would no longer be the core country in the Pacific region. . . . Without the U.S. open market and the U.S. Seventh Fleet, the United States would be of little importance to Asia and the Pacific. Japan and China would become the core countries.[32]

This would keep the United States out of war in the area as well as a liberal system would, but it would keep it out of liberal economic relations as well. It is also unlikely that "finite deterrence" could mean anything but nuclear armament for all the players. What alternatives are there for the United States, and how does military power fit in?

U.S. military commitments in East Asia should be a higher relative priority than they were after the Vietnam War, if only by default, because military requirements for European defense have plummeted. But the increase in relative priority coincides with an absolute decline in forces, so there is not likely to be any redeployment to the Pacific. U.S. planning for major war is no longer "threat-based." No longer does the Pentagon identify a superpower whose location and forces provide the standards by which to measure the adequacy of its own, which can then subsume the capabilities that turn out to be needed for unforeseen minor contingencies. Instead, the United States is moving to maintain a "base force" of standing capabilities for limited contingencies, and a foundation for "reconstitution" of the Cold War level of forces should a new major adversary emerge.[33] To the extent that identified

32. James R. Kurth, "The Pacific Basin versus the Atlantic Alliance: Two Paradigms of International Relations," *The Annals of the American Academy of Political and Social Sciences*, Vol. 505 (September 1989), p. 37.

33. *1992 Joint Military Net Assessment* (Washington, D.C.: Directorate for Force Structure, Resources, and Assessment, J-8, The Joint Staff, August 1992), chaps. 3, 10; Dick Cheney, *Report of the Secretary of Defense to the President and Congress, January 1993* (Washington, D.C.: U.S. GPO,

threats do play a part in current military planning, they lie outside Asia, for example Iran or Iraq. Those countries cannot threaten western survival as the Soviet Union did (although this will change if they get large numbers of nuclear weapons). The only countries anywhere in the world that could recreate a superpower-sized threat early in the twenty-first century are the other great powers of East Asia: Russia, China, and Japan.[34] (See Table 3.)

Power Centers and Instabilities

The future roles of China and Japan highlight how critical the choice of realist or liberal models of international relations is, because some developments

Table 3. Selected Comparisons of Military Forces in East Asia, 1992.

	Ground Force Divisions	Main Battle Tanks	Combat Aircraft	Principal Surface Combatants	Submarines
U.S.A.[a]	4	N.A.[b]	278	110	61
Russia[c]	53	9,800	1,320	54	86
Japan	13	1,210	564	64	17
China	101+	7,500–8000	5,850	54	46
Taiwan	22+	459+	518	33	4
S. Korea	24+	1,800	470	38	4
N. Korea	30+	3,000	732	3+	26
Vietnam	73+	1,300	185	7+	—

NOTES: Excludes independent brigades/regiments/battalions, light tanks, patrol/coastal combatant ships. "+" after numbers indicates high ratios of such smaller units to the large ones tabulated. Tabulations do not indicate relative combat power, due to qualitative disparities and asymmetries in untabulated capabilities.
a. Pacific Command (PACOM).
b. Number not available for PACOM; 15,629 main battle tanks (MBT) listed for total U.S. inventory.
c. Siberian, Transbaykal, and Far East Military Districts.
SOURCE: International Institute for Strategic Studies (IISS), *The Military Balance, 1992–1993* (London: Brassey's/IISS, Autumn 1992), pp. 27, 100, 145–147, 150–154, 161–162, and enclosed map.

n.d.), p. 12. The Clinton administration amended this plan, but the substance did not change significantly. See Secretary of Defense Les Aspin, *The Bottom-Up Review: Forces for a New Era* (Washington, D.C.: Department of Defense, September 1993).
34. Even if the German Problem were reborn, Germany is more constrained by geography and continental institutions than are the large Asian powers.

will look desirable in terms of one and disastrous in terms of the other. By the assumptions of the liberal model, the main problem is to promote liberalization, especially political and economic liberalization in China, and free trade among all. Liberalization in one sphere reinforces the other; as countries become more prosperous they are more likely to become democratic. Thus, it is in the security interest of countries to help each other become rich, even if that widens differences in national capability. If political and economic liberty become universal, peace will be secure and differences in national power beside the point. Commercial competition should displace military competition. The economic development and expanding trade that characterize Asia point to opportunities for mutual profit between the United States and local countries. National competitions for power waste resources, at best, or generate conflicts artificially, at worst.

For realists, ideology is barely relevant. Political fraternity will wilt under other pressures, and differences in power will resolve conflicts of interest. Even if the pacifying effect of political liberalism is accepted, there is the problem that market efficiency may operate within authoritarian polities, yielding material strength without ideological discipline. For realists, it is not in a country's strategic interest for others to get rich unless they can be counted on to remain militarily weak or diplomatically allied. To realists, liberal theory overestimates the value states place on absolute as opposed to relative gains:

> For the United States, which future is preferable: one in which the U.S. economy grows at 25 percent over the next decade, while the Japanese economy grows at 75 percent, or one in which the U.S. grows at only 10 percent while that of Japan grows 10.3 percent? Robert Reich . . . posed that choice in 1990 in a series of meetings with graduate students, U.S. corporate executives, investment bankers, citizens of Massachusetts, senior State Department officials, and professional economists. A majority of every group, with one exception, expressed a preference for the latter outcome. The economists unanimously chose the former, and . . . were surprised that other Americans would voluntarily forgo fifteen percentage points of economic growth in the interest of hampering the progress of one of America's principal trade and financial partners.[35]

It is good for a country other than one's own to have impressive military power as long as the two countries are bonded by the imperative to cooperate

35. Michael Mastanduno, "Do Relative Gains Matter? America's Response to Japanese Industrial Policy," *International Security*, Vol. 16, No. 1 (Summer 1991), p. 73.

against a common threat. Otherwise, its friendship depends on the vicissitudes of international developments, and the wealth that is convertible into military power makes it a potential threat. By liberal logic, other countries are more dangerous if they are lean and hungry than if they are fat and happy. Realists, however, worry that prosperity may just make them muscular and ambitious.

Prospects for China and Japan thus have radically different implications for stability, depending on which models of the causes of war and peace are superimposed on the future. Those prospects have been obscured until recently because analysts tended to consider the power of both in terms of how they lined up in the global conflict with Moscow, and to see them as junior partners. The U.S. reconciliation with China, which turned the tables and made the Soviets confront the strategic planning problem of a two-front war as the United States had earlier, allowed Washington to remain one of the two principal powers in the area even as it withdrew a huge chunk of the forces it had deployed in the area between 1950 and 1972. By the end of the Cold War, only about 17 percent of U.S. military manpower was allocated to Asia, only about 6 percent was deployed forward in the region, and 70 percent of those deployed forward were in Japan and Korea.[36]

Now both Russia and the United States are less dominant in the region. Russia is preoccupied with internal transformation, and its power is drastically reduced from that of the Soviet Union. As a group of sober Russian strategic analysts put it:

> Having retained more than four-fifths of the territory of the USSR, Russia nonetheless accounts for slightly over one-half of the population. It controls (taking into consideration production decline) less than one-half of the Soviet gross national product for 1990. In terms of most parameters . . . Russia has become a middle-sized country. In Europe this is the equivalent of France, Great Britain, and Italy; in Asia, of India, and Indonesia.[37]

To the extent that Russian foreign policy focuses on Asia, it is focused much less on East Asia than on Central Asia and the multiple disorders on Russia's

---

36. *A Strategic Framework for the Asian Pacific Rim: Looking Toward the 21st Century,* Report to Congress (Washington, D.C.: Office of the Assistant Secretary of Defense for International Security Affairs, East Asia Pacific Region, April 1990), p. 5.
37. "Some Theses for the Report of the Foreign and Defense Policy Council," in Foreign Broadcast Information Service (FBIS), *Central Eurasia,* FBIS-USR-92–115, September 8, 1992, p. 54.

southern borders.[38] In the near future, Russia's weakened condition facilitates more cooperation with China (by reducing the threat that Beijing might worry about) while enhancing incentives for it. For example, Russian civilian products are not competitive internationally, and the country's only industrial comparative advantage is in weapons manufacture, but these products are frozen out of the western market while the West tries to prevent either Moscow or Beijing from selling more arms elsewhere.[39] In the longer term, if Russia solves its problems, balance of power concerns are likely to bring back at least modest tension between the two great powers of mainland Asia.[40] Moscow will inevitably be a strategic heavyweight in the region, especially when and if its own economic and political situation stabilizes, but its clout is unlikely to grow as fast as Beijing's or Tokyo's.

The United States remains formally committed to a strategic role in the Pacific, but its military presence has again been attenuated as the flag has come down from Philippine bases, land- and sea-based tactical nuclear weapons have been removed, and defense budget cuts trim the number of forces regularly on station elsewhere in the neighborhood. U.S. political rhetoric minimizes change, but military movement highlights it. There is an important difference on this point between Northeast and Southeast Asia. American deployments in Korea may last for a long time, and those in Japan would be the last to go. The U.S. military role in the northern area has not shifted from substance to symbol, but in the southern part of the region it shifted clearly in that direction after 1973. Whether this matters is a question that brings us back to the opposing implications of the liberal and realist models.

Two potential changes would most focus the issue. These would be China's achievement of a high level of economic development (close to Taiwan's or South Korea's) and Japan's development of a normal amount of military power (a share of national product allocated to the military comparable to the share devoted by other wealthy countries). For those guided by liberal

38. See Sergei Karaganov, "Russia and Other Independent Republics in Asia," in *Asia's International Role in the Post–Cold War Era: Part II*, Adelphi Paper No. 276 (London: International Institute for Strategic Studies, April 1993), pp. 27–29.

39. "Instead of being coopted and integrated, the powerful political and economic interests connected with the Russian armaments industry are being pushed in an anti-Western direction. A side effect of these policies will be, of course, a further shift towards relatively indiscriminate arms sales . . . particularly to China." Karaganov, "Russia and Other Independent Republics in Asia," p. 26.

40. "The Chinese factor is encouraging Russia to retain its political reliance on nuclear containment and . . . strategic alliance with the West." "Some Theses for the Report of the Foreign and Defense Policy Council," p. 57.

theories of the causes of war and peace, such outcomes would be desirable at best and harmless at worst; for American realists, either one should be disturbing.

Even under the conventional economic measurements that kept estimates low, China has grown at an impressive pace since embracing the market. According to the most authoritative U.S. figures for 1991, China's real GNP grew 7 percent, its industrial output 14 percent.[41] In 1992, by one report, the growth rate was a whopping 12 percent.[42] If we take more recent International Monetary Fund (IMF) calculations based on purchasing power parity rather than exchange rates (see below), the results look far more dramatic. *The Economist*, which makes the case that most official statistics for China are meaningless, claims that the average annual growth rate has been nearly 9 percent for fourteen years, and that China's true output is already at least a quarter of U.S. GNP. Its marginal savings rate is also among the highest in the region.[43]

It is not inevitable that recent average rates will continue indefinitely, but if they do, the long-term prospects for the balance of power—global as well as regional—are staggering. Consider the implications of Table 4, based on the most conservative estimates of China's recent economic performance. If the country ever achieved a per-capita GNP just one-fourth that of the United States (about South Korea's ratio today), it would have a total GNP *greater* than that of the United States. That in itself is a limited indicator, since it would not equate to comparable disposable income, but it would still be an epochal change in the distribution of world power. By the same token, Japan's smaller population mitigates the implications of its per-capita income. Japan would need double the American per-capita GNP to exceed absolute U.S. GNP.[44] Similarly, the prospect of Russia's economic development poses

---

41. Central Intelligence Agency, *The Chinese Economy in 1991 and 1992: Pressure to Revisit Reform Mounts*, EA 92-10029 (Washington, D.C.: CIA Directorate of Intelligence, August 1992), p. iii.
42. Nicholas D. Kristof, "China Builds Its Military Muscle, Making Some Neighbors Nervous," *New York Times*, January 11, 1993, p. A8.
43. "China: The Titan Stirs," *The Economist*, November 28, 1992, pp. 3–5; David Shambaugh, "China's Security Policy in the Post–Cold War Era," *Survival*, Vol. 34, No. 2 (Summer 1992), p. 101. See also Charles Horner, "China on the Rise," *Commentary*, Vol. 94, No. 6 (December 1992).
44. Population itself is not a source of power. Indeed, at present China's population is a source of weakness, and will become a greater one if its growth is not curbed. The point is that population makes for power when it is associated with an advanced economy. It is not because of its per-capita income that the United States is the most powerful country in the world; several countries rank higher on that index, but no matter how efficient a Switzerland or Sweden may be, they can never be superpowers. Countries with the most power potential in the twenty-first century will be the ones that combine high rankings in productivity, population, and resources; those with the most actual power will be the ones from among that group who marshal the most military power from that potential.

Table 4. Prosperity and Power Potential.

	China	S. Korea	Japan	USA
Per capita GNP ($)	547.0	4,920.0	22,900.0	20,910.0
(% of U.S.)	(2.6)	(23.5)	(109.5)	
Total GNP ($ billions)	603.5	210.1	2,820.0	5,201.0
(% of U.S.)	(11.6)	(4.0)	(54.2)	
Population (millions)	1,102.4	42.7	123.2	248.8
(% of U.S.)	(443.1)	(17.2)	(49.5)	
Percentage of U.S. per capita GNP needed to equal total U.S. GNP	22.6	582.7	201.9	

SOURCE: U.S. Arms Control and Disarmament Agency (ACDA), *World Military Expenditures and Arms Transfers 1990* (Washington, D.C.: U.S. Government Printing Office, November 1991), pp. 58, 68, 69, 85.

NOTE: This compilation uses 1989 figures from ACDA. The most recent official World Bank data publicly available at this writing, cited below, go only one year later, are incommensurable (listing per-capita income in terms of gross *national* product, but national income in gross *domestic* product), and understate the size of the Chinese economy even more than the above data, citing $370 per capita GNP for 1990. See analysis in "China: The Titan Stirs," *The Economist,* November 28, 1992, pp. 3–5. More realistic data would show much less current disparity between China and the United States, reinforcing the argument in the text of this paper. Cf. World Bank, *World Development Report 1992: Development and the Environment* (New York: Oxford University Press, 1992), pp. 218–223. U.S. government estimates report World Bank figures for 1991 and do not offer figures for China in 1992; see *The World Factbook 1992* (Washington, D.C.: Central Intelligence Agency, n.d.).

less threat to a balance of power than does China's. Even by the conservative estimates, the prospect of China as an economic superpower is not remote. If the IMF calculations are to be believed, that eventuality is much closer. By those numbers, China's economy is four times larger than previously estimated, and the third largest in the world already.[45]

With only a bit of bad luck in the evolution of political conflict between China and the West, such high economic development would make the old

be, they can never be superpowers. Countries with the most power potential in the twenty-first century will be the ones that combine high rankings in productivity, population, and resources; those with the most actual power will be the ones from among that group who marshal the most military power from that potential.

45. Steven Greenhouse, "New Tally of World's Economies Catapults China Into Third Place," *New York Times*, May 20, 1993, pp. A1, A8.

Soviet military threat and the more recent trade frictions with Japan seem comparatively modest challenges. The West will need more than a bit of good luck to avoid clashing with China politically. This is true according to *either* set of assumptions about international relations, realist or liberal. For realists, Chinese power was not a problem for Asia in the second half of the Cold War because the Soviet Union was pinning China down. With that constraint reduced, the only alternatives will be to accept Chinese hegemony in the region or to balance Chinese power. The latter course need not and should not mean a new Cold War in Asia, but it does imply cautious moves toward containment without confrontation—polite containment, which need not preclude decent relations. (Diplomatic discussion should be about "equilibrium" rather than "containment," a loaded term.) If that is infeasible or undesirable, then realists will have to learn to live with Beijing in Asia as other countries have learned to live with the U.S. colossus in the western hemisphere,[46] or hope for the division of Chinese power through the breakup of the country. Disintegration is hardly a fanciful prospect; overcoming disunity has been a historic Chinese problem, a violent one for much of this century, and the current unevenness of development in the country increases centrifugal strains.[47]

The other theoretical approach does not make the question less vexing unless we assume that Chinese politics joins the End of History. Liberal theory is nonchalant about power imbalances only in regard to liberal polities or economies, so unless China embraces democracy and free trade, it may, for internal and ideological reasons, evince all the nasty vices in foreign policy that structural realism ascribes to imperatives imposed by the inter-

46. China might seem less of a problem since it has not intervened as often in neighboring countries in modern times as the United States has, but it has still used force against neighbors and engaged in coercion a number of times since 1949. Moreover, China lost large amounts of territory in the last century and a half and, as Michel Oksenberg suggests, nationalism could emerge "as a substitute for Marxism as a unifying ideology." Quoted in Kristof, "China Builds Its Military Muscle," p. A8.

47. Pressures in this direction come from economic warlordism. For example, in 1990 Guangdong province, transferring resources from the production of rice to cash crops and industry, sought to import rice from Hunan, which demanded above-market prices. Guangdong tried to circumvent the Hunan government and buy directly from producers. "Hunan put troops on its borders to stop the rice shipments; Guangdong countered with its own mobilisation." "Cut Along the Dotted Lines," *The Economist*, June 26, 1993, p. 35. In a different view, however, trends in Chinese unity point in the other direction, toward "diaspora economic power," as cooperation among the PRC, Taiwan, Hong Kong, and Singapore builds an "inter-tribal economy" and fosters trans-governmental Chinese economic hegemony. Joel Kotkin, "China Dawn," *Washington Post National Weekly Edition*, October 12–18, 1992, p. 23.

national system. But the liberal solution for pacifying international relations—liberal ideology—is precisely what present Chinese leaders perceive as a direct security threat to their regime.

Normal Development as a Threat

So should we want China to get rich or not? For liberals, the answer is yes, since a quarter of the world's people would be relieved from poverty and because economic growth should make democratization more likely, which in turn should prevent war between Beijing and other democracies. For realists, the answer should be no, since a rich China would overturn any balance of power. But what can we do about it anyway? American leverage on Beijing after the Cold War is not overwhelming. Active efforts to keep China poor or to break it up are hard to imagine, and would be counterproductive by exacerbating antagonism. Realists at best can passively hope for Chinese economic misfortune. Otherwise, we had better hope that liberal theory about the causes of peace pans out, so that what is good for China turns out to be good for everyone. As with all too many of the problems of security in East Asia, we may begin with a realist diagnosis but be forced into banking on liberal solutions, simply because the costs of controlling the balance of power may be too high.

As for Japan, its democracy ostensibly eliminates grounds for anxiety in one of the liberal perspectives, but limitations in the openness of trade still leave the country as a problem for either liberalism or realism. The main reason that recent trade frictions between Tokyo and Washington have not become a security problem as well as an economic one is that Japan is an unevenly developed great power. Cold War bipolarity obscured the discrepancies among the country's economic, military, and political weights. The situation grew increasingly anomalous as Japan grew richer; it can only seem even more peculiar as the end of the Cold War finishes sinking into everyone's consciousness.

The United States may continue to provide the security guarantee that allowed Japan to remain militarily limited, but the reason to do so will steadily become less obvious as time goes on and the residue of Cold War strategic mentality dissipates. Or, even with attenuated American protection, Japan might dispense with a high level of military power of its own if the threat that it worried about in the Cold War—the USSR—is not replaced by some other. Without U.S.-Russian military domination of Asia, however, can China avoid becoming such a potential threat? The old reasons that Tokyo's political and military roles should remain incommensurate with the country's wealth were peculiar. While it is not at all inevitable that the country will turn away from this peculiarity—it is deeply rooted in Japan's postwar aversion to militarism—there is no reason to assume that new circumstances will not push Tokyo toward more normal great power status. If the economic, political, and military roles were to come into balance, strategic relations would be revolutionized in East Asia and beyond.

After emphasizing the potential danger that China poses for a balance of power, it might seem that realism would prescribe full Japanese armament so that Tokyo could balance Beijing. Unless a bipolar contest between those two Asian giants emerges as the only alternative to Chinese primacy, however, such a prescription misreads the situation. Despite the unbalanced nature of Japan's power, its lopsided economic clout *already* gives it the weight of a hefty great power in a *multipolar* balance. In the near term, if Japan suddenly starts spending two to three times as much on defense and stocks up on nuclear weapons, it will be playing not a balancing role in the region, but a dominating one. The only good reason to want Japan to be a military superpower to balance China in the longer term would be if that were to become the only alternative to a multipolar balance, that is, if Russia and the United States ceased to provide strategic counterweights to China.

Some Americans still want Japan to improve its military and contribute forces to enterprises like the 1991 war against Iraq. They berate Japan for "only" shelling out money for the Persian Gulf War, rather than lives, and argue, "The key question Americans should ask themselves is: 'How long are we prepared to be loyal allies of Japan and act as volunteer Hessians serving Japanese interests, without demanding genuine military reciprocity?'"[48] They are right about the question but wrong about the answer, which should be: "As long as possible." Nothing significant is in the post–Cold War U.S. defense budget for the defense of Japanese interests that would not be there anyway for other purposes. Once Tokyo starts spending blood as well as treasure to support international order, it will justifiably become interested in much more control over that order.

48. Edward Olsen, "Target Japan as America's Economic Foe," *Orbis*, Vol. 36, No. 4 (Fall 1992), p. 496. For a moderate argument in this vein, see David B.H. Denoon, *Real Reciprocity: Balancing U.S. Economic and Security Policy in the Pacific Basin* (New York: Council on Foreign Relations Press, 1993).

As of now, Japan's foreign policy stance bears similarities to what would have been called liberal isolationism in an earlier era; it is based on the logic of "civilian" power.[49] American realists should encourage that stance, not disparage it. Nor should they let theoretical dogmatism preclude taking advantage of exceptions that all great theories have; there is no need to assume that international pressures inevitably dictate that Japanese leaders must become military realists. After all, if Moscow could trade in a realist foreign policy for a liberal one, there is no reason that Tokyo has to do the reverse, or that it must do so sooner rather than later.

The notion that it would be better for Japan to be a regular military power is strategic Old Thinking, the echo of concerns about burden-sharing in the global conflict with communism. When containing Soviet power was a difficult and expensive mission, getting Japan to share the burden made sense. When the burden has been lifted, however, so has the guarantee that Japanese security interests can never diverge from ours. Thinking about Japan as a replacement for the Soviet threat to keep American strategists gainfully employed would be compulsive realism, and perhaps the prevalent trepidations of other Asian nations about Japanese power are a bit hysterical. (After Tokyo's precedent-breaking decision to send troops for the UN mission in Cambodia, Singapore's Lee Kuan Yew was reported to have said that encouraging Japan to engage in peacekeeping was like offering a drink to a recovering alcoholic.) But even if a more heavily armed Japan were to behave as meekly abroad as when it was an American strategic dependency, it is difficult to think of a U.S. interest in the balance of power that would be served, unless Washington withdraws from the region and relies on Tokyo as its proxy.

Neoliberal institutionalist logic, which emphasizes the self-reinforcing dynamics of integrative activities, makes a reasonable case for encouraging a normal role for Japan. Promoting Japanese military participation in multilateral peacekeeping would make especially good sense if the alternative were Japanese remilitarization outside such a framework. As Jack Snyder suggests in response to the Lee Kuan Yew line: social drinking is all right; it is drinking alone that we should worry about. But there is as yet no appreciable impulse to remilitarization from within Japan. Multilateral military integration for Japan should be the U.S. fallback position, not the current objective. A

49. Hanns W. Maull, "Germany and Japan: The New Civilian Powers," *Foreign Affairs*, Vol. 69, No. 5 (Winter 1990/91).

growing political role for Japan could be encouraged and accommodated within non-military international institutions.[50] Why not postpone Japan's development of normal power until the Japanese press for it themselves?

The argument for Japanese military power makes more sense in terms of liberalism, or in terms of economic nationalism divorced from military considerations, than it does in terms of traditional U.S. strategic interests. In one view, the Japanese got a commercial edge over the United States by allocating to civilian investment the extra five-to-eight percent of GNP that was the difference between the Japanese and the U.S. allocation to defense throughout the Cold War. If one believes that only economic power is important, one could want the Japanese to spend more on military forces in order to level the economic playing field. Since its long-standing alliance with Washington and its democratic political system prevent Japan from becoming a military threat to the United States, by this reasoning, it can hardly be worse for Tokyo to divert resources to military power than for Washington to do so.[51]

In absolute terms, Japan's defense budget already ranks high: between third and sixth in the world in recent years (and even second, by some estimates, after the Soviet collapse and the increase in exchange rates).[52] This makes the disproportion in spending all the more significant. Japan has been spending relatively less on military power than any other major state—less than a sixth of the effort of the Cold War superpowers (as a fraction of GNP), and between a fifth and a third of the rates of Britain, Germany, France, China, and India. (See Table 5.) While the Western powers' military efforts

---

50. "For example, of the 150-plus slots allocated to Japan in the United Nations Secretariat, only 88 are now filled." Joseph S. Nye, Jr., "Coping With Japan," *Foreign Policy*, No. 89 (Winter 1992–93), p. 109.

51. Chalmers Johnson does not promote Japanese militarization but sees vested interests in traditional U.S. military strategy as partly responsible for our failure to confront Tokyo's economic challenge. He wants Americans to "recognize that Japan has replaced the USSR as America's most important foreign policy problem," and sees adaptation blocked by "entrenched interests in the preservation of the system of inequalities that characterized Japanese-American relations during the 1960s. . . . the interests of the defense establishment in the role of America as a hegemon athwart the Pacific, of the diplomatic establishment in Cold War dualism, of . . . the Atlanticists in not having to come to grips with problems for which they do not have the requisite skills." Chalmers Johnson, "Japan: Their Behavior, Our Policy," *National Interest*, No. 17 (Fall 1989), pp. 26–27. If the United States and Japan do become more confrontational economically, however, and at the same time modify the traditional one-sided security relationship, does it not become more probable that military tension could arise?

52. Unusually high personnel costs help prevent this level of expenditure from providing a comparable amount of combat power at present. One obstacle to Japanese remilitarization is the difficulty of recruitment to fill even currently low levels of mobilized manpower.

Table 5. Relative Levels of Military Effort by Major States: Military Expenditures as Percentage of GNP.

	1965	1970	1975	1980	1985	1989
U.S.A.	7.6	7.9	5.9	5.3	6.6	5.8
USSR	15.7	14.2	13.7	12.9	12.9	11.7
China	6.8	7.7	13.2	8.8	5.1	3.7
U.K.	5.9	4.8	4.9	5.0	5.1	4.2
France	5.2	4.1	3.8	4.0	4.0	3.7
W. Germany	4.3	3.3	3.6	3.3	3.2	2.8
India	3.7	3.1	3.2	3.2	3.5	3.1
Japan	1.0	0.8	0.9	0.9	1.0	1.0

SOURCE: For 1965–70, *World Military Expenditures and Arms Transfers, 1965–1974* (Washington, D.C.: ACDA, n.d.), pp. 24, 28, 29, 32, 34, 46, 50; for 1975–89, *World Military Expenditures and Arms Transfers, 1990* (Washington, D.C.: ACDA, November 1991), pp. 58, 62, 63, 67, 68, 81, 85.

NB: Data for USSR and China are soft; many other sources estimate higher figures for the USSR.

are now declining, however, Tokyo's is not. Japan's capacity in high technology also suggests that it would have a comparative advantage over most other countries in fielding a modern force if it focused on that goal.

For a realist, a normally armed Japan, unless it is pinned down by a powerful common enemy, is a potential threat. It would be the strongest military power in Asia, and the second-ranking one in the world. The fact that Japan is democratic, in this view, does not bar it from conflict with other democracies[53] (not to mention that some observers doubt whether Japan really is or will remain a democracy in western terms).[54] To keep Tokyo a uni-dimensional superpower, however, means that the United States would have to avoid provoking the Japanese in the economic sphere and avoid making them feel fully responsible for their own fate. All of that cuts against

53. Hisahako Okazaki has called attention to the discomfiting analogy of the seventeenth-century rivalry and war between Britain and the Netherlands, two republics. Cited in Peter J. Katzenstein and Nobuo Okawara, "Japan's National Security: Structures, Norms, and Policies," *International Security*, Vol. 17, No. 4 (Spring 1993), p. 91.

54. Karel van Wolferen, *The Enigma of Japanese Power: People and Politics in A Stateless Nation* (New York: Knopf, 1989). For a more benign and carefully researched view see Gerald Curtis, *The Japanese Way of Politics* (New York: Columbia University Press, 1988). See also Francis Fukuyama and Kong Dan Oh, *The U.S.-Japan Security Relationship After the Cold War*, MR-283-USDP (Santa Monica: RAND Corporation, 1993), pp. 35–40.

arm-twisting over bilateral trade issues, while such pressure is made more likely by U.S. domestic politics. Can American political leaders convince voters either that unfair Japanese trade practices are a myth, or that the United States should "coddle" the Japanese because some academic theory implies that otherwise the United States might have to fight them again? Here liberal theory could rescue realism, if arguments for free trade in U.S. domestic politics were used to help reduce diplomatic friction with Tokyo.

If Japan's power does develop fully, its political friction with other Asian countries—most significantly, China—would grow more than with Washington.[55] When Tokyo had an independent military policy during the past century, that policy was driven by China. All three of Japan's wars (1894–95, 1904–05, 1931–45) originated in disputes related to China. The whole question of balance between these two countries has been a non-issue since 1945 because of the Washington-Tokyo alliance, and stability in Asia has depended on the lack of strategic competition between China and Japan.[56]

Asymmetries would make it hard to estimate the balance of conventional military capability in such a competition, because China is more of a continental power, reliant on ground forces and quantity of weaponry, while Japan is more of a maritime power, reliant on naval and air forces and quality of technology. Confusion about which one had a military edge could be especially destabilizing. Rough parity is more conducive than clear hierarchy to miscalculation and to decisions to gamble on the resort to force.[57]

For Japan to be a big league player, it would have to have nuclear weapons. Neorealists like Kenneth Waltz are happy with that prospect because they see nuclear deterrence as stabilizing, and believe it makes anxieties about conventional military balance beside the point.[58] If that is convincing, balance of power theorists can simply endorse nuclear proliferation as the solution

55. Japan's 1987 decision to breach the symbolic ceiling of one percent of GNP for defense spending alarmed the Chinese because it seemed inconsistent with the warming of superpower relations, and was interpreted as demonstrated intent to become a "political power." Jonathan Pollack, "The Sino-Japanese Relationship and East-Asian Security: Patterns and Implications," *China Quarterly* (December 1990), pp. 718–719.
56. Fred C. Iklé and Terumasa Nakanishi, "Japan's Grand Strategy," *Foreign Affairs*, Vol. 69, No. 3 (Summer 1990), pp. 84–85. As Michael Chambers points out, this could have been due as much to their own underdeveloped capacity to project power as to Cold War constraint.
57. Blainey, *Causes of War*, chap. 8. If it is clear which power in a confrontation is superior to the other, bargaining leverage should be irresistible, since the weaker one knows it can get nothing from resisting except defeat in war.
58. Kenneth N. Waltz, *The Spread of Nuclear Weapons: More May Be Better*, Adelphi Paper No. 171 (London: International Institute for Strategic Studies, Autumn 1981).

to security dilemmas in Asia, and let the United States pack up its strategic bags and come home. It is not clear, though, how many statesmen have the courage of Waltz's convictions.

Chinese-Japanese bipolarity would be a problem for liberal theory as well, if China does not liberalize, since those who tout the "separate peace" among democracies recognize that they fight frequently and with alacrity against non-democracies. Chinese elite attitudes have also not accepted the positive-sum logic of free trade, but remain mercantilist and zero-sum in outlook.[59] "China's leaders encounter great difficulty in accepting the fact that state sovereignty has been overtaken by an era of interdependence in which national boundaries are highly permeable."[60]

By realist criteria, a China and a Japan unleashed from Cold War discipline could not help but become problems. Japan is powerful by virtue of its prosperity, which in turn depends on penetrating foreign markets, which creates political friction with competitors. Because of its bigness and central location in regional geography, China evokes the structural theory of the German Problem; even without evil designs, the country's search for security will abrade the security of surrounding countries. Geographically, the "Middle Kingdom" is close to virtually everyone in East Asia. It is also the strategic pivot between the otherwise distinct subregions of Northeast and Southeast Asia. Individually, countries on the mainland cannot hope to deter or defeat China in any bilateral test of strength; collectively, they cannot help but worry China if they were to seem united in hostility.

If China becomes highly developed economically, the problem would change. Asia would be stable but unhappy, because a rich China would be the clear hegemonic power in the region (like the United States in the western hemisphere), and perhaps in the world. If China remains economically limited, the Americans and Russians recede further from the area, and Japan normalizes the balance among its roles, Japan will be the dominant power in Asia.

For these reasons, and because of Japan's desire to avoid becoming a normal great power, many governments in East Asia dread the prospect of American withdrawal. If a symbolic U.S. presence suffices—and some spokesmen in Asian capitals imply that it would—there is no reason that the

---

59. Michel Oksenberg, "The China Problem," *Foreign Affairs*, Vol. 70, No. 3 (Summer 1991), p. 10.
60. Shambaugh, "China's Security Policy in the Post–Cold War Era," p. 93.

United States cannot remain one of the principal strategic players.[61] It is not probable, however, that a simply symbolic military involvement will suffice outside Korea. There it works because it represents a tripwire.[62] The same presumption cannot exist in Southeast Asia because offshore forces cannot be positioned as a tripwire, because of the legacy of aversion still flowing from the old Indochina War, and because the United States has not cultivated deterrence by indicating its willingness to fight either of the potential threats in the subregion (China or Vietnam). The time that U.S. commitment would actually matter would be when someone called on it to deter or defend against such a specific challenger. At such a moment a symbolic role could well be exposed for what it was—a hesitant and weak commitment, accepted within the United States only by unelected elites (and a fraction of them at best). The United States has been in that position, however, since 1975. When Vietnam had an army of 180,000 in Cambodia in the 1980s, and clashed with Thai troops several times in border skirmishes, Washington remained formally committed by the Manila Treaty to defend Thailand. Was anyone then really confident that the United States would go to war in a big enough way to save Thailand—meaning combat on the ground—if the Vietnamese moved westward? The pretense served by token presence and symbolic commitment can continue, but it scarcely matters unless a test comes.

Southeast Asia is the area of East Asia where U.S. military engagement is least likely, although Washington has a disconcerting habit of going to war over places it had not anticipated (for example, Kuwait) and even where officials had publicly indicated we would refrain (Korea in 1950). Southeast Asia is also where diplomacy to improve balance of power is impeded by visceral American bitterness over the fruitless war there two decades ago. By balance of power criteria, the United States should have repaired relations with Vietnam long ago. Although Vietnam cannot be expected to contain China on its own, there is no strategic reason anymore to keep Hanoi weak. There are of course ample emotional reasons,[63] but winning the Cold War

---

61. For a discussion of alternate U.S. force postures, see James A. Winnefeld, et al., *A New Strategy and Fewer Forces: The Pacific Dimension*, R-4089/2-USDP (Santa Monica: RAND Corporation, 1992).
62. The tripwire concept is capsulized in the answer given by General Foch in 1910 to General Wilson's query about the minimum British force that would be useful to the French: "A single British soldier—and we will see to it that he is killed." Quoted in Barbara Tuchman, *The Guns of August* (New York: Dell, 1963), p. 68.
63. The POW/MIA issue can never be resolved satisfactorily. Testimony of former U.S. officials in summer 1992 and discovery in Soviet archives of the translation of an apparently incriminating

should be counted as more important than not winning the Vietnam War. In the new postwar world, the prospect of economic development makes the power potential of Vietnam, with a population of nearly 70 million, more significant than any other mainland country in Southeast Asia, with the possible exception of Thailand.

Since Vietnam is no longer an extension of Soviet power and influence, no longer occupies Cambodia, has demobilized half of its huge army, has moved to liberalize its economy and (to a lesser degree) its polity, and faces China on its northern border, it is also far less of a threat to the interests of the United States or its friends in the Association of Southeast Asian Nations (ASEAN) than during the Cold War. This would change in the unlikely event that Hanoi decided to reoccupy Cambodia, but Chinese capacity to punish Vietnamese adventurism is stronger than the converse. In the bipolar Cold War world, it may have made sense for the United States to want Vietnam to be weak and vulnerable. In the new postwar world, there is no reason to want that unless Chinese dominance is preferred to some measure of balance.

One way in which limited U.S. military engagement could prove most potent, and U.S. diplomacy most decisive, would be in a situation of regional multipolarity where Washington shifted to playing the role of makeweight or external balancer, as Britain sometimes did on the continent of Europe. That way the United States might be the most important strategic player without having the most potent military force in the region. U.S. deployments, nevertheless, would still have to be substantial rather than symbolic. As time goes on, the rising capabilities of the local states will make the threshold of substantial presence harder for a post–Cold War U.S. defense budget to meet.

It is hard, however, to imagine Washington playing the game of agile external balancer, tilting one way then another, rather than faithful ally. Such unvarnished realism seems out of liberal character. (Divorced from the criterion of defending democracy, how would the mission be described to American voters and taxpayers: defense of markets? defense of economic competitors?) Despite realist criticism of American legalism and moralism, however, the United States is not totally unaccustomed to dumping friends and embracing bitter enemies for balance-of-power purposes. Taiwan discov-

---

North Vietnamese document, whether genuine or not, reinvigorated old suspicions. It is also impossible to prove the negative, that is, that Hanoi never held back any prisoners, in any hiding place, for any time after 1973.

ered that in the 1970s. The most delicate question posed by a balancer role is what it would mean for U.S. relations with Japan, since it implies moving away from the Mutual Security Treaty. Washington would have to make an exception for Japan; otherwise, the move to balancing would be counterproductive, provoking Tokyo to rearm and act independently. With an exception for the Mutual Security Treaty, then, the U.S. role as balancer would be between China and Russia. That, however, implies an unstable tripolar configuration. Playing balancer while still firmly linked with Tokyo could, instead, encourage more Russian-Chinese cooperation, and reversion toward the bipolar groupings of the early Cold War. If the local powers—especially Japan—move more independently anyway, there may be little choice. Otherwise, facile proposals for an American balancer role overlook too many pitfalls.

Cleavages and Casi Belli

Even those who lack faith in liberal guarantees of peace must consider interests as well as power in estimating the odds that states will clash. International anarchy and national anxiety about power are necessary but not sufficient conditions for war. Some conflict of interest, some substantive dispute, some *casus belli* has to enter the equation to provide the impetus to violence.[64] One of the reasons for optimism about peace in Europe is the apparent satisfaction of the great powers with the status quo. While Eastern Europe may be a mess, traditional nationalist, ideological, religious, communal, or resource conflicts appear to have been wrung out of the relationships among France, Germany, Britain, Russia, and Italy. And in Asia, no great power is now as revisionist in its aims for the general international order as Japan was before World War II.

East Asia is less beset by traditional *casi belli* than volatile regions like the Middle East or South Asia. For example, the relative ethnic homogeneity of the major East Asian states reduces the potential for irredentism.[65] Yet there is still an ample pool of festering grievances, with more potential for gener-

64. The fact that intentions matter as well as capabilities is part of the reason that "balance of threat" theory improves on balance of power theory. See Stephen M. Walt, *The Origins of Alliances* (Ithaca: Cornell University Press, 1987).

65. There are still problems of this sort that are not trivial: divided Mongols and Kazakhs, repressed Tibetans, or communal tensions in smaller states like Malaysia.

ating conflict than during the Cold War, when bipolarity helped stifle the escalation of parochial disputes. Endless numbers of scenarios can be dreamed up, and those that are far-fetched provide no useful guidance. But three are worth mentioning to illustrate two simple points. First, far from improbable possibilities exist for miscalculation and escalation. Second, in two of the three cases there is little visible discussion or planning, at least in American circles, for the strategic questions posed by such instabilities.

One example is the discord over who owns the Spratly Islands, in the South China Sea. (See map, p. 33.) China claims all of them,[66] in conflict with claims by Vietnam, the Philippines, Malaysia, and Brunei. In one sense this issue is trivial and hard to see as the source of major conflict, since the islands are tiny, barren, and isolated. (There are similar disputes over the Paracel Islands as well.)[67] That insignificance, however, abets miscalculation and unintended provocation. Moreover, if important amounts of oil or seabed minerals turn up in the area, greed will compound national honor as potential fuel for conflict. The other claimants would probably be unable to contest determined Chinese efforts to occupy the islands. That would leave two alternatives: to roll over and accept the Chinese conquest, conceding PRC dominance in the area, or to regroup and retaliate on some other issue. It is not fanciful to see another Sino-Vietnamese war, or a heating up of the Sino-Japanese dispute over the Senkaku/Diaoyutai Islands in the East China Sea, growing out of the Spratly dispute. Has any part of the U.S. national security establishment seriously considered what if anything to do if China fights with the Philippines and Vietnam over a couple of the Spratlys, Tokyo reacts by fortifying the Senkakus, and Beijing threatens retaliation if the Japanese do not pull back?

A second difficult case, a residue of the Cold War, is a potentially different problem in its own right: Korea. Of all the places in the world where U.S. forces were deployed on behalf of a client state, South Korea is probably the one where deterrence was most effectively and efficiently achieved. It was effective because there was more certain reason to believe that deterrence was necessary there (that is, that in the absence of the U.S. commitment the adversary would attack) than against the Soviet Union. Since the direct attack

66. Beijing and Taipei have overlapping claims, both in the name of one China.
67. See Wayne Bert, "Chinese Policies and U.S. Interests in Southeast Asia," *Asian Survey*, Vol. 33, No. 3 (March 1993), p. 327.

in 1950, Pyongyang has frequently demonstrated its risk propensity in more consistently reckless provocations than any other government in the world: trying to assassinate the South Korean president (in the 1968 Blue House raid, and again in 1974, when Park Chung Hee's wife was killed in the attempt); seizing the U.S.S. *Pueblo* in 1968; hacking American officers to death in the Demilitarized Zone (DMZ) tree-cutting incident of 1976; murdering half the South Korean cabinet with a bomb in Rangoon in 1983; feverishly digging infiltration tunnels under the DMZ; and blowing up KAL Flight 858 in 1987. The presence of American forces has been a permanent and potent reminder of how close Kim Il Sung came to absolute disaster when he tried to invade. The deterrent has been efficient, in turn, because it is small and functions primarily as a tripwire.

Today, pessimists worry about a North Korean nuclear weapons program. Would any government be more willing to do wild and crazy things with such weapons than the one that so regularly perpetrates acts like those mentioned above? Optimists, on the other hand, see Korean unification around the corner. That is plausible if the North Korean regime collapses, perhaps after Kim Il Sung dies. Whether that happens or not, the problem with the nuclear issue is that no likely outcome can be comfortable for other countries.

Even if North Korea were to reverse course, and submit again to the full strictures of the NPT, there would be no better reason for assuming compliance than there was in regard to Iraq before 1991. Pyongyang would have to accept unprecedented and absolutely unlimited inspections to give the West any reasonable confidence that its nuclear activities could be fully monitored. Experience with Iraq made astoundingly clear how much nuclear activity a zealous and secretive government could keep hidden. Yet no government accepts unlimited inspection, which is a virtual abrogation of sovereignty, except in a surrender agreement. The Iraq case also makes clear why preventive attack, however attractive an option it might become, should be written off. Initial confidence that the six-week air war in 1991 had destroyed Iraq's nuclear potential turned out to be terribly wrong. Confidence that buried and hidden facilities in North Korea had been found and eliminated would require not just air attack, but invasion and occupation of the country.

If Korea does unify under Seoul, however, the new government will have powerful incentives of its own for a nuclear deterrent. First, it would be much harder for the United States to maintain its military role in the country if the North Korean threat were gone. Second, the Seoul regime would have new borders with both China and Russia. Third, relations with Japan, always testy, would probably worsen, as Tokyo's apprehensions grew about the prospect of a stronger Korea. Some have speculated that one reason the South Koreans were initially less exercised than Washington about the North Korean nuclear program was that they would not mind inheriting it.

For the third example, suppose democratization continues in Taiwan, as even most American realists hope. What if the result is that Taiwan's independence movement overpowers the Kuomintang, and Beijing fulfills its threat to act militarily to prevent secession?[68] Has the U.S. government seriously tried to figure out what it should or would do in such circumstances? The U.S. Taiwan Relations Act genuflects to "peaceful" reunification, but Washington has made no clear commitment about how it would react to military conflict. For liberals, it was not too hard to dump Taipei in the 1970s when it was an authoritarian regime itself, and when its conquest was not imminent, but a democratic Taiwan would be harder to abandon to a repressive Beijing in a moment of crisis. For realists, nothing could seem more within Beijing's legitimate sphere of influence than the island that all sides have so far recognized as part of China, and it would seem hard to justify major war and the risk of nuclear escalation to defend it after having abrogated the defense commitment so long ago.

Pressures in both directions—defending Taiwan, or standing aside—would be extreme, because the consequences either way could be catastrophic. At the same time, Beijing could hardly to be expected to assume that Washington would intervene, given the evolution of policy since the Shanghai Communiqué; Chinese leaders would have at least as good an excuse to miscalculate as Kim Il Sung in June 1950 or Saddam Hussein in August 1990. This is the scariest of the potential crises.

Traditional preoccupation with Europe, the painful memory of the price of indulging ambitious strategic aims in the Vietnam War, and the late–Cold War entente with China all disposed most American strategists against thinking very hard about potential situations such as those mentioned above. Similarly, the residue of Cold War thinking for pessimists, and the euphoria

---

68. Taiwan's opposition independence party has protested moves toward rapprochement between Taipei and Beijing (such as high-level talks), and has announced in Singapore that "we assert to China and the world: Taiwan is not a part of China." Quoted in Nicholas D. Kristof, "China and Taiwan Have First Talks," *New York Times*, April 28, 1993, p. A8.

over the advance of liberalism for optimists, make it seem fanciful or demented to worry about balancing the power of Germany, Japan, China, or other Cold War friends. But the Cold War is over, and so is the particular realist calculus that went with it; the pacifying logic of liberal theory does not convince everyone as an alternative; and it is doubtful that East Asia will liberalize enough anyway to make new violence improbable. Thinking harder about bad cases is hardly hysterical.

Prospects

The United States now has more leverage in more places on more issues than any other state. This is because there is no other comparable pole, as there was during the Cold War. That fact, in turn, naturally erodes American democracy's inclination to pay significant costs to call the tune in all the regions that it could. Erosion, though, could take a long time before it alters power configurations substantially, or could be reversed by emergence of a significant threat.

The problem for policy is that the analytical basis for prediction cannot limit the range of conditions within which choices will have to be made. Every one of the three basic structural patterns of distribution of power could plausibly evolve. Moreover, realist theory is divided over which should even be preferred. There is also the fourth possibility of a neoliberal solution in which institutionalization of cooperation comes to modify anxiety about relative power, and to cause peace, although the plausibility of that outcome varies inversely with the odds that more intense *casi belli* will develop. The four general possibilities are:

UNIPOLARITY

Unipolarity could develop in two opposite ways. In one, the United States would reenter the region in force, on a scale comparable to the 1950s and 1960s, and become the dominant power. In the other, it would withdraw completely, as Britain did from east of Suez a quarter century ago. The former choice is less probable than the latter. In the latter case, the dominant power would be Japan, in the near term, if it arms more heavily and takes a more active political role, or China, in the long term, if its economic development continues at high rates. The least likely of the great powers to develop a hegemonic position would be Russia, although that could happen if China breaks up and Japan remains restrained and non-nuclear while the United States withdraws. Japan's peculiar strategic passivity, however, has been premised on the Mutual Security Treaty, so the latter combination of developments is hard to imagine.

Domination of Asia by a single great power would be uncomfortable for all but the dominant one, but once accomplished would dampen prospects for major war, for the reasons that Geoffrey Blainey suggests about the stability of hierarchy: "Wars usually end when the fighting nations *agree* on their relative strength and wars usually begin when fighting nations *disagree* on their relative strength."[69] This accords with Robert Gilpin's view that a bipolarity that emerges as a rising power challenges a declining hegemonic state is likely to lead to war,[70] and conflicts with Waltz's argument that bipolarity is stabilizing. It is also a helpful reminder that what is good for stability—that is, strong inhibitions on resort to force—does not necessarily go with what is best for individual countries' independence.

Local states, however, are not likely to allow one among themselves to achieve dominance without a fight. Unlike the states of the western hemisphere who live with the U.S. colossus, several states in East Asia have the capacity to contest a rising threat. As Arthur Waldron has noted, China's role might not be to dominate the region. Rather, in the process of asserting hegemony, Beijing may stimulate arms races (with Japan, Taiwan, Korea, and others) that it does not win. Such a process, complicated by disagreements about what the structure of the system was (with China considering it hierarchical, others seeing it as multipolar), could be quite volatile.

If the system were insecurely hierarchical, and edged toward bipolarity rather than wider balance, it might become more dangerous for the reasons Gilpin suggests in his interpretation of history as a series of hegemonic transitions. Or, if Waltz is correct, and the Cold War analogue is more appropriate than the Peloponnesian, bipolarity could make the structure stable. Even the Cold War model is not entirely reassuring, however, since stability in that case did not begin to emerge until 1963, after fifteen years of probing and scary crises over Berlin and Cuba worked out the bounds of strategic interaction.

69. Blainey, *Causes of War*, p. 122 (emphasis in original).
70. Robert Gilpin, *War and Change in International Politics* (New York: Cambridge University Press, 1981).

BIPOLARITY

Depending on which countries develop their regional power in all its dimensions, bipolar combinations could include any pair among the four current great powers of the area (United States, Russia, China, Japan). Probably the least dangerous combination would be the two peripheral to the region, the Russians and Americans, but without a Cold War between them it is hard to see why they would want to invest as much military and political capital in the region as the states who are fully located there. The most probable bipolar pair, and potentially the most antagonistic, is China and Japan. That would be the one with most potential for war among great powers (for example, with Korea as a bone of contention, as it was a century ago), unless the two somehow established a condominium (which I have heard no regional experts argue is likely).

MULTIPOLARITY

Multipolarity would continue the present situation or some variation with at least three among the United States, Russia, China, and Japan.[71] India could also figure in the balance. As the middle powers develop further, the situation could become more complicated if alignments are fluid. The majority of states might also coalesce against the most troublesome. Except in the unlikely event that Japan's politics and society turned toward militarism again, the great power most likely to feel surrounded and beset would be China.

Multipolarity seems the most likely pattern, if only because it leaves open the widest number of possible combinations. Theory is not consistent on the question of whether multipolarity is more or less stable than the alternatives. Much writing about the classical European balance of power saw multipolarity as most stable for preserving the main actors and preventing major war (although small wars or dismemberment of weak states, especially in the eighteenth century and earlier, were sometimes the price of general equilibrium). Most agree, though, that if multipolarity exists, a balance of five or more powers is more stable than a tripolar configuration, because the

---

71. A hybrid would be a bipolarity of blocs organizing a multipolarity of states, with one alliance led by the continental powers Russia and China, the other by the offshore powers Japan and the United States. This might be fairly stable, given the geographic division, unless smaller states on the continent sought protection from Washington and Tokyo. The relatively even balance of power between the two leading states in each of the blocs might, on the other hand, complicate the functioning of the alliances, making them more similar to the European blocs before 1914 than to those of the Cold War. The vulnerability of the structure to quick realignment could thus make it shaky.

latter can be turned upside down by a shift in alignment by one state. Only if India becomes a full player in East Asia would there be five such power centers. That is less likely than that the United States would drop out and leave a tripolar combination of Russia, China, and Japan. Thus the odds that the particular form of multipolarity will be stable, combined with the odds that some form of multipolarity will exist, are not reassuring.

There is one potential pattern of multipolarity that would be ideal, and that merges conceptually into the institutionalist option discussed below: a consensual pattern modeled on the nineteenth-century Concert of Europe. This would depend on delicate diplomacy, but is not out of the question if the great powers are basically satisfied and can resolve minor grievances by compromise and offsetting concessions. While there is disagreement about whether a concert must rest on a balance of power,[72] the two are certainly compatible. While such a system may have some of the self-reinforcing advantages touted by liberal regime theorists, however, there is little evidence that it can survive the emergence of significant conflicts of interest, and thus that it is anywhere near as much a cause of stability as a reflection of it. The Concert of Europe also depended on a fair amount of ideological homogeneity (not yet evident in East Asia), and when such consensus waned, so did the Concert. Moreover, the right of big states to set the rules for small ones was a more explicit principle than is practical to admit in the more modern international climate.[73] Some sort of concert would be desirable in Asia, although no one should depend on it to solve more than modest disputes. In 1991, however, when Gorbachev proposed something like it—a five-power regional security conference of the United States, the Soviet Union, China, Japan, and India—the idea proved unpopular because it "smacked most inopportunely of a great-power deal, something that is clearly unpopular in the world right now."[74]

---

72. See Paul W. Schroeder, "Did the Vienna Settlement Rest on a Balance of Power?"; Enno E. Krahe, "A Bipolar Balance of Power"; Robert Jervis, "A Political Science Perspective on the Balance of Power and the Concert"; and Wolf D. Gruner, "Was There a Reformed Balance of Power System or Cooperative Great Power Hegemony?"; all in *American Historical Review*, Vol. 97, No. 3 (June 1992).
73. See Richard K. Betts, "Systems for Peace or Causes of War? Collective Security, Arms Control, and the New Europe," *International Security*, Vol. 17, No. 1 (Summer 1992), pp. 24, 27–28. For a more favorable view see Charles and Clifford Kupchan, "Concerts, Collective Security, and the Future of Europe," *International Security*, Vol. 16, No. 1 (Summer 1991).
74. V. Golobnin, quoted in William T. Tow, "Northeast Asia and International Security: Transforming Competition to Collaboration," *Australian Journal of International Affairs*, Vol. 46, No. 1 (May 1992), p. 15.

INSTITUTIONS OVERRIDING IMBALANCES?

What stands out so far is the raft of uncertainties about what distribution of power in East Asia is either likely or desirable. This raises the incentives to look beyond realism for solutions. Neoliberal institutionalism, in linking the logic of self-interested cooperation to the concerns of security policy, offers some other hypothetical possibilities for fostering stability. One hope is that development of regional economic cooperation or integration, for example in ASEAN, will have spillover effects in reducing apprehensions and facilitating confidence in political security (in a sense the reverse of the sequence in Europe, where NATO and security cooperation eased the progress of European unity in other spheres).

Moves to make a security forum out of the ASEAN Post-Ministerial Conference—which includes the United States, Japan, Canada, and South Korea—are modestly promising, as are the revival of the Five Power Defense Arrangement, which ties Britain, Australia, and New Zealand to Singapore and Malaysia, and the growth of intelligence cooperation among ASEAN states. Inhibitions against more integration are strong, however,[75] and even if multilateral security organization succeeded in the ASEAN region, that still leaves out most of East Asia.

Other possibilities have been broached. In 1990, Australia and Canada proposed a Conference for Security and Cooperation and a North Pacific Security Dialogue. Others have proposed utilizing the Asia-Pacific Economic Cooperation (APEC) process to deal with security matters. The Bush administration, preferring continued emphasis on bilateral arrangements, opposed such moves, but the Clinton administration has endorsed them.[76] There is scant evidence, however, that favorable attitudes about developing discussion forums will extend toward more explicit security organization, and some countries have explicitly indicated that they are not interested in agreements for collective action, especially binding defense commitments. The leap from economic multilateralism to multilateral security planning is not yet in sight.[77]

75. Richard Stubbs, "Subregional Security Cooperation in ASEAN: Military and Economic Imperatives and Political Obstacles," *Asian Survey*, Vol. 32, No. 5 (May 1992), pp. 403–409; Leszek Buszynski, "ASEAN Security Dilemmas," *Survival*, Vol. 34, No. 4 (Winter 1992–93), pp. 101–103.

76. Tow, "Northeast Asia and International Security," pp. 14–15, 17–18; Elaine Sciolino, "U.S. to Urge Asia to Build Security," *New York Times*, April 1, 1993, p. A8.

77. David E. Sanger, "Asian Countries, in Shift, Weigh Defense Forum," *New York Times*, May 23, 1993, p. 16; Tow, "Northeast Asia and International Security," p. 18. See also Gerald Segal, "North-East Asia: Common Security or à la Carte?" *International Affairs*, Vol. 67, No. 4 (October

Neoliberal analysis has sometimes emphasized the difficulty of constructing effective multilateral institutions in the absence of hierarchy, when no dominant power bears disproportionate costs in providing collective goods. The United States did so in Asia at the height of the Cold War when it provided the bulk of resources for the United Nations Command in Korea, undertook the one-sided Mutual Security Treaty with Japan (obliging Washington to defend Tokyo, but not the reverse), and shepherded the Southeast Asia Treaty Organization (SEATO), the broadest alliance in the region, through its two decades of existence. The United States is not about to shoulder such burdens now, nor is any other great power.

The most ambitious institutionalist alternative to relying on balance of power to keep peace, hypothetically, is a genuine collective security arrangement. The idea became vaguely popular again as a result of the end of the Cold War, and has been broached in regard to Asia by Soviet and other proposals, but it does not offer much for Asia. First, the fundamental logic of the concept is dubious. It is no accident that collective security schemes have seldom if ever worked elsewhere, and that the situations in which the concept is said to have been validated (NATO's organization for deterrence, or the UN wars for Korea and Kuwait) are ones in which hegemonic or balance-of-power dynamics operated behind the facade of collective security rhetoric.[78] Second, Asia is behind Europe in the development of integrative organizational forms that could be appropriate foundations. The Asian counterparts to NATO, the Conference on Security and Cooperation in Europe (CSCE), the Western European Union (WEU), or the European Economic Community (EC) have been found in Southeast Asia, just one corner of the huge region. The most significant security analogue, SEATO, is defunct. Third, and most fundamental, no consensus on norms or status or supranational order is shared by all major states of East Asia.

Policies

Either general approach to explaining international relations, realism or liberalism, leaves open many possible predictions for Asia. Only more specific

---

1991), pp. 763–765, and David Youtz and Paul Midford, *A Northeast Asian Security Regime: Prospects After the Cold War*, Public Policy Paper No. 5 (New York: Institute for East-West Studies, 1992).

78. For detailed arguments see Betts, "Systems for Peace or Causes of War?"

theories within these broad schools offer clear predictions, which means that there is not yet any wide analytical consensus to serve as a basis for prescription. I nevertheless venture some recommendations consistent with a prudent synthesis of the theories. These recommendations are offered in terms of U.S. interests, rather than the disinterested perspective of a Man from Mars. Thus, for example, the prospect of hierarchy would worry me only if the dominant power is other than the United States. American hegemony in East Asia is not however, on my list of preferred options, because it is not worth the cost of attempting to achieve it.

In regard to objectives, we should think in terms of one main goal, a conventional but heavily qualified one. First, the principal U.S. strategic aim should be to prevent the emergence of a hierarchical regional system under any dominant power other than the United States. This is not just because the United States has economic interests in East Asia that might be obstructed. The implications of a locally hegemonic power go beyond the region. A China, Japan, or Russia that grows strong enough to overturn a regional balance of power would necessarily also be a global power that could reestablish bipolarity on the highest level.

Second, this strategic aim should not necessarily take priority under all circumstances. Efforts to prevent dominance by a single power center in East Asia should be limited if the contender for dominance has a genuinely democratic government. The level of tradeoffs with nonstrategic interests (for example, absolute economic gains), or of acceptable costs and risks in strategic competition, should vary with the odds that a rival (in terms of national power) will be unfriendly and dangerous. There is good reason to believe that such odds are lower with kindred democracies. This is not beyond doubt, especially for realists, but restraint is still recommended because friction with such countries risks being counterproductive by damaging the grounds for amity while failing to achieve the desired outcome in the realm of power.

Empirical support for the pacifying impact of constitutional democracy is firmer than for the assumption that economic interdependence breeds peace.[79] In a reasonable synthesis of realist and liberal theory, therefore, a

79. See the compilations in the appendices to Doyle's "Liberalism and World Politics"; and Zeev Maoz and Bruce Russett, "Normative and Structural Causes of Democratic Peace, 1946–1986," *American Political Science Review*, Vol. 87, No. 3 (September 1993). In a thorough review of theories on causes of war, Jack Levy concludes that, "This absence of war between democratic states comes as close as anything we have to an empirical law of international relations," and that "liberal economic theories are consistent with the absence of wars among democracies but would

country with a liberal economy but an illiberal polity should warrant at least as much concern as the old Soviet Union ever did, since it poses the prospect of economic power without political restraint. The possibility of this combination in China's future, together with the country's size, makes it the great power in the region about which U.S. strategists should worry most over the long term.[80] Gambling that democracy will underwrite peace is a reasonable risk, but compounding the wager by gambling that wealth will produce democracy some time in the future is compromising balance of power norms too much. Linkage of trade terms to internal political reforms, with careful consideration of counterproductive effects, may not always be wrongheaded.[81] In the Cold War, realism subordinated U.S. concern with human rights in China to strategic cooperation against the Soviet Union, but after the Cold War, supporting liberal political values in China is compatible with concern about balance of power.

In regard to policy, institutions to foster cooperation should be promoted, since they may help and cannot hurt, as long as such efforts do not lull governments into indifference to imbalanced power. That danger is not likely. It is most probable that if such institutions do develop and prosper they will, as in Europe, emerge from alliances based on common political and strategic interests, rather than transcend or subvert them.

In regard to power politics we should think in terms of a sequence of options and fallback positions. First, if a concert of great powers in East Asia is feasible, we should seek it. Second choice would be regional bipolarity under the old Cold War leaders, Russia and the United States, although this

---

incorrectly predict a lower overall war involvement for democratic as opposed to nondemocratic states." Levy, "The Causes of War: A Review of Theories and Evidence," in Philip Tetlock, et al., eds., *Behavior, Society, and Nuclear War,* Vol. 1 (New York: Oxford University Press, 1989), p. 270. For deductive arguments that economic interdependence causes conflict, see Waltz, *Theory of International Politics,* chap. 7. The case most often cited for such arguments is Japan's attempt to achieve autarky by force. See Michael A. Barnhart, *Japan Prepares for Total War: The Search for Economic Security, 1919–1941* (Ithaca: Cornell University Press, 1987). Liberal critics argue that the character of modern interdependence, particularly the trans-nationalization of production as distinct from interdependence based on trade in raw materials, contradicts realist arguments based on examples such as Japanese imperialism in the 1930s or western oil dependence in the 1970s. See Rosecrance, *Rise of the Trading State,* pp. 144–150.

80. For a discussion of conditional prospects for democratic reform, see Andrew Nathan, "China's Path from Communism," *Journal of Democracy,* Vol. 4, No. 2 (April 1993), which notes at the outset that "in October 1992 Party Secretary Jiang Zemin summarized two of the reasons why the regime has been able to stabilize itself since 1989: economic growth and political repression" (p. 28).

81. See Roger W. Sullivan, "Discarding the China Card," *Foreign Policy,* No. 86 (Spring 1992).

option is not very plausible. Third in acceptability should be a multipolar balance which continues to include the unusual U.S.-Japan alliance, allowing Japan to contribute less than its economic share to the military balance. Regarding China and Russia, Washington should pressure whichever of the two most threatens others in the region. Fourth choice should be to accept regional dominance by any of the other three great powers if it is, by that time, a securely democratic state. Fifth preference should be bipolarity of some combination of local powers. Our last choice should be to promote a global coalition to contain whatever non-democratic superpower develops and comes to dominate East Asia.

For most of these alternatives it makes sense for the United States to retain close to its current level of forces in Northeast Asia. Numbers in Korea could be thinned out slightly (although there is not much left to cut) since it does not take much to provide a tripwire. It would be mistaken, however, to eliminate the U.S. presence there before cutting it to the bone everywhere else in the world except the Middle East. Investment in deterrence should vary not just with the stakes at issue but with threats to them: although U.S. interests in Korea are not as great as in Europe, instability and sensitivity of deterrence are higher in Korea, so the strategic payoff from deployments there is greater.

In regard to Southeast Asia, the United States should stay out of direct combat over the Spratlys, but make clear that it reserves the right to provide military assistance to countries whose claims are negated by force. Washington should end economic warfare against Vietnam and encourage that country's development in order to help balance Chinese power and to support tendencies to political liberalization in Hanoi; such a double gamble, too risky in regard to a big country like China, is not as risky in regard to a weak one like Vietnam. As for Taiwan, Washington should plan to provide arms in the event of a clash between Taipei and Beijing, but not to enter the fight directly. The first point should be made clear to Beijing, the second need not be, in order to allow uncertainty to buttress deterrence.

In any case, the U.S. government should examine directly its commitment to Taiwan and decide, one way or the other, about how far to go. If the decision is that Taiwan's autonomy should be defended with American force, that should be made clear to Beijing. What should be avoided at all costs is the dangerous but all-too-precedented combination of pre-crisis ambiguity followed by a decision to intervene directly against attack; such a stance reduces deterrence and invites miscalculation and escalation.

Asia's relative importance to the United States has been obscured by the traditional U.S. interest in Europe, recent preoccupation with the Middle East, and the residue of distaste from the Vietnam War. Emerging questions about balance of power in the region have been avoided because of liberal faith in the progress of peace and realist habits of mind grounded in the Cold War. Potential *casi belli* in the area have been overlooked by most Americans because interstate violence in East Asia (except for the Indonesian invasion of East Timor) was driven by global bipolarity, now defunct. These oversights should make Asia the most fertile ground for adjusting and reinventing strategic concepts in the post–Cold War era.

Arms and Affluence

Military Acquisitions in the Asia-Pacific Region

Desmond Ball

By the early 1990s, the Asia-Pacific region had experienced a sustained build-up of modern conventional weapons systems for the better part of a decade. The fact that this build-up continued regardless of the end of the Cold War—indeed, in many countries in the region, it quickened during the late 1980s—has been a cause of both concern and wonderment. According to some recent press accounts: "Asia is rushing to arm itself as never before";[1] "Southeast Asian countries have recently gone on a military spending spree";[2] China is also now engaged in an "arms buying spree";[3] "Asia's armories are bulging, . . . conventional arms abound, and more are flooding in";[4] and there is a "new Asian arms race" underway which "bodes ill for a region already racked by ancient animosities and border disputes."[5] Moreover, for many commentators, "the new Asian arms race" is not only profoundly disturbing; it also defies rational explanation. The *Economist* recently observed that the end of the Cold War "has brought perhaps the deepest peace that Asians have known this century," and then posed the question: "What accounts for the

Desmond Ball is a Professor in the Strategic and Defence Studies Centre, Australian National University, Canberra. He is the author of Politics and Force Levels: The Strategic Missile Program of the Kennedy Administration *(University of California Press, 1980);* Can Nuclear War Be Controlled? *(International Institute for Strategic Studies, 1981);* Pine Gap: Australia and the U.S. Geostationary Signals Intelligence Satellite Program *(Allen & Unwin, 1988);* Building Blocks for Regional Security: An Australian Perspective on Confidence and Security Building Measures (CSBMs) in the Asia/Pacific Region *(Australian National University, 1991); and* Signals Intelligence in the Post–Cold War Era: Developments in the Asia-Pacific Region *(Institute of Southeast Asian Studies, 1993).*

This is a revised version of a paper prepared for presentation at the *Seventh Asia-Pacific Roundtable on Confidence Building and Conflict Reduction in the Pacific,* organised by the ASEAN Institutes of Strategic and International Studies (ASEAN ISIS), and held in Kuala Lumpur, Malaysia, June 6–9, 1993. It is published with the permission of ISIS Malaysia and the *Roundtable.*

1. Jonathan Sikes, "Asia Puts Its Wealth in Military," *Washington Times,* February 12, 1990, p. 7.
2. James Clad and Patrick Marshall, "Southeast Asia's Quiet Arms Race," *Chicago Tribune,* May 23, 1992, p. 21.
3. Tai Ming Cheung, "Loaded Weapons: China in Arms Buying Spree in Former Soviet Union," *Far Eastern Economic Review,* September 3, 1992, p. 21.
4. "Asia's Arms Race," *Economist,* February 20, 1993, p. 19.
5. Clad and Marshall, "Southeast Asia's Quiet Arms Race."

International Security, Vol. 18, No. 3 (Winter 1993/94), pp. 78–112

paradox of Asia furiously strapping on the armour when it has seldom been more at peace?"[6]

What lies behind this alarmist rhetoric? This article describes the overall scale and principal characteristics of the regional military acquisitions during this period of relatively sustained build-up; it offers a range of explanations for the acquisitions; it assesses the implications of the acquisitions for regional security; and it discusses the prospects for constraints, controls, and confidence-building measures in the region. It concludes that there is no arms race underway in the region, but that there are some disturbing features of the current acquisition programs, and that these must be addressed by regional security policy-makers and analysts if they are not to overwhelm the more positive aspects of the emerging post-Cold War security architecture in the region.

Regional Defense Spending

Through the mid and late 1980s, regional defense expenditure increased at an unprecedented rate. Given the decline in defense spending in the United States, Europe, and the former Soviet Union since 1989, this has resulted in a doubling of the Asian share of the world military expenditure over the past decade. Although gross figures should be treated carefully, it is likely that defense expenditures in East Asia and Australasia in 1992 amounted to some $105 billion (figures are in U.S. dollars unless otherwise indicated), and that this will increase to more than $130 billion by 1995—by which time it will equal that of all Europe (not counting the states of the former Soviet Union).

In the case of arms imports to the region, Asia's share of world expenditure on arms transfers rose from 15.5 percent in 1982 to 34 percent in 1991.[7] In 1991, three countries in the Asia-Pacific region—South Korea, China and Thailand—ranked in the top ten arms importers in terms of contracts con-

6. "Asia's Arms Race," *Economist*, February 20, 1993, p. 19.
7. Ian Anthony, Agnes Couraddes Allenbeck, Paolo Miggiano, Elisabeth Skons, and Herbert Wulf, "The Trade in Major Conventional Weapons," in Stockholm International Peace Research Institute (SIPRI), *SIPRI Yearbook 1992: World Armaments and Disarmament* (Oxford: Oxford University Press, 1992), p. 308.

cluded; two others—Taiwan and Burma—ranked in the top ten in terms of the value of arms actually delivered.[8]

There are, of course, significant differences in the rates of growth of defense expenditures throughout this vast and disparate region. In Northeast Asia, where defense budgets are generally an order of magnitude greater than in Southeast Asia ($10–35 billion, as compared to $1–2 billion for ASEAN countries), the rate of growth remains very high. In South Korea, for example, the defense budget for fiscal year (FY) 1993 is 9.8 percent higher than the FY 1992 budget ($12.3 billion compared to $11.2 billion).[9] In Taiwan, the defense budget for FY 1994 will be 12.6 percent greater than that for FY 1993.[10] In China, the increase for 1993 is 12.5 percent, which is the fourth consecutive year that it has grown by a double-digit percentage.[11] Only in Japan has the rate of growth slowed, with the two percent growth in 1993 being the smallest increase in 33 years.[12] On the other hand, in Southeast Asia, the picture is rather different, with the high growth rates of the late 1980s having given way to little real growth in most defense budgets since 1991 (apart from Singapore, where the defense budget is pegged to six percent of gross domestic product [GDP] and has therefore continued to increase with the growth of GDP, and Burma, where the repressive regime has announced that its defense budget will increase by nearly 10 percent in 1992–93).[13] Nevertheless, even where real growth has stopped, the increases through the late 1980s permitted much larger allocations to capital acquisition programs, and these will generally be sustained through the 1990s.

There are several important features of these defense modernization programs. In Southeast Asia, defense forces have been restructured from counter-insurgency capabilities to modern, high-technology forces, with increased emphasis on maritime (including land-based air) capabilities. Even South Korea, where the principal military threat is a land offensive across the Demilitarized Zone (DMZ) by the North Korean Army, plans to allocate some 60 percent of the (increasing) defense budget over the next five years

---

8. Richard F. Grimmett, *Conventional Arms Transfers to the Third World, 1984–1991* (Washington, D.C.: Congressional Research Service, Library of Congress, July 20, 1992), pp. 60, 72.
9. Anthony Spellman, "Asian Reports," *Armed Forces Journal International*, March 1993, p. 19.
10. "Military Budget Projected for NT $300 Billion," *China Post*, September 15, 1992, p. 16.
11. Paul Lewis, "Chinese Budget Soars for 4th Year," *Defense News*, March 22–28, 1993, p. 13.
12. "Defense Budget Increase Small," *Current News* (Washington, D.C.: Current News Analysis and Research Service, Office of the Assistant Secretary of Defense for Public Affairs, Department of Defense), April 1, 1993, p. 14.
13. Paul Beaver, "Flashpoints," *Jane's Defence Weekly*, June 6, 1992, p. 986.

to the Air Force and Navy, rather than "the usual 40 percent."[14] In Japan, the Maritime and Air Forces accounted for some 72.1 percent (37.6 and 34.5 percent respectively) of the procurement vote for the three services in 1992.[15]

Throughout the region, there is a significant degree of consistency in the acquisition programs. The more particular enhancements include:

- national command, control and communications (C^3) systems;
- national strategic and tactical intelligence systems;
- multi-role fighter aircraft, with maritime attack capabilities as well as air-superiority capabilities (e.g., F-16s and F-18s);
- maritime surveillance aircraft (e.g., P-3s);
- anti-ship missiles (e.g., *Harpoon* and *Exocet*);
- modern surface combatants—destroyers, frigates, ocean patrol vessels;
- submarines;
- electronic warfare (EW) systems;
- rapid deployment forces.

Some Explanations of the Regional Acquisition Programs

There is no single-factor explanation for the robust arms acquisition programs of the past decade. Rather, there are at least a dozen factors involved, which have obtained to greater or lesser extents and in varying combinations in different countries at different times during this period. Moreover, military and geostrategic factors, such as threat perceptions or arms race dynamics, have generally been less determinate than other considerations.

ECONOMIC GROWTH AND INCREASING RESOURCES FOR DEFENSE

Most of East Asia has experienced extraordinary economic growth over the past couple of decades, which has provided the largesse for the weapons acquisition programs. Indeed, it seems that the rates of economic growth provide the single best indicator of increases in defense expenditures throughout the region. In the case of the ASEAN countries, for example, a series of studies of the relationship between defense expenditure and economic growth from the early 1960s through to the late 1980s have consistently

14. "Bigger Role for Forces," *Jane's Defence Weekly*, August 8, 1992, p. 22.
15. Kensuke Abata, "JDA Spends Less Yen on More Contracts," *Jane's Defence Weekly*, May 8, 1993, p. 15.

shown that there is a close and positive correlation between them.[16] Those countries with the highest rates of growth of gross national product (GNP), such as Singapore and Malaysia, have had the highest rates of increase of defense spending, while those with slower economic growth, such as Indonesia and the Philippines, have had the slowest increases in defense spending.

In fact, while the correlation between defense expenditure and GNP growth has been very close, with increases in GNP being reflected in proportional increases in defense expenditure, the proportionality has been generally less than unity. In other words, the rate of growth of defense expenditure has generally been less than the rate of growth of GNP, so that defense spending as a percentage of GNP has generally fallen over the past decade. In the case of Indonesia, for example, it fell from 3 percent in 1981 to 1.6 percent in 1991; in Malaysia, it fell from 5.8 percent in 1981 to 3.4 percent in 1991; and in Thailand, it fell from 3.8 percent in 1981 to 2.6 percent in 1991. Only in Singapore has the percentage remained fairly constant—and that is precisely because the defense budget has been officially "pegged" at 6 percent of GDP.[17]

THE REQUIREMENTS OF ENHANCED SELF-RELIANCE

In the light of the end of the Cold War and the changing regional security environment, many countries in East Asia have determined to enhance their defense self-reliance to enable them to deal better with regional contingencies on the basis of their own resources. (Some countries, of course, such as China, Vietnam and Indonesia, had adopted policies of self-reliance or "national resilience" in the 1960s.)

For most countries in the region (partial exceptions are North and South Korea, China and the countries of Indochina and South Asia), increasing self-reliance against regional contingencies involves a primary emphasis on defense of the maritime approaches. In the case of Australia's defense strat-

---

16. See, for example, Geoffrey Harris, "The Determinants of Defense Expenditure in the ASEAN Region," *Journal of Peace Research*, Vol. 23, No. 1 (March 1986), pp. 41–49; David D.H. Denoon, "Defence Spending in ASEAN: An Overview," in Chin Kin Wah, ed., *Defence Spending in Southeast Asia* (Singapore: Institute of Southeast Asian Studies, 1987), pp. 48–71; and Andrew L. Ross, "The International Arms Trade, Arms Imports, and Local Defence Production in ASEAN," in Chandran Jeshurun, ed., *Arms and Defence in Southeast Asia* (Singapore: Institute of Southeast Asian Studies, 1989), pp. 1–41.
17. Singapore Ministry of Defence, *Defence of Singapore 1992–1993* (Singapore: Public Afairs Department, Ministry of Defence, August 1992), p. 46.

egy, for example, the official policy information paper, *The Defence of Australia 1987*, states that: "The fundamental importance of the sea and air gap [around northern Australia] to our security gives high priority to maritime (naval and air) forces capable of preventing an adversary from substantial operations in the area."[18]

For some countries in the region, such as the ASEAN countries, the maritime demands of increasing self-reliance are requiring a radical reorientation of planning and capabilities away from internal counter-insurgency operations to the maritime theatre. In the case of other countries, such as Japan and Australia, the maritime build-ups are, in contrast, more part of a relatively long-established strategy.

The requirements of greater self-reliance are several. To begin with, greater self-reliance requires independent surveillance, warning, and intelligence capabilities to monitor regional developments, especially in the maritime approaches or "sea-air gaps." The centrality of independent national intelligence capabilities to a policy of self-reliance is even more pronounced where such a policy is pursued through a defensive or non-offensive posture, as is commonly the case in the Asia-Pacific region (as, for example, the postures of Japan, China, Indonesia and Australia). As the Japanese Defense Agency (JDA) has stated in connection with Japan's enhancement of its technical intelligence collection capabilities: "It is highly important for Japan, which follows an exclusively self-defensive posture, to maintain warning and surveillance in its territory and in surrounding airspace and waters and to collect and process information necessary for such defense. Such activities must be carried out constantly, both in peacetime and in time of emergency."[19]

The most cost-effective approach to greater self-reliance tends to involve the employment of maritime strike capabilities, since the most vulnerable point for opposing forces is generally in the maritime approaches, where they can be hit with surface-to-surface or air-to-surface anti-ship missiles.

THE DRAWDOWN OF U.S. PRESENCE AND CAPABILITIES IN THE REGION

One of the principal security concerns in East Asia since the end of the Cold War is uncertainty about the future of the U.S. presence in the region.

---

18. The Hon. Kim C. Beazley, *The Defence of Australia 1987* (Canberra: Australian Government Publishing Service, 1987), p. 31.
19. Japan Defense Agency, *Defense of Japan 1984* (Tokyo: Japan Defense Agency, 1984), p. 110.

The bases, facilities, and forces which were maintained in the Philippines have now all been removed. Some of these have been redistributed elsewhere in the region, especially to Hawaii and the U.S. west coast and to lesser extents to Japan and Singapore, but some have been withdrawn from the region entirely. Overall, U.S. capabilities in the region are likely to be reduced by perhaps 20 percent over the next several years as compared to the end of the 1980s. The reduction in capabilities in the Pacific will almost certainly include one aircraft carrier and possibly two; several squadrons of aircraft (amounting to about half a fighter wing, or 15 percent of the strength of the Pacific Air Forces at the end of the Cold War); and several tens of thousands of Army personnel from Japan and South Korea. The scale of reductions in the Asia-Pacific region, in terms of "forward presence" capabilities, is illustrated in Figure 1.[20]

The reductions in U.S. defense capabilities in the Pacific are proportionally much less than those which have befallen European deployments; they are really quite modest when compared to the decline in former Soviet capabilities in the Far East/Western Pacific; and there is little real prospect of any more extensive reductions in U.S. capabilities in the Pacific through the rest of the 1990s. On the other hand, many regional security officials and analysts remain apprehensive about the future of the U.S. presence in the region. U.S. attempts to assuage regional concerns by reiterating facts and figures about the volume and importance of U.S. trade with and investment in the region, and by noting that defense cuts have fallen less than proportionally on Pacific deployments, have generally been to little effect. Washington has, quite simply, accorded insufficient political attention to the region. The belief is widespread in many Asian capitals that the United States might not maintain the will, and perhaps over the longer term might lose the economic capacity, to ensure that no other power in the region will become ascendant.

FEARS OF "THE DRAGONS"

Many of the smaller countries in East Asia are concerned that, with the drawdown of the U.S. presence and capabilities in the region, there will be increasing competition between the major regional powers. As Lee Kuan Yew reportedly stated in early 1990, the "medium-size political powers . . .

20. U.S. Joint Chiefs of Staff, *Joint Military Net Assessment 1992* (Washington, D.C.: U.S. Joint Chiefs of Staff, August 1992), Section 8, p. 7.

Figure 1. U.S. Forward-Presence Trends in the Pacific.

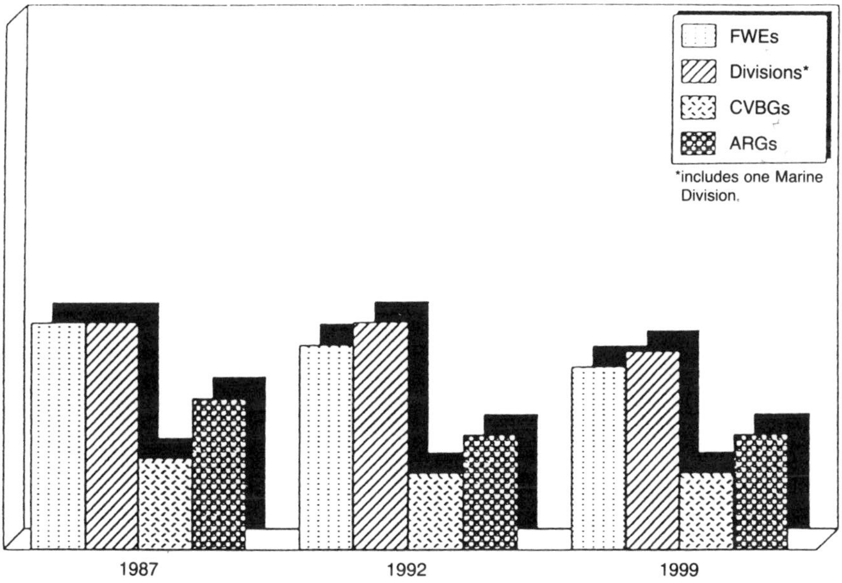

FWEs
Divisions*
CVBGs
ARGs
*includes one Marine Division.

1987 1992 1999

FWE Fighter Wing Equivalent
CVBG Aircraft Carrier Battlegroup
ARG Amphibious Readiness Group

Source: *Joint Military Net Assessment 1992* (Washington, D.C.: U.S. Joint Chiefs of Staff, August 1992), p. 8-7.

are bound to compete for power. This is simply human nature."[21] The increasing power projection capabilities of Japan and China, and to a lesser extent India, are generating considerable disquiet.

Japan is already involved in maritime operations out to 1000 nautical miles, which takes it almost as far south as the Philippines. In regional terms, Japan already has a substantial and very modern naval force, including some 100 maritime combat aircraft, 64 major surface combatants (6 destroyers and 58

21. Cited in Jonathan Sikes, "Asia Puts Its Wealth in Military," *Washington Times*, February 12, 1990, p. 7.

frigates), and 14 submarines. It is in the process of building several *Yukikaze*-class destroyers equipped with the *Aegis* system; it is modernizing its submarine fleet; it is planning to acquire tanker aircraft to extend the range of its air coverage; and it is considering the acquisition of "defensive" aircraft carriers. These Japanese developments have attracted the attention of defense planners in China, Taiwan and South Korea, and have also raised some apprehensions in Southeast Asia.

China's capabilities for operating in the Western Pacific are also growing. The Chinese Navy is acquiring a new class of destroyer (*Luhu*, or Type 052), upgraded versions of the *Luda*-class destroyers, a new class (*Jiangwei*) of missile frigates, and new classes of resupply and amphibious assault ships for sustaining operations farther from shore and for longer periods. China's power-projection capabilities in the South China Sea have been enhanced with the construction of an airbase and anchorages on Woody Island in the Paracel Islands, and the acquisition of an air-to-air refueling capability for its naval air forces. China is also acquiring several types of modern aircraft from Russia—including Su-27 *Flanker* strike/fighters (24 of which have already been delivered, with possibly another 48 to come), some of which are expected to be based on Hainan Island; MiG-31 *Foxhound* interceptor fighters (24 of which are currently being delivered, with the possibility of local manufacture of up to 200 in the future); and possibly even Tu-22M *Backfire* supersonic bombers. For the longer term, China's defense planners remain actively interested in the acquisition of some aircraft carrier capability.

These Chinese developments are generating strong apprehensions throughout East Asia. Some countries, such as Taiwan and South Korea, feel a compelling need to counter some of the new Chinese capabilities with their own programs. Others are more disturbed by the lack of transparency attending the Chinese acquisitions, with respect to the strategic purposes of the new capabilities as well as the ultimate dimensions of the Chinese buildup. In Southeast Asia, there is concern about the possibility that China might be able to assert supremacy over the South China Sea. In East Asia more generally, there is fear of the possibility that there could be some form of arms race between China and Japan in the first decade of the next century that would inevitably embroil the rest of the region.

Some developments involving India are also affecting East Asia. Although India's naval expansion has been stalled by budgetary constraints over the past few years, India remains committed to plans for the acquisition of another aircraft carrier, more surface combatants, more *Dornier*-288 long-range maritime patrol aircraft, and a modern conventional and nuclear-powered submarine fleet. It is also gradually developing its naval and air facilities on the Andaman and Nicobar Islands, which are only 80 nautical miles from the north coast of Sumatra.

Although India's reach into East Asia will remain very limited, the possibility of active Sino-Indian competition would have some disturbing implications for the region. It has figured, already, in China's support for the repressive regime in Burma—for which, in return, China has reportedly received access to a naval base on Hanggyi Island in the Bassein River at the mouth of the Irrawaddy, which it is building for Burma, as well as to a site for a monitoring station on Burma's Coco Island, just north of India's Andaman Islands. More ominously, there is the possibility of a nuclear arms race between India and China.[22]

THE INCREASING SALIENCE OF REGIONAL CONFLICT

One of the more unfortunate consequences of the end of the Cold War is the likely increase in regional conflict. Not only has the salience of regional conflict been enhanced in relative terms by the disappearance of the East-West conflict, but the end of that conflict has "removed the tempering mechanism" that often served to keep regional tensions under control.[23]

In East Asia, there remains much fertile ground for regional conflict. There are numerous issues of simmering and potential conflict involving competing sovereignty claims, challenges to government legitimacy, and territorial disputes. An outline summary of more than a score of conflict issues is given in Table 1.

Most of these issues are unlikely to lead to inter-state conflict. Some could well be resolved through negotiation, possibly involving the institution of joint surveillance and development zones encompassing the areas of disputation; others are quiescent, such as the Philippines' claim to Sabah; and others will remain essentially internal matters, such as the insurgency movements in Indonesia and the Philippines. Nevertheless, all of them remain sources of tension, suspicion, and misunderstanding. In all cases, the parties

22. See Sandy Gordon, "The New Nuclear Arms Race?" *Current Affairs Bulletin*, Vol. 69, No. 6 (November 1992), pp. 28, 29.
23. James Clapper, Director of the Defense Intelligence Agency (DIA), "Testimony to the Senate Armed Services Committee, January 22, 1992," *Regional Flashpoints Potential For Military Conflict* (Washington, D.C.: United States Information Service, January 24, 1992), pp. 1–2.

Table 1. Sovereignty, Legitimacy and Territorial Conflicts in East Asia.

- Competing Soviet/Russian and Japanese claims to the southern Kurile Islands, referred to by the Japanese as "the Northern Territories, namely, Kunashiri, Etorofu and Shikotan Islands, an integral part of Japanese territory, illegally occupied by the Soviet Union."[a]
- The unresolved dispute between Japan and South Korea over the Liancourt Rocks (Takeshima or Tak-do) in the southern part of the Sea of Japan.[b]
- Divided sovereignty on the Korean Peninsula, where some 1.4 million ground forces of the Republic of Korea and North Korea remain deployed against each other across the demilitarized zone (DMZ).
- Competing sovereignty claims of the Chinese regimes on mainland China and Taiwan.
- The unresolved dispute between Japan and China over the Senkaku (Diaoyutai) Islands in the East China Sea.
- The armed communist and Muslim insurgencies in the Philippines.
- The continuing claim of the Philippines to the Malaysian state of Sabah and its adjacent waters.
- The strong separatist movement in Sabah.
- Competing claims to the Paracel Islands (Xisha Quandao or Quan Doa Hoang Sa) in the South China Sea, contested by China and Vietnam.
- Competing claims to the Spratly Islands in the South China Sea, contested by China, Vietnam, Brunei, Malaysia, Taiwan and the Philippines.
- Border disputes between China and Vietnam.
- Boundary dispute between Indonesia and Vietnam on their demarcation line on the continental shelf in the South China Sea, near Natuna Island.[c]
- Border disputes between Vietnam and Cambodia.
- Boundary dispute between Vietnam and Malaysia on their off-shore demarcation line.
- The Bougainville secessionist movement in Papua New Guinea.
- The Organisasi Papua Merdeka (OPM) resistance movement in West Irian/Irian Jaya.
- The continuing resistance to Indonesian rule in East Timor.
- The Aceh independence movement in northern Sumatra.[d]
- The dispute between Malaysia and Singapore over ownership of the island of Pulau Batu Putih (Pedra Branca), some 55 km east of Singapore in the Straits of Johore.[e]
- The competing claims of Malaysia and Indonesia to the islands of Sipadan, Sebatik, and Ligitan, in the Celebes Sea, some 35 km from Semporna in Sabah.[f]
- Border dispute between Malaysia and Thailand.[g]
- Residual conflict in Cambodia.
- Continued fighting between government and resistance forces in Laos.[h]
- Residual communist guerilla operations along the Thai-Lao border in northeast Thailand.[i]
- Border conflicts between Thailand and Burma.[j]

concerned maintain at least a "watching brief" on the issues. Neighbors are also concerned about the implications of the issues for neighborhood stability.

It is noteworthy that about a third of the conflicts listed in Table 1 involve disputes over maritime boundaries and off-shore territorial claims. These include the dispute between Russia and Japan over the southern Kurile Islands or "Northern Territories"; between Japan and China over Senkaku

- The Shan, Kachin, Karen secessionist, communist insurgent, and pro-democracy rebellions in Burma.[k]
- Insurgency in Bangladesh.
- Hostilities along the Burma-Bangladesh border.[l]
- Territorial disputes between China and India.

NOTES:

a Japan Defense Agency, *Defense of Japan 1990* (Tokyo: Japan Defense Agency, 1990), p. 47.

b Ewan W. Anderson, *An Atlas of World Political Flashpoints: A Sourcebook of Geopolitical Crisis* (New York: Facts on File, 1993), p. 117.

c "Indonesia Invites Vietnam to Resolve Boundary Dispute," *Jakarta Post,* July 27, 1992, p. 1; and "Jakarta Hopes to Settle Sea-Border Issue With Hanoi," *Straits Times,* June 5, 1993, p. 11.

d Hugo Gordon, "Tensions Soar in East Asia as Superpowers Leave Region," *Washington Times,* August 8, 1991, p. 8.

e "Malaysian State Claims Island," *Asian Defence Journal,* October 1991, pp. 92–93; "Singapore Welcomes Malaysia's Offer of Talks on Disputed Islands," *Asian Defence Journal,* November 1991, pp. 113, 116; and N. Balakrishnan, "Tangled Ties: Island Issue Looms Large in Malaysia-Singapore Row," *Far Eastern Economic Review,* July 2, 1992, p. 21.

f P.K. Katharason, "Indonesians Detain Our Boat Off Sipadan," *The Star* (Kuala Lumpur), July 11, 1991; and "Row Over Islands Will Not Dampen Ties: Malaysian Minister," *Indonesian Observer,* February 4, 1992, p. 2.

g "Dispute Over 1977 Malaysia-Thailand Boundary Pact," *Asian Defence Journal,* April 1993, p. 85; and "Border Panel to Discuss Demarcation Problems," *Bangkok Post,* June 17, 1993, p. 8.

h "Fighting Between Lao Government and Resistance; Thailand Closes Border," *SWB (Summary of World Broadcasts)* (Caversham Park, England: BBC Monitoring), Part 3: Far East, January 11, 1992), p. i.

i Robert Karniol, "Thai Crackdown on Laotian Rebels," *Jane's Defence Weekly,* July 25, 1992, p. 11.

j Bertil Lintner, "Burma-Thailand, Collective Insecurity: Series of Raids, Incursions Increase Border Tension," *Far Eastern Economic Review,* December 3, 1992, pp. 22–23.

k See Bertil Lintner, *Outrage: Burma's Struggle for Democracy* (London and Bangkok: White Lotus, 1990).

l Bertil Lintner, "Burma's New Front," *Far Eastern Economic Review,* January 9, 1992, pp. 21–22.

Island in the East China Sea; between Malaysia and Singapore over the island of Pulau Batu Putih in the Straits of Johore; between Malaysia and Indonesia over the islands of Sipadan and Ligitan in the Celebes Sea; and, perhaps the most important potential maritime flashpoint, the competing claims to the Paracel and Spratly Islands in the South China Sea, contested by China, Vietnam, Brunei, Malaysia, Taiwan, and the Philippines.

These maritime conflict issues are proving to be very significant in shaping the defense modernization programs underway in East Asia. Together with other factors discussed in the previous sections, they drive the requirement for greater maritime surveillance capabilities, including ground-based signals intelligence (SIGINT) systems and sophisticated maritime reconnaissance aircraft.[24] They are also generating requirements for particular combat capabilities, such as longer-endurance surface combatants, platforms able to launch anti-ship missiles, and longer-range aircraft. (Malaysia, for example, has included in the performance specifications required of its new fighters the ability to conduct operations with certain payloads and for certain times on station over the area of the South China Sea and the particular Spratly Islands that it claims.)

THE REQUIREMENTS FOR EEZ SURVEILLANCE AND PROTECTION

The promulgation of 200-mile Exclusive Economic Zones (EEZs) under the Third United Nations Conference on the Law of the Sea (UNCLOS III) has generated requirements for surveillance and power-projection capabilities over resource-rich areas which, for many states in the region, are greater than their land areas.

In Malaysia, "the protection of the economic interest of the country in the Exclusive Economic Zone" was introduced as "a new element" in the 1986–90 five-year defense plan;[25] the defense allocation was significantly increased in the 1991–95 plan, and the principal reason given for the increase was the need to "[improve] the capability and efficiency of the country to control and safeguard the Exclusive Economic Zone."[26]

THE BROADENING OF REGIONAL SECURITY CONCERNS

Throughout the Asia-Pacific region, security concerns are broadening to include economic and environmental issues. Economic security involves not only the protection of critical sea lines of communication (SLOCs) but also increasingly the protection of fish stocks and other marine resources. With regard to SLOC protection, Japan—which "relies heavily on other countries for the supply of natural resources, energy, food and many other materials

---

24. Desmond Ball, *Signals Intelligence in the Post–Cold War Era: Developments in the Asia-Pacific Region* (Singapore: Institute of Southeast Asian Studies, 1993), pp. 85–96.
25. *Fifth Malaysia Plan 1986–1990* (Kuala Lumpur: National Printing Department, 1986), p. 545.
26. Malaysian Ministry of Finance, *Economic Report 1990/91* (Kuala Lumpur: 1990), p. 28.

which are indispensable to national existence"[27]—has established a requirement to "secure the safety of maritime traffic" through surveillance and escort operations out to 1000 nautical miles.[28]

Many countries in the region are also very concerned about the increasing illegal activity in the South China Sea and surrounding access-ways, such as piracy, smuggling, and unlicensed fishing. This concern has generated new requirements for maritime surveillance capabilities and maritime constabulary operations.

Environmental issues are now also on the security agenda in East Asia. Global pollution, desertification, deforestation, and the greenhouse effect, with the attendant issue of rising sea levels, are all real problems in this region. Large-scale oil spills in the Malacca Straits or the South China Sea could do irreparable damage to maritime life and other offshore resources. Deforestation in Malaysia and Kalimantan is already portending adverse environmental effects in Southeast Asia.[29] Rapid industrialization is causing a dramatic increase in carbon dioxide emissions. Global warming threatens to drown the coastal lowlands in which economic activity is frequently concentrated.

In addition, environmental issues will become an increasing source of international disputes. The externalities of environmental degradation are not confined to the national borders of the countries in which the noxious activity is generated; costs are frequently borne by those who receive no benefit from the activity. Conflicts will increasingly occur over attribution of responsibility for offshore pollution and damage to marine resources, desertification, acid rain, rising sea levels, and "environmental refugees."

The requirements of monitoring SLOCs and EEZs, and of monitoring oil spills and other pollution and the possible movement of "environmental refugees," all demand greater maritime surveillance capabilities. Other economic and environmental problems are likely to also require escort, offshore patrol, and maritime constabulary capabilities.

PRESTIGE

It is evidently the case, at least in some instances, that the acquisition of sophisticated weapons systems is due as much to the attendant prestige as

---

27. Japan Defense Agency, *Defence of Japan 1990* (Tokyo: Japan Defense Agency, 1990), p. 116.
28. Ibid.
29. See Philip Hurst, *Rainforest Politics: Ecological Destruction in Southeast Asia* (Kuala Lumpur: Abdul Majeed & Co., 1991), chaps. 1–3.

to any geostrategic considerations. The possession of high-technology weapons systems, and the demonstrated ability to operate and maintain them, is regarded as an indicator of political and economic modernization. F-16 fighter aircraft and frigates equipped with sophisticated electronic systems serve as status symbols much as national airlines and space programs do.

TECHNOLOGY ACQUISITION AND REVERSE ENGINEERING

In some cases, modern weapons systems are being acquired because of their new technologies, which might be transferred to the civil sector. Many modern technologies, such as satellite launch vehicles and super-computers, are dual-use, so that investments for defense purposes can also stimulate indigenous commercial developments. Small numbers of modern fighter aircraft can be used to introduce new composite materials; combat information systems aboard modern frigates provide access to integrated data-management systems; and advanced electronic warfare systems are at the leading edge of communication and signal processing technologies. There is no doubt that some countries, such as China, have acquired small numbers of certain modern weapons systems for the purposes of "reverse engineering" and technology transfer.

CORRUPTION

The involvement of the military in economic and commercial activities in many parts of East Asia has produced instances where military greed and impropriety have figured in many major acquisition programs. In Thailand, for example, the widespread practice of "commissions" or "kickbacks" to senior military decision-makers, sometimes amounting to as much as 35–40 percent of a contract, has raised the possibility of "a corruption-driven procurement process" in which weapons are bought more because of the "kickbacks" than for any national security requirement.[30] According to one arms sale specialist, for example, "the important thing to remember when you sell to the Thai military is not what a weapon can do, it's how much it can produce in under-the-counter payments."[31]

---

30. Tai Ming Cheung, "Officer's Commission: Arms Procurement Driven By Profit Rather Than Need," *Far Eastern Economic Review,* July 2, 1992, p. 13.
31. Cited in Kenneth Stier and Bao Anyou, "The Bitter Truth Behind Thailand's Khaki Commerce," *Asia, Inc.*, October 1992, p. 36.

SUPPLY-SIDE PRESSURES

With the end of the Cold War and the reductions in defense budgets in the United States, Europe and the former Soviet Union, arms manufacturers are having to ply their wares more actively in Asia in order to compensate for the decline in their home markets.[32] The retirement of enormous amounts of conventional weaponry from the U.S., Soviet, and European inventories has also produced large stocks of surplus arms and equipment which governments and manufacturers are willing to sell at cut-rate prices. It is, in the judgement of the *Economist*, "the greatest buyers' market ever."[33]

The Russians are evidently willing to sell virtually anything to anybody with the cash to pay, or even the products to barter. China has already signed several arms contracts with Russia, including those for the Su-27 and MiG-31 fighters, and has discussed a wide variety of other acquisitions, including Tu-22M *Backfire* bombers, Il-76 Airborne Warning and Control System (AWACS) aircraft, surface-to-air missiles, early-warning and air defense radar systems, T-72 main battle tanks, armored vehicles, and naval surface combatants.[34] Russia is selling Malaysia some 18 MiG-29 fighters, and has agreed to accept part of the payment in palm oil, fabrics and other goods.[35] Russia has also offered to sell MiG-35 anti-tank helicopters to Malaysia;[36] *Scud* missiles and advanced versions of the MiG-21 fighter aircraft to Indonesia; and submarines, helicopter gunships, armored fighting vehicles and patrol boats to other ASEAN countries.[37] In February 1993, Indonesia announced that it was buying 39 ships from Germany (16 *Parchim* class corvettes, 12 landing ships, two supply ships, and nine *Condor*-2 class minesweepers—about one-third of the former East German Navy),[38] reportedly for "the bargain price of $35 million."[39]

32. See David Silverberg, "Manufacturers Struggle to Identify Future Markets," *Defense News*, August 27, 1990, p. 12; and Kenneth J. Stier, "U.S. Companies Struggle to Win Asian Arms Supply Race," *Journal of Commerce*, January 30, 1991, p. 4.
33. "Asia's Arms Race," *Economist*, February 20, 1993, p. 20.
34. See Tai Ming Cheung, "Loaded Weapons."
35. "Russia is Willing to Accept Malaysian Items for MiGs," *Wall Street Journal*, March 3, 1993, p. 11; and Michael Mecham, "Malaysia Buys MIG-29s, F/A-18Ds," *Aviation Week & Space Technology*, July 5, 1993, pp. 24–25.
36. Bilveer Singh, "The Russians Are Coming," *Business Times* (Singapore), February 10, 1993, p. 24.
37. Michael Vatikiotis and Tai Ming Cheung, "Bearing Arms: Russia Poised to Sell Weapons in Asean," *Far Eastern Economic Review*, December 24–31, 1992, p. 20.
38. See "Germany to Build Submarines for RI [Republic of Indonesia]," *Indonesian Observer*, February 5, 1993, p. 1; and Michael Richardson, "Indonesia to Acquire One-Third of Former E. German Navy," *International Herald Tribune*, February 5, 1993, p. 7.
39. Vatikiotis and Cheung, "Bearing Arms."

PREEMPTION OF POSSIBLE INTERNATIONAL RESTRAINTS ON ARMS TRANSFERS

A more proximate factor involved in some of the recent acquisitions is a concern that the glut of weapons systems and associated equipment might not last for much longer, and hence that purchases should be concluded while stocks last and before international constraints are imposed on arms transfers. According to U.S. officials, for example, China is "moving quickly to acquire as much military capability as possible before the international community closes the door on the sale of advanced military technology."[40]

ACTION-REACTION OR ARMS RACE DYNAMICS

The characterization of the regional military acquisition programs as "an Asian arms race" has a singular deficiency: it does not accord with any generally accepted definition of the term "arms race." Any arms race should have two principal features: first, a very rapid rate of acquisitions, with the participants stretching their resources in order to ensure that they remain at the head of the race; and, second, some reciprocal dynamics in which developments in the defensive and offensive capabilities of one adversary are matched by attempts to counter the advantages thought to be gained by another. Thus, the continued acquisition of new weapons capabilities becomes an interactive process in which the arms requirements of one party depend upon the known, assumed, or anticipated capabilities of the forces of the other party or parties.

There is little of this in the current acquisition programs in the region. Defense budgets are continuing to increase in real terms in only half a dozen countries in the region. The proportions of GDP being allocated to the defense vote—a key indicator of national commitment to any race—are generally decreasing throughout the region. There are few unambiguous cases of particular acquisitions in one country leading to either imitative or offsetting acquisitions by others. Perhaps the clearest exception concerns the acquisition of advanced fighters in Southeast Asia, where Singapore's decision to purchase F-16s does seem to have acted as something of a stimulant for the subsequent Indonesian and Thai F-16 acquisitions, as well as fueling Malaysia's interest in a strike fighter.[41] Even in this instance, however, other con-

40. David A. Fulghum, "China Exploiting U.S. Patriot Secrets," *Aviation Week & Space Technology,* January 18, 1993, p. 20.
41. See Tai Ming Cheung, "Shoulder to Shoulder: ASEAN Members Strengthen Ties," *Far Eastern Economic Review,* March 22, 1990, pp. 25–26.

siderations were at least as strong, including the central importance of air defense and strike capabilities in enhanced self-reliance. More generally, imitative dynamics have entered the acquisition processes through concerns common to many defense establishments that their capabilities for surveillance of air and sea approaches and of activities in disputed maritime areas be as effective as those of their neighbors, and of particular countries to reap the prestige that is attendant on the acquisition of modern technology and to demonstrate that they are just as capable of operating and maintaining high-technology systems as their neighbors.

Themes in Regional Acquisition Programs

There are significant common themes apparent in the acquisition programs currently in progress in the region. East Asia is, of course, an extremely diverse region, with extraordinary disparities in national economic resources and military capabilities, and significant differences in security concerns and threat perceptions, in light of which the degree of consistency in the acquisition programs is all the more remarkable.

NATIONAL COMMAND, CONTROL, AND COMMUNICATIONS (C^3) SYSTEMS

The requirements for enhanced self-reliance induced by the end of the Cold War, the expiration of bipolarity, the drawdown of the U.S. presence and the increasing salience of regional contingencies are reflected in the centrality of modern command, control, and communications (C^3) systems in the current regional acquisition programs.

Many countries in the Asia-Pacific region went through the Cold War dependent upon the United States for their defense in the paramount contingency, Communist aggression. There was little need for national defense planning staffs and structures, independent operations concepts and doctrines, joint-service cooperation, or independent communications and other supporting infrastructure. Defense planning was done in Washington or Honolulu, and operational concepts and doctrines were formulated by the relevant U.S. commands. The services required inter-operability with their U.S. counterparts (for example the Japanese Maritime Self-Defense Agency with the U.S. Navy, and the South Korean Army with the U.S. Army) rather than with the other arms of their own forces. The most important communications systems were those designed and maintained by the United States for communication between regional capitals and Washington, and between

U.S. commands and local commanders in the theatre, rather than between national capitals and their national forces.

Now, however, self-reliance is dictating the construction of national command centers and joint-force headquarters, and the design and development of nationally based communications systems and facilities. The Japan Self-Defense Agency is building a new headquarters in Tokyo to provide, *inter alia,* more centralized control over the operations of the service and defense intelligence agencies.[42] In South Korea, the headquarters of each service are being relocated to a common site in a suburban area of Taejon City in the center of the country.[43] Singapore has built a new Ministry of Defense headquarters, complete with a "hardened underground central operations control centre" at Bukit Gombak, some 7.5 km south of Kranji, which will be linked through microwave and fiber-optic channels to an island-wide command, control, communications and intelligence network.[44]

NATIONAL TECHNICAL INTELLIGENCE SYSTEMS

Throughout the Asia-Pacific region, there has been a significant expansion in technical intelligence (especially SIGINT) capabilities and operations over the past decade, and this is expected to continue over the foreseeable future.[45] The enhancement of SIGINT capabilities is due to the requirements of greater self-reliance, the increasing need for maritime surveillance information, and the need to collect electronic order of battle (EOB) information on the communications and electronic systems of neighbors and potential adversaries for electronic warfare purposes.

Independent intelligence collection capabilities are an essential ingredient of more self-reliant defense postures. As an official of the Japan Defense Agency recently stated, with regard to the enhancement of the JDA's SIGINT capabilities: "In the cold war era the world moved in teams, and as a member of the American-led team, our judgment was not so important. Now Japan needs its own ability."[46] South Korea remains reliant on the U.S. intelligence system for strategic early warning, but the Ministry of National Defense has

42. David E. Sanger, "Tired of Relying on U.S., Japan Seeks to Expand Its Own Intelligence Efforts," *New York Times*, January 1, 1992, p. 6.
43. Ministry of National Defense, *Defense White Paper 1990* (Seoul: Ministry of National Defense, Republic of Korea, 1991), p. 152.
44. "Singapore Plans C^3I Network," *Defense News*, March 4, 1991, p. 14.
45. See Ball, *Signals Intelligence in the Post–Cold War Era*, especially chapters 4 and 5.
46. Cited in Sanger, "Tired of Relying on U.S., Japan Seeks to Expand Its Own Intelligence Efforts."

recently described the requirement for national South Korean capabilities as follows: "Reducing this reliance on U.S. forces will require the acquisition of reconnaissance aircraft and intelligence-gathering equipment as a substitute for those belonging to the U.S. forces, as well as improvement of early warning and battleground surveillance capabilities and development of command, control, communication and intelligence (C^3I) systems."[47]

In the case of Australia, the *Review of Australia's Defence Capabilities* in 1986 argued that "a high level of intelligence self-reliance" was "central" to greater defense self-reliance;[48] and the subsequent policy information paper, *The Defence of Australia 1987*, reiterated that "a high level of capability in strategic intelligence is fundamental" to a more self-reliant defense posture.[49] And as New Zealand Prime Minister David Lange stated when announcing the decision to establish the satellite communications (SATCOM) SIGINT station at Waihopi on December 2, 1987:

> This Government is committed to the pursuit of a more self-reliant defence policy. This involves greater independence in intelligence matters. . . . To further enhance our own intelligence capabilities a defence satellite communications station will be constructed in the Waihopi Valley, near Blenheim. . . . The station will mark a new level of sophistication in our independent intelligence capability.[50]

Many of the new SIGINT acquisitions are designed to collect maritime surveillance information. In Japan, for example, the stations at Miho on Honshu and at Shiraho on Ishigaki-Shima at the southern end of the Ryuku archipelago (some 260 km east of Taiwan) are equipped with large circularly disposed antenna arrays (CDAAs) and are designed to provide ocean surveillance over the Japanese SLOCs from Japan south to the Philippines and east to Guam.[51]

Many countries in the region are also acquiring advanced airborne SIGINT capabilities, again primarily for ocean surveillance purposes. For example, the Japan Maritime Self-Defense Force (JMSDF), which currently operates

---

47. Ministry of National Defense, *Defense White Paper 1990* (Seoul: Ministry of National Defense, Republic of Korea, 1991), p. 152.
48. Paul Dibb, *Review of Australia's Defence Capabilities: Report to the Minister for Defence* (Canberra: Australian Government Publishing Service, March 1986), pp. 6, 60–64, and 115–117.
49. Beazley, *The Defence of Australia 1987*, p. 34.
50. The Rt. Hon. David Lange, Prime Minister for New Zealand, "Defence Satellite Communications Station," Press Statement, December 2, 1987, pp. 1–2. See also "NZ Spy Base Plan Gives Self-Reliance," *Australian*, December 7, 1987, p. 15.
51. See Ball, *Signals Intelligence in the Post–Cold War Era*, pp. 43–46, 93.

two EP-2J SIGINT aircraft, is acquiring four much more capable EP-3 SIGINT aircraft.[52] China now operates several EY-8 SIGINT aircraft, equipped with the BM/KZ-8608 electronic intelligence (ELINT) system designed to monitor shipborne radar emissions.[53] South Korea is planning to acquire some dozen SIGINT aircraft, which will be used for ocean surveillance as well as for more general SIGINT collection.

As discussed below, most countries in the region are rapidly developing their electronic warfare (EW) capabilities. It has been widely recognized that defense operations on the modern battlefield cannot be effectively conducted without comprehensive and real-time intelligence concerning the adversary's electronic order of battle—i.e., catalogues of the plethora of communications systems, radars, and other electromagnetic emitters which might be expected in the area of operations. The EOB data required for the design of appropriate EW capabilities is being collected by new ELINT systems of various sorts and levels of sophistication.

MULTI-ROLE FIGHTER AIRCRAFT

Most countries in the region are currently acquiring significant numbers of advanced multi-role fighter aircraft—i.e., fighters with maritime attack capabilities as well as air defense capabilities.[54] According to one estimate, it is likely that "about 3000 new fighters and strike aircraft will be procured this decade by Asia-Pacific countries," while an approximately equal number of existing aircraft will be upgraded with new mission avionics and armaments.[55] Some 1500 of these new fighters will be deployed by four Northeast Asian air forces—China (about 550), Taiwan (466), Japan (400), and South Korea (160). In Southeast Asia, the ASEAN countries are likely to acquire some 300 new fighters and strike aircraft through this decade. (In South Asia, India and Pakistan are likely to acquire about 1000 such aircraft.)

---

52. Ibid., p. 46.
53. Ibid., p. 56.
54. For up-to-date tables listing new fighter aircraft acquisitions, surface combatants equipped with anti-ship missiles, new surface combatant acquisitions, airborne maritime surveillance capabilities, submarine capabilities, acquisitions of airborne early warning and control (AEW&C) systems, and acquisitions of signals intelligence (SIGINT) aircraft in the Asia-Pacific region, see Desmond Ball, *Trends in Military Acquisitions in the Asia-Pacific Region: Implications for Security and Prospects for Constraints and Control*, Working Paper No. 273 (Canberra: Strategic and Defence Studies Centre, Australian National University, July 1993), Tables 2–8, pp. 30–45.
55. Prasun Sengupta, "Forecast Asia-Pacific: Tension Remains," *Aerospace*, September 1992, p. 54.

In most cases, the capability for maritime attack operations has been an important factor in these new fighter programs. In China, for example, the Su-27 *Flankers* and the B-7 *Hong* fighter-bombers are being configured for anti-ship operations. Similarly, in Southeast Asia, all the new fighters and strike aircraft are being equipped with *Exocet* or *Penguin* anti-ship missiles.

MARITIME RECONNAISSANCE AIRCRAFT

It is estimated that current programs will involve the acquisition of more than 120 new maritime reconnaissance aircraft in the region,[56] almost doubling present inventories of these aircraft. The Japan Maritime Self-Defense Force, for example, is planning to acquire as many as 74 P-3C long-range maritime patrol (LRMP) aircraft, while South Korea is acquiring eight to ten P-3Cs. Thailand has three Dornier-228 LRMP aircraft, with another two planned, and has three P-3A/Bs in the process of delivery. Further south, Australia and New Zealand maintain nineteen P-3C and six P-3K *Orions* respectively. The P-3s are all equipped to carry *Harpoon* anti-ship missiles.

In Southeast Asia, the maritime capability requirements are relatively rudimentary. Apart from Thailand, which has a particular interest in LRMP aircraft with anti–submarine warfare (ASW) capabilities because of concerns about submarine activities in the eastern Indian Ocean, the ASEAN countries are principally interested in surface surveillance capabilities, with coastal surveillance and monitoring of EEZs being at least as important as military surveillance. Singapore, Thailand, Malaysia, Indonesia, and Brunei are all modernizing their airborne surface surveillance capabilities. Singapore currently operates four E-2C *Hawkeyes,* which perform maritime surveillance missions in addition to their primary airborne early warning function. (Acquisition of an additional two to four E-2Cs is under consideration.) For "dedicated maritime surveillance" operations, Singapore has ordered four Fokker F-50 *Maritime Enforcer* Mark II aircraft (with an additional two on option), which are expected to achieve initial operational capability in 1994.[57] Thailand currently operates several different types of maritime surveillance aircraft, including three Fokker F-27 *Maritime Enforcer* Mark I aircraft, in addition to its LRMP capabilities. Malaysia currently operates three C-130H maritime patrol aircraft, and is planning to acquire four light maritime sur-

---

56. Ibid.
57. "Singapore Orders F-50 Maritime Enforcer Mk.II," *Asia-Pacific Defence News,* June 7, 1991, p. 6; and "The JDW Interview," *Jane's Defence Weekly,* October 12, 1991, p. 684.

veillance aircraft. Indonesia operates two C-130H maritime patrol aircraft, 18 *Searchmasters*, and three Boeing *Surveillers*. The Indonesian Navy is also acquiring six CASA/IPTN CN-235 medium-range maritime patrol aircraft. And Brunei has ordered three CASA/IPTN CN-235s.[58]

MODERN SURFACE COMBATANTS

Some 200 new major surface combatants are programmed for procurement in East Asia through the 1990s, with about another 50 under serious consideration. These include the 13,000-ton light aircraft carrier being acquired by Thailand (with delivery scheduled for 1996); four (and possibly eight) U.S. *Arleigh Burke*–class *Aegis* destroyers, with a displacement of some 7200 tons, being acquired by Japan; more than a hundred new frigates; and more than a hundred corvettes and ocean patrol vessels in the 1000–1500 ton range. It is also likely that by the end of the decade both China and Japan will also have made definite decisions to acquire some aircraft carrier capabilities. In addition, it is likely that more than 200 new minor surface combatants (corvettes, fast attack craft, missile patrol boats, etc.) will also have been procured in the region.

ANTI-SHIP MISSILES

There are already more than 300 surface combatants in East Asian navies equipped with modern anti-ship missiles such as *Harpoons* and *Exocets*. Between them, these combatants have some 1600 anti-ship missile launchers. These numbers are likely to be more than doubled through the course of the 1990s, as most of the new combatant acquisitions will be equipped with extensive surface-to-surface missile suites.

The most capable of these missiles is the *Harpoon*, which is currently in service with six navies in the region (Japan, South Korea, Indonesia, Singapore, Thailand and Australia). Almost all of the other navies in the region have either indigenously produced anti-ship missiles (e.g., the Chinese C-801 and the Taiwanese *Hsiung Feng* II) or *Exocet* missiles. Even Brunei now has three missile patrol craft, each equipped with two *Exocet* MM-38 missiles. When the Philippines takes delivery of three *Cormoran*-type missile patrol boats by 1995, every country in the region will possess modern shipborne anti-ship missiles.

---

58. "ASEAN Special Report: Options for Defence," *Jane's Defence Weekly*, February 22, 1992, p. 294.

In addition, most of the new fighter aircraft and long-range maritime patrol aircraft being introduced into the region are also equipped with anti-ship missile capabilities—*Harpoon*, *Exocet* or *Penguin* anti-ship missiles.

SUBMARINES

East Asian navies currently possess about 100 submarines, although many of the *Romeo*-class submarines possessed by China and North Korea are no longer operational. (In addition, India currently has some 18 submarines.) More than three dozen new submarines are planned for acquisition during the 1990s. Most of these new boats will be deployed in Northeast Asia, with Japan in the process of building another dozen, South Korea acquiring at least nine Type 209s, and Taiwan seeking to acquire some six to ten boats. To the south of the region, Australia is in the process of building six new *Collins*-class submarines to replace the six *Oberon*-class boats built in the 1960s.

In Southeast Asia, only Indonesia currently maintains a submarine capability, with two Type 209 *Cakra* class boats commissioned in 1981 and refitted in 1986–87, and three additional Type 209s ordered from Germany for delivery in 1995–96.[59] However, Malaysia has decided to acquire two to four submarines later in the 1990s, and Thailand and Singapore are seriously considering the acquisition of small numbers of submarines.

ELECTRONIC WARFARE CAPABILITIES

Most countries in East Asia are rapidly developing their electronic warfare capabilities, including their maritime EW capabilities. This reflects the widespread efforts in the region to achieve national self-reliance, the general recognition of the value of EW as a "force multiplier," the defense modernization programs (which necessarily include significant electronic components), and the ability of many countries in the region to produce advanced electronic systems (or the desire to promote the development of indigenous electronic sectors through local design and production).

In East Asia, Japan is clearly the leader with respect to the acquisition of advanced EW equipment, with all the major combatant platforms of the JMSDF equipped with such systems—e.g., the HLQ-101 and HLR-108 ESM systems installed on ASW aircraft, the NOLQ-1 EW suite on the *Hatsuyuki* and *Shirane* helicopter destroyers and the *Hatakaze* and *Sawakaze* guided mis-

59. Charles Bickers, "Indonesia Continues Its Naval Build-Up," *Jane's Defence Weekly*, January 30, 1993, p. 4; and "Germany To Build Submarines for RI."

sile destroyers, and the NOLR-6 system on the *Amatsukaze* guided missile destroyer and some *Yamagumo*-class vessels.[60]

Although the scale of recent acquisitions of advanced weapons systems elsewhere in East Asia is generally somewhat less in quantitative terms than those of Japan, they are nevertheless impressive and are invariably also being equipped with advanced EW systems. For example, Indonesia's six *Van Speijk* frigates are equipped with "state-of-the-art" EW systems; Singapore is acquiring the advanced Shipboard Electronic Warfare System (SEWS) for its six *Victory*-class corvettes; Australia is installing the Raytheon AN/SLQ-32 (V)2 and Thorn/EMI ESM systems on its new FFG-7 and ANZAC frigates; and Malaysia intends to equip the new frigates it is acquiring from Britain with the GEC-Marconi *Mentor* EW suite, which provides a comprehensive threat warning, surveillance, target indication, and direction-finding (DF) capability.[61]

RAPID DEPLOYMENT FORCES

Most countries in the region have either recently established or are in the process of developing some form of rapid deployment force, typically of brigade or light divisional size, designed to be deployed to possible areas of operation (AOs) at short notice and to fight as more or less self-contained units. For example, Australia has an Operational Deployment Force (ODF) consisting of two infantry battalions and supporting armor and airborne units. In 1984, Indonesia formed a Rapid Reaction Strike Force (Paksukan Pemukul Reaksi Cepat, or PPRC), which consists of an infantry airborne brigade (with one battalion ready to react to any location within the archipelago within twelve hours), a Marine battalion landing team, two fighter/ground attack squadrons, twelve C-130 *Hercules* for airlift, and about a dozen naval support vessels.[62] In the late 1980s, the Chinese People's Liberation Army (PLA) formed about ten battalion-sized rapid reaction units designed "for rapid deployment anywhere along China's borders or in the South China Sea."[63] In 1988, the PLA Navy also created a special rapid reaction force,

---

60. Ball, *Signals Intelligence in the Post–Cold War Era,* pp. 47–48, 83.
61. Ibid., pp. 81–84, 96.
62. Bob Lowry, *Indonesian Defence Policy and the Indonesian Armed Forces,* Canberra Papers on Strategy and Defence No. 99 (Canberra: Strategic and Defence Studies Centre, Australian National University, 1993), pp. 83, 93–94.
63. Gary Klintworth, *China's Modernisation: The Strategic Implications for the Asia-Pacific Region* (Canberra: Australian Government Publishing Service, 1989), p. 43.

supported by an array of new amphibious assault ships and landing craft.[64] In 1989, Malaysia began development of a Rapid Deployment Force which is currently based on a reinforced battalion group but which will grow to divisional strength (about 12,000 troops) by the turn of the century; based at Mersing on the southeast coast of the peninsula, it is to be equipped with new transport aircraft, medium-lift helicopters, amphibious assault ships, light tanks, amphibious infantry combat vehicles, and light field guns.[65] Singapore maintains "a reinforced infantry battalion on 24-hour standby to respond to any exigencies,"[66] and has announced plans to develop an air-mobile rapid deployment division (tentatively designated No. 12 Division), which is to be equipped with new utility helicopters and integral mechanized armor and artillery systems.[67]

Net Assessment of Military Acquisitions for Regional Security

The recent trends in military acquisitions in the region evince a mixed and very complex picture. Some of the most significant factors are entirely non-military, such as the availability of economic resources and the perceptions of prestige attendant upon high-technology aerospace programs. There are also many different types of weapons systems involved, some of which are relatively defensive, while others are more offensive (e.g., maritime strike and other power projection systems) and thus more likely to stimulate counter-acquisitions and crisis instabilities.

Overall, the generally high rates of growth in defense expenditures through the 1980s have lessened in the early 1990s, with some important exceptions in Northeast Asia (China, Taiwan and South Korea). On the other hand, even where real growth in defense spending has stopped, most regional defense budgets now contain relatively high allocations for capital procurement, which are likely to be maintained over the foreseeable future. A critical question is whether these allocations will be able to support the continued acquisitions of new capabilities as well as the replacement of

64. Jim Bussert, "The Chinese Navy—A Pacific Wild Card," *Defense Electronics*, July 1992, p. 50.
65. Anthony Spellman, "Rapid Deployment Forces on Horizon for Malaysia, Singapore," *Armed Forces Journal International*, April 1991, p. 36; David Saw, "Malaysia Looks Beyond Its Deal of the Decade," *Armed Forces Journal International*, June 1992, pp. 32–33; and Peter Howard and Ian Kemp, "The Jane's Interview," *Jane's Defence Weekly*, September 26, 1992, p. 32.
66. Singapore Ministry of Defence, *Defence of Singapore 1992–1993*, p. 23.
67. Spellman, "Rapid Deployment Forces on Horizon for Malaysia, Singapore."

systems acquired in the 1980s, and hence whether or not a new round of real increases in procurement budgets might be expected in the later 1990s.

At the least, the general commitment to greater self-reliance will remain unabated. This can be regarded as a healthy trend. The national self-confidence generated by the achievement of greater self-reliance and the acquisition and maintenance of modern, high-technology weapons systems can serve to promote regional confidence. In Indonesian terms, "each country's *Ketahanan Nasional* (National Resilience) is the precondition of achieving *Ketahanan Regional* (Regional Resilience)."[68]

On the other hand, it is critical that these acquisition programs do not lead to a regional arms race. Since the requirements for defense self-reliance cannot be defined without some consideration of the capabilities possessed by neighbors and potential adversaries further afield, there must come a point when further acquisitions begin to generate counter-programs, to the detriment of both self-reliance and regional security.

Several aspects of the current acquisition programs are disturbing. To begin with, these programs are proceeding in an atmosphere of uncertainty and some lack of trust. Uncertainty and suspicion are fueled by a relative lack of transparency in the region with respect to the long-range objectives and motivations behind the current acquisition programs, as well as the particular force elements of these programs. Tensions are already being induced in the region by attempts by some countries to discern the purposes and intentions of their neighbors. For example, an espionage controversy that damaged relations between Malaysia and Singapore in late 1989 was reportedly due, at least in part, to Singapore's efforts to collect information on Malaysia's "recent $1.6 billion arms deal with Britain."[69]

In addition to the absence of transparency, misunderstanding is also caused by the lack of any common threat perceptions throughout the region. Some countries are more concerned than others about India's power-projection capabilities, some are more concerned about the increasing Chinese capabilities, and some are more worried about the plans and intentions of their

68. See A. Hasnan Habib, "Technology for National Resilience: The Indonesian Perspective," in Desmond Ball and Helen Wilson, eds., *New Technology: Implications for Regional and Australian Security,* Canberra Papers on Strategy and Defence No. 76 (Canberra: Strategic and Defence Studies Centre, Australian National University, 1991), pp. 60–65, 76.

69. See Suhaini Azuam, "Neighbourly Interest: Spy Accusation Reveals Regional Suspicions," *Far Eastern Economic Review,* December 21, 1989, pp. 20–26; and Holman Jenkins, "Dwindling Supports Throws Status Quo Into Sea of Change," *Insight,* January 14, 1991, pp. 26–28.

nearer neighbors. Justifications for particular acquisitions, no matter how well articulated, might simply not ring true in these circumstances, leading to misunderstandings and unanticipated and unfortunate reactions.

The "offensive" character of some of the new weapons systems being acquired is also cause for concern. Many of the new acquisitions (such as the maritime attack aircraft, modern surface combatants, and submarines, all equipped with anti-ship missiles) involve strike capabilities with offensive connotations. Unfortunately, for many countries they provide the most cost-effective basis for self-reliance; in some cases, such as that of Australia, a viable posture of self-reliance would not be possible without some minimal strike capabilities. Yet these capabilities are the most likely to generate counter-acquisitions.

This applies particularly to new fighter aircraft acquisitions. Air power is at the forefront of the force modernization programs in the region, but it is also a principal means of projecting power in the region. Air power is inherently (although not only) offensive. The quantitative and qualitative enhancements of air power are perhaps the most likely to trigger unanticipated and undesired arms acquisition competitions.

Other acquisitions, such as submarines and long-range anti-ship missiles, are more disturbing in terms of their implications for crisis stability. The underwater environment is particularly opaque, and underwater operations are particularly subject to uncertainty, confusion, loss of control, and accidents. Similarly, over-the-horizon targeting of long-range anti-ship missiles raises the prospect of errors and miscalculation. Inadvertent escalation becomes increasingly likely.

Prospects for Constraints and Controls

It is clear that, at least in the short term, there is little possibility that countries in the Asia-Pacific region will engage in arms control or multilateral security dialogues which will constrain their force development plans and programs. Most countries in the region are committed to robust acquisition programs and can provide both the funds and the strategic justifications for them. In any case, the region currently lacks any machinery by which the processes of dialogue and cooperation could have any constraining impact. Some confidence and security building measures (CSBMs) are currently being instituted, however, which offer the prospect of constraints in the longer term.

In this context, the essential "building blocks" are those which address the more likely points of tension and misunderstanding which attend the acquisition programs, and hence alleviate the possibilities for reciprocal acquisitions, miscalculations and inadvertent escalation. The basic "building blocks" are transparency and dialogue.

TRANSPARENCY

A critical requirement is to encourage much greater transparency with respect to major arms acquisition programs and strategic objectives. Mechanisms are needed for discussion and sharing of information on security perceptions and threat assessments (including intelligence assessments of general regional security developments as well as particular issues such as refugee movements, piracy, and terrorism); major weapons acquisition programs; military exercises and forward deployments; and defense doctrines and operational concepts.

Various official Australian government statements over the past half-decade provide something of a model for the sort of public disclosure which is both possible and necessary. The *Review of Australia's Defence Capabilities,* issued in March 1986, provides a detailed and comprehensive explanation of the basis and rationale of the structure of the Australian Defence Force (ADF).[70] The policy information paper on *The Defence of Australia 1987,* issued by the Minister for Defence in March 1987, provides a comprehensive overall explanation of the basis of Australian defense policy and planning, including the concepts of self-reliance and "defense in depth."[71] In December 1989, the Minister for Foreign Affairs and Trade, Gareth Evans, issued a major statement on *Australia's Regional Security,* which describes Australia's regional security interests and policies, including not just the military but also the diplomatic, economic, and development assistance dimensions, and explains the Australian policies of "comprehensive engagement" for Southeast Asia and "constructive commitment" for the South Pacific.[72] In August 1990 the Royal Australian Air Force (RAAF) issued *The Air Power Manual,* which

---

70. Dibb, *Review of Australia's Defence Capabilities,* p. v.
71. Beazley, *The Defence of Australia 1987,* pp. vii-x.
72. Gareth Evans, Minister for Foreign Affairs and Trade, *Australia's Regional Security* (Canberra: Management Information Processing, Department of Foreign Affairs and Trade, December 1989).

describes the basic doctrine and operational concepts for the employment of air power in the defense of Australia.[73]

The publication of similar statements by regional governments should be encouraged—with, however, an awareness of the limitations that some regional socio-political cultures impose on open government. Australia could offer to provide assistance to regional planners with respect to planning methodologies and techniques, such as program budgeting and five-year (and more forward) defense planning. The development and publication of long-term defense plans and their conceptual bases would allay some of the uncertainty in the region.

Transparency would also be enhanced by the establishment of a public registry containing information on arms acquisitions. The idea of an international arms register was widely and seriously discussed in the late 1980s, and on December 9, 1991, the United Nations General Assembly passed Resolution 46/36L on "Transparency in Armaments," which calls upon the UN Secretary-General to establish a register of conventional arms, including both holdings and transfers, covering such systems as main battle tanks, armored personnel carriers, combat aircraft, attack helicopters, large-calibre artillery systems, warships, and missiles or missile systems. However, the information required is to be of a very general nature and will not include the particular models or types of equipment, small arms (which still dominate the battlefield in most regional conflicts), the financial terms of sales (which would indicate whether a supplier is "dumping" the equipment), or important details of extant holdings. It is, nevertheless, a useful first step in an evolutionary process of providing transparency and promoting restraint.[74]

In April 1992, the Malaysian Minister for Defence, Datuk Seri Mohammed Najib bin Tun Abdul Razak, proposed that a "regional register" be established both to support the UN regime and so that "suspicion could be minimised and managed" in the Asia-Pacific region itself.[75] Such a regional registry, while being wholly compatible with the categories and collection processes

---

73. Royal Australian Air Force, *The Air Power Manual* (Canberra: Air Power Studies Centre, Royal Australian Air Force, August 1990).
74. See David Anderson, "Transparency in Arms Transfers: The Arms Registry," paper prepared for the 89th Interparliamentary Union (IPU) Conference, New Delhi, April 12–17, 1993.
75. The Hon. Datuk Seri Mohammed Najib bin Tun Abdul Razak, "Towards Cooperative Security and Regional Stability: The Malaysian View," in David Horner, ed., *The Army and the Future: Land Forces in Australia and South-East Asia* (Canberra: Directorate of Departmental Publications, Department of Defence, 1993), p. 137.

of the UN regime, could be configured to address those deficiencies in the broader regime and provide greater illumination of other particular matters of concern to regional policy-makers and analysts.

As with all the other important avenues for promoting CSBMs in the region, however, the issues with respect to transparency are not straightforward. Transparency is not a neutral strategic value. The effect of transparency is different for countries with more "defensive" as opposed to "offensive" defense postures, as well as for those countries more dependent upon arms imports rather than indigenous production. It can expose vulnerabilities (in both intelligence collection and force structure capabilities). Uncertainty about the capabilities of potential adversaries sometimes serves to enhance deterrence (or to induce caution).

In addition, particular problems and sensitivities obtain in the Asia-Pacific region. The widespread and extensive acquisitions over the past decade notwithstanding, many countries still maintain only very limited stockpiles of some critical weapons systems and ordnance. For example, the holdings of precision-guided munitions (PGMs) by the Royal Australian Air Force are so small that they "would not last one day of intensive operations at the higher level."[76] Thailand has only sixteen *Harpoon* anti-ship missiles. A full public listing of stocks of these sorts of systems could undermine the credibility of many defense postures in the region, thus diminishing regional resilience.

For many Asian defense establishments, a high level of public transparency is simply unacceptable at this stage. Many governments are unwilling to disclose their real levels of defense expenditure, let alone their orders of battle or the particulars of their operational deployments and stockpiles. Nevertheless, they may be willing to discuss these matters at "a professional level," behind closed doors, with senior officials from other defense establishments. It may well be that the most promising path to greater transparency in the region will be dual-track, with some information, such as general defense doctrines and major weapons acquisitions, being disclosed publicly, but other information, such as operational concepts and details of deployments and acquisitions, being disclosed only to professional counterparts.

76. Air Marshal S.D. Evans, "Air Power in the Defence of Australia: The Strategic Context," in Desmond Ball, ed., *Air Power: Global Developments and Australian Perspectives* (Sydney: Pergamon-Brassey's Defence Publishers, 1988), p. 122.

INSTITUTIONALIZED REGIONAL SECURITY DIALOGUE

The most fundamental building block for regional security cooperation and confidence-building is the institutionalization of regional security dialogue. Such dialogue should lead to better appreciation of the concerns, interests and perceptions of the participating countries, enhancing mutual understanding and trust, and preventing misinterpretations, misunderstandings and suspicions likely to cause tensions and even conflict. More generally, institutionalized dialogue would serve as a mechanism for managing some of the uncertainty that presently confounds regional security planners and analysts. However, too much should not be expected from the dialogue process in terms of agreed solutions to regional security problems, at least through the rest of the 1990s. The task for the near term, as Mahathir bin Mohamad stated more than a decade ago with respect to regional dialogue on economic cooperation, is "the tedious one of getting to know each other."[77] It could well take more than a decade for the developing dialogue processes within the region to produce sufficient mutual understanding, confidence and trust for resolving or managing substantive regional security issues.

Informal dialogue processes, such as the increasing frequency of meetings of defense chiefs and other high-level officers throughout the region, are extremely important. However, these need to be complemented by some degree of institutionalized dialogue mechanisms. Regularly scheduled meetings and exchanges of information and views would have a better chance of continuing through periods of less tranquil political winds than *ad hoc* visits and meetings; they could also provide a mechanism for maintaining lines of communication when other lines have been cut by political storms, and hence of ameliorating the effects of such storms on regional relations. A degree of institutionalization which included the preparation of agendas would also serve to focus and to provide some continuity to the dialogue.

There have been some very significant developments in this area over the past few years. The most important of these is the ASEAN Post-Ministerial Conference (PMC) process. In 1990, the notion of using the PMCs of the meetings of the ASEAN Foreign Ministers as a forum for regional security

---

77. Mahathir bin Mohamad, "'Tak Kenal Maka Tak Cinta'," in *Asia-Pacific in the 1980s: Toward Greater Symmetry in Economic Interdependence* (Jakarta: Center for Strategic and International Studies, May 1980), p. 18.

dialogue was informally raised within the ASEAN Institutes of Strategic and International Studies. The essence of the notion was that the ASEAN PMC was already a well-established mechanism for bringing together the six nations of ASEAN and their "dialogue partners," and that it was practicable to extend it in membership to include other Asia-Pacific countries and in agenda to include regional political and security issues. In June 1991, the ASEAN Institutes recommended to their governments that they move to effect this proposal.[78] The proposal was discussed by the ASEAN Ministers at the Twenty-fourth ASEAN Ministerial Meeting in Kuala Lumpur on July 19–20, 1991; a Joint Communiqué issued on July 20 stated that the ASEAN PMC was an "appropriate base" for addressing regional peace and security issues.[79] This was endorsed at the Fourth ASEAN Summit in Singapore in January 1992.

Several attendant developments are needed if the ASEAN PMC process is to accommodate fully the requirements of an institutionalized regional security dialogue. To begin with, the PMC arrangements need to become more fully multilateralized, both in membership, to include the so-called "non-like-minded" (China, Russia, Vietnam, Laos, and North Korea), and in agenda preparation, to broaden the purview beyond essentially ASEAN concerns. This development is already underway: China and Russia have been invited as guests to the ASEAN Ministerial Meetings since 1991, and Laos and Vietnam have now also been invited.[80] It is likely that these four countries will effectively be full "dialogue partners" on political and security matters by 1994. In addition, the PMC process must be supported by the development of some institutionalized infrastructure at both the official and non-governmental levels. This development is also now underway at the official level. In June 1991, the ASEAN Institutes of Strategic and International Studies proposed that there be instituted a "senior officials meeting [SOM] made up of senior officials of the ASEAN states and the dialogue partners" to support the ASEAN PMC process (e.g., with respect to the preparation of agendas and meeting arrangements).[81] The first of the SOMs was held in

78. ASEAN Institutes of Strategic and International Studies (ISIS), *A Time For Initiative: Proposals for the Consideration of the Fourth ASEAN Summit,* June 4, 1991, pp. 4–5.
79. *Joint Communiqué of the Twenty Fourth ASEAN Ministerial Meeting, Kuala Lumpur, July 19–20, 1991,* p. 5.
80. See Jusuf Wanandi, "Developments in the Asia-Pacific Region," paper prepared for a symposium on *The Changing Asia-Pacific Scene in the 1990s: Security, Cooperation and Development* (Beijing: China Center for International Studies, August 10–12, 1991), p. 26.
81. ASEAN ISIS, *A Time For Initiative,* p. 5. For further discussion of the role of SOMs, see His

Singapore in May 1993, and included discussion of proposed multilateral approaches to regional peace and security.[82] On the other hand, proposals for non-governmental support structures remain under development; they warrant strong encouragement.

The PMC and attendant processes remain focused, of course, on the more foreign policy aspects of security, rather than the military dimension. However, there have also been important developments with respect to institutionalized defense dialogue over the past couple of years. Arrangements for regular discussions between defense intelligence officials, albeit mostly on bilateral bases, now involve each of the ASEAN countries and many of the dialogue partners. In April 1992, Malaysian Minister for Defense Najib announced that Malaysia was "willing to host the first of a proposed series of Asia-Pacific security dialogue meetings," to which each participant "could send a delegation made up of various representatives of their security [i.e., defense] agencies, both military and civilian."[83] The first of the "Najib talks" took place in Kuala Lumpur in June 1993. Such meetings will provide a forum for discussion of such matters as defense assessments, operational concepts, defense planning, exercises and weapons acquisitions which would be important for regional transparency but which remain out of bounds for public disclosure.

Conclusions

It is necessary to stress that the development of regional cooperative security and confidence-building measures to the point where they become a significant aspect of the regional strategic architecture will not be easy. The Asia-Pacific region is very disparate: quite different security perceptions obtain, outstanding territorial and legitimacy conflicts require resolution, and there is very little tradition of security cooperation, at least on a multilateral basis. The issues themselves are generally complex, and the practical and operational factors involved in the establishment of effective CSBM regimes are extremely demanding.

Excellency Dr. Taro Nakayama, Minister for Foreign Affairs of Japan, "Statement to the General Session of the ASEAN Post-Ministerial Conference," Kuala Lumpur, Malaysia, July 22, 1991, pp. 12–13; and Wanandi, "Developments in the Asia-Pacific Region," p. 27.

82. Peter Gill, "U.S. Takes New Line On Regional Security," *Australian Financial Review*, March 2, 1993, p. 12.

83. Najib, "Towards Cooperative Security and Regional Stability," p. 137.

However, the fact that the exercise will not be easy is not an excuse for inaction. The need for regional CSBMs is too important for that. Rather, it means that policy-makers, officials and security analysts will have to devote increasing attention and resources to the practical and operational considerations involved in institutionalizing greater regional cooperation. The initial steps or "building blocks" will necessarily be modest. The place to start is with dialogue and other measures designed to enhance mutual understanding and confidence in the region. The critical question is whether or not the arrangements for enhanced regional cooperation can be instituted to the point where they can enable the effective management of the extraordinary changes and the increasing complexities and uncertainties which characterize the emerging security environment in the Asia-Pacific region.

Part II:
The Implications of the Rise of China

Hegemon on the Horizon?

China's Threat to East Asian Security

Denny Roy

Northeast Asia has been relatively peaceful for the past forty years. The post–Cold War era, however, will bring new security challenges to the Asia-Pacific region. Perhaps the most serious of these challenges involves China's expected emergence as a major economic power in the near future. While a developed, prosperous Chinese economy offers the region many potential benefits, it would also give China the capability to challenge Japan for domination of East Asia.

China's recent economic growth signals a change in East Asia's distribution of power and draws renewed attention to Chinese foreign policy. What are the consequences of Chinese economic growth for regional security?[1]

I argue that a burgeoning China poses a long-term danger to Asia-Pacific security for two reasons. First, despite Japan's present economic strength, a future Chinese hegemony in East Asia is a strong possibility. China is just beginning to realize its vast economic potential, while Japan's inherent weaknesses create doubts about the ability of the Japanese to increase or sustain

The author is grateful to two anonymous reviewers for their helpful comments on earlier drafts of this article. The views expressed herein are the author's own, and not necessarily those of his employer.

Denny Roy teaches in the Department of Political Science at the National University of Singapore.

1. There are a few recent studies which mention, but do not analyze in detail, the possible threat posed by a stronger China. See Gerald Segal, "The Coming Confrontation Between China and Japan," *World Policy Journal*, Vol. 10, No. 2 (Summer 1993); Zakaria Haji Ahmad, "Japan and China in Pacific Asia's Evolving Security Environment," *Global Affairs*, Vol. 8, No. 1 (Winter 1993), pp. 27, 28; A. James Gregor, "China's Shadow Over Southeast Asian Waters," *Global Affairs*, Vol. 7, No. 3 (Summer 1992); and Nicholas D. Kristof, "The Rise of China," *Foreign Affairs*, Vol. 72, No. 5 (November/December 1993). Kristof hints at two theoretical assumptions that might provide a basis for understanding China's external behavior in the future: he writes that China has "a sense of wounded pride, the annoyance of a giant that has been battered and cheated by the rest of the world." China will "seek a more powerful role, because that is what great powers are supposed to do" (pp. 70, 72). His conclusions, however, are very general: he says China may try to "resolve old quarrels in its own favor," including attacking Taiwan, but also that Chinese foreign policy will not be aggressive or irresponsible (pp. 59, 70–72). William H. Overholt briefly, but directly, examines the impact of a wealthier China on regional security; Overholt, *China: The Next Economic Superpower* (London: Weidenfeld and Nicolson, 1993), chap. 6. Overholt, however, emphasizes the positive consequences of a developed China, not the potential dangers.

International Security, Vol. 19, No. 1 (Summer 1994), pp. 149–168

their present level of economic power. China also faces less resistance than Japan to building a superpower-sized military. Second, a stronger China is likely to undermine peace in the region. Economic development will make China more assertive and less cooperative with its neighbors; China's domestic characteristics make it comparatively likely to use force to achieve its political goals; and an economically powerful China may provoke a military buildup by Japan, plunging Asia into a new cold war.

Asia's Future: China or Japan as Number One?

With the United States apparently committed to a drawdown of its global military forces, the Asia-Pacific region seems to have a vacancy for a successor hegemon. Many analysts expect Japan to inherit this mantle on the basis of its impressive economic strength and influence.[2] Nevertheless, two formidable obstacles stand between Japan and hegemony: the instability of Japanese economic strength and the weakness of Japan's armed forces.

Japan's inherent economic vulnerabilities amply justify Frank Gibney's term "fragile superpower."[3] The fragilities include Japan's lack of natural resources and consequent dependence on foreign supplies of raw materials; an aging workforce (Japanese now lead the world in life expectancy, which will result in a higher proportion of retirees to workers); a labor shortage (coupled with strong resistance to importing foreign labor); a declining savings rate; and a dangerously unfavorable corporate capital-to-debt ratio. Like the United States, Japan has begun to move production to developing countries with lower labor costs, which threatens to erode its economic base and to increase unemployment.[4] These characteristics and developments may undermine the long-term stability of Japanese economic power. Bill Emmott argues that the sun is now setting on Japan's economic heyday; the surplus of Japanese capital is declining and "may disappear altogether as early as

---

2. Works that support the view of Japanese dominance in Asia are Chalmers Johnson, "Where Does Mainland China Fit in a World Organized into Pacific, North American, and European Regions?" *Issues & Studies*, Vol. 27, No. 8 (August 1991), p. 12; Walden Bello, "Trouble in Paradise," *World Policy Journal*, Vol. 10, No. 2 (Summer 1993); and Steven Schlossstein, *The End of the American Century* (New York: Congdon and Weed, 1989).
3. Frank Gibney, *Japan: The Fragile Superpower* (Tokyo: Charles E. Tuttle, 1987).
4. Andrew Pollack, "A 'Made in Japan' Label Is Getting Harder to Find," *International Herald Tribune*, August 30, 1993, p. 1.

1995."[5] Economic growth will be impeded by claims for financial compensation from victims of Japanese aggression in the Pacific War, which may run into the hundreds of billions of dollars.[6] Finally, the political environment of the post–Cold War era, with its increased interest in trade blocs and "managed trade," is likely to prove less favorable to Japanese economic growth. The massive trade surplus that has become Japan's "staff of life"[7] is in jeopardy, and Japan's relatively small, stingy home market could not compensate for the opportunities lost due to protectionism that now looms in the bigger overseas markets. Since Japan's "bicycle economy" requires continuous forward movement to prevent collapse, even a slowdown could have serious ramifications.

Japan's military weakness is the other principal obstacle to Japanese hegemony. Rather than an "economic superpower," Japan is really an incomplete major power. As long as the Japanese choose not to expand their capacity to project military power, they will lack the abilities to protect their economic interests abroad and to exert decisive global political influence.

Tokyo also faces strong disincentives against attempting to deploy military forces commensurate with its economic strength. Consequently, the Japanese government is unlikely to undertake heavy rearmament in the absence of a serious new threat (such as a stronger China, discussed below). One problem with increased military spending is that it would erode some of Japan's economic strength. Japan would begin to suffer the financial drain that it largely avoided during the Cold War by relying on U.S. protection.

More serious are the political disincentives. The great majority of Japanese still oppose an increase in either the size or the role of their armed forces. Japanese also overwhelmingly support the "peace constitution" forbidding armed forces (now interpreted to mean forces capable of threatening neighboring countries), and are disinclined even to take up arms in defense of the Japanese home islands, let alone undertake campaigns of conquest overseas.[8]

---

5. Bill Emmott, "The Limits to Japanese Power," *Pacific Review,* Vol. 2, No. 3 (1989), p. 179.
6. Associated Press, "Japan may face claims of up to $290b from WWII victims," *Straits Times* (Singapore), September 9, 1993, p. 4.
7. George Friedman and Meredith LeBard, *The Coming War with Japan* (New York: St. Martin's Press, 1991), p. 386.
8. A recent poll asked Japanese, "What will you do if Japan is attacked by a foreign country?" Less than half of the respondents said they would fight the invaders; most of the remainder responded, "I don't know." Paul D. Scott, "The New Power of Japan," *Pacific Review,* Vol. 2, No. 3 (1989), pp. 187, 188n. See also Peter J. Katzenstein and Nobuo Okawara, "Japan's National

Significantly, this pacifism appears to be based more on circumstances than on principle.[9] The Japanese know that a military resurgence in their country would provoke other Asian-Pacific countries to form an anti-Tokyo coalition that might eventually strangle Japan.[10] While balancing is sometimes inefficient,[11] prompt and efficient anti-hegemonic balancing against Japan is virtually assured by the lingering legacy of fascist Japan's Asia policy in the 1930s and early 1940s.

Present circumstances—a relatively weak China and Russia, an engaged but non-threatening United States, and the region's historical fear of Japanese military power—thus rule out an unprovoked Japanese military buildup, leaving Japan dependent on others for protection and unable to qualify as a hegemonic candidate. A change in these circumstances, however, could spark a *reactive* Japanese rearmament, discussed below.

If Japan is an overachiever that has to a large degree transcended its handicaps, China has long been a perennial underachiever. Despite its large territory and population, substantial natural resources, and the economic vigor demonstrated by Chinese everywhere except inside the People's Republic, China's various economic development strategies have posted disappointing results since the intrusion of the West during the Qing Dynasty heralded the end of the ancient order.

But with the economic reforms implemented by Deng Xiaoping and his protegés, China now shows signs that it is beginning to realize its economic potential. China's economy grew by 12.8 percent in 1992, helped greatly by $11 billion in foreign investment, and by another 13 percent in 1993 (in contrast, Japan's economy grew just 3.3 percent in 1993).[12] The International Monetary Fund recently reported that based on "purchasing power parity" statistics, China has the world's third largest economy.[13] Even at a more

---

Security: Structures, Norms, and Policies," *International Security*, Vol. 17, No. 4 (Spring 1993), p. 101.

9. The main arguments in Japan against rearmament tend to be economic and political rather than ethical. Katzenstein and Okawara, "Japan's National Security," p. 116.

10. As the Japanese discovered earlier in the century, threatening states generally prompt other states to balance against them. See Stephen M. Walt, *The Origins of Alliances* (Ithaca, N.Y.: Cornell University Press, 1987), pp. 17–26.

11. John Mearsheimer, "Back to the Future: Instability in Europe After the Cold War," *International Security*, Vol. 15, No. 1 (Summer 1990), pp. 15–16.

12. Carl Goldstein, et al., "Get Off Our Backs," *Far Eastern Economic Review*, July 15, 1993, p. 69; "Prices and Trends," *Far Eastern Economic Review*, Jan. 27, 1994, p. 58.

13. Susumu Awanohara and Lincoln Kaye, "Number Games," *Far Eastern Economic Review*, July 15, 1993, p. 74.

modest annual growth rate of 8 to 9 percent, the target declared by China's economic czar Zhu Rongji, China's economy will double in size within nine years. Indeed, the biggest worry among the leadership in the former "sick man of Asia" these days is how to keep the economy from growing too rapidly.

China's sudden economic surge raises the possibility that early in the next century, China will be a more powerful country than Japan. To the "Japan As Number One" argument[14] that Japan will soon replace the United States as the world's strongest economic power, others reply that "Japan will never become number one. . . . China is growing so much faster that it will overtake Japan before Japan has a chance to overtake the United States."[15]

Taken as a whole, China is still profoundly poor, and probably faces many setbacks en route to prosperity. Several problems threaten to prevent China's growth into an economic superpower. The most serious is the possibility of fractionalization—the breakup of the Chinese empire into several autonomous states—a tendency that has been accelerated by China's recent economic success.[16] Another hurdle is continued state ownership of much of China's economy. Employing about one-third of the urban Chinese workforce, these state-owned industries are largely unprofitable; some 40 percent of them operated in the red in 1991. Yet Beijing is reluctant to shut them down, fearing massive unemployment and consequent social unrest.[17] Other difficulties include a chronically high population growth rate, which exacerbates unemployment and siphons capital investment away from industry and into less productive sectors such as housing and environmental protection; inflation, the "running dog" of rapid economic growth; and widespread official corruption and profiteering.[18]

Nevertheless, China holds several important economic and political advantages that may make Beijing's long-term prospects for an Asia-Pacific hegemony better than Japan's.

In the economic sphere, China combines its high growth rate with a large territorial and population base (in contrast with Japan's small territory and

---

14. Terminology borrowed from Ezra F. Vogel, *Japan As Number One* (New York: Harper & Row, 1979).
15. Segal, "The Coming Confrontation Between China and Japan," p. 27.
16. Ibid., p. 27.
17. David Shambaugh, "China in 1991: Living Cautiously," *Asian Survey*, Vol. 32, No. 1 (January 1992), p. 26.
18. K.C. Yeh, "Macroeconomic Issues in China in the 1990s," *China Quarterly*, No. 131 (September 1992), pp. 503–504, 516.

medium-size population). This gives China a huge potential domestic market—over a billion customers within its own borders. Indeed, the special economic zones on China's eastern coast already send many of their "exports" to the Chinese interior.[19] In contrast, Japan lacks a large domestic markets and is thus vulnerable to protectionism. China's natural resource endowments are also far superior to those of Japan. The Chinese are self-sufficient in food production and supply most of their own energy needs, while the Japanese depend heavily on imports.

Another possible Chinese economic advantage is what Andrew Brick terms "Greater China": a network of ethnic Chinese with proven entrepreneurial prowess throughout the region. Chinese minorities in Southeast Asia, most of whom still speak the dialects of their ancestral home provinces in the PRC, own disproportionately large shares of their adopted states' capital. In Indonesia, for example, where Chinese account for only 5 percent of the population, they control 75 percent of the country's wealth.[20] Given the choice of doing business with Japan or the PRC, the overseas Chinese are likely to prefer customers, suppliers, and investors with whom they share language, culture, and ancestry. The overseas Chinese network gives China a significant long-term edge in the competition to establish an economic empire in East Asia.

China also has an important political advantage over Japan. To dominate the region, either Japan or China would need much larger military forces. China's edge is that the region would be more accommodating to a buildup of Chinese military power than to a Japanese buildup. The reason is historical. Although the foreign policy of the PRC has hardly been pacific, China's record of aggression pales in comparison with that of Japan in this century. Where China has been militarily assertive, as with its punitive invasion of Vietnam in 1979 and its recent threats to use force against Taiwan and rival claimants of disputed islands in the South China Sea, its neighbors have been relatively tolerant.

While the Japanese government has irritated other Asian countries by its seeming reluctance to acknowledge the full magnitude of Japan's atrocities during the Pacific War, the Chinese government has sought to assure the

19. Bruce Cumings, "The Political Economy of China's Turn Outward," in Samuel S. Kim, ed., *China and the World* (Boulder, Colo.: Westview, 1989), pp. 217, 218.
20. Andrew B. Brick, "Chinese Water Torture: Subversion Through Development," *Global Affairs*, Vol. 7, No. 2 (Spring 1992), p. 97.

region that "China does not seek hegemony now, nor will it do so in the future, even when it is economically developed."[21] Beijing and its apologists have steadily counter-attacked the "China threat" argument as an attempt by anti-China Westerners "to sow discord between China and its neighboring countries and to destroy China's plans of reunification and economic development."[22] There is substantial sympathy for China's position within the region. For example, Singapore Senior Minister Lee Kuan Yew, the dean of Southeast Asian statesmen, said after Beijing lost its bid to host the 2000 Olympic Games, "America and Britain succeeded in cutting China down to size. . . . The apparent reason was 'human rights.' The real reason was political, to show Western political clout."[23] Malaysian Prime Minister Mahathir Mohamad displays a similar attitude. "The U.S. is saying we are threatened by China," he says. "But I don't see the threat from China as being any worse than the threat from the U.S."[24] Anna Dominique Coseteng, a Philippine senator, recently said that although the Chinese "have been around the Philippines for 3,000 years, [they] have not shown any signs of wanting to control government policies or interfere in our affairs."[25] Korean scholar Sang Joon Kim assures us it is "highly unlikely that China will use its power and resources to support an aggressive or expansionist policy."[26]

This is not to deny that East Asians are concerned about China's recent military upgrading program. They clearly are. But the predominant sentiment throughout the region is appeasement.[27] There is no serious support for any response stronger than trying to get the Chinese "incorporated into a multilateral security framework."[28] Thus, there is a double standard in East Asia: a Chinese military buildup, while not welcomed, is acceptable; a Japanese

---

21. The quotation is from Chinese Foreign Minister Qian Qichen, in Michael Richardson, "China Said to Court Asians as a Buffer Against U.S.," *International Herald Tribune,* July 24–25, 1993, p. 1.
22. Wei Zhengyan, "China's Diplomacy in 1993," *Beijing Review,* January 17–23, 1994, p. 15.
23. *Straits Times,* October 14, 1993, p. 1.
24. "Give Bosnia Back," *Asiaweek,* August 11, 1993, p. 21.
25. "A Colossus Stirs," *Asiaweek,* January 27, 1993, p. 25.
26. Sang Joon Kim, "Korea, China and a New Order for Peace in Northeast Asia," *Korean Journal of International Studies,* Vol. 24, No. 2 (Summer 1993), p. 137.
27. Yong Pow Ang's commentary is typical: "Rather than fret over China's defence build-up, the ASEAN countries would do well to accommodate the inevitable rise of China as a regional superpower." Yong, "ASEAN Should Accommodate China's Rise as Superpower," *Straits Times,* August 10, 1993, p. 27.
28. Yoichi Funabashi, "The Asianization of Asia," *Foreign Affairs,* Vol. 72, No. 5 (November/December 1993), p. 84.

defense buildup is not. Several Asian countries have complained loudly even about Japan's participation in United Nations peacekeeping operations.

While a Japanese military buildup would likely galvanize the region into forming an opposing coalition, the region appears prepared to tolerate a Chinese buildup, and would probably not form a balancing alliance unless China's external behavior became significantly more threatening than it is now. China thus faces far weaker political constraints against building a superpower-sized military capability—an important prerequisite of hegemony—than Japan.

If China can avoid disintegration, its inherent long-term economic and political advantages justify the expectation that during the first decade of the next century the "Middle Kingdom" is likely to become the most powerful country in East Asia.

The Impact of a Strong China on Regional Security

The prospect of Chinese dominance has important ramifications for peace in the region. A stronger China would endanger East Asian security in two ways. First, China would be tempted to establish a regional hegemony, possibly by force. Second, the rise of Chinese power might trigger a response from Japan, bringing East Asia under the shadow of a new bipolar conflict.

ECONOMIC DEVELOPMENT AND CHINESE FOREIGN POLICY

While some scholars argue that ancient China established a track record of benevolent hegemony,[29] two patterns in the foreign policy of the PRC suggest that neighboring countries might find life with a powerful China unpleasant. First, China has from time to time behaved in ways offensive to the rest of the world, seemingly undaunted by the possible consequences of negative global opinion.[30] Second, China has shown its willingness to use force to settle disputes, even when its own territory is not under attack.[31]

China as a threat, using force

---

29. Chen Jian writes, "Territorial expansionism or imperialism as known in the West was never an active part of Chinese civilization." Chen, "Will China's Development Threaten Asia-Pacific Security?" *Security Dialogue*, Vol. 24, No. 2 (June 1993), p. 194.
30. A. James Gregor makes this observation in "China's Shadow Over Southeast Asian Waters," *Global Affairs*, Vol. 7, No. 3 (Spring 1992), p. 5.
31. China's incursion into Vietnam in 1979 was evidently intended to punish Hanoi for invading Cambodia. China entered the Korean War to rescue its communist ally North Korea. The Chinese have also used force against Vietnam to defend their disputed claim to the South China Sea islands; territorial self-defense might be claimed in that case, but only dubiously.

If a relatively weak and developing China has established such patterns, would a stronger, developed China abandon them? The question of whether economic development will make Chinese foreign policy more pacific or more assertive divides commentators roughly into two theoretical camps. The liberal position holds that prosperity will make China behave more peacefully, while realists argue that greater economic strength would embolden a unified China to expand its political influence in the region, perhaps to the grief of its neighbors. An evaluation of the primary arguments for both these positions suggests that the realists have the stronger case.

Two arguments are commonly advanced in support of the liberals' prosperity-causes-peace proposition. The first is that economic development leads to political liberalization, and with it greater government accountability to the demands of the mass public. Historically, democratic peoples have rarely if ever chosen to fight each other. Thus, peaceful relations could be expected between a democratized China and the United States, Japan, and the other liberalizing states in the region.[32]

Unfortunately, this prediction, and the argument upon which it is based, may never be tested. The establishment of a liberal democracy in China is extremely unlikely in the foreseeable future.[33] The obstacles are daunting, and since crushing the student rebellion in Tiananmen Square, Beijing has shown little interest in further political liberalization. Even if China does eventually begin to respond to pressures for liberalization, many observers, including the Beijing regime itself and many Chinese intellectuals, see "soft authoritarianism," in which the state allows considerable economic freedom but retains tight control over politics, as a more likely model for the Chinese than Western-style democracy.[34] In any case, prosperity will not automatically result in meaningful mass public input into China's foreign policy decisions. Without democratization within, there is no basis for expecting more pacific behavior without.

A second argument for the pacifying effects of Chinese prosperity is the interdependence argument. According to this view, China is aware that its

32. See, for example, Winston Lord, "China and America: Beyond the Big Chill," *Foreign Affairs*, Vol. 68, No. 4 (Fall 1989); and Gaston J. Sigur, "China Policy Today," *Department of State Bulletin*, Vol. 87, No. 2119 (February 1987). The literature on the war involvement of democracies is summarized in Nils Petter Gleditsch, "Democracy and Peace," *Journal of Peace Research*, Vol. 29, No. 4 (November 1992).
33. See, for example, Shambaugh, "China in 1991," p. 31.
34. See Denny Roy, "Singapore, China, and the 'Soft Authoritarian' Challenge," *Asian Survey*, Vol. 34, No. 3 (March 1994).

economic development depends on maintaining financial, trade, and diplomatic ties with other countries. Dependence on the outside world will therefore, it is argued, deter Beijing from contemplating any acts that might offend foreign governments or jeopardize China's access to international capital, technology, and markets.[35] The same international links that promote Chinese prosperity also ensure Chinese docility.

Problems with the interdependence argument, however, weaken its persuasiveness. First, economic interdependence may heighten rather than defuse political tensions.[36] The threat or practice of economic coercion has sometimes driven states to war. If used against China, this strategy might backfire, pushing Beijing to try to establish direct control over the foreign resources and markets the Chinese consider vital to their well-being.

A second weakness of the interdependence argument is that in China's case, the deterrence value of interdependence is severely limited. In the past, the liberal capitalist countries have proven greatly reluctant to pressure Beijing, and this pressure, when applied, has produced poor results. Western governments easily succumb to the ageless warning against "isolating" China; Japan, the first to break ranks and lift post-Tiananmen trade sanctions against China, opposes "applying an abstract yardstick of human rights to foreign aid."[37] For their part, the Chinese leaders have learned from past experience that the threat of collective international punitive action against them is largely a paper tiger.[38] In the most recent confirmation of their view, the perpetrators of the Tiananmen massacre were first runners-up in the competition for the right to host the 2000 Olympic Games.

Finally, interdependence may be doomed by its own success. Throughout its modern history, China has been an economically backward country trying to catch up with the earlier-industrializing West and Japan. This has been a common goal of the various developmental strategies pursued by the PRC

35. An example of this view is Kim, "Korea, China, and a New World Order," pp. 135–137.
36. Stephen Van Evera, "Primed for Peace: Europe After the Cold War," *International Security*, Vol. 15, No. 3 (Winter 1990/91), p. 33n. Michael W. Doyle adds that the pacifying effects of interdependence are minimized in relations between "liberal" (e.g., the United States, Japan, Western Europe) and "nonliberal" countries (e.g., China). "Kant, Liberal Legacies, and Foreign Affairs, Part 2," *Philosophy and Public Affairs*, Vol. 12, No. 4 (1983), p. 326.
37. Then–Prime Minister Kiichi Miyazawa, quoted in Lin Binyan, "The Beijing-Tokyo Axis Against Human Rights," *New Perspectives Quarterly*, Vol. 9, No. 1 (Winter 1992), p. 32.
38. Deng himself reportedly dismissed the possibility of serious international sanctions by saying the world finds China "too big a piece of meat." Roger W. Sullivan, "Discarding the China Card," *Foreign Policy*, No. 86 (Spring 1992), p. 21.

since its inception.[39] An "open door" to the international economy, with heavy dependence on imports of capital and technology and exports of low-to-middle-end manufactures, is China's most successful strategy to date. But dependence means vulnerability. Like all national governments, the Chinese leaders are naturally inclined to "control what they depend on [from abroad] or to lessen the extent of their dependency."[40] Dependence is a necessary evil, part of the price that capital-poor, developing economies must pay to achieve rapid modernization. The security threat of vulnerability to economic coercion is compensated for by the security benefit of a growing economy, the basis of future military and political strength. Enmeshment in the world economic system also promises quicker development than the alternative strategy of autarky. The opportunity costs of interdependence thus remain low for developing countries, while the costs of securing their own sources of necessary resources are prohibitively high. But as a developing country becomes strong and wealthy relative to the other states in the system, both the benefits it realizes from interdependence and the costs of establishing its own sphere of influence decrease. Today's weak China has to suffer the vulnerabilities of interdependence, but tomorrow's strong China will not. The more powerful China grows, the less it needs the aid and approval of the other major powers to get what it needs. Over the long term, interdependence cannot offer other countries much hope of reining in a burgeoning China.

Realists would not in any case expect prosperity to make China more pacific. If the international behavior of states is strongly influenced by threats and opportunities governments perceive in the international system, as realists assume, then China's growth from a weak, developing state to a stronger, more prosperous state should result in a more assertive foreign policy. Specifically, says Christopher Layne, "rising powers," or states that have acquired the prerequisites of major power status, "seek to enhance their security by increasing their capabilities and their control over the external environment."[41] Strong countries are also more assertive than lesser powers in both defining and defending their interests.[42] As China fulfills its economic

39. Cumings, "The Political Economy," pp. 204, 205.
40. Kenneth N. Waltz, *Theory of International Politics* (New York: McGraw-Hill, 1979), p. 106.
41. Christopher Layne, "The Unipolar Illusion: Why New Great Powers Will Rise," *International Security*, Vol. 17, No. 4 (Spring 1993), p. 11.
42. Jack Levy, *War and the Modern Great Power System, 1495–1975* (Lexington: University Press of Kentucky, 1983), pp. 11–19; Layne, "The Unipolar Illusion," p. 8n.

potential, it will conform to these patterns. A growing economic base will increase opportunities for China to establish greater control over its environment, while simultaneously decreasing the costs of doing so. An economically stronger China will begin to act like a major power: bolder, more demanding, and less inclined to cooperate with the other major powers in the region.

The realist argument has powerful historical support. A stronger China will be subject to the same pressures and temptations to which other economically and militarily powerful countries of recent history succumbed, including Britain, Nazi Germany, the Soviet Union, and the United States. Each sought to dominate the part of the globe within its reach (although the particular character of each hegemony varied, from relatively benign to malign).

CHINA IS PRONE TO USING FORCE

The impact of a strong China on Asia-Pacific security becomes more clear if we compare the consequences of a dominant China with those of a dominant Japan. For several reasons, a strong China is more likely to use force in pursuit of its goals in the region than a strong Japan, even a powerfully rearmed one.

First, while the Japanese government is democratic and stable, the Chinese government is a typical Third World regime: authoritarian and unstable. Steven David argues that these latter characteristics create war-proneness.[43] David points out that since Third World governments are not democratic, their accountability to the mass public is limited, which increases the possibility that ruling elites will go to war for their own purposes against the wishes of the majority. An authoritarian regime may even embark on hostile overseas adventures against its country's interest if the regime expects this will help it maintain its own political power. Militarism and hyper-nationalism, partly facilitated by state control of the media, are more prevalent in the Third World, making their populations more supportive of adventurism. Finally, the leaders of Third World states are more likely to undertake ag-

43. Steven R. David, "Why the Third World Still Matters," *International Security*, Vol. 17, No. 3 (Winter 1992/93), pp. 131–140. In specifying which states make up the "Third World," David explicitly excludes China (p. 127). Nevertheless, I categorize China as a Third World state and find David's observations applicable to China.

gressive action abroad to divert the public's attention from domestic political problems.

China is subject to all of these factors. Both its state and society are unstable. A single party monopolizes power, suppressing serious dissent, and authority is located in persons rather than institutions. Presiding over a sprawling, largely destitute, populous empire, the central government lives in constant fear of insurrection. To the familiar problems of poverty are now added the new problems of rapid, uneven economic growth, including massive corruption and a growing disparity between the rich and the poor. Consequently, as David Shambaugh observes, China may "become more confrontational externally, even as it becomes more fragmented internally."[44]

A second reason why China is more likely to use force than Japan is that China is a dissatisfied power, while Japan is a status-quo power.[45] Japan has benefited enormously from the current international order, it is relatively comfortable with interdependence,[46] and it has a constitution that forbids offensive military action. China, on the other hand, is still trying to recover territory and prestige lost to the West during the *bainiande ciru* ("century of shame"). China's irredentist claims have brought sharp disagreements with Britain, Taiwan, Vietnam, Japan, India, and Malaysia, among others. Its fear of exploitation and conquest by foreigners remains strong.[47] The Chinese leadership perceives the international environment as primarily hostile, and their own place within it insecure. The Soviet Union is gone, but the Chinese believe the United States "has never abandoned its ambition to rule the world, and its military interventionism is becoming more open."[48] Beijing is deeply resentful of attempts by the United States and others to foment "peaceful evolution," which Chinese leaders fear will result in social and

---

44. David Shambaugh, "China's Security Policy in the Post–Cold War Era," *Survival*, Vol. 34, No. 2 (Summer 1992), p. 89.
45. Segal, "The Coming Confrontation Between China and Japan," p. 29.
46. Japanese scholar Seizaburo Sato says most Japanese now accept the idea that "the international game has changed from a game based on military power, to a game based on economic capabilities." The Japanese therefore accept interdependence, not only because it is believed to uphold peace, but also because they "realize that other countries are also dependent on Japan." Indeed, "for Japanese, interdependence is an improvement on vulnerability." Seizaburo Sato, "Japan Ascendant," *Peace and Security*, Vol. 7, No. 1 (Spring 1992), p. 4.
47. In official Chinese commentaries, for example, Western criticism over Chinese human rights abuses, China's treatment of Tibet, and similar issues is inevitably attributed to alleged Western plans to divide and weaken China.
48. The quotation is from a high-level Chinese report leaked to the press. Nicholas Kristof, "The Rise of China," *Foreign Affairs*, Vol. 72, No. 5 (November/December 1993), p. 73.

political chaos and the destruction of their plans for China's economic development. Although they have submitted out of necessity, the Chinese remain highly averse to interdependence, and to subjection to international norms and regimes.[49]

Accordingly, unlike Tokyo, the Chinese government sees the use of force as a serious policy option. Indeed, Chinese leaders speak much more belligerently at home than abroad.[50] Even in official public statements, China continues to renew its threat to attack Taiwan if the island declares itself independent of the mainland, and refuses to rule out the use of force to settle the South China Sea islands dispute.

Finally, China is better able to mobilize its population for war than Japan. As we saw above, Japan would have difficulty fielding large armies for self-defense, let alone foreign military adventures. Thomas Berger concludes that even if the Japanese government decided to undertake a major military buildup, "given the existing culture of anti-militarism they would encounter strong opposition from the general populace as well as from large sections of the elite."[51] This is a formidable barrier to Japan's use of force in defense of its interests overseas.

China, however, has no such problem. The multi-million-member People's Liberation Army has obediently carried out a variety of unsavory orders from Beijing, including the attacks by PLA "volunteers" on American and South Korean troops in Korea, the occupation of Tibet, the punitive incursion into Vietnam, and the slaughter of unarmed demonstrators in Tiananmen Square. It could be counted on to enforce China's hegemonic imperatives as well.

If China is prone to using force, Chinese economic development carries with it the problem of making more force available for Beijing to use.[52]

---

49. Michel Oksenberg, "The China Problem," *Foreign Affairs*, Vol. 70, No. 3 (Summer 1991), p. 10; Shambaugh, "China's Security Policy," pp. 92–93.
50. An example: during a speech to the People's Liberation Army general staff in late 1992 that was later leaked to the Hong Kong *South China Morning Post*, Chinese President Yang Shangkun said the Chinese government had decided to acquire an aircraft carrier and to settle the Spratly Islands controversy by force if Vietnam did not accept Chinese terms by 1997. He also reportedly said, "Hostile forces in the international arena might get burned if they don't behave well," and specifically mentioned the United States as a potential opponent. Report in the *South China Morning Post*, reprinted as "China Prepared to Use Force, Says Yang in Tough Speech," *Straits Times*, December 15, 1992, p. 1.
51. Thomas U. Berger, "From Sword to Chrysanthemum: Japan's Culture of Anti-militarism," *International Security*, Vol. 17, No. 4 (Spring 1993), p. 147.
52. This is because, as Stephen Walt notes, "modern military power is based largely on industrial capacity." Walt, "The Case for Finite Containment: Analyzing U.S. Grand Strategy," *International Security*, Vol. 14, No. 1 (Summer 1989), p. 11.

JAPAN'S RESPONSE TO CHINESE GROWTH

China and Japan are natural rivals. Both the Japanese and the Chinese see themselves as rightful leaders of the region. Historical and geographic factors in the Sino-Japanese relationship make them highly susceptible to conflict.

One of the most important historical factors is the memory of the Pacific War, during which Japan invaded and pillaged much of China. Recent Sino-Japanese relations underscore the fact that a past history of conflict between two nations makes them more likely to perceive each other as security threats, increasing the possibility of future conflict between them.[53] Since the war, the Chinese have been extremely sensitive to, and highly critical of, hikes in Japan's defense spending, the deployment of Japanese peacekeeping troops overseas, and other indications of increased Japanese military activity. Many Chinese seem convinced that a rearmed Japan means a militaristic Japan.[54] For their part, the Japanese have expressed concern over China's recent assertiveness, including Beijing's pushy approach toward resolving ownership over the disputed Spratly Islands; recent Chinese reiteration of ownership of the Senkaku Islands, which Japan also claims to own; and expansion of China's capability to project military power, including the acquisition of in-flight aircraft refueling technology. In August 1992, Tokyo publicly warned China against purchasing an aircraft carrier, which the Chinese were rumored to be considering. The legacy of the Pacific War seems to have reinforced the security dilemma, causing China and Japan to interpret all military activities by the other side as offensive threats.

Another potential source of Sino-Japanese tension is competition for Southeast Asia. Ancient China and modern Japan have each claimed a sphere of economic influence in this resource-rich and rapidly industrializing region of nearly half a billion people. With powerful and growing export-oriented economies, both China and Japan have voracious appetites for raw materials and a pressing need to expand their share of overseas markets.

China and Japan also have similar but competing strategic interests in the region. One such interest centers on the South China Sea. The Spratly and Paracel Islands, claimed by China for their potential a. oil fields, fisheries and military bases, straddle the key sealane between the Strait of Malacca

53. David J. Myers, "Threat Perception and Strategic Response of the Regional Hegemons: A Conceptual Overview," in Myers, ed., *Regional Hegemons: Threat Perception and Strategic Response* (Boulder, Colo.: Westview, 1991), p. 13.
54. See, for example, Sun Zhengao, "The Security Situation in Northeast Asia," *Korean Journal of International Studies*, Vol. 24, No. 2 (Summer 1993), pp. 164–165.

and Japan, the route traveled by ships bearing some 90 percent of the oil the Japanese consume. The combination of technological improvements now underway in the Chinese military and the construction of air and naval bases on Chinese-occupied islands will soon give China the ability to restrict the flow of shipping through the South China Sea—in effect, to cut Japan's jugular vein.

Serious conflict in this potentially explosive relationship will be averted if both sides remain non-threatening. But the growth of China into an economic powerhouse might upset this fragile calm. If the important trends of the present continue into the near future, Japan and China will soon be concurrent great powers for the first time in history. Neighboring great powers without a more threatening common enemy are natural enemies of each other. With the waning of U.S. and Russian power in the region, Japan and China are each likely to identify the other as its most dangerous potential adversary, with negative consequences for their economic and diplomatic cooperation.

One of these consequences could be a major Japanese military buildup. The argument is often made that a stronger China is desirable as a potential balancer against Japan. But no "check" on Japanese military power is presently needed; the risk of encirclement provides sufficient deterrence. On the contrary, an increase in Chinese power will make large-scale Japanese rearmament *more* likely, not less. Japan's anti-militarist sentiment constrains the Japanese from making the first move. The Japanese would consider a large military buildup only if they felt seriously insecure. But a large increase in China's economic strength, coupled with a corresponding growth in Chinese military power, would give China the capability to threaten Japan's economic and political survival. In such circumstances, the Japanese would feel compelled to respond.[55]

China's rapid economic growth also raises the possibility of a regional power transition of the type some theorists have identified as extraordinarily dangerous.[56] In the power transition scenario, a major power with a relatively

55. Thomas Berger concludes that for domestic reasons, "it is highly unlikely that the Japanese would set out to become a military superpower." Nevertheless, "if a serious threat to Japan's security arose" and if the United States were unwilling or unable to guarantee Japan's protection, "the Japanese government would be compelled to consider a dramatic expansion of Japan's military capabilities." Berger, "From Sword to Chrysanthemum," pp. 147–148.
56. A.F.K. Organski and Jacek Kugler, *The War Ledger* (Chicago: University of Chicago Press, 1980); Robert Gilpin, *War and Change in World Politics* (Cambridge: Cambridge University Press, 1987).

high growth rate is projected to overtake the slower-growing or declining dominant power. Political tensions between the two rise as the threatened dominant power fears it will lose its control over the international system, while the rising challenger begins to flex its newfound muscle by demanding self-serving changes in the system. Robert Gilpin says the natural consequence of these tensions is a "hegemonic war."[57] Although power transition theory deals with the international system, its logic also seems applicable to a regional rivalry for control of East Asia between a dominant but mature Japan and a rising China. The conclusion: serious political tensions between China and Japan are certain, and military conflict is likely, if China's economic power continues to grow rapidly relative to Japan's.

Although a delicate peace now prevails between China and Japan, it would probably not survive China's emergence as a top-rank economic and military power. The international systemic pressures that typically produce tensions in such cases will be intensified by Beijing and Tokyo's common but conflicting hegemonic aspirations and by their history of poor relations. It is important to note that a Sino-Japanese cold war would not require that Japan revert to the aggressive, imperialist foreign policy that it pursued during the Pacific War, only that it becomes a "normal" major power, counting military force among its strategic options.

In the U.S.-Soviet Cold War, each of the superpowers had its own distinct sphere of influence, and conflicts were generally limited to peripheral areas. This helped preclude a major war. In a Sino-Japanese cold war, however, Southeast Asia would be an area of primary interest to both contestants, increasing the chances of direct major power conflict. In this sense, the new East Asian cold war would be more dangerous than the previous Cold War.

Conclusions

China represents a greater long-term threat to East Asian security than Japan. If behavior reflects capabilities, China's potential to build a larger economy also makes it more likely to be assertive and uncooperative. China is more prone to using force than Japan, and will likely remain so after its economy has grown, because the Chinese government is authoritarian, unstable, wants to redress the status quo, and can mobilize large military forces with

57. Gilpin, *War and Change in World Politics,* pp. 208–209.

comparative ease. China is also harder to deter than Japan, because it is less vulnerable to economic coercion, and will be even less dependent on outside suppliers as its economy continues to develop. Furthermore, past experience gives Beijing good reason not to take the threat of economic sanctions seriously.

How should the United States and the other major Asia-Pacific powers prepare for the Chinese challenge? Three general strategies are possible. The first would be to suppress China's economic growth and thereby preempt its development into a superpower. This might be attempted through a cutoff of economic contact with China, similar to U.S. policies toward North Korea, Cuba and, until recently, Vietnam.

This option, however, stands little chance of success. An economic embargo is politically impossible in the case of China. Even if the governments in Asia, Western Europe, and North America could be persuaded that such a strategy was strategically sound, their fears of missed economic opportunities and cheating by coalition partners would remain major barriers. Furthermore, economic suppression of China, while perhaps precluding one form of security threat from China, would likely create others, including massive outflows of Chinese economic refugees, Chinese vulnerability to territorial challenges by bordering states, and the breakdown of centralized control over China's nuclear weapons arsenal. An economically retarded, chaotic China is scarcely more desirable than a highly prosperous, united China.

A second policy option would also aim at undercutting China's potential strength, but by another means: strategic economic engagement designed to increase regionalism within China's borders. The current trend in China is toward a decline in control by the central government in Beijing and greater leeway for regional authorities to run their own economic and political affairs.[58] The United States and other capitalist countries could attempt to foster this tendency by providing information and incentives to encourage their nationals who do business in China to target the regions most committed to free market reforms and least responsive to Beijing's control. China's capitalist business partners could also push for arrangements that would promote greater regional autonomy, undermining the central government's control over local prices, profits, and wages. The goal would be to strengthen the linkages between individual Chinese provinces and foreign states, and to

58. Segal, "The Coming Confrontation Between China and Japan," p. 27; Harry Harding, *A Fragile Relationship* (Washington, D.C.: Brookings Institution, 1992), p. 305.

weaken the links between the provinces and Beijing, making regional governors less likely to cooperate with attempts by the central government to marshal resources for campaigns of overseas conquest or coercion.

However, an open attempt by the United States and other foreign governments to foment fractionalization in China would also be counterproductive. This policy would convince the Chinese their worst fears of Western neoimperialism were correct. Chinese nationalism would increase, and links between Beijing and the provinces would likely grow stronger rather than weaker as more Chinese saw the need to work together against the apparent attempt by foreigners to divide and conquer. Such a policy would also alienate America's Asia-Pacific allies, who would wonder why the more distant and powerful United States was taking such an aggressive approach when so many of them are prepared to accommodate a strong China. Without their cooperation, U.S. efforts to shape Chinese development could not succeed.

In short, openly attempting to thwart China's economic growth by imposing an embargo or encouraging national disintegration would probably not work, and would likely backfire by increasing Beijing's insecurity and hostility toward the West.

A third possible strategy for the major powers would be to continue their participation in China's economic development, encouraging positive behavior when feasible (e.g., Most Favored Nation trade status as a reward for progress in human rights), and organizing an anti-China coalition only if and when threatening behavior occurs. While the free flow of capital and goods may be providing nourishment for a future hegemon, it also helps promote regional autonomy, political liberalization, and cross-cutting linkages between various parts of China and the outside world. From a political standpoint, it is far better to rely on the free market than initiatives by foreign governments to achieve these goals. Nevertheless, this strategy requires the other major powers and the ASEAN states to be prepared to react swiftly to undue assertiveness by the stronger China of the near future. A powerful China provides another reason for a continuing U.S. military presence in the region. It may also breathe new life into the shaky U.S.-Japan alliance. In the meantime, multilateral security regimes might focus on persuading China to limit its power-projection weapons systems and to agree to shared or divided ownership of the South China Sea Islands.

In the absence of an ideal solution, continuing to abet China's growth, while hoping defensive balancing will not be necessary, is the least problematic option for the outside world. Continued and unrestrained economic engagement conveys implicit acquiescence to the possibility of an economically and militarily powerful China, with all its attendant risks. But this approach has its positive points as well: it is the least threatening from China's perspective, and it allows for the possibility that unrestrained trade and investment will continue to weaken the central government's control over the provinces, reducing Beijing's potential for foreign aggression. This strategy also recognizes the limits on the ability of outside countries, even powerful ones, to manipulate China. Michel Oksenberg correctly points out that "America has periodically sought to produce a China more to its liking. The efforts have always ended in massive failure."[59] It may well be inescapable that China's destiny remains in its own hands.

From the point of view of the rest of the world, the ideal China, perhaps, would be a medium-sized China, with an economy and military forces about the size of present-day Japan's. While continuing to export goods of increasing quality, this more prosperous China could also provide surplus capital for investment abroad and a vast market for foreign imports, finally fulfilling the dream of nineteenth-century Western traders. The Chinese might also maintain qualitatively improved but numerically smaller military forces structured for rapid deployment to China's borders and coastal waters, but not far beyond. This mid-size China would be a prominent economic and political player in the region, engaging in diplomatic give-and-take with the other major powers, but not a hegemon.

Unfortunately, current developments foretell an economically gigantic China with a historic fear of foreigners, a distaste for cooperation, and an interest in developing a blue-water navy and long-range air combat capabilities.[60] These may be the first signs of what will develop into the greatest threat to the region's stability since the Pacific War.

---

59. Oksenberg, "The China Problem," p. 14.
60. Michael T. Klare, "The Next Great Arms Race," *Foreign Affairs*, Vol. 72, No. 3 (Summer 1993), pp. 136–152; Gregor, "China's Shadow Over Southeast Asian Waters," pp. 7–8.

China's Illusory Threat to the South China Sea

Michael G. Gallagher

The rebirth of Chinese power after five hundred years of decline is one of the major events of this decade: "The rise of China, if it continues, may be the most important trend in the world for the next century."[1] And indeed, on the economic side of the ledger China has turned in a stunningly impressive performance over the last fifteen years. Economic growth has averaged 9 percent since 1978. China's 1993 growth rate was 13 percent.[2] In 1994, industrial output is expected to top 15 percent. Fast-paced economic growth has made mainland China a favorite of foreign investors. In the first nine months of 1993, $15 billion (U.S.) was spent by overseas investors in the China market.[3]

China's leadership has apparently decided to invest a portion of that new wealth in a major upgrading of the combat power of the People's Liberation Army (PLA). Special attention is being paid to the buildup of air and seapower. This combination of rapid economic growth and increasing military strength has many, in Asia and elsewhere, wondering exactly what the Chinese intend to do with their newly acquired power: "China has increasing weight to throw about. But its neighbors still question whether this weight will be thrown behind efforts to build a more secure and stable Asia."[4]

One focus of this concern over Chinese intentions is the Spratly Islands. At the far end of the South China Sea from the Chinese mainland, this collection of stony outcroppings and islets is perhaps the main source of international tension in Southeast Asia with the end of the Cold War. In a world of shrinking natural resources, the mainland Chinese have clearly stated what flag they think should fly over the potentially oil-rich island group: "these islands and reefs are within Chinese territory and other coun-

Michael G. Gallagher holds a doctorate in international studies from the University of Miami. He has lived and taught in Hong Kong and Nanjing, and in Miami at the University of Miami and Florida International University. He had published articles on Chinese environment and technology issues.

1. Nicholas D. Kristof, "China's Rise," *Foreign Affairs*, Vol. 72, No. 5 (November/December 1993), p. 59.
2. Ibid., p. 61.
3. "China Speeds on to the Market," *The Economist*, November 20, 1993, p. 35.
4. "A Job for China," *The Economist*, May 1, 1993, p. 18.

International Security, Vol. 19, No. 1 (Summer 1994), pp. 169–194

tries are definitely not allowed to invade and occupy them."[5] Ominous statements of that sort have driven people to worry that China's growing economic and military strength may tempt it to expand at the expense of its neighbors in Southeast Asia. "Beijing's buildup on Hainan and Woody Island [the largest island in the Paracels group], signal[s] an inclination to dominate the South China Sea by force rather than negotiate shared control with the other claimants to the Spratlys."[6]

The head of the Malaysia Institute of Maritime Affairs, Hamzah Ahmad, feels that China is seeking to replace the United States and Russia as the region's main military power. "China should not attempt to revive the Middle Kingdom mentality and expect tribute from Southeast Asia," he declared in October 1993.[7]

But fears of a looming conflict over the Spratly Islands may be premature. China's huge size and tremendous numbers may no longer be a decisive advantage in the competition for the control of the Spratly Islands. The growing wealth of its maritime rivals, and their willingness to invest in high-technology weaponry, combined with serious political constraints, both international and domestic, on overseas adventures, have diminished any military advantages China might at one time have enjoyed over its neighbors.

This paper is divided into four sections. The first discusses the basis for the dispute over the Spratly Islands, and includes an examination of the terrorial claims of China and its rivals, the significance of the Spratly Islands dispute in international politics, and what tactics the Chinese have used in the past to exert their control over the contested islands. The next section analyzes the military balance between China and some of its smaller neighbors. Their military modernization efforts are described briefly, and the potential problems facing the Chinese in any military operations against the Spratly Islands are analyzed. The section that follows it describes some of the international political and economic constraints on aggressive action in the South China Sea. The concluding section discusses the domestic problems now facing China and how they might affect Chinese behavior with regards to the South China Sea.

---

5. John Garver, "China's Push Through the South China Sea: The Interaction of Bureaucratic and National Interests," *The China Quarterly*, December 1992, p. 1015.
6. Michael T. Klare, "The Next Great Arms Race," *Foreign Affairs*, Vol. 72, No. 3 (Summer 1993), p. 142.
7. "Trick or Treat," *The Economist*, July 10, 1993, p. 29.

Background of the Dispute

To a casual observer, it might seem strange that the Spratly Islands could be the flashpoint for a major international confrontation. Of the 230 islands that make up the Spratly group, only seven are more than 0.1 square kilometers in area.[8] Thity is the largest island in the group; claimed by the Philippines, it is less than one mile long and just 625 yards wide.[9] Many of these so-called islands are merely rocky outcroppings that are underwater at high tide.

These minuscule islands, however, possess significance well beyond their actual size. The islands sit astride sea routes through which twenty-five percent of the world's shipping passes, including the supertankers carrying the petroleum that fuels the economies of Japan, Taiwan, and South Korea. Large quantities of oil may also lie beneath the islands as well: a December 1989 Chinese report claimed that the sea floor surrounding the Spratly Islands may contain from 1 billion to 105 billion barrels of oil.[10] In addition, the area is a rich fishery: 2.5 million tons of fish were harvested from the waters around the islands in 1980.

China's growing economic success and its huge and expanding population suggest why China would be excited by the opportunity to gain control of such large, virtually untapped natural resources. The Chinese assert that their claim to the Spratly Islands dates back 1700 years to the time of the Han Dynasty. But the only independent confirmation of Chinese claims to the Spratlys dates from 1867, when a British survey ship discovered a group of fishermen from Hainan working the area's rich fishing grounds.[11] Despite the sparseness of historical evidence to support their claims to the islands, the Chinese have been forthright about their intention to claim those resources. In February 1992, China's National People's Congress passed a declaration stating that the Spratlys Islands were an integral part of Chinese territory. China's claims to the Spratlys are easier to understand when one

---

8. Stephen Parksmith, "Spratly Claims Conflict," *Asian Pacific Defence Reporter: Annual Reference Edition* (1993), p. 48.
9. Parksmith, "Spratly Claims Conflict." Thity's small size certainly makes it useless as a site for an airstrip, unless one is using light fixed-wing aircraft, helicopters, or VTOL aircraft, of which China has none. Along with the runway itself one has to have an airfield infrastructure as well.
10. Garver, "China's Push Through the South China Sea."
11. Parksmith, "Spratly Claims Conflict," p. 48.

realizes that the Chinese regard control of the ocean's resources as vital to their nation's continued existence.[12]

Claims to the resources of the South China Sea have been backed by China's willingness to use force to compel recognition of its rights. In January 1974 Chinese forces drove South Vietnamese naval forces out of the Paracel Islands after a sharp clash in which one South Vietnamese corvette was sunk and two destroyers were damaged. Chinese and Vietnamese forces skirmished a second time in the South China Sea in March 1988. This time the two navies fought over the disputed Johnson Reef in the Spratly islands, far to the south of the 1974 Paracels clash. Chinese forces sank three Vietnamese supply ships, killed seventy-two Vietnamese, and captured nine.[13] By the end of 1988 the Chinese had occupied six atolls in the Spratly Islands. China continued its expansionist activities in the Spratlys when it occupied Da Lac reef in July 1992. Vietnam swiftly protested the Chinese move, demanding that the Chinese remove their forces from the disputed reef. By spring 1992, the prospect of an armed clash over who controlled the Spratlys was drawing the attention of Japan and the United States. During a spring 1992 visit to Malaysia, then U.S. Undersecretary of Defense for Policy Paul Wolfowitz declared that the parties to the dispute "must not resort to military force to try to sort that mess out."[14]

Along with the use of force, China has throughout the 1970s and 1980s used fishing fleets, the dispatch of "oceanographic" vessels carrying high-ranking naval and civilian personnel on cruises through the disputed areas, and the construction of airfields, blockhouses, and other facilities in both the Paracels and Spratly Islands to make China, if not first claimant on the scene, at least the party on the spot with the most muscular presence. China may be practicing Cold War "salami tactics," absorbing the South China Sea in small bits so as to avoid a violent response from potential adversaries.

During the 1970s, Vietnam was China's only competitor in the Paracels. In contrast, presently China must share the Spratly Islands with other nations. China has garrisoned seven atolls, but Vietnam has occupied twenty-one atolls, the Philippines has placed troops on eight, and the Malaysian flag

---

12. "In order to make sure that the descendants of the Chinese nation can survive, develop, prosper and flourish in the world of the future, we should vigorously develop and use the oceans." Garver, "China's Push Through the South China Sea," p. 1019.
13. Michael Richardson, "Spratlys Increasing Cause for Concern," *Asian Pacific Defense Reporter*, October–November 1992, p. 37.
14. Ibid.

flies over two atolls.[15] Although outside confirmation for Chinese claims to the Spratly Islands date from the 1860s, other countries can marshal evidence to support their claims as well. Vietnamese claims to the islands date from 1862 and 1865, when cartographic surveys of the South China Sea showed the islands as part of Vietnam. The Philippines' claims date from 1938, when Manila tried to interest Japan in a joint occupation.[16] In 1971, Philippine President Ferdinand Marcos fairly summed up the non-Chinese view of the Spratly dispute when he declared the islands "derelict and disputed."[17]

Apart from the declared parties to the Spratly dispute, any reasonable examination of the situation in the South China Sea must consider the attitudes of both the wealthiest and the largest of the Association of Southeast Asian Nations (ASEAN) states, Singapore and Indonesia. Among the nations of Southeast Asia the tiny city state of Singapore is by far the most prosperous and technologically advanced, but its government is acutely aware of its dependence on the unimpeded flow of shipping through the Malacca Straits and the open waters of the South China Sea beyond. The Singaporean Air Force chief, Brigadier General Bey Soo Khiang, expressed his nation's anxieties concerning its vulnerability in post–Cold War Asia in an early 1993 speech. "The reduction of the American military presence in the Asia-Pacific region is likely to be destabilizing. . . . We will then have a region fraught with potential for a competition for influence. To avert becoming another Kuwait, or suffering the tragedy of being bullied by a bigger and stronger power, countries will attempt to strengthen their national resilience."[18]

Indonesia, freed from fears of foreign domination by its huge size and a population of 180 million, nonetheless has always been jealous of its prerogatives as the largest power in Southeast Asia. Remembering Indonesia's disastrous relations with China in the 1960s, which culminated in the overthrow of President Sukarno, the generals in Jakarta probably feel that they have every reason to be wary of China's intrusion into the South China Sea. Nervousness over Chinese expansionism certainly pushed along Indonesia's February 1993 stopgap purchase of thirty-nine vessels from the former East German navy and the follow-on plans to construct twenty-one modern frig-

15. Parksmith, "Spratly Claims Conflict," p. 49.
16. Ibid.
17. Ibid.
18. Denis Warner, "Interdependence a Regional Cornerstone," *Asian Pacific Defense Reporter*, February–March 1993, p. 16.

ates in local shipyards.[19] Indonesia's concern for its image as the great regional power also displays itself in its representatives' public attitudes towards attempts to enhance military and political cooperation in Southeast Asia. "We don't want to see the region amalgamated," one Indonesian diplomat bluntly stated during ASEAN's May 1993 foreign ministers' meeting held in Singapore.[20]

The Military Equation

Table 1 suggests that China would be capable of bringing vastly superior military strength to bear in any armed confrontation over the Spratly Islands. Overwhelming numbers would support China's leaders if they one day decided to expel rival claimants from the disputed islands.

The bulk of China's modern weaponry has been purchased at garage-sale prices from the increasingly decrepit military of the Russian Republic. Over the last two years the PLA has bought up to $2 billion worth of Russian arms. These include one hundred A300 SAM missiles and twenty-six Su-27 Flanker fighter aircraft.[21] Combined with an inflight refueling capability,

Table 1. Naval and Air Forces Available to China, Selected ASEAN Countries, and Vietnam.

	Combat Aircraft	Large Warships	Patrol Craft (SSM)	Submarines
China	5000	54	860 (207)	46 + 5 SSN
Malaysia	69 + 6 armed helos	4 frigates	37 (8)	0
Singapore	192 + 6 armed helos	6 corvettes	24 (6)	0
Indonesia	81	17 frigates	48 (4)	2
Vietnam	185 + 20 armed helos	7 frigates	55 (8)	0

NOTES: Aircraft totals include naval air forces; patrol craft include gun and torpedo boats; SSM = Surface-to-Surface Missiles, SSN = attack submarines.

SOURCE: Compiled from International Institute of Strategic Studies, *The Military Balance 1993–94* (London: Brassey's, 1993), pp. 145–165.

19. Tai Ming Cheung, "Instant Navy," *The Far Eastern Economic Review,* February 18, 1993, p. 11.
20. Michael Vatikiotis, "The First Step: ASEAN Takes the First Step on Security Concerns," *Far Eastern Economic Review,* June 3, 1993, p. 18.
21. Tai Ming Cheung, "Sukhois, Sams, Subs: China Steps Up Arms Purchases From Russia," *Far Eastern Economic Review,* April 16, 1993, p. 23.

which the Chinese have acquired from the Iranians, the highly maneuverable, Mach 2–plus Flankers could provide air cover for Chinese warships flying from airfields on Hainan Island. As of April 1993 the Chinese were said to be negotiating with the Russians for an additional twenty-six Flankers and two Kilo-class diesel-powered submarines, which would provide a much-needed upgrade for the PRC's submarine fleet, most of whose boats are based on 1950s Soviet designs. Other deals rumored to be under discussion include the acquisition of another seventy Flankers, fifty Mach-3 MiG-31 high-altitude interceptors, additional Kilo-class submarines, and an undisclosed number of Tu-26 Backfire long-range bombers.[22] Armed with anti-shipping cruise missiles, the Backfires would be a serious threat to shipping as far south as the Malacca Straits.

Since China is still a relatively poor nation, the best way for it to acquire a modern air force may be to build a foreign-designed aircraft locally. A recent story reported that the Russians had offered to develop for the Chinese air force a brand new fighter for as little as $500 million.[23] With performance falling between the MiG-29 and the MiG-31 high-altitude interceptor, the proposed aircraft would have Russian electronics and engines, but would be built in Chinese factories upgraded by Russian engineers. The Chinese were supposedly planning to produce the new aircraft at the rate of 100–150 a year, according to the Russians, but considering China's fiscal and technical constraints, a more realistic figure may be fifty aircraft a year.[24]

However, China's rivals for control of the Spratly Islands have not been standing idly by while the PRC stockpiles weaponry. In July 1993, Malaysia announced its decision to buy eighteen MiG–29s and eight McDonnell Douglas F-18s as part of its military modernization program. Although the exact dollar amount of the MiG-29 deal remained undisclosed, the Russians, eager to dispose of an estimated one hundred MiGs left undelivered by the collapse of the former Soviet Union, offered Malaysia generous terms in return for the sale, including the manufacture of spare parts either through a joint partnership or a local Malaysian company.[25] In June 1992, GEC-Marconi of the United Kingdom agreed to build for the Royal Malaysian Navy two

22. Michael Richardson, "China's Buildup Rings Alarm Bells," *Asian Pacific Defense Reporter*, February–March 1993, p. 11.
23. Tai Ming Cheung, "China's Buying Spree, " *Far Eastern Economic Review*, July 8, 1993, p. 24.
24. Ibid.
25. Michael Mecham, "Malaysia Buys MIG-29s, F/A18Ds," *Aviation Week and Space Technology*, July 5, 1993, p. 25.

modern frigates for approximately $425 million.[26] Equipped with *Seawolf* missiles capable of knocking down both aircraft and low-flying cruise missiles, and with *Exocet* anti-shipping missiles, these up-to-date vessels, operating in conjunction with the new MiGs and F-18s and the missile-armed patrol craft already in Malaysia's possession, would provide a credible defense of Malaysia's claims in the South China Sea. This would be particularly true if the frigates and the new fighter aircraft were based at Jesselton, in the Malaysian province of Sabah on Borneo. From Jesselton it is only 250 miles to the easternmost fringes of the Spratly group, a very short flight at Mach 2–plus speeds, and only half a day's steaming time for the new frigates when they enter Malaysian service in the second half of this decade. Malaysia intends to build a potent military force by the first few years of the twenty-first century, having announced plans to jump the percentage of its growing GDP that it spends on military affairs from 2 percent to 6 percent over the next 10–15 years.[27] By the early 2000s, Malaysia could be the owner of a military machine that, at least in qualitative terms, would be the equal of any country in region, including China.

Singapore is an often overlooked factor in Southeast Asia's military balance. With a population of only 2.5 million, the tiny city-state is in the process of building a military force to match the growing sophistication of its economy. With 192 aircraft (including F-16s and E2C early warning aircraft) and a high level of training, Singapore's air force is already the most potent in Southeast Asia. The Navy's six *Victory*-class corvettes and six *Sea Wolf* missile patrol craft are armed with U. S. *Harpoon* and Israeli *Gabriel* anti-shipping missiles.[28]

Singapore's industrial base is annually becoming more capable of supplying the armed forces' needs from domestic sources. The local defense industry is dominated by Singapore Technologies Incorporated. Singapore Technologies is a holding company with forty-six subsidiaries, 12,000 employees and $1.2 billion (U.S.) in annual sales.[29] Local shipyards are producing *Victory*-class corvettes for home use and for export. The local armaments industry is now capable of manufacturing 155mm heavy artillery, composite armor

26. "Frigates for the Royal Malaysian Navy," *Asian Pacific Defense Reporter*, June–July 1992, p. 31.
27. "Russia Muscles In," *The Economist*, July 17, 1993, p. 34.
28. International Institute for Strategic Studies (IISS), *The Military Balance 1993–94* (London: IISS, 1993), p. 160.
29. David Boey, "A Firm Product Base," *Jane's Defense Weekly*, April 4, 1993, p. 37.

panels for the Singaporean Army's armored personnel carriers, and improved antitank missile warheads. Local industry, in cooperation with local and foreign firms, has developed extensive maintenance and refit capabilities for both ships and aircraft. In 1991, plans were made for the purchase of twelve additional F-16s to enhance the air force's striking power. More significantly for any future operations in the South China Sea, Singapore announced plans to buy two more maintenance E2C early warning aircraft, creating a total force of six.[30] Each twin-engine E2C is capable of tracking up to 250 potential airborne targets simultaneously and, if based at nearby airfields (e.g., Malaysian Sarawak), would be able to loiter in the vicinity of the Spratly Islands, giving adequate warning of the approach of any hostile forces.

Economically, Indonesia is still lagging behind star performers like Malaysia and Singapore, but its military does have its modern components. Alone among ASEAN states, Indonesia operates its own submarine force, and possesses an inflight refueling capability. The Indonesian air force also flies twelve F-16s, while the navy's frigates and patrol craft are armed with *Exocet* and *Harpoon* anti-shipping missiles.[31]

By the year 2000, moreover, the island nation's poverty may be a receding memory for many of its citizens. With an average annual growth rate of 5.5 percent, and an export economy shifting from reliance on oil to increasing emphasis on manufactured goods, Indonesia is likely to have the money available for continued military modernization. An agreement earlier this year to purchase up to one-half of the old East German Navy and plans to construct 21 modern frigates are signs that Indonesia's rulers are committed to a strong modernization effort. While the East German warships are obsolescent, they do provide a welcome increase in the Indonesian navy's numbers. (Modernizing these aging vessels, particularly the 16 *Parchim*-class frigates may, however, turn out to be prohibitively expensive.[32]) Along with boosting the size of its navy, Indonesia is giving its air force greater striking power with the June 1993 agreement with Great Britain to purchase Hawker Hunter light attack aircraft, scheduled for delivery in 1996.[33]

30. Tai Ming Cheung, "Staying Smart," *Far Eastern Economic Review,* May 12, 1991, p. 18.
31. IISS, *The Military Balance, 1993–94,* p. 149.
32. Tai Ming Cheung, "Instant Navy," p. 11.
33. "Minister Views Purchase of UK Jet Fighters," Jakarta Radio, June 15, 1993, Foreign Broadcast Information Service: East Asian Edition, No. 114 (June 16, 1993), p. 40.

Geography

Geography is another difficulty the Chinese must cope with in the event of an armed confrontation over the Spratly Islands. The main Chinese naval bases in the South China Sea, Yulin on Hainan Island and Zhanjiang, the headquarters of China's South Seas Fleet on the mainland, are much farther from the disputed islands than are the bases of potential enemies. Chinese surface forces facing serious opposition in the waters surrounding the Spratly Islands would require effective air cover in order to survive. Currently, the People's Liberation Army Air Force (PLAAF) lacks modern aircraft with the range, speed, and maneuverability necessary to protect a large Chinese naval force operating in the Spratly group. The Flankers and the Backfire bombers discussed earlier would certainly help reduce Chinese problems in this area, but would by no means solve them.

The initial order of twenty-six Flankers, even with inflight refueling capability (which the Chinese do not have yet on a large scale), would not be able to provide more than a very small force, reduced further by the usual difficulties concerning maintenance, to cover Chinese ground and naval forces in the Spratly Islands. Even with the seventy additional Flankers and the introduction of the projected Russian-designed, Chinese-produced fighter aircraft mentioned above, the Chinese could still face serious difficulties in providing effective air cover over the Spratly Islands. Again the question of inflight refueling capacity dominates any discussion of Chinese air operations in the South China Sea. Even with a sizable tanker force available, which is a highly questionable proposition before the early 2000s, the Chinese would still not be able to mount more than limited aerial operations over the disputed islands. The tanker aircraft themselves would also be vulnerable to attack, while they were in transit over the open waters of the South China Sea, from long-legged aircraft such as the MiG-29 and the F-18.

Since it is likely that Chinese naval forces would have to operate in the vicinity of the Spratly Islands with only limited air support, they would often be forced to fend for themselves in the event of air attack. Here Chinese prospects are dismal. Chinese naval vessels are adequately equipped with short-range antiaircraft guns, but ships equipped with modern antiaircraft missile systems are virtually nonexistent. At the start of 1994, in the entire People's Liberation Army Navy (PLAN) there were only four ships—a *Jiangdong*-class frigate, two *Jiangwei*-class frigates, and one brand new *Luhu*-class destroyer—equipped with surface-to-air missile (SAM) systems.[34] In 1993, China commissioned the first of the *Luhu*-class guided-missile destroyers. A substantial improvement over previous classes of Chinese surface warships, the *Luhus* are still only equipped with French-made *Crotale* SAM systems. The *Crotale's* seven-nautical-mile range would provide little defense against aircraft mounting 50–100-mile-range *Exocet* and *Harpoon* missiles.

With the demise of the Soviet Union, China now has the world's second largest submarine fleet, after the United States. But all of the PLAN's diesel-powered boats are based on 1950s Soviet designs. Only forty-six of the fleet's one hundred boats are on active duty.[35] As for the five Chinese-built *Han*-class nuclear attack boats in PLAN service, only two boats are believed to be fit for duty due to maintenance and technical problems.[36] Additionally, the twin afflictions of obsolescence and poor maintenance may make Chinese submarines excessively noisy when submerged, making China's submarine fleet vulnerable to modern anti–submarine warfare technology. Chinese acquisition of Russian *Kilo*-class boats would only mitigate, not entirely solve this problem. Limited funding makes it unlikely that China would be able to purchase more than a few of these modern vessels, and the establishment of a shipyard to construct the submarines on Chinese soil is unlikely before the late 1990s at the earliest. If tensions over the Spratly Islands erupt into a crisis over the next several years, China could find itself in the unenviable position of being able to field only a relatively small amount of mostly foreign-manufactured modern weaponry, operating far from any safe haven, against potential adversaries armed with increasingly up-to-date equipment, much of it manufactured locally.

Military Modernization

China's lack of SAM-equipped warships and its creaky submarine fleet only serve to highlight a fact that is often left out of any discussion about China's ability to threaten its neighbors militarily: the PLA is very large, but is deficient when it comes to the sinews of warfare in the 1990s.

34. R.N. Moore, *Jane's Fighting Ships, 1993–94* (Coulsdon, Surrey, U.K.: Jane's Information Group, 1993), pp. 117, 127.
35. Tai Ming Cheung, "Lacking Depth," *Far Eastern Economic Review,* February 4, 1993, p. 11.
36. Ibid.

Chinese military technology is still as much as twenty years behind the West. One major obstacle is lack of money. The 1992 PLA budget stood at $7.4 billion (U.S.), or double its 1988 level.[37] The total cost for the initial buy of twenty-six Sukhois and two Kilo boats is expected to be in the $1.5–2 billion range.[38] Even though expenditures for arms purchases are likely to be spread out over a period of several years, such amounts would still represent a sizable chunk of the PLA's procurement budget.

China's military industry has a well-documented history of problems with reverse engineering. The most modern domestically designed aircraft is the J-8II, an F-4 equivalent based on a 25-year-old design. The PRC is supposedly developing a Tornado equivalent, the H-7, which may first have flown in 1989. The Chinese claim the H-7 will enter squadron service by the mid-1990s. The H-7 is rumored to be short of lightweight composite materials in its airframe, and not to have a fly-by-wire flight control system.[39] Sometimes Chinese copies of foreign-designed weapons never see the light of day: Chinese duplicates of the Soviet T-62 tank and the MiG-23 fighter-bomber are examples of weapons that never reached the production line. One reason for these failures may be that the PLA has the tendency to rush a new weapon into service without a thorough debugging.[40] Lack of extensive automation or computerized quality control also hamper the PLA's efforts to close the technology gap with the outside world.

Modern Chinese-produced weaponry has often proved itself ineffective. Towards the end of the 1991 Gulf War, Iraqi shore batteries fired two of China's much-publicized Silkworm missiles at the battleship USS *Wisconsin* and its escorting destroyer, HMS *Gloucester.* One missile disintegrated and fell into the sea. The second missile was shot down by a *Sea Dart* missile fired by the *Gloucester*.[41]

Ironically, Chinese efforts to cannibalize the military technology of the old Soviet Union may not help the PLA very much in its drive to upgrade its combat power. First, it was not just Chinese but also Soviet equipment that failed to affect the outcome of the Gulf War: Iraqi tank crews watched im-

---

37. Tai Ming Cheung, "Sukhois, Sams, Subs."
38. Ibid.
39. Richard A. Bitzinger, "Arms to Go: Chinese Arms Sale to the Third World," *International Security,* Vol. 17, No. 2 (Fall 1992), p. 98.
40. Ibid., p. 99.
41. Norman Friedman, *Desert Victory: The War for Kuwait* (Annapolis: Naval Institute Press, 1991), p. 210.

potently as the shells from the guns on their supposedly first-line Soviet-made T-72 tanks bounced off the armor of the oncoming American M1 tanks.[42] Secondly, the tremendous economic problems bedeviling the Russian Republic, along with the independence of the former Soviet republics, has reduced the Russian military to a state bordering on collapse. Whatever political order rises from the ruins of the former Soviet Union, the sprawling Soviet-era military research and development apparatus will require many years to rebuild. Russian military procurement has, according to one source, been cut "savagely," falling 32 percent in 1991, and by another 68 percent in 1992.[43] Unless the PRC can overcome its inability to successfully develop and, especially, to mass-produce modern military equipment, the PLA faces the high probability of merely being locked into a higher level of technological obsolescence than is now the case.

International Constraints on Chinese Behavior

Great powers are often viewed by their smaller neighbors with deep suspicion, and the fear that one nation will become overwhelmingly powerful tends to drive that country's rivals into each other's arms.

Starting in the early 1970s, the Five Power Defense Arrangement (FPDA) has provided an embryonic network for military cooperation among ASEAN and outside powers. Including Singapore, Malaysia, Britain, Australia, and New Zealand, the FPDA has over the last twenty years sponsored joint air exercises at the Payar Lebar airport in Singapore, including 1992 exercises that involved aircraft from Malaysia, Singapore, and Australia.[44] In July 1992 Vice Admiral Soedibyo Rahardjo, the chief of staff of Indonesia's armed forces, and Brigadier General Lee Hsien Yang of Singapore, the armed forces chief of staff and son of Singapore's former prime minister Lee Kuan Yew, signed an agreement to establish joint anti-piracy patrols between their two nations. The two countries' navies agreed to set up a direct communication link to coordinate action against the growing threat that piracy poses to the region's shipping. The signing of the anti-piracy accord coincided with the

42. Ibid., p. 234.
43. "Russia's Armed Forces: The Threat That Was," *The Economist*, August 28, 1993, p. 18.
44. Denis Warner, "First Big Steps Towards Regional Security," *Asian Pacific Defense Reporter*, June-July 1992, p. 11.

seventh bilateral air exercises between Indonesia and Singapore. Interestingly, the exercises included simulated attacks on shipping.[45]

Singapore-Indonesian defense cooperation goes beyond agreements over piracy and bilateral air exercises, however, extending to the development of a joint bombing range on Sumatra.[46] While the 1992 anti-piracy agreement and the joint air exercises hardly represent military cooperation on the scale of the NATO Cold War alliance, they have laid down a foundation on which future cooperation could be built.

But the ASEAN nations are still reluctant to transform what has been an economic and political relationship into a military one. At a 1992 conference on regional security held in Singapore, Lt. Colonel Philip Su, then Singapore's assistant chief of the general staff, expressed the hope that bilateral military exercises would be transformed into multilateral ones. Colonel Su even raised the possibility of the joint development of weapons systems, but stopped short of suggesting that ASEAN become a full-fledged military alliance, saying that given the lack of a clearly defined enemy, a treaty of military alliance, rather than bringing ASEAN states together, might only drive them apart.[47]

Such public disavowals may be only to provide cover for ASEAN members, particularly Indonesia, that are fearful of the loss of sovereignty that the establishment of a formal alliance, with its joint command arrangements and frequent consultation among members, might entail. For despite Colonel Su's protestations that a formal military arrangement among ASEAN states would lack a discernible adversary, China is the only plausible target for any ASEAN military cooperation. Japan, despite its impressive economic power, is likely to remain a military dwarf as long as the U.S.-Japan security treaty remains intact. Trade differences aside, the United States supports Japan's campaign for a seat on the UN Security Council, and continues to seek Japan's cooperation on a broad array of political issues ranging from North Korea's nuclear program to dealing with prickly regional leaders like Malaysia's Prime Minister Mohammed Mahathir.[48] Suggesting that not everyone in the region is frightened of Japan, one proposal floated at a January 1992

---

45. Michael Richardson, "Crackdown on Piracy," *Asian Pacific Defense Reporter*, October–November 1992, p. 34.
46. Tai Ming Cheung, "Staying Smart."
47. Warner, "First Big Steps," p. 10.
48. "That's What Friends are For," *The Economist*, February 26, 1994, p. 34.

regional conference in Kuala Lumpur called for a regional ASEAN defense force equipped by Japan on a concessionary basis.[49]

From the standpoint of international public opinion, the ASEAN states are in a much better position *vis-à-vis* China than Vietnam was in the 1970s and 1980s. Chinese moves against Vietnam during that period were based on a unique set of circumstances: China's 1974 gains in the Paracels were acquired at the expense of the soon-to-be-extinct government of South Vietnam, which had been judged a pariah in the court of international public opinion. Even in the United States, South Vietnam's only ally, there was an overwhelming desire to purge as quickly as possible the painful and divisive memories of the war. In their plans to destroy South Vietnamese ambitions in the Paracels, the Chinese could also count on their new strategic relationship with Washington. Having already given up its South Vietnamese allies for lost, the United States would hardly be in the mood to jeopardize its new quasi-alliance with China against the Soviet Union.

In 1988, a communist-ruled Vietnam was again an international outcast due to its 1978 invasion of Cambodia. Two hundred thousand Vietnamese troops were mired in a protracted guerrilla war against the Khmer Rouge. China used Thailand as a conduit for funneling weapons to its Khmer Rouge allies. Mikhail Gorbachev's Soviet Union, Hanoi's main armorer and banker, was in full retreat from superpower status and was attempting to shrink its international commitments as rapidly as possible. The security of their erstwhile ally was not uppermost in the minds of Soviet policy makers as they sought to rebuild their relationship with their old rivals, the Chinese. The Chinese had astutely judged the international situation to be favorable to them before they drove the Vietnamese Navy away from Jones Reef in the Spratly Islands. They had displayed similar good judgment during their 1979 invasion of Vietnam, when they refrained from aggressive action in the South China Sea, for fear of bringing the then–vastly superior Soviet fleet down on their backs in defense of Moscow's Vietnamese clients.

Since the 1979 Chinese invasion, Vietnam has pulled out of Cambodia and opened its economy to foreign investment. With the lifting of the U.S. trade embargo in early 1994, this new cloak of international acceptance may give Vietnam greater protection against Chinese aggression, despite a 50 percent reduction in its armed forces, than at any time since the immediate aftermath

---

49. Michael Vatikiotis, "Brave New World," *The Far Eastern Economic Review*, January 30, 1992, p. 19.

of the 1979 Sino-Vietnamese War, when Hanoi enjoyed both military superiority over the PLA and the benefit of a security treaty with the now defunct Soviet Union.

Vietnam's ASEAN neighbors may also be able to draw upon international respectability. With the exception of the Philippines, all the ASEAN states are enjoying rising levels of prosperity. Forms of government range from Malaysia's machine-style politics, to Indonesia's mild authoritarianism, to Singapore's nanny-style paternalism. While none of these governments is fully democratic, they present a more pleasant face to the world than China's present regime. Any major Chinese military action to clear its rivals out of the Spratly Islands is likely to cause a level of international protest second only to that which followed the Iraqi seizure of Kuwait. More importantly, given the island groups' strategic position astride main shipping routes, large-scale violence over the Spratly Islands has a good chance of bringing larger powers onto the scene.

Worried about potential for violence in post–Cold War Asia, the governments of Singapore, Thailand, and Malaysia have offered port facilities to the United States. Even Indonesia, usually among the most reluctant of ASEAN members when it comes to inviting outsiders to assist in the region's troubles, signed an agreement in the fall of 1992 allowing the United States Navy the use of the state-owned Ptpal dockyard in Surabaya.[50] With Thailand, the United States carries out forty mostly small-scale joint exercises every year.

Depending on the magnitude of the problem, the United States might simply decide to increase its arms sales to the countries that felt most anxious about Chinese intentions. This policy has been followed for many years with regards to Taiwan. Along with the October 1992 agreement to sell Taiwan 150 F-16 fighters, the United States has quietly shared Patriot missile technology with the Republic of China and has licensed the construction of *Perry*-class frigates in Taiwanese shipyards. Additional U.S. moves to bolster Taiwan as a counterweight to mainland Chinese ambitions include discreet talks with Taiwan's military leadership and the agreement to sell Taiwan sixty-eight Supercobra attack helicopters.[51] All the ASEAN states already use at

50. Michael Richardson, "Indonesia Opens Commercial Door to U.S.," *Asian Pacific Defense Reporter*, October–November 1992, p. 33.
51. Gary Klintworth, "Rich, And Now Powerful, " *Asia Pacific Defense Reporter*, October–November 1992, p. 36.

least some American equipment, so a policy of containing China by building up the militaries of its rivals would be relatively easy to implement.

Apart from military and diplomatic maneuvers to block any threat from China, the ASEAN states are trying to deter any aggressive moves in their direction by fostering economic ties with the Chinese. Singapore has sought to broaden economic ties with the PRC: Lee Kuan Yew recently set off for China with 150 senior government and business officials in tow. In May 1993 a Singaporean delegation signed an agreement in China to develop a 27-square mile zone near Suzhou. The Suzhou development zone has already attracted $1.1 billion in investments, mostly from overseas Chinese investors, and may garner up to $20 billion. In June 1993, Prime Minister Mahathir of Malaysia signed $600 million worth of agreements in China. He declared it his most successful trip as prime minister. Malaysian exporters are finding that China's rising living standards are taking up some of the slack as Japan's economy was stalled.[52]

The ASEAN states' growing economic ties with China raise the following question. Given the economic carrot the Chinese can dangle in front of the business people of Southeast Asia, wouldn't it be easier for the ASEAN countries to go along with China's claims in the South China Sea rather than put an increasingly profitable relationship at risk?

However, the Spratly Islands sit astride vital sea lanes and possess important natural resources. A nation, if it has the means, will usually seek to prevent a hostile power from gaining control of important lines of communication and natural resources. For example, for centuries it was standard British policy to prevent enemy nations from gaining control of the Low Countries, which would have threatened London's control of the North Sea and the English Channel. And as noted above, the ASEAN states possess ever more capable military forces. Given the obvious technological defects of Chinese naval and air forces, there is no real reason for China's neighbors in Southeast Asia to submit to Chinese bullying. In fact, if a confrontation does take place in the South China Sea over the next several years, China's opponents, aware of the low technological level of China's sea and air forces, may simply decide that China is bluffing.

Also, while China can provide ever more lucrative opportunities for trade and investment, the China market is not the only game in town. Singapore,

---

52. "Trick or Treat," *The Economist*, July 10, 1993, pp. 28–29.

for example, is the world's largest manufacturer of computer hard disk drives, and has large markets in North America, Europe, and Japan. In 1993, Singapore's exports to China surged by 77.2 percent, but they also jumped by 38 percent with Japan, and a healthy 58 percent with Malaysia.[53] Malaysia's electronics industry accounts for 36 percent of its manufacturing, and grew at a 25 percent annual rate in 1993; it still depends more on exports to Japan, America, and Europe than on the China market.[54] The Lippo group, a growing Indonesian multinational corporation, does a great deal of business in China, but apparently tries to limit its exposure in China by having some projects financed mostly by foreign partners: "We see ourselves as a bridge for overseas capital looking to get into China," said James Riady, Lippo's deputy chairman.[55]

But if Southeast Asian governments should keep in mind their nations' economic interests in dealing with China over the South China Sea, why shouldn't Beijing consider its own trade and investment interests when deciding what action to take over the Spratly Islands? By the fall of 1993, $83 billion (U.S.) in direct investment had been pledged to the China market by foreign investors.[56] In November 1993, German companies signed $2.8 billion worth of contracts with Chinese customers.[57] The big Thailand-based conglomerate Charoen Pokphand (CP) has plans in the works for a $3 billion petrochemical plant near Shanghai.[58] China desperately needs foreign capital to finance its infrastructure development, including its power needs. The Nomura Research Institute calculates that China needs 20,000 megawatts of new generating capacity per year, but domestic producers can only supply 12,000 megawatts.[59] Thus China must seek out overseas investors. Two Chinese firms, the Harbin Group and Shanghai United, have signed technology transfer agreements with Westinghouse. Another Chinese firm, the Dongfang group, is hoping for joint venture agreements with Siemens, Hitachi, and General Electric.[60]

53. N. Balakrishnan, "High Octane Growth," *The Far Eastern Economic Review*, January 20, 1994, p. 44.
54. Ibid.
55. "Southeast Asia's Octopuses," *The Economist*, July 17, 1993, p. 62.
56. "China Speeds on to Market," p. 35.
57. Ibid.
58. "Southeast Asia's Octopuses, " p. 61.
59. "Power Surge: Electricity in China," *The Economist*, March 19, 1994, p. 82.
60. Ibid.

A stable international environment is usually viewed as beneficial to trade and foreign investment. Given both economic and military risks, Chinese leaders would have to ask themselves if islands that are barely noticeable on the map are really worth the risk of even a temporary disruption of the impressive flow of foreign investment into their country.

Domestic Constraints on Chinese Behavior

In addition to economic enticements, rivals with growing arsenals, and diplomatic difficulties, problems within China itself may place additional limits on Chinese actions beyond the borders of the PRC. Indonesian and Malaysian strategists have pointed out that China's defense spending has grown by 20 percent over the last two years, but what they have failed to discover (or to mention) is where the new money is going within the PLA's sprawling infrastructure. Public statements concerning the PLA's post–Cold War strategy constantly say that China needs to form a well-equipped rapid reaction force designed to be deployed quickly to trouble spots on China's frontiers. But of the 3 million PLA soldiers now on active duty, less than one-fourth are in units scheduled to be modernized. With the government paying only a portion of their operating expenses, these units are being forced to go in to sideline business activities. The newly modernized units are reportedly to be stationed across China, but there is to be an especially heavy concentration of modernized units in Northeast China to defend Beijing.[61] These units are also receiving much of the modern equipment that is reaching the PLA. Chinese strategists say that the three armies are deployed to defend China's capital from any possible threat from the increasingly run-down Russian Far Eastern Command. But with such a large part of the PLA left out of the modernization effort, the primary mission of the three armies may be to protect the Chinese leadership from any future internal unrest.

Chinese society has developed a web of hairline cracks from the frenetic pace of the transition from a command to a free-market economy. China's fast-growing economy has sparked an urban inflation rate of 20–26 percent annually.[62] A similar burst of inflation in 1988 helped set the stage for the

61. These units are the 38th army at Baoding in Hebei Province, the 39th Army at Dalian in Liaoning Province, and the 54th Army at Xinxiang in Henan Province. Tai Ming Cheung, "Quick Response," *Far Eastern Economic Review*, January 14, 1993, p. 19.

62. "China Prepares for a Summer of Discontent," *The Economist*, April 9, 1994, p. 35.

uprising in Tiananmen Square in 1989. With private enterprise comprising an ever-growing share of China's GDP, power is flowing out of Beijing into the provinces and the hands of individuals. Thriving Guangdong Province, for example, gets only 3 percent of its investment capital from the central government.[63] In 1992, Guangdong provincial officials decided that the central government charged too high a price for oil, and purchased a tanker-load of Kuwaiti oil instead. In a 1992 incident, officials in Hunan province were so upset by neighboring Guangdong's attempts to bypass them by buying rice directly from Hunanese farmers that they ordered regional PLA troops to the Guangdong-Hunan border to block rice shipments. Guangdong officialdom responded with its own mobilization.[64] This renewed provincial rivalry coincides with a growing income gap between prosperous coastal provinces like Guangdong and Fujian, and poverty-stricken interior provinces like Gansu, which in 1991 had a per capita income of $75, compared to $350 in Shanghai.[65]

People in China are no longer dependent for their livelihoods on the *Danwei,* the state-controlled work units that formerly dominated every aspect of a worker's life. Many state employees nowadays just stop by their workplaces to pick up their paychecks, which merely supplement the income from the jobs they hold in the bustling private sector. In a society where housing and medical care were once virtually free, enterprises are prodding their employees to buy their own housing, and doctors and nurses are now demanding bribes for treatment.[66]

Entire villages of illegal migrants from the countryside have grown up on the fringes of most large Chinese cities. Since these places do not have Communist Party–run street committees, it has become very difficult for Chinese Public Security to control the transients' comings and goings. China may have up to 100 million people drifting across the country in search of work.[67] Moreover, ten percent of the urban population may be underemployed. China's long history is dotted with great rebellions whose basic material was the jobless and the homeless. The Chinese government's disquiet over the situation was reflected in the Shanghai newspaper *Wenhuibao*: "The floating population, which exists without the normal controls, is fertile

63. "Cut Along the Dotted Lines," *The Economist,* June 26, 1993, p. 35.
64. Ibid.
65. Ibid.
66. "Why China's People are Getting Out of Control," *The Economist,* June 12, 1993, p. 42.
67. Ibid.

soil for the growth of secret societies. If they get together and form organizations, then the large group of people without a steady income will be a great threat to stability. If they join with the millions of unemployed in the cities, then the results will be even more unimaginable."[68]

The people left behind in the villages of China's vast countryside are also feeling the effects of their nation's rapid economic development. Widening economic opportunities have led to rampant official corruption, much of it in the countryside. Local officials extort money from the peasants under the guise of special "taxes," including fees levied on old radios and televisions, and forced "loans" from peasants to local bureaucrats in return for dubious IOUs.[69] In some parts of the countryside, refusal to give in to this extortion can lead to jail, with one's family forced to pay in return for one's release. Hong Kong newspapers reported 200 incidents of peasant unrest in 1992 alone.[70] The most dramatic incident took place in 1993 in Sichuan Province's Renshou County. Thousands of peasants showed their outrage over an excessive road-building fee by storming local government offices and taking local officials hostage. People's Armed Police units dispatched to quell the rioting were themselves cornered by large mobs of angry peasants, which they dispersed with tear gas.[71] The destruction of the old social contract, the epidemic of petty corruption, and the creation of a huge class of undocumented and possibly uncontrollable transients are trends, that, if they continue over the next few years, are likely to divert the attention of China's leadership far away from the reefs and islets of the Spratly Islands.

It could be argued that a short, sharp war in the South China Sea might be just what China's leaders need to divert the Chinese people's attention away from problems at home. History is filled with such instances: for example in 1982, Argentina's military junta thought an easy victory over the tiny British garrison in the Falklands would shore up its shaky position at home. But the wars that China has fought since 1949 indicate a different pattern. Chinese leaders seem to like having their domestic house in order before they tackle foreign enemies. When China entered the Korean War in November 1950, communist control of the mainland was unchallenged. Chiang Kai-shek and the remnants of the Nationalist armies had fled to

68. Ibid.
69. Anthony Blass, Carl Goldstein, and Lincoln Kaye, "Get Off Our Backs," *Far Eastern Economic Review*, July 15, 1993, p. 68.
70. Ibid.
71. "The Revolt of the Peasants," *The Economist*, June 19, 1993, p. 33.

Taiwan in disarray; although ragtag groups of Nationalist soldiers were still loose in the remote jungles of Southwest China, they posed no threat to the Communists' domination of mainland China. China intervened in Korea strictly for reasons of international prestige and national security. Mao Zedong felt that China could not tolerate the destruction of a fellow communist government in North Korea by the U.S.-led United Nations forces. More importantly, with the Americans driving towards the Yalu River, the Chinese government was anxious about the potential threat to Manchuria, China's main industrial region.

China's last war, the 1979 invasion of Vietnam, was also fought against a background of foreign threats and domestic peace. In December 1978, Vietnam had invaded Cambodia and toppled from power Beijing's Khmer Rouge allies. Vietnam's principal ally and China's main adversary, the Soviet Union, had taken over the former U.S. Navy base at Cam Ranh Bay. China's leaders, fearing Russian encirclement and disturbed by what they believed to be a steep decline in U.S. ability to fend off Soviet expansionism after the fall of South Vietnam, felt they had to go to war to demonstrate to their enemies that China could deal with challenges to its security without outside assistance.

Within China itself, however, the political situation was calm. Deng Xiaoping and his fellow economic reformers had swept most of the remaining Maoists from power and had tightened their control over the government. In 1978, Deng Xiaoping had started the program of economic reforms that was to make China one of the great economic success stories of the 1990s.

China's quiet intervention in the Vietnam War during the 1960s was the only occasion when Beijing has intervened militarily beyond its frontiers during a time of domestic crisis. The Cultural Revolution, Mao's last great effort to ideologically purify China and eliminate his political enemies, riddled China with factional feuds from one end of the country to the other. Fighting took place in China's far-western province of Xinjiang. In 1967, regional PLA units stationed in the big industrial city of Wuhan revolted against Beijing in support of local government leaders. Despite the turmoil, the Chinese dispatched 50,000 engineering and air defense troops to North Vietnam. The reasons for that deployment were the same ones that led to the Korean War intervention: defense of an ally and worries over the security of Chinese territory from foreign attack. China's relations with the United States had been in a deep-freeze since Korea. With the U.S. Air Force bombing Hanoi and the Americans sending 500,000 troops to South Vietnam, China's leaders decided not to take any risks with their nation's security.

But the 1965–68 deployment was limited in nature and for purposes of deterrence only. At the beginning of 1965, for example, the Chinese and North Vietnamese air forces conducted joint exercises which were restricted to within twelve miles of the Chinese border.[72] Chinese air defense and engineering troops arrived in North Vietnam with no fanfare, and fired on American aircraft only in self-defense or in the defense of their North Vietnamese allies. Beijing was very careful to signal to Washington the exact conditions under which it would enter the war in force: "The Chinese People's Liberation Army now stands ready, in battle array. We shall not attack; if we are attacked, we will certainly counterattack."[73]

Chinese officials who pushed for a more aggressive policy towards the United States could find themselves in serious trouble. Luo Ruiqing, the PLA Chief of Staff in the mid-1960s, clashed with Defense Minister Lin Biao over the seriousness of the threat to China posed by the American buildup in Vietnam. Both men agreed that some danger existed, but Luo argued for increased defense spending to counter what he felt to be the heightened danger of American attack. Mao Zedong, not wishing to be distracted from the crisis of the Cultural Revolution, sided with his protege Lin,[74] and Luo Ruoqing was relieved of his command in 1966. After the Tet offensive in early 1968, the Chinese, seeing that the United States was looking for way out, withdrew their forces from North Vietnam.

What the examples of Korea and the two wars involving Vietnam show is that Chinese leaders carefully balance China's domestic situation against the nature of any external threats. In both the Korean War and the 1979 invasion of Vietnam, domestic stability in China allowed Beijing a free hand overseas. Only in the case of the 1965–68 intervention in Vietnam did Chinese leaders decide to involve themselves on foreign soil while their country suffered from domestic conflict. Even then, the Chinese dispatch of troops to North Vietnam had limited defensive goals, was carried out quietly, and was quickly

72. Allen S. Whiting, *The Chinese Calculus of Deterrence: India and Indochina* (Ann Arbor: University of Michigan Press, 1975), p. 175.
73. According to Whiting, this statement meant that China would not enter the war unless it was physically invaded: "This wording excluded any ground combat with American troops unless and until American troops crossed the border" into China. Ibid., p. 185.
74. Gerald Segal, *Defending China* (Oxford: Oxford University Press, 1985), p. 169.

terminated once the danger of a U.S. attack on China had died away. This suggests that Beijing will behave cautiously if faced with the combination of internal unrest and the threat of foreign war.

Conclusion

Today, the PLA's largest source of relatively modern military technology is the military-industrial complex left behind by the former Soviet Union. The generals of the PLA should not forget the uselessness of Soviet armor during the Gulf War. Geography also argues against easy Chinese success in any military operations against the Spratly Islands. Even if all the reported sales of Russian military equipment are consummated, China, due to the distance of the Spratly Islands from major Chinese bases, would find it difficult to maintain a continuous air umbrella with a large force of aircraft over the ships of its South Sea Fleet. Considering the PLAN's lack of SAM-equipped warships, the absence of effective air cover might place the PLAN in the same fatal situation as the *Prince of Wales* and *Repulse* were fifty years ago when Japanese warplanes sent them to the bottom of the South China Sea. Even if the PLAN had many SAM-equipped vessels on hand, they might not help Chinese forces operating in the vicinity of the Spratly Islands. Much of China's weaponry, as we have already seen, is simply not very good. Results for the Chinese could be disastrous if they came up against a force armed with even a small number of "smart" weapons. Such a situation is almost certainly unavoidable since China's regional rivals are growing in both wealth and technological prowess. During the 1982 Falklands War, fewer than half a dozen Argentine aircraft armed with *Exocet* missiles sank the modern British destroyer *Sheffield* and several other vessels. A few more hits, particularly on one of the all-important aircraft carriers, could have cost Britain the war. China is so poorly equipped for the type of short, destructive high-tech fighting that was the hallmark of the naval warfare around the Falklands that one analyst recently declared: "An expansionist maritime policy is not an option given the current state of the [Chinese] fleet's equipment and training."[75]

The ASEAN states are slowly moving in the direction of increased military cooperation, with China being the only possible target of such efforts. The

---

75. Moore, *Jane's Fighting Ships: 1993–94*, p. 55.

fast-paced economic growth of most ASEAN states has made them very popular with foreign investors, particularly those from Japan and Taiwan. Their economic star status, in tandem with the Spratly Islands' location along important sea lanes, almost certainly guarantees a major international outcry and open-handed assistance for these states in the event of aggressive action by China. China could face the same type of diplomatic isolation and drop-off in foreign investment that it suffered in the wake of the massacre in Tiananmen Square. Even Vietnam, with its new openness to foreign investment, would no longer be the isolated target of opportunity it once was. Violent Chinese action in the Spratly Islands would make other nations believe that China was an East Asian version of Saddam Hussein's Iraq, shattering China's carefully crafted public relations image as a poor nation lifting itself up by its own efforts to join the ranks of the advanced nations.

The force of domestic pressures may set another obstacle in the path of China's maritime ambitions. Much of the PLA's re-equipment program and troop deployment patterns may be at least partially dictated by the need to guard against new outbreaks of internal disorder. Eleven Chinese provinces suffered from peasant unrest in 1992.[76] Brought on by the most spectacular economic transformation since Japan finished its modernization at the beginning of this century, the shredding of China's social fabric is likely to continue. In the last few years of the twentieth century, the PLA and its political masters may have little time for foreign adventures.

If the mainland Chinese want to acquire a larger slice of the resources of the South China Sea, they are probably going to have to negotiate for it. Perhaps in recognition of this situation, the Chinese in August 1993 opened talks with Vietnam aimed at sorting out the two sides' territorial claims in the South China Sea.[77] China's ASEAN neighbors, along with efforts to widen economic ties with China, are engaged in diplomatic efforts of their own to head off any potential crisis. Over the last eighteen months, Singapore, Malaysia, and Indonesia have pushed for exchange visits of defense officials and officers with China in the hope of reducing chances for any misunderstandings.[78]

Broadening opportunities for trade, continued negotiations, and the deterrents to Chinese action already discussed make it unlikely that a major

76. Blass, Goldstein, and Kaye, "Get Off Our Backs," p. 68.
77. Politics and Current Affairs Section, *The Economist*, August 28, 1993, p. 4.
78. Michael Richardson, "China's Military Secrecy Raises Questions," *Asian Pacific Defense Reporter*, June–July 1993, p. 24.

military confrontation over the Spratly Islands will erupt in the near future. The situation should be monitored carefully, however. Since its creation in 1949, the People's Republic of China has often displayed great astuteness in the conduct of its foreign policy. The opening of relations with the United States in the 1970s and China's use of the 1990–91 Gulf Crisis to pull itself out of the public relations quicksand of Tiananmen are proof. But the Chinese retain the very human capacity for self-delusion. China's last war, the 1979 invasion to "punish" Vietnam, cost the PLA heavily. A month of heavy fighting bought the Chinese 20,000 casualties and little else. The Chinese were forced to withdraw behind their borders without the satisfaction of having inflicted serious damage on the battle-hardened Vietnamese army. But considering the rewards of continued peace, outsiders can hope that Chinese decision makers will avoid past mistakes and what could be a major tragedy not only for China, but for the prosperity and stability of East Asia as well. A war over the dribs and drabs of land that make up the Spratly Islands would be a sorry way indeed to start off the Pacific Century.

East Asia and the "Constrainment" of China

Gerald Segal

The remarkable economic growth in East Asia depends on further modernization of political and social systems throughout the region. Stability and growth also depend on the development of an international system that restrains non–status quo powers and develops mechanisms for managing and resolving conflicts short of war. There is little doubt that the single most important state in East Asia is China: a China that collapses in chaos, or is aggressive in the region, can wreck the prosperity of the region.

Is regional security in East Asia impossible when China is strong? Is regional insecurity especially likely when a rising China is insecure about whether it can sustain its rise, and whether others will allow it to rise? How should other states deal with the state that may be the single largest force for change in the global balance of power?

Sadly, the debate on these questions is often unsophisticated. On the one hand the dominant "engagement" school argues that China can be neutered as a challenge to the status quo, by giving it incentives to join regional and global society. The engagement school believes that there is no need to think in terms of a balance of power because stability will be provided by states anxious not to lose the benefits of economic interdependence.[1] There is another school of

Gerald Segal is a Senior Fellow at the International Institute for Strategic Studies, Director of the Economic and Social Research Councils Pacific Asia Programme, and Co-chairman of the European Council for Security Cooperation in Asia-Pacific.

This work is the result of extensive interviews in nearly every country in East Asia in 1994–95. All interviews were on a confidential basis. But the author would like to thank the following people for commenting on all, or parts of an earlier draft of this article: Sidney Bearman, Barry Buzan, Bates Gill, Paul Godwin, Harlan Jencks, Ellis Joffe, Gary Klintworth, Michael Leifer, Paul Monk, Jonathan Pollack, Michael Swaine, David Shambaugh, Allen Whiting, and the anonymous reviewers for *International Security*.

1. For example see Kishore Mahbubani, "The Pacific Impulse," *Survival*, Vol. 37, No. 1 (Spring 1995); James Richardson, "East Asian Stability," *The National Interest*, No. 38 (Winter 1994–95); Morton Abramowitz, "Pacific Century: Myth or Reality," *Contemporary Southeast Asia*, Vol. 15, No. 3 (December 1993). Some of the engagement school is struggling with ways to add a dose of realism. See the notion of "conditional engagement" and "virtual alliances" as discussed in a study program on China currently underway in the Council on Foreign Relations. I am grateful to Jim Shinn of the Council for an opportunity to see the work in progress.

International Security, Vol. 20, No. 4 (Spring 1996), pp. 159–187

thought that China must be "contained." The containment school argues that the balance of power in East Asia is becoming dangerously unstable.[2]

The notions of "engagement" and "containment" are left over from the Cold War, and for that reason alone they are insufficient categories of analysis for the special problem of coping with a rising China. Instead, this article argues that engagement is a vital, necessary but insufficient policy towards China. China is a powerful, unstable non–status quo power.[3] Those states whose interests are in conflict with China should defend those interests by constraining China where they can. Formulating a policy of "constrainment" requires an assessment of whether China's neighbors and powers further afield are strong enough to resist China. I argue that they are, but that it also requires the will to do so. The evidence presented below suggests that most states lack the will to constrain China. A careful look at recent trends, and especially responses to China's activity in the South China Sea, reveals that China is not constrained by concerns that it might damage its increasingly important economic interdependence with East Asia. I identify the risks of a policy that engages China through interdependence but does not also constrain its undesired behavior, and suggest the possibilities for the success of a more constraining policy.

China and East Asia: Balancing Room?

Balancing and constraining China in East Asia might appear at first glance to be an impossible task. China is 68 percent of East Asian territory and some 65 percent of the East Asian population (See Figure 1.)[4] These fundamental bases

2. Paul Dibb, *Towards a New Balance of Power in Asia,* Adelphi Paper No. 295 (London: International Institute for Strategic Studies [IISS]/Oxford University Press, May 1995). See related arguments in Richard K. Betts, "Wealth, Power and Instability: East Asia and the United States after the Cold War," *International Security,* Vol. 18, No. 3 (Winter 1993–94); Aaron Friedberg, "Ripe for Rivalry: Prospects for Peace in a Multi-polar Asia," ibid.; and Barry Buzan and Gerald Segal, "Rethinking East Asian Security," *Survival,* Vol. 36 No. 2 (Summer 1994). These issues have become a trendy and sometimes vibrant focus of debate. See, e.g., Shannon Selin, *Asia-Pacific Arms Buildup,* Working Paper No. 6 (Vancouver: University of British Colombia, Institute of International Relations (1994); Andrew Mack and Pauline Kerr, "The Evolving Security Discussions in the Asia-Pacific," *The Washington Quarterly,* Vol. 18, No. 1 (1995); and Jonathan Pollack, "Sources of Instability and Conflict in Northeast Asia," *Arms Control Today,* November 1994.

3. Gerald Segal, *China Changes Shape,* Adelphi Paper No. 287 (London: IISS/Oxford University Press, March 1994). On the optimist side see William Overholt, *The Rise of China* (New York: Norton, 1993); and most recently, Jim Rohwer, *Asia Rising* (New York: Simon & Schuster, 1995). For a range of academic views see Thomas Robinson and David Shambaugh, eds., *Chinese Foreign Policy* (Oxford: The Clarendon Press, 1994).

4. Figure 1 and Table 1 were produced by Digby Waller, the Defence Economist at the International Institute for Strategic Studies.

Figure 1. Percentage of East Asia by population, land, GDP, defense spending, exports.

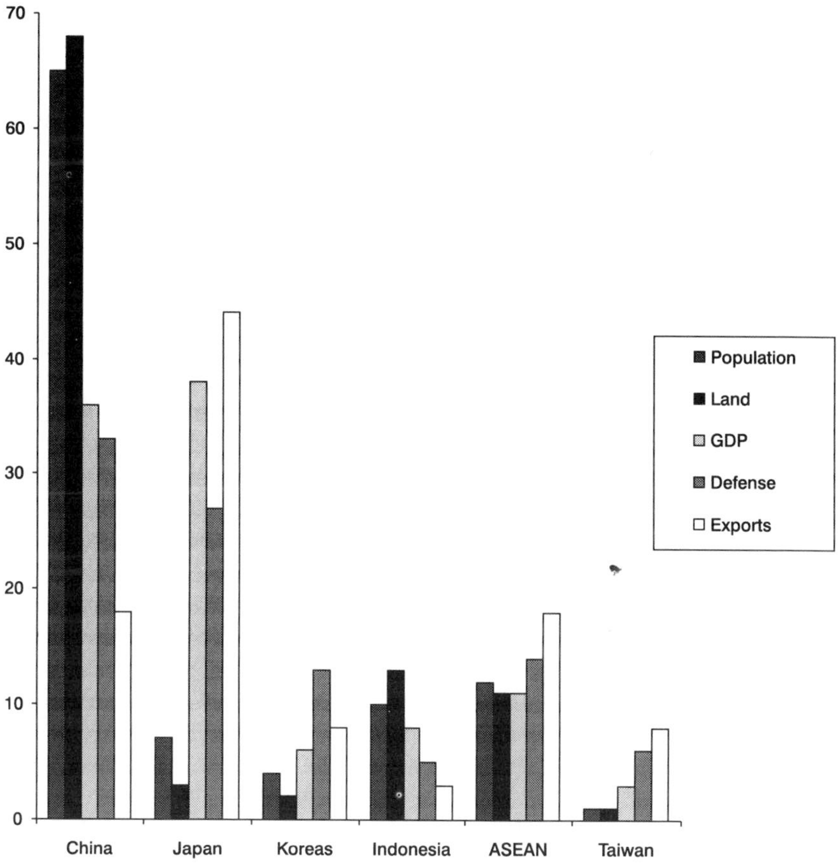

NOTE: All figures are for 1994, except exports (1993). ASEAN figure does not include Indonesia; China figures include Hong Kong.

of power are relatively unchanging. The only other region in the world where the balance of power is so dominated by a single state is North America. The contrast to the far more balanced European condition is striking.[5]

5. Perhaps it is precisely because the European theater seems so susceptible to complex balances, and East Asia seems so unsuited, that the European balances have received so much analytical attention, and East Asian balances are virtually virgin analytical territory. Henry Kissinger, *Diplo-*

The imbalances in terms of size and population in East Asia have existed for centuries—indeed longer in East Asia than anywhere else in the world. The result has been a centuries-old, distinctly unbalanced pattern of international relations. Before the coming of European imperialism (only in strength in the seventeenth century), the political units were rarely engaged with one another. When they were, the nature of the balance of power depended overwhelmingly on whether China was strong. A strong China cast a long shadow over its smaller neighbors. When China was weak, the neighbors were far more free to engage in relations with only parts of China and were not subject to significant Chinese pressure. Some of China's neighbors, most notably Japan and Korea, did manage to develop the basis of healthy, strong and independent political cultures, but they knew that their independence depended overwhelmingly on China remaining weak. The peoples of Southeast Asia were far less successful in organizing strong and persistent political entities, and therefore this region was much more deeply affected by the patterns of interaction set during the era of European domination and then by the overlay of the Cold War in the second half of the twentieth century. When the Cold War overlay was lifted (much earlier in East Asia than in Europe), both the relatively strong states of Northeast Asia, and the much weaker ones in Southeast Asia, knew that the future pattern of international relations in their region depended on whether they had a strong or weak Chinese neighbor.[6]

The Chinese empire spent most of the twentieth century in tatters. In 1850 China was still, nominally, the world's largest economy, but by the end of the nineteenth century it was losing territory all around its rim to rapacious foreigners. By the end of the twentieth century, China has regained only a little of what it lost. Apart from offshore islands taken from Taiwan, islands in the South China Sea, and the prospect of regaining Hong Kong in 1997, the boundaries of the Chinese state are little changed from the late nineteenth century. The result is an irredentist China with a boulder rather than just a chip on its shoulder.

China can afford to shoulder the boulder because in the intervening century China has gone from basket case to economic boom. As geo-economic histori-

---

macy (New York: Simon & Schuster, 1994); Richard Rosecrance, "A New Concert of Powers," *Foreign Affairs*, Vol. 71, No. 2 (Spring 1992), pp. 64–82; Coral Bell, *The Post-Soviet World* (Canberra: Strategic and Defence Studies Centre, 1992); John Mearsheimer, "Back to the Future: Instability in Europe After the Cold War," *International Security*, Vol. 15, No. 1 (Summer 1990), pp. 5–56. See also William Pfaff, *The Wrath of Nations* (New York: Simon & Schuster, 1993).

6. Gerald Segal, *Rethinking the Pacific* (Oxford: The Clarendon Press, 1990).

Table 1. Countries as a Percentage of East Asia.

	Population	Land Surface	GDP 1994 (1992)	Military Spending 1994 (1992)	Exports 1993 (1992)
China & HK	65.2	68.3	35.7 (33.8)	33.3 (32.5)	18.1 (17.6)
Indonesia	10.4	13.4	7.6 (8.0)	5.4 (5.0)	3.3 (3.3)
Japan	6.8	2.7	37.5 (38.3)	27.0 (26.7)	44.4 (45.3)
Vietnam	3.9	2.4	0.7 (0.7)	1.3 (1.4)	0.3 (0.2)
Philippines	3.6	2.2	2.1 (2.3)	2.3 (2.2)	0.9 (1.5)
Thailand	3.2	3.7	4.6 (4.7)	5.4 (6.1)	3.9 (3.7)
S. Korea	2.4	0.7	5.6 (5.8)	9.9 (9.1)	7.9 (7.9)
Taiwan	1.2	0.2	2.8 (2.9)	6.4 (6.3)	8.3 (8.5)
N. Korea	1.2	0.9	0.3 (0.4)	3.2 (4.0)	0.1 (0.1)
Malaysia	1.1	2.4	2.1 (2.1)	3.3 (4.4)	4.3 (4.0)
Singapore	0.2	0.0	0.8 (0.9)	1.8 (1.6)	8.2 (7.7)

SOURCES: International Institute for Strategic Studies, World Bank, IMF. Gross domestic product (GDP) and defense spending rates are purchasing-power parity (PPP). Exports are for merchandise and invisibles.

ans have pointed out, there does seem to be some strong correlation between economic power and the ability of empires to satisfy their territorial claims. But China's sustained economic growth is still in its early stages. As Table 1 shows, China is far from being a dominant power in East Asia according to many measurements of power. It is true that its relative economic and military power is increasing, but sustained economic growth in China only seems possible in a very decentralized political and economic system.[7] China is also hobbled by weak leaders, massive social problems, and internal migration said to number between 100 and 150 million people.[8] In short, China is much weaker than it appears at first glance.

Nevertheless, China still feels that it has legitimate claims to territory and to increased status in East Asia and the wider world. The challenge for East Asia and the wider world is whether China should be allowed to take the territory, power and status that it claims, or whether it should be constrained while it is still relatively vulnerable.

East Asia need not travel "back to the future," if only because so many East Asian states, most notably Japan, are much stronger than they were in pre-

7. The process and problems of Chinese decentralization are discussed in David Goodman and Gerald Segal, eds., *China Deconstructs* (London: Routledge, 1994).
8. Paul Smith, "The Strategic Implications of Chinese Emigration," *Survival*, Vol. 36, No. 2 (Summer 1994).

European times. The international system is also very different. China's growth depends to a great degree on being economically and perhaps even politically interdependent with the international system, and that openness might well be put at risk by aggressive irredentism. China's prospects for growth depend on other states providing markets for its goods, raw materials and investment for its economy, and information and technology for its development. Thus there clearly is a basis for East Asians and the wider world to manage a growing China, but East Asian powers must be prepared to take steps to do so.

WILL EAST ASIA BALANCE?

Objective conditions for balancing China are not the same as real policies to do so. In the nineteenth century the key to ensuring a balance against a strong adversary was developing a sufficient commonality of interests to hold together a coalition. The strategy also depended on there being a core of relatively strong states who were prepared to articulate and then act upon such a commonality of interests. In East Asia there may be a commonality of interest, but there seems to be little will to articulate let alone act upon shared interests.

The fracture lines in East Asia are clear enough. First, in East Asia a wide range of capabilities confronts China. As Figure 1 and Table 1 show, there are few states that might qualify as a great power, but a large number of middle or smaller powers. Only two countries have more than 100 million people (Japan and Indonesia). Only Australia and Russia have huge territories on China's scale, but both have small populations. Russia is a great power, but only to someone looking from Europe.[9] Its backside in Asia is vulnerable, especially given the fact that, apart from Japan, it was the last to seize large swaths of territory from a weak China. Koreans are still divided, but even if united would still be the smallest state in Northeast Asia. The Association of South-East Asian Nations (ASEAN) states are mostly aspiring middle powers and in any case their combined gross domestic product (GDP) is less than that of Australia and New Zealand combined. Indonesia is the only substantial ASEAN power, and it is the most distant from China.

---

9. Michael Bradshaw, *The Economic Effects of Soviet Dissolution* (London: Royal Institute of International Affairs, 1993); and Bradshaw, *Siberia in a Time of Change*, No. 2171 (London: Economist Intelligence Unit, 1992). See also Andre Voskressenski, "Current Concepts of Sino-Russian Relations and Frontier Problems in Russia and China," *Central Asian Survey*, Vol. 13, No. 3 (1994); and Gerald Segal, *The Soviet Union and the Pacific* (London: Unwin Hyman for the Royal Institute of International Affairs, 1990).

Second, the East Asians have a range of different interests regarding China. In some cases, some people raise questions about the loyalty of large parts of the population that are ethnic Chinese.[10] Because ethnic Chinese are a majority of the population in Singapore, many in the region suspect any Singaporean keenness on close co-operation with China on Chinese terms. On the other hand, in Taiwan there is also a majority ethnic Chinese population, but because many of them fled the communist take-over of the mainland and value their current prosperity and independence, they generally are more hostile towards mainland China. The attitudes of Koreans towards China are dominated by their perception of how it affects the conflict over the unification of Korea.

Alone among the major players, Japan has no significant ethnic Chinese population, but it does have a tradition of independence from and rivalry with China. Indonesia has a more powerful (but still small) ethnic Chinese population, but a less consistent, albeit sometimes intense worry about China.[11] These two countries might have been expected to work more closely together in thinking about China, but both have had their eyes on other challenges. Indonesia has seen itself as playing a leading role on the ASEAN or Non-Aligned stage, while Japan has remained bound into an alliance with the United States and sees its role as on the global and most notably the G-7 stage. It is almost as if Japan, because of its behavior in China in the 1930s and 1940s, has avoided thinking long and hard about how to handle China.[12] Indonesia has, until recently, simply considered China as not much constraint on its behavior.

Because of these different positions towards, and interests in China, the states of East Asia have interacted with China in very different ways. Japan and Korea have found that their trade and investment relations are increasingly focused on China's northern coastal areas. Russia does most of its business with North-east China, while Hong Kong and Taiwan focus on southern coastal China.[13] States farther from China have less clear-cut regional relationships. Singapore, much like the European or "Anglo-Saxon" states of the Pacific rim, does a great

10. Tim Huxley, *Insecurity in the ASEAN Region* (London: Royal United Services Institute, 1993); and Amitav Acharya, *A New Regional Order in South-East Asia*, Adelphi Paper No. 279 (London: IISS/Oxford University Press, May 1993). See also Michael Leifer, *ASEAN and the Security of Southeast Asia* (London: Routledge, 1989).

11. Michael Leifer, *Indonesia's Foreign Policy* (London: Allen and Unwin for the Royal Institute of International Affairs, 1983).

12. Kenichiro Sasae, *Rethinking Japan-U.S. Relations*, Adelphi Paper No. 292 (London: IISS/Oxford University Press, December 1994).

13. Goodman and Segal, *China Deconstructs*, on different regions.

deal of business with central coastal China. In short, there are signs that the decentralization within China is reflected in the more fragmented relationship that the outside world is developing with China.

The fragmented attitude to China is also evident on key East Asian issues. Concern over the proliferation of nuclear weapons in North Korea affects China's relations with other states in Northeast Asia, but has little resonance in Southeast Asia. Concern over ethnic Chinese populations is a factor in China's relations in Southeast Asia, but has no role in Northeast Asia. China's difficult negotiations regarding entry into the World Trade Organization (WTO), or its violation of international copyright agreements, are of primary interest to states with the most developed service sectors, and have little role in Sino–Southeast Asian relations. Thus there is a clear tendency for states to take different views of China, and for China to be able to play on such differences.

Because East Asia is generally fragmented, the result, in a third feature of the region, is the relative lack of East Asian institutions or even a clear sense of regional international society.[14] The ability to balance and constrain China does not only depend on the existence of such institutions. Nevertheless, most East Asians understand that it is in China's interest that such institutions do not develop, especially in the security sphere. As the strongest and rising power, it is in China's interest to deal with its neighbors bilaterally, and to seek to reduce any efforts to "internationalize" aspects of foreign policy that would result in more actors being capable of working together to balance China.

China is not the main reason for the slow development of APEC (Asia-Pacific Economic Cooperation), but it is an important factor in the long term. In the shorter term, a primary problem has been the tension between those who wish to see what is essentially a non-white East Asian group (Malaysia's proposal for an East Asia Economic Caucus, or EAEC), and those who see the benefit of a more open trans-Pacific APEC.[15] Obviously an EAEC has less chance of remaining economically open, and certainly less ability to resist a growing China that in 1995 became the largest economy in the region, according to World Bank purchasing power parity (PPP) calculations of GDP.

The very tentative nature of East Asian regionalism is even more evident in the security realm. The ASEAN Regional Forum (ARF)—an informal collection

---

14. David Dewitt, "Common, Comprehensive and Cooperative Security," *The Pacific Review*, Vol. 7, No. 1 (1994); and Paul Evans, "Building Security," *The Pacific Review*, Vol. 7 No. 2 (1994).
15. "ASEAN and Regional Security," *Strategic Survey 1994–1995* (London: IISS/Oxford University Press, 1995).

of states in Asia-Pacific (as well as the European Union)—makes no pretense of seeking to shape the security policy of member states. Even its most ardent supporters acknowledge that the ARF will not begin to consider matters of conflict resolution for many years. Cynics may see the ARF as little more than a gentleman's dining or golf club, because no one is willing to articulate the nature of the primary security concern: China. Even in the parallel, non-governmental track-two process of CSCAP (Council on Security and Cooperation in Asia-Pacific), China has been able to block significant membership for Taiwan. From the Chinese point of view, it is advantageous not to have an effective collective or even co-operative security system, for it is inevitable that such a system would be primarily intended to constrain the largest power.[16] As one ASEAN official put it, China and its neighbors know that if East Asians do not hang together, they will certainly hang separately.

Does Interdependence Restrain China?

The analysis so far suggests that there are objective conditions, but little propensity, for China to be balanced and restrained by East Asians. One reason for the lack of will to constrain China is the assumption, as stated by the "engagement" school, that China will be restrained by the need for economic interdependence. In 1993–94 this question was tested on the anvil of Hong Kong policy. The answer seemed to be that Chinese behavior was to some extent constrained, but for a complex and perhaps unique series of reasons.[17]

16. For some indication of Chinese thinking, unofficially, see the *Kyodo* report of a high-level Chinese policy document reportedly opposed to regional security schemes. January 29, 1995, in British Broadcasting Corporation (BBC), Summary of World Broadcasts (SWB), Far East (FE/) 2216/G1. See also Huang Fan-zhang, "East Asian Economics: Development, Cooperation Prospects, and China's Strategy" in Barbara Bundy, et al., eds., *The Future of the Pacific Rim* (London: Praeger, 1994). A good Western analysis appears in Bonnie Glaser and Banning Garrett, "Multilateral Security in the Asia-Pacific Region and its Impact on China's Interests: Views from Beijing," *Contemporary Southeast Asia*, Vol. 16 No. 1 (June 1994). The author is also grateful for insights from Susan Shirk based on her "track two" dialogue with the Chinese on these issues. See also Denny Roy, "Hegemon on the Horizon? China's Threat to East Asian Security," *International Security*, Vol. 19, No. 1 (Summer 1994); John Garver, "China's Push Through the South China Sea," *The China Quarterly*, December 1992; Harry Harding, "A Chinese Colossus," *Journal of Strategic Studies*, Vol. 18, No. 3 (September 1995).

17. See a wide-ranging discussion in the UK House of Commons Foreign Affairs Committee in *Relations Between the UK and China in the Period up to and Beyond 1997* (London: HMSO, March 1994). See also Percy Cradock, *Experiences of China* (London: John Murray, 1994); and Gerald Segal, "A Clearer Fate for Hong Kong," *The World Today*, February 1994.

When the new British Governor, Chris Patten, proposed democratic reforms in defiance of Chinese wishes, China's first instinct was to shout and threaten dire consequences, seemingly in disregard of its economic interests in a stable Hong Kong. At first glance, China's policy offered scant support for the notion of restraint through interdependence. And yet China soon found that the bluster failed to cow the people of Hong Kong into rejecting the Patten proposals, and Beijing was unwilling to carry through on most of its dire threats. In effect it adopted a wait-and-see approach and took part in local elections, hoping that it might do well enough to undermine Patten in a more subtle fashion. When it failed to do so in the elections to the Legislative Council in September 1995, China still did not revert to its dire threats, and instead carefully tried to isolate Governor Patten.

Beijing's bite amounted to something less than its bark, in part because policy towards Hong Kong was no longer simply a matter of central government fiat. Too many people in the more decentralized Chinese political and economic system have a stake in stability in Hong Kong. Whether due to the "Red Princes"—the wealthy and powerful children of senior leaders—or the local authorities in southern coastal China, the result was a more fragmented and pragmatic Chinese policy. To the extent that these decentralized forces in China drew some of their power from their international connections, the Hong Kong case provided evidence that China's hand was stayed by interdependence. More accurately, this was evidence of how China can be constrained by interdependence, even in the teeth of opposition from the central government.

While the Hong Kong case is often explained away as unique, it was far more difficult to dismiss the importance of the next major test of the notion that China could and would be constrained by economic interdependence.

The South China Sea Case

China has never hidden its claim to complete sovereignty in the South China Sea. Ever since China emerged from the distractions of the Cultural Revolution, it has sought carefully to extend its control of these disputed waters.[18] China has insisted on its unshakable legal claim to the region, although it has frustratingly never explained the legal basis of its policy nor defined the precise limits of its claim. China signed but has not yet ratified the 1982 United Nations

18. Lo Chi-kin, *China's Policy Towards Territorial Disputes* (London: Routledge, 1989); Mark Valencia, *China and the South China Sea*, Adelphi Paper No. 297 (London: IISS/Oxford University Press, July 1995); Michael Gallagher, "China's Illusory Threat to the South China Sea," *International Security*, Vol. 19, No. 1 (Summer 1994).

Convention on the Law of the Sea. Beijing has given no indication that it would accept international arbitration of its claim to sovereignty over every bit of territory in the region. China has been reluctant to take the issue to the International Court of Justice (ICJ) in part because, like all the other claimants (Taiwan, Vietnam, Malaysia, Philippines, Brunei), its claim to sovereignty is weak.[19] China has applied the continental shelf principle in defining its maritime claims in the Yellow and East China Sea, but claims the South China Sea on the basis of "historic use and administration."[20] However, China has clearly not had continuous and effective control, administration, and governance of the territory, as the latter principle calls for. And even if some sovereignty claims would be upheld by the court, the tiny outcrops in the sea do not appear to be legally qualified to justify exclusive economic zones of 200 nautical miles or even more extensive con- tinental shelves. Only 26 features in the Spratly group are above water at high tide and the largest has a land area of less than half a square kilometer. None has ever sustained a permanent population. Continental shelf claims from states surrounding the Spratlys are likely to be seen as much stronger by the ICJ.

It appears, as Michael Swaine of the RAND Corporation has suggested, that Chinese claims "have more to do with power than law."[21] Clearly the Chinese do not feel that they have to negotiate with anyone about this issue. The furthest reaches of the South China Sea stretch some 1800 km from undisputed Chinese territory on Hainan island, and touch Natuna island (in the south of the South China Sea) held by Indonesia.[22] China moved south in stages, taking the Paracel islands from Vietnam in 1974, and then building an airstrip on the islands capable of handling fighters and transport aircraft. In the 1980s China extended its control into the more southerly Spratly group. The most publicized clash in the Spratlys came in 1988, when several Vietnamese ships were destroyed in one engagement.

19. Valencia, *China and the South China Sea;* and Mark Valencia with Jon M. Van Dyke and Noel Ludwig, "The Solution for the Spratly Islands Ought to Look Like This," *International Herald Tribune,* October 10, 1995.

20. In June 1995, in the midst of a new period of anxiety in Southeast Asia about the South China Sea, Chinese archaeologists claimed to have found porcelain fragments there dating back to the Song Dynasty (960–1279). *Xinhua* (China's News Agency) on June 13, 1994, in SWB FE/2332/G7.

21. Michael Swaine quoted in *Far Eastern Economic Review,* April 13, 1995, p. 25. For a classic example of the Chinese line of argument see the interview with a Chinese State oceanographic official in *Wen Wei Po,* April 17, 1995, in SWB FE/2284/G1–3. See also *Ta Kung Pao,* February 26, 1995, in SWB FE/2241/G/1–2.

22. For a careful analysis of the legal issues, see Daniel Dzurek, "China Occupies Mischief Reef in Latest Spratly Gambit," *International Boundary Research Unit Boundary and Security Bulletin* (London), April 1995, pp. 65–71.

By the early 1990s, the six rival claimants were all busy reinforcing their postures and seeking contracts with foreign firms to explore for oil and gas. In August 1990, Chinese Premier Li Peng declared in Singapore that China was prepared to put aside the question of sovereignty and jointly develop the Spratlys. But it soon became clear that China was not in fact interested in anything that might "internationalize" the problem, and refused any serious efforts at multilateral negotiations.[23] China's position was far better pursued in bilateral relations where it could pick off one rival after another. In October 1991, at an unofficial but Indonesian-sponsored (and Canadian-financed) meeting of the claimants to the Spratlys, China joined in the agreement to resolve matters peacefully and to avoid unilateral action. It seemed as if China would be constrained from extending control of the South China Sea by its concerns about appearing to be a regional bully and about losing the benefits of economic interdependence.

In February 1992 China promulgated the "Law on Territorial Waters and Adjacent Areas," but this was more a political symbol than a necessary legal procedure in the pursuit of territorial claims.[24] In 1992 Chinese officials appeared to accept the terms of a July 22 five-point ASEAN declaration on the South China Sea, which agreed that force should not be used to change the status quo.[25] Beijing agreed that opportunities for joint development should be explored, although China made clear that it agreed to nothing that would constrain its sovereign rights in the region. Various discussions were held, many of the most important ones under the auspices of Indonesia (a non-claimant to the Spratly group), but no agreements were reached.

By 1994 both China and Vietnam were becoming more adept at developing contacts with Western countries and corporations. Vietnam even began to modernize its armed forces, including the acquisition of SU-27 aircraft.[26] Vietnam also grew bolder in asserting its right to explore for oil and gas, and evidence seemed to be growing that there were exploitable reserves in the area.[27] Vietnam was set to join ASEAN (by July 1995) and was feeling far less

23. This has been a steady refrain. See *Xinhua,* May 11, 1995, in SWB FE/2301/G/1.
24. Michael Leifer, "Chinese Economic Reform and Security Policy: The South China Sea Connection," *Survival,* Vol. 37 No. 2 (Summer 1995); and Esmond Smith, "China's Aspirations in the Spratly Islands," *Contemporary Southeast Asia,* Vol. 16, No. 3 (December 1994).
25. *The Straits Times* (Singapore), July 31, 1992.
26. *Jane's Defence Weekly,* May 20, 1995, p. 3; *Flight,* May 24, 1995, p. 24.
27. Michael Richardson, "Strategic Signpost for Asia" in *Asia-Pacific Defence Reporter Annual Reference Edition,* Vol. 21, No. 6–7 (December 1994–January 1995), pp. 49–51. See also Ho Limpeng, "The Spratly Islands: Asian Flashpoint," *Navy International,* September 1994, pp. 257–259. On oil finds see *International Herald Tribune,* May 25,1995.

of a pariah. In August 1994 China grew concerned about Vietnam's oil prospecting activities with foreign companies in the Spratlys; in several incidents in the summer and autumn, Vietnamese forces chased off Chinese boats operating in Vietnamese-controlled waters in the Spratlys.[28] Vietnam was clearly seeking to tie its fate in the South China Sea to that of Western oil companies, hoping thereby to add to its strength and deter China. This was not so much a policy of constraining China through China's interdependence with the outside world, as constraining China through a mixture of precise use of military force and use of Vietnamese interdependence with the outside world. The question was whether this clever strategy was too clever by half, and whether China would be constrained.

The end of 1994 was also a time when China was finding itself in deeper conflict with the West, and the United States in particular, over trade disputes and entry into the WTO. But China got into this problem in part because it was feeling less constrained by the international system. Some Chinese officials had incorrectly calculated that because the United States had recently abandoned the linkage of trade and human rights, Western powers would no longer use the linkage of foreign policy issues to constrain Chinese behavior. But the late 1994 trade disputes demonstrated that China was set for a much longer and more complex dispute with the United States on trade issues. This was a difficult time for China, because it was being asked to accept that from now on it would be more, not less, bound by the international system. The Chinese were aware that they were soon to become a major food and fuel importer and thus ever more dependent on the global market for vital supplies.[29] As it could see the implications of becoming more dependent on the outside world, China chose to resist the process as much as it could. The decision to acquire at least 10 (and possibly as many as 22) Kilo-class submarines from Russia was part

28. *Xinhua*, October 17, 1994, in SWB FE/2130/G/2; and *South China Morning Post International Weekly*, August 27, 1994, p. 6. See also Mark Valencia, "Dancing with the Chinese Dragon" in *Trends*, August 27, 1994; and *Far Eastern Economic Review*, October 13, 1994, p. 29.

29. Reports in 1994 suggested that China became a net oil importer in November 1993. It turned out that these initial assessments were premature. In the first quarter of 1995 Chinese oil exports were 4m tonnes, down from 4.2m in the same period in 1994, but still higher than China's import total of 2.45m tonnes which was up from 2.43m. See *Reuters*, May 8, 1995. Estimates suggest China will need to import 100m tonnes by 2010. See Valencia, *China and the South China Sea*. On China's food dependence see a report by The Worldwatch Institute cited in "Malthus Goes East," *The Economist*, August 12, 1995. In that context, it is significant that whereas the Spratly islands have proven to be rich in marine resources, oil has not yet been found in major quantities. The Natuna gas field in the south of the region is the world's largest. See GMA-7 Television (Philippines), June 18, 1995, in SWB FE/2335/B/4; and *World Resources 1994–95* (Oxford: Oxford University Press, 1994).

of a much wider program to modernize Chinese naval forces and extend their power-projection capability.[30] And so, in September 1994 when the Philippine armed forces detained 55 fishermen from China who tried to set up structures on one of the islands claimed by the Philippines, China felt it had to respond. As in the past when China used force to defend what it defined as its national interest, Beijing found itself making policy on the fly.[31]

Although the Spratly islands themselves might not have been very important, the region provided a real test of whether China would be constrained by economic interdependence. While it may not be surprising that China felt it needed to deliver a message that it would not be pushed around, it surprised most observers that China would, for the first time, come into conflict with an ASEAN member. The conventional wisdom in East Asia was that China would no doubt continue to take territory claimed by Vietnam, but it would not encroach on territory claimed by ASEAN states. The argument was that China needed to be on good terms with ASEAN states in order to keep the flow of investment and technology from these states. Any use of force against such pro-Western states would also threaten relations with the developed world as a whole. But the conventional wisdom was wrong.

There is little evidence upon which to reconstruct China's decision-making process, but it seems likely that the general propensity to use force to regain territory claimed by China would not have caused much dispute in Beijing. What might well have been more disputatious was the timing and the target. It seems that the specific operation was launched by the Guangzhou Military Region and South China Fleet, even though some, such as the Foreign Ministry, might have been expected to oppose such action at that time. But at a time of uncertainty in Beijing leadership politics, and with some parallels to the 1974 Paracels incident and the 1988 clash with Vietnam in the Spratlys, it would have been more possible for local commanders to operate under what they thought were standard procedures and strategies that did not require formal approval in Beijing.[32]

30. *Janes Defence Weekly*, March 18, 1995, p. 3. More generally see Jun Zhan, "China Goes to the Blue Water," *Journal of Strategic Studies*, Vol. 17, No. 3 (September 1994).
31. The pattern of Chinese action in such circumstances is discussed in Gerald Segal, *Defending China* (Oxford: Oxford University Press, 1985).
32. This is a difficult subject and I am grateful for the views of Paul Godwin on the matter. For some additional insights see *Kuang Chiao Ching* (Hong Kong) No. 271 (April 16, 1995) in SWB FE/2301/G/1–3. See also the view of Admiral Lanxade who was in China in the relevant months, in *Cols Bleus* (Paris), May 6, 1995.

In choosing to take on an ASEAN state in the South China Sea, China was taking a political risk of souring relations with ASEAN and scaring off foreign investors. On the other hand, in choosing the weakest ASEAN member, the Philippines, China chose the softest target. In choosing the state that had ejected American forces from their bases, it also tested American intentions in the most cautious manner. Thus sometime in the three months before the end of January 1995, China sent at least nine naval vessels to Mischief Reef.[33] This was not the most southerly territory taken by China, but it was the first time it had seized territory claimed by an ASEAN state. Chinese forces arrested Philippine fishermen, built structures on the island, and left troops in place to guard what many analysts expect will turn into a Chinese naval facility and possibly even an airstrip. Philippine forces confirmed the action on February 8 and found they could do nothing to reverse the situation.

What is the significance of the mischief on the reef? The most obvious change in the status quo was that China had unambiguously violated the 1992 ASEAN understanding by using force against an ASEAN member.[34] China claimed that it was only acting in keeping with its sovereign claims; at least for public consumption, it insisted that it had only erected shelters for fishermen. When Western intelligence resources were finally focused on Mischief Reef, it became clear that China had built military structures and stationed People's Liberation Army (PLA) units on a long-term basis. Although Chinese officials admitted in private to Western governments that these were indeed PLA units, in public China continued to assert that this was the benign action of Chinese fishermen and that using force to eject Filipino fishermen was not the same as an attack on an ASEAN member. In any case, China asserted that this was a form of self-defense because the territory was its own. Some Chinese even suggested that the lesson to be learned was the need to expand Chinese forces very rapidly in order to seize the region quickly and thereby avoid such political inconveniences as China would endure in the first half of 1995.[35] China was clearly taking a risk in taking on an ASEAN member and it also risked feeding the sense in the wider world that China would sacrifice economic relations if

---

33. Aptly named by the British Admiralty, Mischief Reef is more than 1,100 km from Hainan, and less than 240km from the coast of the southern Philippine island of Pauline.

34. Those who seek to minimize the importance of the incident on Mischief Reef note that China did not "use force" in the sense of the 1988 clash with Vietnam where troops were killed. But China clearly did "use force" to eject the Philippine fishermen and then placed naval forces on the Reef to deter counter-attack.

35. *China News Digest*, April 26, 1995; and *Xinhua* on April 20, 1995, in SWB FE/2284/G/1; and *Kuang Chiao Ching* (Hong Kong) No. 271 (April 16, 1995), in SWB FE/2301/G/1–3.

this were the only way to satisfy territorial claims and obtain vital energy resources. The main question, and the test of the significance of the Mischief Reef operation, depended on the way in which other people reacted to the Chinese operation and whether China had indeed put at risk the benefits of interdependence.

The initial reaction from ASEAN states was stunning silence, or at least the nearest thing to it that diplomats can muster. In private, ASEAN officials were furious that they had been humiliated by China. The Philippines fumed, in part at their own failures, and soon took out their anger by destroying some Chinese markers on other reefs elsewhere in the Spratlys. But what was most striking was the absence of any formal ASEAN complaint that blamed China for breaking the 1992 understanding. Various countries in the region issued statements regretting the rise in tension and calling for all parties to avoid the use of force: hardly statements of robust deterrence. Behind closed doors, ASEAN officials concluded that they could do little about Chinese activity and that therefore discretion was the better part of valor. They saw no reason to issue statements that condemned China if they could do nothing to back them up. If "Finlandization" described a state that constrained its policies because it lived next door to a neighbor too powerful to challenge, then the states of Southeast Asia were "ASEANized." Of course, this ASEAN version of Finlandization was a self-fulfilling strategy: if no concern were articulated, then no one could be asked to help. If no one helped, then nothing could be done.

ASEAN foreign ministers issued a joint statement that expressed concern about recent activities but declined to identify either the problem or the fact that China was the one who had seized territory. Even these limited moves were made only because the Philippines "made a diplomatic scene" and demanded that something be said to China.[36] China apparently did not even have to pay a public relations price. When China humiliated Vietnam in 1974 and 1988, the Vietnamese had shouted from the moral high ground about Chinese aggression. In 1995, however, meetings of ASEAN officials suggested that there was no unanimity on how to handle China and great reluctance to criticize China explicitly for its actions on Mischief Reef.[37] China found that it could more easily defeat ASEAN members than it could Vietnam.

On April 2–4, 1995, at an already planned meeting with Chinese officials behind closed doors in Hangzhou, the Chinese were apparently presented with

36. *Far Eastern Economic Review,* April 6, 1995.
37. *International Herald Tribune,* April 21, 1995.

a unified ASEAN expression of concern over Chinese actions (informally over dinner). Beijing was "asked" to cease building military structures on disputed islands.[38] The ASEAN officials had asked for the issue to be considered formally at the meeting, but China refused and ASEAN backed down. From China's point of view, the fact that the meeting was routine and secret, and that the message was only delivered informally over dinner, meant that China could feel that it had little price to pay for its actions.

However, while China had humiliated ASEAN, in so doing it may have stimulated forces that it had rather left dormant. As Vietnam had shown after the setback of 1988, a Chinese triumph can stimulate the vanquished to work on a better strategy. After defeat by China, Vietnam sought the benefits of interdependence with Western oil companies, turned itself into a target of opportunity for Western multinationals rather than a target for abuse by Western governments, and sought support by joining ASEAN. The new Vietnamese strategy of deterrence appeared to cause China to avoid taking on Vietnam in 1995 and to seek instead a more vulnerable and less costly target.

The states in the cross-hairs were those ASEAN countries that suddenly found that China was prepared to take them on directly. China was apparently unconstrained by economic interdependence. The action on Mischief Reef demonstrated that engaging China was not a sufficient strategy.

IS ANYONE LEARNING LESSONS?

The initial reaction to Mischief Reef and subsequent events in ASEAN and beyond was low-key. But as 1995 developed, the main actors tried to come to terms with the fact that their hope in the restraining qualities of interdependence was misplaced. Difficult choices now had to be made. As different states groped for a policy, they went off in different directions. In the process, there were signs that while most were not prepared to try to constrain Chinese behavior by organizing a more effective counter-balance of power, such a strategy, if adopted, might have some effect.

THE UNITED STATES. U.S. policy towards China, as in many other aspects of American foreign policy in the 1990s, was hard to judge.[39] There were obvious flip-flops—none more glaring than the case of the Clinton administration's temporizing and then refusal in 1994 to link Most Favored Nation trading

38. Philippines GMA-7 Television, April 10, 1995, in SWB FE/2276/B1. See also *Far Eastern Economic Review*, April 20, 1995, p. 12.
39. Harry Harding, "Asia Policy to the Brink" in *Foreign Policy*, No. 96 (Fall 1994).

status to an improvement of China's human rights record. On the other hand, this same American administration took a tougher line on trade issues, and even liberalized relations with Taiwan.

In the defense field, there was also a range of policies on view. On the one hand, the United States resumed military-to-military contacts, including ship visits. And yet the war games played in American defense academies pitted U.S. forces against China (with a 2010 scenario).[40] When an American aircraft carrier jousted with Chinese military units on October 27–29, 1994, off the Chinese coast, this demonstrated that at least some influential people in the Department of Defense were concerned about how to deal with a rising Chinese military power.[41] Following events on Mischief Reef, Stanley Roth of the National Security Council was quoted as expressing support for the Philippines' efforts to stop "Chinese intrusions," American officials looked for ways to bolster security ties with Japan, and the new Marine Corp commandant, General Charles Krulak, expressed deep concern about China's long-term intentions.[42]

On the other hand, Admiral Richard Macke, then commander of American forces in the Pacific, said in Singapore in March 1995 that Asia and the West must accept the fact that China will develop a modern navy including aircraft carriers intended to project power overseas.[43] In May 1995, U.S. Chief of Naval Personnel Admiral Zlatoper, when rejecting the argument of a study suggesting that China was the main challenge to the Asian balance of power, reportedly argued that China might even be part of a Gulf War–style joint defense strategy to deal with regional crises.[44]

The confused state of American policy in East Asia and towards China was encapsulated in the somewhat contradictory content of the newly revised American strategy for Asia-Pacific published in February 1995. It argued for a greater concentration on traditional friends in the region, but one had to read between the lines to appreciate that China was seen as the main challenge to the regional balance of power. Therefore, implicitly, increased U.S. reliance on its allies would show increasing concern about Chinese intentions.[45]

40. *Defense News*, January 30, 1995, pp. 1, 26.
41. *International Herald Tribune*, December 15, 1994.
42. Associated Press, April 2, 1995; *International Herald Tribune*, June 23, 1995; *Far Eastern Economic Review*, September 28, 1995, p. 32.
43. *International Herald Tribune*, March 8, 1995; Richard C. Macke, "A Commander in Chief Looks at East Asia," *Joint Forces Quarterly*, Spring 1995, esp. pp. 12–13.
44. *Reuters*, May 3, 1995, referring to Dibb, *Toward a New Balance of Power in Asia*.
45. *U.S. Security Strategy for the East Asia–Pacific* (Washington, D.C.: Office of International Security Affairs, Department of Defense, February 1994). See also William Perry speech to China's National Defense University in Beijing on October 18, 1994, in *Defense News*, Vol. 9, No. 81 (1994).

In effect the United States stayed on the sidelines while the security situation deteriorated. It was fully five months after the incident on Mischief Reef that the United States managed to cobble together a formal statement on the incident. The State Department declined to single out any state in the region as the main problem, and instead issued a general statement of "concern" about the freedom of navigation.[46] But by then Sino-American relations were in a tailspin, triggered by the granting of a visa to the Taiwanese president so he could receive an honorary degree at Cornell University. When Sino-Taiwanese relations subsequently deteriorated so badly that China closed air and sea lanes in the Taiwan Straits in order to test-fire missiles, it had become clear that the Spratly issue was only part of a much wider worry about China's propensity to use force, relatively unconstrained by the risks that it might damage economic interdependence in East Asia. It remained unclear, and indeed a major uncertainty for the future, whether China was constrained from attacking Taiwan by an understanding that the United States would help Taiwan resist. The United States remained ambiguous about whether it was offering Taiwan such balance-of-power protection, but for the time being even such an uncertain deterrent seemed to be holding China at bay. Not even such a limited strategy was on offer for those who might wish to resist China in the South China Sea.

JAPAN. The East Asian country that seemed to be having the most significant debate about China was the only other indigenous major power in East Asia, Japan. Well before the events on Mischief Reef, Japanese officials were expressing increasing concern, mainly privately, about Chinese intentions and the resolve of the United States to guarantee East Asian security. With signs that China seemed increasingly willing to throw its weight around, Japan became willing to express its concerns more explicitly. Even in the midst of chaotic Japanese domestic politics and debates about whether it should identify more strongly with Asia or the West, officials in Tokyo were speaking more openly of the need for a robust attitude towards China.[47]

Japanese officials helped nudge the United States in 1995 to revise its strategy in Asia-Pacific and in particular to place far greater stress on working with traditional allies. U.S. officials pointed out to Japanese officials that the litany of challenges to security in the report were mostly identified with China. When the Japanese prime minister visited China in May 1995, Japan edged closer to

46. *Reuters*, May 10, 1995; and *Korea Times*, May 15, 1995.

47. These points are in part based on discussions at a closed seminar at the UK Foreign Office in March 1995. See also "A Question of Balance," *The Economist*, April 22, 1995.

a full apology for its wartime behavior, but the talks, heavily leaked in the Japanese press, were robust in raising difficult security issues where Japan felt China was not acting in the best interests of regional and global security.[48] Japan's reaction to the incident at Mischief Reef drew a warning from Japanese officials, especially in terms of Japanese anxiety to keep the sea lanes in the region open.[49] Japan's Defense White Paper published in June expressed explicit concern with China's more aggressive policy in the South China Sea and called for an improvement in the quality of Japanese forces as a result.[50] In August, Japanese fighters attempted but failed to intercept Chinese fighters that overflew the disputed Senkaku islands.[51]

When China tested a nuclear device in May 1995 just after the renewal of the Nuclear Non-proliferation Treaty (NPT), Japan took the opportunity to send a more general warning to China that if it took action opposed by its neighbors and the international community, it should expect punishment. Japan reduced its grant aid to China by a symbolic amount, but the action was, especially for the usually cautious Japanese, a loud signal of serious worries about Chinese behavior. At the time of the fiftieth anniversary of the surrender of Japan in 1945, Japan and China engaged in increasingly nasty exchanges, each accusing the other of being the greater risk to regional stability. Japanese officials expressed increasing concern that China was trying to exert pressure in new forms. China tried to tell Japan what terms it could use for dealing with the Taiwanese, as the host for the 1995 APEC summit in Osaka. Coupled with increasing frustration over China's blocking of progress on the negotiation of an zero-level comprehensive nuclear test ban treaty, Japanese officials in various ministries found China increasingly difficult to handle.[52]

AUSTRALIA. Perhaps the most thoughtful assessment of the changing balance of power in Asia came from Australia. As the architect of APEC, Australia was worried about what it saw as a stubborn impulse in ASEAN to set the Asia-Pacific agenda and to relegate the Anglo-Saxon countries on the rim to a more marginal role. In public, Australian officials spoke of the need to join Asia; even

48. *UPI*, May 1, 1995. See various reports on the visit in SWB FE/2295/G/1–6.
49. *Agence France Presse* from Tokyo, March 8, 1995; and *International Herald Tribune*, April 4, 1995.
50. *Reuters*, June 30, 1995; *South China Morning Post Weekly*, July 8, 1995, p. 9.
51. *China News Digest*, August 30, 1995.
52. For evidence on these issues in the public domain see *Xinhua*, July 3, 1995, in SWB FE/2347/G/1; *Kyodo*, August 30, 1995, in SWB FE/2396/E/1; Liu Jiangyong, "Distorting History will Misguide Japan," *Contemporary International Relations*, Vol. 5, No. 9 (September 1995); *Kyodo* on pro-Taiwan forces in *Daily Yomiuri*, September 22, 1995; and Ryuichi Otsuka on the test ban in the *Daily Yomiuri*, September 21, 1995.

the normally outspoken Australian Foreign Minister, Gareth Evans, was careful not to condemn China's seizure of Mischief Reef.[53] But the new Australian defense strategy in December 1994 was even more explicit than the 1995 revision of American strategy in identifying China as the major challenge to regional security. In a more detailed presentation of the case, the architect of the Australian review, Paul Dibb, set out the case for concern in a less diplomatic form of words.[54] Implicit in the Australian approach was a sense that its opening to Asia was perhaps misjudged in its undue emphasis on ASEAN states.[55] While it was necessary to work with Indonesia in particular, the Australians increasingly felt that most other ASEAN states were especially hostile to a more important Australian role in Asia. Australians were finding that their closest friends (and most important trade partners) were in Northeast Asia and their closest ally was still the United States. Like the Americans, Australia worried that ASEAN was drifting towards the temptation of a non-white EAEC in which a more powerful China would be far less constrained and far more able to set an anti-Western agenda. Thus in December 1995, when Indonesia unexpectedly signed a defense accord with Australia, departing for the first time from its "non-aligned" posture, there was evidence that at least some of the middle powers of East Asia were beginning to grow seriously worried about China.

TAIWAN. Of the East Asian states, it was always assumed that Taiwan would take the toughest line towards China because it was defending its *de facto* independence. It was certainly true that Taiwanese officials were consistently among the firmest in warning about the consequences of a rising China. Yet when the attention turned to the South China Sea, Taiwan was caught between its desire to resist Chinese pressure and its view that the South China Sea belonged to China.[56] In the PLA operation in 1988 in the Spratlys, a Taiwanese military station had reportedly supplied fresh water to Chinese forces, and on March 25, 1995, Taiwanese forces fired on Vietnamese supply vessels. In April 1995, Taiwan announced meetings with Chinese officials about co-operation in oil exploration in the East and South China Sea, and cancelled a naval patrol

53. Gareth Evans was in Malaysia at the time. See Malaysian Television on February 17, 1995, in SWB FE/2232/B/2.
54. Dibb, *Towards a New Balance of Power.*
55. Gareth Evans on March 20, 1995, reported by *Reuters* from Sydney on March 20, 1995. On the defense White Paper, see *Far Eastern Economic Review,* December 15, 1994, pp. 18–20.
56. Various reports in mid-April 1995 from Taiwanese media in SWB FE/2276/F1; and *Far Eastern Economic Review,* April 13, 1995, p. 29.

in the South China Sea when the tension surrounding Mischief Reef seemed to be rising. In August 1995, the number of mainland Chinese fishermen working on Taiwanese-owned boats was reported to be rising sharply.[57]

The root of Taiwan's ambivalence toward the Spratlys was the gradual emergence of a stronger sense of self-definition. This drew Taiwan's concern away from the Spratlys, and much closer to home. Following President Lee's 1995 pre-election campaign trip to Cornell University, relations between Taiwan and China took a sharp turn for the worse. Beijing rattled its missiles in a summer and autumn of tension, and yet Taiwan received no support from anyone in the region.[58] China's leaders resorted to ultra-nationalist policies, in large part for domestic consumption, at a time of weak leadership in Beijing. China seemed to be paying little attention to the fact that a Taiwan Straits crisis might hinder the flow of investment and trade across the straits. Like the Spratly case, the Taiwan crisis demonstrated the extent to which China seemed unconstrained by either a balance of power or the logic of economic interdependence.

ASEAN. The policies of the ASEAN states were the most fluid. Although their formal response to events in 1995 was to avoid public attacks on China, it was clear that ASEAN officials felt the need to demonstrate that they could constrain Chinese behavior at least in some symbolic fashion. What they achieved was not much, but perhaps just enough of a sense that China was listening, even if it was not prepared to change its behavior.

When China's relations with the United States deteriorated over Taiwan, and Japans relations with China went sour because of nuclear tests, ASEAN found that China was more willing than before to listen to appeals for good behavior. Beijing needed to avoid antagonizing everyone at the same time.[59] Ahead of the ARF meeting in Brunei on August 1, 1995, ASEAN officials persuaded China to promise at least cosmetic changes in policy. While in Brunei, China's Foreign Minister Qian Qichen insisted that China still had sovereignty over the entire South China Sea, but declared that China was willing to resolve disputes according to the Law of the Sea. Qian also agreed to discuss the issue in a

57. In 1994, some 21,000 mainland fishermen sailed on Taiwanese fishing boats. *International Herald Tribune*, April 5, 1995; *The Economist*, April 29, 1995. On fishing boats, see *China News Digest*, August 30, 1995.

58. "Tensions Across the Taiwan Strait," *China News Analysis*, No. 1543 (September 15, 1995).

59. For the formal Chinese statement, and evidence of its linkage of the ARF to the poor state of relations with the United States, see *Xinhua*, August 1, 1995, in SWB FE/2371/G/5; and *Wen Wei Po* on August 1 in SWB FE/2372/G/1.

multilateral forum with ASEAN. While none of this was strictly new—China had already signed the 1982 Law of the Sea convention and had discussed the Spratly issue in Hangzhou in April 1995—the tone at least reflected a recognition of the need to ease ASEAN worries. China agreed to a bit more transparency on military matters, although its officially published defense data is notoriously unreliable.[60] Perhaps most importantly, China seemed prepared to sign agreements with Indonesia for gas supplies from the Natuna field in the southern Spratly islands, thereby apparently putting a practical end to its claim of ownership, at least in the short term.[61]

The more cooperative behavior from China showed that Beijing worried about a coalition being built against it, and that if the states of East Asia could begin to articulate and act upon a shared concern with China, then Beijing might well alter its policies. Signs of the depth of concern in ASEAN before the ARF meeting were not as coherent as they might have been, but ASEAN states certainly showed that China had crossed an important line.

THE PHILIPPINES. The Philippines, having been shocked by the initial Chinese action in January 1995, was also among the most vociferous in warning about the long-term threat. The Philippine armed forces were in no position to take on China on their own, but in the aftermath of the incident on Mischief Reef, Manila did authorize an increase in defense spending. Philippine naval units also destroyed seven Chinese markers on other islands in territorial waters just east of Mischief Reef, although they did not take on Chinese forces remaining on Mischief Reef, nor did they challenge Chinese naval vessels operating in disputed waters.[62] The Philippine navy arrested 62 Chinese fishermen just south of Mischief Reef on March 25, 1995, and charged them with illegal possession of firearms and explosives, and illegal entry.[63] In the months following the incident there were exaggerated worries among Philippine leaders about China posing a threat to the main islands of the Philippines,[64] at the same time as the Philippines engaged in mostly clever diplomacy intended to

60. China published a "White Paper" on arms control in November 1995 that suggests it does not feel it needs to be any more transparent, only that it must pretend to be so. See the text in *Xinhua* on November 16, 1995, in SWB FE/2463/S1/1–10.
61. *Kyodo*, August 1, 1995, in SWB FE/2372/S1/1 for the ARF statement. Also *Financial Times*, July 31, 1995; *Business Times* (Singapore), August 2, 1995; *The Economist*, August 5, 1995; *International Herald Tribune*, August 4; and ibid., October 7, 1995. For further details on the ARF see *PacNet*, No. 29 (August 18, 1995); *PacNet*, No. 31 (September 1, 1995).
62. Philippines GMA-7 Television on April 24, 1995, in SWB FE/2287/B/1.
63. Philippines GMA-7 Television on April 11, 1995, in SWB FE/2277/B/3.
64. *UPI*, April 19, 1995.

raise consciousness among ASEAN partners about the need to take a more robust line towards China.

China agreed to discuss a "code of conduct" with the Philippines, but refused to do so on a multilateral basis. As China realized that the Philippines was scoring diplomatic points, China warned that others should not "misinterpret" its intentions, an ambiguous remark that could cover a multitude of possible reactions in the future.[65] Other Chinese comments warned the Philippines that it "would bear all the consequences" if it continued to "cling obstinately to its course."[66] But it was Beijing that shifted ground at the ARF meeting, agreeing at least to discuss the Spratly issue in a multilateral dialogue with ASEAN, among other things. Oddly, the Philippines then proceeded to undermine its good efforts in raising consciousness about China by negotiating a "code of conduct" bilaterally with Beijing.[67] Perhaps lessons had not been learned after all.

MALAYSIA. Of course, ASEAN states were not immediately attracted to the notion of multilateral negotiations about territorial disputes because they had so many unresolved disputes among themselves. ASEAN states also had a range of other reasons for turning a deaf ear to Philippine concerns. Malaysia, with its large ethnic-Chinese minority, might have been expected to take a firm line against an extension of Chinese power. But as Prime Minister Mahathir has grown more confident about his ability to manage the Chinese majority at home, he has been happy for them to seek economic benefits from new trade ties with China. He has also seen China as a crucial anti-Western ally in his struggle to develop an EAEC and to shut out the Anglo-Saxon states across the Pacific. China has been more than willing to support this aspiration and happy to hear Mahathir say that "we no longer regard China as a threat."[68]

SINGAPORE. As Malaysia shifted to a more sympathetic stance towards China, Singapore viewed the change as a vindication of its own more long-standing pro-China tilt. As a tiny, mainly ethnically-Chinese state in a sea of non-Chinese, Singapore has natural worries about its survivability. Thus it in effect (but never formally) welcomes a degree of worry by its ASEAN neighbors about China's intentions. It has taken a special role in helping China modernize, and in providing China with oil processing and other facilities in

65. *Reuters,* May 10, 1995; *Xinhua,* May 16, 1995, in SWB FE/2306/G1.
66. *Ta Kung Pao,* May 17, 1995, in SWB FE/2310/G/1–2.
67. *Xinhua* on August 11, 1995, in SWB FE/2381/G/9; GMA-7 Television (Philippines) on August 9 and *Xinhua* on August 9, both in SWB FE/2379/B/3. See also *Financial Times,* August 11, 1995.
68. *Financial Times,* February 10, 1993.

the region.[69] It is also one of the few ASEAN states that has no real or even potential territorial disputes with China. Singapore appreciates, however, that it is in a vulnerable position and must take care not to be seen to be too sympathetic to China's position. Hence, Premier Goh Chok Tong suggested in Beijing that China's rising power, arms spending, and activities in the South China Sea were "stirring anxiety" in the region. Although this was a belated response, Singapore felt that it could not afford to be seen to be silent when China was picking on a fellow member of ASEAN.[70]

INDONESIA. Perhaps the most important and firm response in ASEAN to China's moves in the South China Sea came from Indonesia. The Indonesians were always the most likely leaders of ASEAN and simply by virtue of their size stand as a middle power without their ASEAN colleagues. But because of various factors in post-war regional politics, Jakarta has seen fit to take a back seat in ASEAN. Yet everyone knows that Indonesia has an uneasy relationship with China. As China worked its way down through the Spratly group, and seemed undeterred about taking on an ASEAN member, it looked likely that China would carry on to the southernmost reaches of the South China Sea. As Chinese aspirations in effect reached Natuna island and the proven natural gas reserves (said to be the world's largest) in the region, Jakarta began to wake up to the threat it had allowed to develop unhindered. At a workshop in Surabaya in 1993 organized by Indonesia to discuss Chinese claims to the Spratly islands, China presented a map showing that the southern reaches of its claim included the Natuna gas field. Indonesia now realized that it was no longer neutral in the discussions about the South China Sea. In preparation for the ASEAN Regional Forum in July 1994, Indonesia asked its ASEAN partners to support a formula that would have cut back the area of the Chinese claim in the South China Sea. But Indonesia's supposed partners turned it down, preferring to take the immediate benefits of good trade relations with China rather than risking confrontation.[71] Indonesia grew more concerned.

In July 1994, Jakarta asked China to clarify whether its territorial claims extended to the Natuna region, but China refused to respond. After the Mischief Reef incident, Indonesia decided that the silence meant that China did claim the gas fields, and in April 1995 Indonesia began air patrols in the region around Natuna. Indonesian officials had been reluctant to characterize China

69. For example as reported by *Reuters* on January 6, 1995.
70. *Dow Jones News Service*, May 15, 1995; *Reuters*, May 14, 1995.
71. *Far Eastern Economic Review*, August 11, 1994, p. 18.

as a threat,[72] but in a marked change of tone, the commander of the Indonesian armed forces said in April that it was especially important to modernize Indonesia's air force in order to deal with the Chinese challenge in the South China Sea.[73] Thereafter the Indonesian Foreign Minister Ali Alatas was reported to have obtained Chinese clarification that its South China Sea claims did not include the Natuna gas field, and that China would apply the UN Law of the Sea Convention to the entire South China Sea.[74]

AND CHINA AGAIN. While it remains uncertain just how much China is constrained by its ARF declaration in August 1995, China clearly felt sufficiently constrained by a wave of protest and signs of increased vigilance in East Asia to moderate its diplomatic position. Events in the Taiwan Straits and the South China Sea did not appear to support the notion that Chinese expansionism would be constrained by fear of damaging economic interdependence, but it did seem that China was worried about what looked like early steps in building a regional, anti-China coalition. China seemed to understand that it could be the target of a balance of power, and that it had to alter policy accordingly.

Conclusion: Constructing a Constrainment Strategy

This analysis tells us some important things relevant to the three main questions in the China debate.

First, what is the nature of the China that interacts with the outside world? It is clear that China is a far more complex actor than ever before. Reforms in all their splendor and squalor have ensured that, for all China's authoritarian features, it makes less and less sense to talk of a single Chinese foreign policy. The timing and nature of Chinese activity in the South China Sea during 1995 have been seriously complicated by regional economic interests and regional military forces. Divisions in policy making in Beijing have also been evident, most especially in the linked tensions concerning Taiwan and even Sino-American relations. While those doing economic business with China have known it for a while, those in the diplomatic business are learning that talking to a handful of Chinese leaders in Beijing does not provide a sure sense of Chinese policy.[75]

---

72. *Far Eastern Economic Review,* April 27, 1995, p. 28.
73. *Suara Karya* newspaper (in Indonesian) on April 11, 1995, in SWB FE/2277/B2–3. See also tough comments by the armed forces commander cited by *Reuters* on May 31, 1995.
74. *Antara* (Jakarta) newsagency, on July 21, 1995, in SWB FE/2363/B/1–2.
75. Michael Swaine, *China: Domestic Change and Foreign Policy* (Santa Monica: RAND, 1995); Susan Shirk, *The Political Logic of Economic Reform in China* (Berkeley: University of California Press, 1993);

Precisely because Beijing recognizes that the outside world is learning to appreciate the complexity of modern China, there has been a marked tendency for Chinese leaders to resort to increasingly extreme nationalism in order to build unity in a post-ideological age. Chinese, whether they be dissidents or Party bosses, believe that, in the pithy phrase of Geremie Barme, "to screw foreigners is patriotic."[76] And yet many foreigners do not recognize the new nationalism as a sign of China's weakness. It should be recognized that China is an incomplete great power, with all the uncertainties that we learned to live with in the case of that incomplete superpower, the Soviet Union.

Second, is China learning to live with the constraints of interdependence? The optimists would have us believe that it is: witness its eventual signature on the NPT. But even if China is learning, it only does so under serious pressure. It certainly is a slow learner who is far too keen to rewrite the textbooks. China's determination to change the WTO before the WTO changes China is a case of how hard China fights to reject the constraints of economic interdependence. China's behavior in the South China Sea and across the Taiwan Straits in 1995 also suggests either that China does not feel that the fruits of economic interdependence are at risk when it pursues its irredentist agenda or seeks greater international status, or else that these are short-term prices worth paying for a greater good.[77] In short, economic interdependence does not seem to constrain China as much as many might have hoped.

Third, does China bend to pressure? Can it be constrained? It is remarkable how often one hears that we must understand the Chinese point of view in order to recognize why they are unwilling to bend to external pressure. We are told that China is unique and the Chinese strategic culture simply does not operate like that of other powers. According to this notion, China will never play by the rules of international society or be constrained by a balance of power.

But the evidence from East Asia in 1995 suggests a central conclusion of this article, that Chinese behavior can be moderated by concerted pressure. It was

Richard Yang and Gerald Segal, eds., *Chinese Economic Reform and Defence Policy* (London: Routledge, forthcoming 1996).

76. Geremie Barme, "To Screw Foreigners is Patriotic," *China Journal*, No. 34 (July 1995); and Allen Whiting, "Chinese Nationalism and Foreign Policy After Deng," *China Quarterly*, Summer 1995. For an earlier version of the argument see Michel Oksenberg, "China's Confident Nationalism," *Foreign Affairs*, Vol. 65, No. 3 (Winter 1986–87).

77. It is worth noting that in 1995 China shocked those supporting the notion of a Mekong river development zone, and those who thought China was learning to play by the rules of economic interdependence, by suddenly and sharply reducing flows of water to the delta. *The Economist*, November 18, 1995.

fear of such a concert of power that led China to soften its line at the ARF. In earlier years China signed the NPT because the international community kept up the pressure. China does sign arms control agreements—for example with Russia—when it feels it is dealing with a powerful and tough adversary.

China's policy will remain softer only if pressure is maintained. That is a lesson of trade disputes with China, for once the pressure is off, Chinese leaders go back to doing what they want to do. Thus, for example, if the Japanese and others want China to accept a full Comprehensive Test Ban Treaty, they will have to keep forcing China to pay a price in terms of loss of aid if it continues testing or blocking the negotiations. If Indonesia wants to keep its Natuna gas fields, or keep China from threatening Jakarta in order to keep prices low, then Indonesia will have to galvanize its ASEAN colleagues to keep criticizing undesired Chinese actions, and to do so in even clearer terms.

Emphasis on pressuring China and skepticism about the immediate constraining power of economic interdependence are not meant to suggest that it is necessary to embark on a confrontational strategy towards China. The goal is to integrate China into the international system. Most people would like to see a stable, secure, pluralist, and peaceful country. Sadly, China is none of those things at the moment, in part because it has not yet accepted the constraints inherent in real interdependence with the outside world.

A policy intended to constrain China, much like the one that managed relations with the Soviet Union, is intended to tell China that the outside world has interests that will be defended by means of incentives for good behavior, deterrence of bad behavior, and punishment when deterrence fails. In 1995, China was offered only the first element regarding the South China Sea, and hints of the second element. The result was an unconstrained China. In the same year, when China rattled missiles at Taiwan, there was far more deterrence, although the haziness of the signals left China free to carry on threatening Taiwan. On trade issues in 1995, China was forced to improve its terms for entry into the World Trade Organization as the West held firm to its demands. When China faced punishment for violation of intellectual property agreements, it capitulated to American demands. Constrainment of China can work, but its neighbors and powers further afield need to appreciate that they must act in a concerted fashion both to punish and to reward China; they must use elements from a strategy of engagement as well as the balance of power.

Learning to constrain China is a necessity for all great powers, but most immediately for the East Asians. The ASEAN states seem the least prepared for the difficult task. The largest among them, Indonesia, has the most important role in deciding whether ASEAN is Finlandized. Japan, which dominates a very different configuration of power in Northeast Asia, once looked likely to be similarly Finlandized. But in recent years Japan has begun to move, often surprisingly adroitly, to treat China as a risk that must be constrained and trained.

The key to constraining China is of course the United States. But American policy towards China and East Asia has been and still is incoherent. The longer-term indicators are not for anything much better. Of course the United States cannot be expected to "hold the ring" in East Asia unless the states of the region want and help it to do so. Northeast Asians have made some strides in this direction, but Southeast Asians, apart from Indonesia, have not. For the time being, it is the United States that provides the oxygen of security for the maritime states of East Asia. But without a serious debate in East Asia and the United States about how to constrain China, doubts are bound to grow about whether the United States will continue to keep maritime East Asia from asphyxiation.

China's New "Old Thinking"

The Concept of Limited Deterrence

Alastair Iain Johnston

One overlooked aspect of the growth of China's power in recent years is a disturbing set of ideas in the Chinese military about nuclear weapons.[1] Some of these ideas are old, others are new. What has not changed in the post–Cold War era is a deeply rooted hard *realpolitik* worldview that nuclear weapons buy both soft power (international status and influence) and hard power (militarily operational power). What is new are more comprehensive and consistent doctrinal arguments in favor of developing a limited flexible response capability. From the late 1980s on, Chinese strategists have developed a concept of "limited deterrence" (*you xian wei she*) to describe the kind of deterrent China ought to have. While the the concept is still evolving, limited deterrence, according to Chinese strategists, requires sufficient counterforce and countervalue tactical, theater, and strategic nuclear forces to deter the escalation of conventional or nuclear

Alastair Iain Johnston is Assistant Professor of Government at Harvard University, where he is also a Faculty Associate with the Olin Institute of Strategic Studies and the Fairbank Center for East Asian Research.

The author wishes to thank Patrick Garrity and the participants in the Center for National Security Studies Workshop on Regional Nuclear Forces and the Future of Nuclear Weapons, and Karl Eikenberry, Paul Godwin, Lisbeth Gronlund, Harlan Jencks, Stan Norris, Michael Pillsbury, David Shambaugh, David Wright, and especially Tom Christensen for comments, criticism, and input. A number of U.S. and Chinese officials who must remain nameless also deserve much thanks. None of these people is responsible for the analysis.

1. John Lewis's group at Stanford has produced excellent histories of the Chinese nuclear weapons program. See John Wilson Lewis and Xue Litai, *China Builds the Bomb* (Stanford, Calif.: Stanford University Press, 1988); John Wilson Lewis and Hua Di, "China's Ballistic Missile Programs: Technologies, Strategies, Goals," *International Security*, Vol. 17, No. 2 (Fall 1992), pp. 5–36; and John Lewis and Xue Litai, *China's Strategic Seapower: The Politics of Force Modernization in the Nuclear Age* (Stanford, Calif.: Stanford University Press, 1994). Chong-pin Lin has written an important study of nuclear thinking up to the mid-1980s; Lin, *China's Nuclear Weapons Strategy: Tradition within Evolution* (Lexington, Mass.: Lexington Books, 1988). But there are only a handful of articles on doctrinal issues in the late 1980s. See Harlan Jencks, "PRC Nuclear and Space Programs," in Richard Yang, ed., *Yearbook on PLA Affairs 1987* (Kaohsiung: Sun Yat-sen Center for Policy Studies, 1988); Arthur S. Ding, "PLA in the Year 2000: Nuclear Force and Space Program," in Richard Yang, ed., *Yearbook on PLA Affairs 1988–89* (Kaohsiung: Sun Yat-sen Center for Policy Studies, 1989); J. Mohan Malik, "Chinese Debate on Military Strategy: Trends and Portents," *Journal of Northeast Asian Studies*, Vol. 9, No. 2 (Summer 1990), pp. 3–32; and Xue Litai, "Evolution of China's Nuclear Strategy," in John C. Hopkins and Weixing Hu, eds., *Strategic Views from the Second Tier: The Nuclear Weapons Policies of France, Britain, and China* (New Brunswick, N.J.: Transaction, 1995).

International Security, Vol. 20, No. 3 (Winter 1995/96), pp. 5–42

war. If deterrence fails, this capability should be sufficient to control escalation and to compel the enemy to back down.

China does not presently have the operational capabilities to implement this vision of limited deterrence, however. Rather, the doctrine appears to establish a wish-list of capabilities from which Beijing must choose within the economic, technological, and arms control constraints the nuclear program faces. To the extent that these constraints are lifted or modified, China may well pursue the development of forces to suit this doctrine. Whether or not China's leaders decide to "storm" the nuclear program and to double or triple China's quantitative capabilities depends, in part, on perceptions about the credibility of its deterrent in the face of U.S. ballistic missile defense (BMD) systems. Even if there is no surge in the size of Chinese forces, we should expect China to continue the development of more accurate mobile inter-continental ballistic missiles (ICBMs), a limited sub-strategic nuclear missile capability, a larger submarine-launched ballistic missile (SLBM) capability, technologies that will improve the penetrability of warheads in the face of space and ground-based BMD, and the command, control, communications, and intelligence (C^3I) necessary for directing nuclear forces at different levels of nuclear confrontation.

Recent commentary on Chinese nuclear forces has missed many of these doctrinal arguments and has underestimated the degree of innovation going on within the military strategy community in the last eight or so years.[2] Western scholarship on Chinese nuclear thinking has been hampered by a dearth of authoritative materials. But in recent years a relative flood of new, heretofore untapped primary materials published in military journals and books by strategists associated with the Academy of Military Sciences, the National Defense University, the General Staff Department (GSD), and the Strategic Missile Forces (SMF—also known as the Second Artillery), among other military units, has made its way into U.S. university libraries. This article begins to fill the gap in scholarship on Chinese nuclear thinking by looking at the arguments about nuclear doctrine that have appeared in these sources.

The article begins with a brief look at the past and present role of nuclear weapons in Chinese security policy, and then moves to a discussion of the central elements of limited deterrence as defined by Chinese strategists. While conclusions about nuclear thinking in China are necessarily tentative given the intense secrecy that surrounds the nuclear program, the primary materials used

---

2. See, for instance, Hua Di's comments in the *New York Times*, October 26, 1994, p. A10; and Xue, "Evolution of China's Nuclear Strategy."

in this article provide some intriguing insights into the arguments of nuclear strategists.[3] The article then focuses on the gap between the operational requirements of limited deterrence and current Chinese nuclear capabilities, and some of the variables that might affect closure of this gap.

The Role of Nuclear Weapons

China's decision-makers and strategists have displayed a consistently *realpolitik* worldview since 1949. Even as China has become more engaged in international economic and security institutions in the 1980s and 1990s, the preferred ends have predominantly remained the preservation of territorial integrity and foreign policy autonomy, the defense of political power by the communist leadership in Beijing, and the growth of China's influence commensurate with its self-ascribed status as a major power. From this perspective, the world is, in the main, a threatening place where security and material interests are best preserved through self-help or unilateral security.[4] A rich state and a strong army (*fu guo qiang bing*) are inextricably linked, and form the basic road to security.[5]

Given this worldview, China's leaders and strategists alike have been consistently concerned about China's relative military power. Mao Zedong was no strategic Luddite and he believed that China had to reach the most advanced world levels in air, sea, land, and nuclear capabilities in order for China to "stand up" in international politics.[6] Recent writings on nuclear strategy have also made the general point that the greater one's military capabilities, the

3. All translations of titles and quotations in these materials are the author's, unless indicated otherwise.

4. See, for instance, Li Shisheng, "Guanyu guoji xin zhixu ji ge wenti de tan tao" (A preliminary discussion of several problems relating to the new international order), *Shijie jingji yu zhengzhi* (World economics and politics) [hereafter, *Shijie jingji*], No. 10 (1992); Gu Yan, "Duli zizhu shi Mao Zedong waijiao sixiang de linghun" (Independence and autonomy is the spirit of Mao Zedong's foreign policy thinking), *Shijie jingji*, No. 2 (1994); Zhao Huaipu and Lu Yang, "Quanli zhengzhi yu xianghu yicun" (Power politics and interdependence), *Shijie jingji*, No. 7 (1993). For a discussion of the social-Darwinian flavor of Chinese analyses of international economics, see Huang Yasheng, "China in the New International Political Economy: Perspectives and Problems" (Cambridge, Mass.: Harvard Center for International Affairs [CFIA], unpublished ms., 1995).

5. Chen Chongbei, Shou Xiaosong, and Liang Xiaoqiu, *Weishe zhanlue* (Deterrence strategy) (Beijing: Academy of Military Sciences, 1989) pp. 200–205.

6. Song Shilun, *Mao Zedong junshi sixiang de xingcheng ji qi fazhan* (The formation and development of Mao Zedong's military thought) (Beijing: Academy of Military Sciences Press, 1984), pp. 214–215; and Thomas J. Christensen, *Useful Adversaries: Grand Strategy, Domestic Mobilization and Sino-American Conflict, 1947–1958* (Princeton, N.J.: Princeton University Press, forthcoming), chap. 6.

greater the awesomeness of the state, and the more likely one is to determine conflict outcomes to one's advantage.[7]

Given this causal relationship, Chinese leaders and strategists have agreed that nuclear weapons can play a critical role in improving both China's international status and its military power.[8] Nuclear weapons have been seen as a ticket into the major power club. Mao remarked in early 1958, "As for the atomic bomb, this big thing, without it people say you don't count for much. Fine, then we should build some."[9] More recently, one Chinese strategist stated plainly: "If [China] did not have strategic nuclear power, people would look down upon us and our country's major power status would be hard to establish and preserve."[10]

Chinese leaders and strategists have agreed that nuclear weapons, in addition to buying status, have a general military utility. In the 1960s and 1970s, for instance, acquisition decisions were driven in part by a desire to be able to hit specific countervalue and soft counterforce targets.[11] This faith in the military value of nuclear weapons has not wavered much since. In 1983, Deng

7. Liang Minglun and Zhao Youzi, "Shilun wo jun weilai hetong zhanyi zuozhan de zongti gouxiang" (Preliminary discussion of the comprehensive notion of our military's future coordinated war-fighting campaigns), in National Defense University Research Department, ed., *Gao jishu ju bu zhanzheng yu zhanyi zhanfa* (High tech limited war and campaign methods) (Beijing: National Defense University [NDU] Press, 1994) p. 88; Liu Zhenwu and Meng Shaoying, *Xiandai jundui zhihui* (The command of modern military forces) (Beijing: NDU Press, 1993), pp. 408–409.

8. As Mao's comments in a speech to the Politburo in April 1956 implied, nuclear weapons could improve both China's influence and status, as well as its ability to deter the U.S. threat: "If we are not to be bullied in this world, we cannot do without the bomb." Mao Zedong, "On the Ten Major Relationships" (speech April 25, 1956), in *Selected Works of Mao Zedong* (Beijing: People's Publishing House, 1977), Vol. 5, p. 288. As a result, the ballistic missile and nuclear weapons program has been a top priority of the state science, technology, and military bureaucracies, and according to the CIA, consumed about two-thirds of military R&D funds through the late 1970s. See U.S. Central Intelligence Agency, *Chinese Defense Spending, 1965–79* (Washington, D.C.: National Foreign Assessment Center, July 1980), p. 5; and Lewis and Xue, *China Builds the Bomb.*

9. Huang Cisheng and Wang Lincong, "Shilun Mao Zedong de he zhanlue sixiang" (Preliminary discussion of Mao Zedong's thinking on nuclear strategy), in *Quan jun Mao Zedong junshi sixiang xueshu taolun wen jing xuan* (Selected essays from the all-Army academic meeting on Mao Zedong's military thought) (Beijing: Academy of Military Sciences Press, 1992), Vol. 1, p. 602.

10. Su Qianming, "Shilun changgui liliang yu zhanlue he weishe liliang xiang jiehe" (Preliminary discussion of the linkages between conventional power and strategic nuclear deterrence power), in ibid., Vol. 2, p. 566. In the words of a 1993 study on military command, China's nuclear forces are an "important pillar of our country's great power status." Liu and Meng, *Xiandai jundui zhihui*, p. 391. The mere possession of nuclear weapons is not sufficient to bestow major power status, however. Some argued that China had to maintain a level at least comparable to that of other "middle level nuclear powers" (e.g., France and Britain), or else it could lose its important position in the strategic triangle. See Yang Xuhua and Cai Renzhao, *Junshi weishe xue gailun* (Introduction to military deterrence) (Taiyuan: Shuhai Press, 1989) p. 303.

11. Lewis and Hua, "China's Ballistic Missile Programs."

Xiaoping described the basic deterrent effect of nuclear weapons this way: "You have some [nuclear missiles], and we also have some. If you want to destroy us, then you yourself will receive some retaliation."

Even after Deng's "strategic decision" of 1985 that China no longer had to prepare to fight an early, large-scale and nuclear war,[12] and even after the collapse of the Soviet Union in 1991, the military role of nuclear weapons has not changed appreciably in commentary by Chinese strategists. As a recent analysis of military command noted, China's strategic missile forces "enormously strengthen our army's real power and nuclear deterrence capability, and are playing an increasingly important role in carrying out our country's active defense strategy."[13]

The military security value of nuclear weapons, moreover, promises to increase, according to many Chinese strategists. An interagency meeting in February 1987 organized by the General Staff Department's (GSD) chemical defense department[14] concluded that since other states were continuing to develop nuclear and chemical weapons, then nuclear war in the future could not be completely ruled out. China's military had to be prepared to fight under nuclear and chemical warfare conditions, despite the 1985 strategic decision.[15] A 1988 study of limited nuclear war concluded that "nuclear weapons not only cannot be pushed off the stage of warfare, but rather will develop continuously; the question is how to develop the role they will play in future wars."[16]

12. The strategic decision in 1985 codified a more relaxed estimate of the probability of a massive Soviet thrust into China from the north and northwest, based on the expanding Sino-American strategic relationship and improved Sino-Soviet relations.

13. Liu and Meng, *Xiandai jundui zhihui*, p. 391. A study of combined operations noted that "only by possessing a great power to destroy the enemy can we decide the fate of a war, increase the awesomeness of our army and state, and produce a long-term effective deterrent." Liang and Zhao, "Shilun wo jun weilai hetong zhanyi," p. 88. See also Zhang Baotang, "Dui xin shiqi zhanlue daodan budui zhanlue jianshe ji ge wenti de chu tan" (Initial exploration of several questions relating to the strategy for building the Strategic Missile Forces in the new period), in NDU Research Department, Military Construction Research Institute, ed., *Jundui xiandaihua jianshe de sikao* (Thoughts on the building of a modernized military) (Beijing: NDU Press, 1988), p. 412.

14. The GSD chemical defense department handles nuclear, chemical, and biological weapons defense issues, including the nuclear explosion detection network, civil defense activities, and nuclear and chemical de-contamination forces. See General Staff Department Chemical Defense Department, ed., *Fang hua bing shi* (The history of the chemical defense troops) (Beijing: Peoples Liberation Army Press, 1990). Other institutions represented at the meeting included the Ministry of Foreign Affairs (MFA), Ministry of Nuclear Industry, Ministry of Health, the Operations and Intelligence Departments of the GSD, the Academy of Military Sciences (AMS), and the National Defense University.

15. Ibid., p. 182.

16. Hu Yanlin, "Weilai zhanzheng hen keneng shi yi chang you xian he zhanzheng" (The future war could very well be a limited nuclear war), in NDU Curriculum Research Office, ed., *Junshi sixiang luncong* (Essays series on military thought) (Beijing: NDU Press, 1988), p. 373.

Another analyst argued that in the post–Cold War period, improved political relations between the United States and Russia, drastic cuts in their arsenals, and increased attention towards conventional high-tech regional conflicts have all reduced the deterrent value of nuclear weapons for the superpowers. But for medium-size nuclear states, the role of nuclear weapons will increase, since there are inherent contradictions between the interests of these states on the one hand and U.S. hegemony and its vision of a new world order on the other. Moreover, non-nuclear but "nuclear oriented" states will continue their efforts to develop nuclear weapons, and improve their status and bargaining power in regional politics. Thus, by implication, China will continued to need nuclear weapons.[17]

Recent Innovations in Chinese Nuclear Thinking

Given the dearth of open Chinese materials on China's nuclear doctrine and force posture,[18] there has been some debate among Western scholars as to precisely how Chinese strategists have thought about the utility of nuclear weapons. There have been three general views in the West. The first has used "minimum deterrence" to characterize Chinese nuclear doctrine: the Chinese, it is argued, believe that a small number of warheads sufficient to inflict unacceptable damage on a handful of enemy cities constitutes a credible deterrent. China's force structure—by the 1980s relying primarily on around fifty single-warhead, relatively inaccurate inter-continental and intermediate-range ballistic missiles (ICBMs and IRBMs)—could do nothing else.[19] A second view

17. Suo Kaiming, "The Role of Nuclear Weapons on the Future," paper presented to International School on Disarmament and Research on Conflicts [ISODARCO] Beijing Arms Control Seminar, October 1992, pp. 4–7. According to another military author, "following the continuous development and improvement in science and technology, [China] will certainly have the capabilities to approach and catch up to the advanced countries in terms of the quality of nuclear weapons." Su, "Shilun changgui liliang," pp. 565, 568. For a similar exhortation, see Yang and Cai, *Junshi weishe*, p. 306.

18. Lewis and Hua contend that up until the early 1980s, there were very few discussions about strategy to guide technical decisions made by warhead or missile designers. See Lewis and Hua, "China's Ballistic Missile Programs," pp. 5–6. This is confirmed by the small number of articles on nuclear strategy from 1974–87 in *Junshi Xueshu* (Military Studies), an authoritative military journal that is limited to officers at the regiment level and above. See Zhao Qinde and Wu Xianshun eds., *Junshi xueshu suoyin 1974–1987* (Index to *Military Studies*) (Beijing: Academy of Military Sciences, 1988).

19. See Lewis and Hua, "China's Ballistic Missile Programs," p. 21. A senior strategist in the Academy of Social Sciences, Wu Zhan, acknowledged that many Western analysts thought that the term "minimum deterrence" best described Chinese forces. See Wu Zhan, "Shilun zhanlue jingong wuqi" (Preliminary discussion of strategic offensive weapons), in *Meiguo yanjiu cankao*

contends that Chinese strategists have never genuinely accepted minimum deterrence, but instead lean toward some form of limited war-fighting or flexible response.[20] A third view has focused on the "Chineseness" of China's deterrent: China has been deeply influenced by a strategic tradition that stresses minimalism, ambiguity, flexibility, and patience. Thus it has constructed a unique, relatively small proto-triad, has been deliberately ambiguous about targeting and launch doctrine, and has balanced caution and bravado to keep adversaries uncertain about their ability to achieve nuclear or conventional victory.[21]

Fueling this debate was the public propensity of Chinese officials and strategists to reject the term "deterrence" as a description of what Chinese nuclear forces were supposed to do. Even today, some Chinese strategists still insist that China does not practice deterrence but adheres to a doctrine of "defense" (*fangyu*) or "self-protection" (*zi wei*).[22] And behind the public discourse, when

---

ziliao (Reference materials on American studies), No. 7 (1985). A senior official in the Ninth Academy, the institute in charge of nuclear weapon design, used the term to describe Chinese forces in comments at the 1994 ISODARCO Beijing Arms Control Seminar. For other characterizations that essentially describe minimum deterrence, see Robert Sutter, "Chinese Nuclear Weapons and Arms Control Policies: Implications and Options for the United States," Congressional Research Service, Report for Congress, March 25, 1994, pp. 14–15; and Alastair I. Johnston, "Chinese Nuclear Force Modernization: Implications for Arms Control," *Journal of Northeast Asian Studies*, Vol. 2, No. 2 (June 1983) pp. 13–28.

20. See Jencks, "PRC Nuclear Programs"; Malik, "Chinese Debate"; and Paul Godwin, "Changing Concepts of Doctrine, Strategy and Operations in the Chinese People's Liberation Army, 1978–1987," *China Quarterly*, No. 112 (December 1987), pp. 584–587.

21. Lin, *China's Nuclear Strategy*.

22. Avery Goldstein reports that in his conversations with Chinese analysts in 1991 they insisted that deterrence was hegemonistic in character since it involved the threat of force to compel an adversary to act in a way that was contrary to its interests. See Avery Goldstein, "Robust and Affordable Security: Some Lessons from the Second-Ranking Powers During the Cold War," *Journal of Strategic Studies*, Vol. 15, No. 4 (December 1992), p. 516. See also Chen Peiyao, "Ze yang kandai he weishe zhanlue" (How should we approach nuclear deterrence strategy?), in *Shijie jingji*, No. 5 (1987) pp. 39–44; Sun Xiangming, "Zhanlue lilun ji ge wenti zhi wo jian" (My views on several questions in strategic theory), *Zhongguo junshi kexue* (Chinese military sciences), No. 3 (1990), in *Renmin daxue, Fuyin baokan ziliao—junshi* (People's University reproduced periodical materials—military affairs) [hereafter *Fuyin baokan ziliao—junshi*], No. 6 (1990), pp. 65–66; and Hu Guangzheng and Xiao Xiandu, *Yingxiang dao ershiyi shiji de zhengming* (Contention that will have influence into the 21st century) (Beijing: Peoples Liberation Army Press, 1989), pp. 139–140. However, from the late 1980s on, particularly in internal circulation materials, Chinese strategists increasingly used "deterrence" to characterize the mission of Chinese forces. See Chen Weimin, "Weishe lilun yu guofang jianshe" (Deterrence theory and national defense construction), *Shijie jingji*, No. 3 (1989), p. 47. A recent book on the U.S.-Soviet arms race and arms control noted plainly: "Capitalist states use deterrence, socialist states use deterrence; large states use it, medium and small states use it. We must not only not oppose, but must also take advantage of nuclear deterrence that is favorable for peace and development." Wang Yang, ed., *Mei Su junbei jingsai yu kongzhi yanjiu* (Research in the U.S.-Soviet arms race and arms control) (Beijing: Academy of Military Sciences Press, 1993), p. 172.

"deterrence" was used, there was a fair degree of ambiguity about what the term meant when used to characterize Chinese nuclear doctrine.

In the last few years, however, in a range of newly available materials published in "internal circulation" military journals and books, one can now discern the outlines of a rough consensus about nuclear doctrine, a consensus that is closer to the second group of Western analyses. Around 1987, the Strategic Missile Forces began to redress the neglect of research on doctrine by starting up a nuclear campaign theory (*zhanyi lilun*) research program that focused on detailed operational issues.[23] Around the same time, the Chinese Navy's Military Studies Research Institute conducted studies on the use of SLBMs for retaliation singly or in coordination with the SMF's ICBMs.[24] Out of these and other research programs has come an emerging agreement that China should rely on what is now termed "limited nuclear deterrence" (*you xian he weishe*). Chinese strategists now explicitly distinguish "limited deterrence" from "minimum deterrence" and from what they sometimes call "maximum deterrence" (e.g., counterforce war-fighting doctrines of the United States and the Soviet Union). In limited deterrence, nuclear weapons play a critical role in the deterrence of both conventional and nuclear wars as well as in escalation control (intrawar deterrence) if deterrence fails. In other words, nuclear weapons have a wider utility than proponents of minimum deterrence would suggest. The deterrent and war-fighting value of nuclear weapons, in the eyes of these strategists, has not declined over the past decades, but has, in fact, increased. These arguments are based on two major sets of assumptions, namely, that the advent of nuclear weapons does not fundamentally change the nature of warfare, and that deterrence rests on the operational usability of nuclear weapons. What follows is an analysis of these assumptions, after which I discuss how these assumptions are embodied in the operational concepts of limited deterrence.

---

23. These included military technology development and its effects on nuclear counterattacks, the character and form of nuclear counterattacks, applications of nuclear firepower, the command and control of nuclear campaigns, the political and logistical aspects of nuclear campaigns, training exercises for nuclear campaigns, the defense and survivability of nuclear capabilities, and the principles and methods of the adversary's nuclear attack. See Liu Tieqing, Rong Jiaxin, and Chang Jinan, "Zhanlue daodan budui zhanyi lilun tixi chuyi" (Our views on the structure of the campaign theory of the Strategic Missile Forces), in NDU Research Department, ed., *Zhanyi jiben lilun xintan* (New explorations of the basic theory of campaigns) (Beijing: NDU Press, 1989), pp. 323–324.
24. See Jiang Shenggong, "Dui haijun zhanyi xue lilun tixi de sixiang" (Thinking about the structure of the theory of naval campaigns), in ibid., pp. 206–207.

A NUCLEAR REVOLUTION?

In contrast to U.S. proponents of the assured-destruction concept of deterrence, most of the Chinese strategists who write on nuclear questions explicitly reject the notion that nuclear weapons have overturned Clausewitz's axiom that warfare is the continuation of politics. They accurately note the arguments of the nuclear revolutionists that since nuclear war will be too difficult to control, and since the outcomes are so horrific for all states, there can be no political purpose for which nuclear weapons would be worth using (as opposed to wielding), but then they will go on to criticize this normative argument on three grounds, one descriptive, one political, and one military.[25]

Descriptively, according to some Chinese strategists, the causes of nuclear war and its consequences are not directly linked. The causes of nuclear war exist objectively (interstate conflict, the aggressiveness of hegemonism, etc.) and are necessarily political since the decision to use nuclear weapons would have to be motivated by some political choice or goal. The consequences of nuclear war are a result of such variables as technology, command skills, and geography.[26] Thus, whether a state can objectively achieve its political goals through nuclear war, *and* whether a state is motivated by political goals when using nuclear weapons, are two different things. The latter possibility still exists and thus Clausewitz's axiom cannot be overturned.[27]

Politically, the anti-Clausewitzian view of nuclear weapons leads to "blind opposition" to nuclear weapons, according to one analyst. This ignores the

---

25. See Xia Zhengnan, "He zhanzheng bu zai shi zhengzhi de jixu le ma?" (Is nuclear war not the continuation of politics?), *Zhongguo junshi kexue* (Chinese military science), No. 2 (1989), reprinted in *Fuyin baokan ziliao—junshi*, No. 10 (1989), p. 30. For a minority voice in defense of the nuclear revolution view, see Zhao Qinxuan, "Shilun he zhanzheng bu zai shi zhengzhi de jixu" (Preliminary discussion on nuclear war not being a continuation of politics), *Waiguo junshi xueshu* (Foreign military studies), No. 2 (1989), reprinted in *Fuyin baokan ziliao—junshi*, No. 5 (1989), pp. 17–19.
26. Wang Pufeng and Guo Shanyi, "He zhanzheng be keneng gaibian 'zhanzheng shi zhengzhi de jixu' de yuanli" (Nuclear war cannot change the basic principle that 'war is a continuation of politics'), *Zhongguo junshi kexue* (Chinese military science), No. 3 (1990), in *Fuyin baokan ziliao—junshi*, No. 6 (1990), pp. 43–46; Zhao Fusheng and Zhang Chengliang, "He zhanzheng yu zhengzhi guanxi de sikao" (Thoughts on the relationship between nuclear war and politics), in *Quan jun Mao Zedong junshi sixiang*, Vol. 1, pp. 592–594; Liu Kaitong, "Suowei he shidai luoji yu dang jin shijie xianshi" (So-called 'logic of the nuclear age' and present world reality), in *Shijie jingji*, No. 12 (1990), p. 34.
27. Fang Diansheng, "He wuqi de faming he shiyong gaibian bu liao zhanzheng de zhengzhi benzhi" (The invention and use of nuclear weapons cannot change the political nature of war), in NDU Curriculum Research Office, ed., *Junshi sixiang luncong* (Essay series on military thought), (Beijing: NDU Press, 1988), pp. 47–48.

objective fact that nuclear weapons exist and that "the complete destruction of nuclear weapons is already impossible."[28]

Militarily, the critique goes, the opponents of Clausewitz's dictum exaggerate the uncontrollability of nuclear war and thus undermine the credibility of deterrence threats. If a state is incapable of using nuclear weapons short of provoking mutual suicide, then deterrence threats are not credible.[29] The implication is, then, that credible deterrence at least assumes that nuclear war is controllable and thus, logically, that there are achievable political goals in nuclear war. Some strategists point to the Gulf War as a good example of the political utility of nuclear weapons: one Chinese analysis asserts that the United States deployed 800–900 nuclear weapons against Iraq, and that usability provided a deterrent effect that conventional weapons could not have replaced.[30]

The predominant view appears to be that the nuclear revolution does not by itself eliminate the possibility that states (including China) can use nuclear weapons in wartime for achievable political ends. Chinese strategists rebut the normative argument that nuclear weapons are unusable with a descriptive argument that exhibits little sensitivity to the paradoxes of nuclear deterrence or to its technical and political fragility.

WHAT DETERS?

There is still some ambiguity among Chinese strategists about what deters a nuclear attack in the first place.[31] In discussions of the U.S.-Soviet "balance of terror," one often finds the argument that the credible threat of inflicting unacceptable damage on the enemy is, in principle, the source of deterrence. Often a discussion of deterrence begins by citing Henry Kissinger on the three main elements of deterrence: the capability to inflict unacceptable damage, the

---

28. Zhang Jianzhi, "Dui caijun jiben lilun wenti de tantao" (Preliminary investigation of questions concerning the basic theory of disarmament), in *Guoji caijun douzheng yu Zhongguo* (China and the international disarmament struggle) (Beijing: Current Affairs Press, 1987), p. 52.

29. Wang and Guo, "He zhanzheng be keneng gaibian," p. 43.

30. Liu Mingshou and Yang Chengjun, *Gao jishu zhanzheng zhong de daodan zhan* (Missile warfare in high-tech wars) (Beijing: NDU Press, 1993), p. 177.

31. The Chinese term for deterrence—*wei she*—is ambiguous. It literally means to use awesomeness, or latent power, to terrorize. Often the concept is described by a four character idiom—*yin er bu fa*—meaning to "draw the bow but not shoot." This leaves two somewhat contradictory impressions. One is of massive, undifferentiated, virtually automatic retaliation—an image closer to assured destruction visions of deterrence. The other is a threat of accurately targeted, precise, almost surgical violence—an image closer to war-fighting notions of deterrence.

will to do so, and the clear communication of both capabilities and will.[32] However, when it comes to more detailed discussions of how to communicate a credible deterrent threat, the arguments have moved in two different directions.

One view is essentially similar to what Robert Powell calls the "spectrum of risk." Drawing from Thomas Schelling's concept of "threats that leave something to chance," Powell argues that one way to make credible an otherwise incredible threat to commit mutual suicide through nuclear retaliation is for a state to threaten to take discretely rational moves that increase the probability that subsequent moves may lead to mutual destruction. In other words, if state A relies on a spectrum of risk, it must act in ways which *could* begin an unravelling process. Whether this unravelling occurs depends on state B's reaction to this initial move. The fear that "explosive escalation" might occur through incrementally risky steps would make the implicit deterrent threat more credible.[33]

Chinese strategists are not as explicit as Schelling and Powell about the manipulation of risk. However, in the past this may have been China's implicit approach to deterrence. Chinese strategists may have believed that rhetorical bravado and apparently risk-acceptant behavior in the face of superior U.S. and Soviet capabilities communicated a willingness to begin a confrontational sequence that might spin out of control should the other side persist in challenging China. In some of the more recent writings on nuclear strategy, there are also hints of this sort of deterrence calculus. Usually this entails a recognition that nuclear war is hard to control, and that once the nuclear threshold has been crossed, a full-scale nuclear war could easily break out.[34] A more explicit version of this contends that the automation of nuclear responses, due to the need for a rapid response at the earliest warning of a nuclear attack, increases the chance of miscalculation.[35] The implication, then, is that deterrence may rest on the initiation of risk-acceptant behavior, which could plausibly lead confrontation past the nuclear threshold.

---

32. Liu, Rong, and Chang, "Zhanlue daodan budui," p. 326.
33. Robert Powell, "The Theoretical Foundations of Strategic Nuclear Deterrence," *Political Science Quarterly*, Vol. 100, No. 1 (Spring 1985), pp. 75–96.
34. Fang, "He wuqi de faming he shiyong," pp. 45–46; Sang Zhonglin and Xiao Kaishi, "Wo jun zhanyi lilun de yanjiu ying zeng qiang 'he guannian'" (We must strengthen the 'nuclear concept' in our army's campaign theory), in NDU Research Department, *Zhanyi jiben lilun xintan*, p. 802.
35. Chen, "Ze yang kandai he weishe," p. 43.

The second and more common view about what deters comes closer to Powell's notion of "the spectrum of violence." In this case the possibility of explosive escalation is assumed to be low because nuclear war is assumed to be controllable. Instead, side B is deterred when it comes to believe that side A can bear as much or more pain or destruction than B.[36] Deterrence is achieved by both punishment and denial; that is, threats to inflict future pain on B (made credible by the destruction already inflicted and received by A) also imply that A will escalate to the point where B is denied victory.

Again, Chinese strategists are not this explicit about spectrum-of-violence thinking. But a number emphasize that deterrence rests on a credible ability to fight an actual nuclear war (*shi zhan nengli*). "Without the prerequisite that nuclear weapons could possibly be used in a real war, then nuclear weapons cannot be political tools and have deterrent value. If we do not have the determination and real capability to dare implement a nuclear attack on the enemy through powerful retaliation, then our nuclear power loses its deterrent value in constraining the outbreak of nuclear war."[37] Another study of military strategy notes simply that the greater the applied warfare capabilities of a state, the greater the deterrent effect. If deterrence breaks down, then one must resort to the operational use of nuclear weapons to deter further escalation, and to "strive to fight and win a nuclear war" (*li zheng da ying he zhanzheng*).[38] This means having the ability and will to do everything from intimidating the enemy through deployments, exercises, and tests, to selectively injuring the enemy and incrementally increasing psychological pressure on it, to irreparably damaging its ability to fight, escalate, or prolong nuclear war.[39] War deterrence fails when a state's war-fighting capability is weak or doubted by the enemy; intrawar

---

36. Powell, "Theoretical Foundations," p. 81.
37. Zhao and Zhang, "He zhanzheng," p. 592. See also Hu and Xiao, *Yingxiang dao ershiyi shiji*, p. 143; Wang Wenrong, Ma Bao'an, and Liu Hongji, "Mudi, fangshi, liliang: wo guo xin shiqi junshi zhanlue de san ge jiben wenti" (Goals, methods, and strength: three basic questions in our country's military strategy in the new period), *Guofang daxue xuebao* (NDU Journal), No. 1 (1989) in *Fuyin baokan ziliao—junshi*, No. 4 (1989), pp. 47–48.
38. Peng Guangqian and Wang Guangxu, *Junshi zhanlue jianlun* (A brief discussion of military strategy) (Beijing: Peoples Liberation Army Press, 1989), pp. 160; see also pp. 84–85.
39. Guan Jixian, *Gao jishu jubu zhanzheng zhanyi* (Campaigns in high tech limited wars) (Beijing: NDU Press, 1993), p. 43. See also Liu and Meng, *Xiandai jundui zhihui*, p. 410, and Lin Zhaochong, "Xiandai weishe zhanlue man tan" (Informal discussion of modern deterrence strategy), in Academy of Military Sciences Strategy Department, eds., *Hua shuo zhanlue* (Talking about strategy) (Beijing: Academy of Military Sciences Press, 1987), pp. 59–60.

deterrence fails when a state does not have the capacity to continue to inflict damage on the enemy.[40] In essence, compellent actions have deterrent effects.

The second view predominates in Chinese writings on nuclear deterrence, but it has in common with the first view that deterrence should not be mutual. In other words, for deterrent threats to be credible, China cannot be deterred or perceived to be deterred by the adversary's threats. In an interesting appropriation of historical language to "Sinify" the concept, some Chinese strategists claim that the goal of deterrence is, in Sun Zi's words, "to defeat the enemy without fighting."[41] The use of this phrase implies that deterrence is one-sided, and that it can have active political payoffs (compellent effects) rather than merely passive ones (deterrent effects). This is a very different image than the one that U.S. theorists of assured destruction have used to describe deterrence, that of two people in a roomful of gasoline, each holding matches. It would seem, then, that many Chinese strategists view deterrence as the product of a very real ability to inflict damage on the enemy in a competitive nuclear duel. They are, apparently, uncomfortable with the assured destruction notion of deterrence.

LIMITED DETERRENCE, LIMITED WAR-FIGHTING

Chinese writings reveal a bewildering array of classifications and typologies of deterrence.[42] Only a handful of these, however, have been used explicitly to describe China's deterrent: defensive, self-defensive, minimum, eclectic, and limited. The consensus appears now to be, however, that "minimum deterrence" does not describe what Chinese forces are supposed to do. Rather the preferred term is "limited deterrence."

---

40. One discussion of conventional limited war that parallels the nuclear discourse notes that counterattacks or actions designed to "teach a lesson" all have intrawar deterrence effects; they convince the enemy of China's willingness and ability to inflict further damage. See Wang Houqing, Wang Chaotian, and Huang Dafu, *Ju bu zhanzheng zhong de zhanyi* (Campaigns in limited wars) (Beijing: NDU Press, 1990), pp. 97–98.

41. Chen, "Ze yang kandai he weishe," pp. 40–42; Xu Guangyu, *He zhanlue zongheng* (The ins and outs of nuclear strategy) (Beijing: NDU Press, 1987), p. 358; Liu Huaqiu, "Sun Zi Bing Fa yu dang dai he weishe" (Sun Zi's *Art of War* and contemporary nuclear deterrence), paper presented to the Second International Symposium on Sun Zi's *Art of War*, Beijing, October 1990.

42. I have come across at least 20 types: offensive, defensive, passive, active, punitive, positive, immediate, general, strong, medium, weak, minimum, maximum, assured, self-defensive, offensively defensive, superior, balanced, eclectic, and limited. See, for instance, Liu, "Sun Zi Bing Fa"; Lin, "Xiandai weishe"; Zhang, "Dui caijun jiben lilun"; Yang and Cai, *Junshi weishe;* and Peng and Wang, *Junshi zhanlue.*

For Chinese strategists, minimum deterrence requires only the ability to carry out a simple, undifferentiated countervalue second strike. The adversary's people and social wealth are held hostage, and the fear of unacceptable damage deters any first strike. Any measures that might reduce the destructiveness of nuclear war are destabilizing. A very few warheads, anywhere from a handful to several tens, are sufficient; thus a state that accepts minimum deterrence readily accepts qualitative and quantitative inferiority.[43] A number of Chinese strategists now explicitly reject minimum deterrence as a viable option for China. The main argument is that minimum deterrence capabilities are in practice too vulnerable to a disarming first strike, and thus have little deterrence value. Moreover, a minimum countervalue assured second-strike capability is useless for controlling any escalatory competition or for achieving intrawar deterrence. "A number of people have the view that one only needs a few nuclear weapons to scare people and that is sufficient. This view is a product of a lack of understanding of the real meaning of nuclear deterrence and the relationship between nuclear deterrence and actual warfighting; it is biased and harmful and we ought to take the lead and correct it."[44]

At the other end of the spectrum is what Chinese strategists call maximum deterrence. This essentially describes what Chinese analysts believe are the characteristics of U.S. and Soviet nuclear doctrine. This doctrine maintains that since it is difficult to determine what the adversary may consider unacceptable countervalue damage, in order to deter one has to have superior war-fighting and war-winning capabilities. The goal is to develop a first-strike advantage such that in a crisis one can eliminate enemy capabilities while reducing one's own losses.[45] Chinese strategists reject this doctrinal orientation for both political and technological reasons: this is the strategy pursued by hegemonistic powers and contravenes China's commitment to No First Use (NFU);

---

43. Peng and Wang, *Junshi zhanlue*, p. 160; Lin, "Xiandai weishe," p. 50. This conceptualization essentially parallels what some have called the assured destruction school. Charles Glaser, "Why Do Strategists Disagree about the Requirements of Strategic Nuclear Deterrence?" in Lynn Eden and Steven E. Miller, eds., *Nuclear Arguments: Understanding the Strategic Nuclear Arms and Arms Control Debates* (Ithaca, N.Y.: Cornell University Press, 1989). See also Robert Jervis, *The Meaning of the Nuclear Revolution: Statecraft and the Prospect of Armageddon* (Ithaca, N.Y.: Cornell University Press, 1989), p. 75.
44. Liu and Meng, *Xiandai jundui zhihui*, p. 409. See also Zhang, "Dui caijun jiben lilun," pp. 56–57.
45. Peng and Wang, *Junshi zhanlue*, p. 161; Zhang, "Dui caijun jiben lilun," pp. 56–57. This description parallels the arguments of the damage-limitation school in the United States. See Glaser, "Why Do Strategists Disagree," p. 113.

moreover, China does not have the economic or technological wherewithal to build this kind of deterrent.[46]

Between these two extremes stands limited deterrence, the preferred descriptive term used by Chinese strategists. The term appeared as early as 1987. At that time its definition did not differ much in character from minimum deterrence. One strategist contended, for example, that limited deterrence was suitable for economically and technologically weak states. The ability to inflict unacceptable damage with a few hundred warheads aimed at enemy cities "and other targets" was sufficient.[47] Another noted that the goal of limited (also called eclectic) deterrence was to develop a mutually assured destruction second-strike capability and thus maintain strategic stability.[48]

Over time, however, Chinese strategists have drawn the distinctions between minimum and limited deterrence much more sharply and have given the latter a distinctly limited counterforce–war-fighting flavor. A number of Chinese strategists now argue that a limited deterrent means having enough capabilities to deter conventional, theater, and strategic nuclear war, and to control and suppress escalation during a nuclear war. That is, a limited deterrent should be able to respond to any level or type of attack from tactical to strategic, and the initial response should be calibrated to the scope of the initial attack.[49] Limited deterrence thinking appears to entertain war-winning possibilities. War-winning *does not* mean achieving complete political-military victory over an adversary at any level of violence and dictating political terms at the end of war, but it does mean inflicting enough counterforce and countervalue damage on the enemy such that it backs down and is thus denied victory.

The war-fighting orientation of limited deterrence is obvious from the list of targets that Chinese strategists consider appropriate. The consensus seems to be that China's limited deterrent ought to be able to hit a range of countervalue and hard and soft counterforce targets. The authors of one recent study on modern military command argued, for example, that China's SMF had the following wartime operational tasks:

---

46. Chen, "Weishe lilun," pp. 49–50.
47. Lin, "Xiandai weishe," p. 50.
48. Zhang, "Dui caijun jiben lilun," pp. 56–57. There was some confusion in Zhang's analysis about deterrence. In places he implied that China's "eclectic" (*zhezhong*) deterrent belongs in the assured second-strike category of strategies (p. 53). Elsewhere, however, he implied that war-fighting strategies—a different category—were examples of "active defense," a term used to describe China's overall military orientation (p. 59).
49. Peng and Wang, *Junshi zhanlue*, p. 162; Xu, *He zhanlue zongheng*, p. 368.

- to strike enemy strategic missile bases and weapons stockpiles, major naval and air bases, heavy troop concentrations, and strategic reserve forces, and thus destroy the enemy's strategic attack capabilities;
- to strike at the enemy's threater through strategic political and military command centers and communication hubs, thereby weakening its administrative and command capabilities;
- to strike the enemy's strategic warning and defense systems;
- to strike the enemy's rail hubs, bridges, and other important targets in its transportation networks;
- to strike basic industrial and military industrial targets;
- to strike selectively at several political and economic centers so as to create social chaos; and
- to launch warning strikes in order to undermine the enemy's will to launch nuclear strikes, and thereby contain nuclear escalation.[50]

These are very different and much more demanding targets than those for minimum deterrence. To hit these and to retain the ability to engage in protracted escalation suppression, a limited deterrent would require far more than a handful of inaccurate second-strike warheads. Indeed, Chinese strategists argue that it requires a greater number of smaller, more accurate, survivable, and penetrable ICBMs; SLBMs as countervalue retaliatory forces; tactical and theater nuclear weapons to hit battlefield and theater military targets and to suppress escalation; ballistic missile defense to improve the survivability of the limited deterrent; space-based early warning and command and control systems; and anti-satellite weapons (ASATs) to hit enemy military satellites.[51]

---

50. See Liu and Meng, *Xiandai jundui zhihui*, pp. 392, 401, 405. For similar target lists, see also Yang and Cai, *Junshi weishe*, pp. 304–305; Liu, Rong, and Chang, "Zhanlue daodan budui," pp. 322, 328; Academy of Military Sciences, *Junshi zhanlue* (Military strategy) (Beijing: Academy of Military Sciences Press, 1987), p. 235; Guan, *Gao jishu jubu zhanzheng*, p. 112. This list suggests that Xue is inaccurate in arguing that China's strategists are only interested in "area targeting theory." Xue, "Evolution of China's Nuclear Strategy," p. 180.

51. See Liu and Yang, *Gao jishu zhanzheng*, pp. 170–171; Liu, Rong, and Chang, "Zhanlue daodan budui," p. 330; Liu Jixian, Wang Tangying, and Huang Shuofeng, *Guofang fazhan zhanlue gailun* (Introduction to national defense development strategy) (Beijing: NDU Press, 1989), p. 161; Song Zhi, "Ben shijie mo ge zhuyao guojia de junshi zhanlue he women de duice" (The military strategy of each major state at the end of this century and our countermeasures), in Academy of Military Sciences Operations Analysis Research Department, ed., *Guoji xingshi yu guoji zhanlue* (The international situation and international strategy) (Beijing: Academy of Military Sciences Press, 1987), p. 73. There has probably been some debate as to the relative priority among these systems for limited deterrence. Song Zhi argued that most of China's new missiles should be placed on SLBMs. Others argue that a limited deterrent should rely on mobile land-base systems, making use of smaller warheads and improved reaction times. See Liu, Rong, and Chang, "Zhanlue daodan

Limited deterrence also suggests a launch strategy that puts a premium on destroying as many enemy military capabilities as possible before these are used (or at least as many as is necessary to deny the enemy victory). This creates tension with China's official no-first-use (NFU) pledge, made in 1964 after its first nuclear test. Given quantitatively inferior capabilities, a political goal of denying the adversary victory, and a target set that includes the adversary's nuclear weapons, command and control and other point targets, it would make sense militarily to strike first in a crisis. While some strategists note that the NFU pledge carries political image benefits—it means, for instance, that China's retaliatory use of nuclear weapons would be justified in world opinion—many also appear to believe it is a considerable military handicap. Strategists with the SMF Command College have argued that, in comparison to the superpowers, NFU gives China's capabilities a "passive nature," among other quantitative and qualitative weaknesses.[52] The NFU pledge leads to an emphasis on detecting and surviving an initial counterforce strike—hence the importance of early warning, dispersal, and concealment, and the utter lack of transparency on the size of China's forces.[53] Very often one finds strategists arguing abstractly in favor of first strikes in conventional and nuclear war, even while claiming that China is committed to a second strike posture (*hou fa zhi ren*).[54]

That a number of Chinese strategists chafe at the possible operational restrictions imposed by NFU is obvious from several discussions of the ideal timing of China's "nuclear counterattack" (*he fanji*). These analysts stress that the first response to an attack must be immediate and extremely rapid. While this is a reaction to an aggressive action taken by the enemy, it is not at all clear that China's forces should wait until this initial action is complete. In other words, there are intriguing hints of interest in launch-on-warning or launch-under-early attack.

This is the import of comments on the operational responsibilities of the SMF in an authoritative work on strategy compiled by the Strategy Department of the Academy of Military Sciences with input from, among other units, the

budui," p. 330; Liu and Yang, *Gao jishu zhanzheng,* p. 173; Zhang Jinxi and Wang Xiancun, "Mao Zedong junshi sixiang yu wo guo de he zhanlue lilun" (Mao Zedong military thought and our country's theory of nuclear strategy), *Junshi Zhishi* (Military knowledge), No. 5 (1988), reprinted in *Fuyin baokan ziliao—junshi,* No. 8 (1988), p. 18.

52. Liu, Rong, and Chang, "Zhanlue daodan budui," pp. 328–329.

53. Sang and Xiao, "Wo jun zhanyi lilun," pp. 806–807.

54. Guan, *Gao jishu jubu zhanzheng,* pp. 110–111.

Operations Department of the GSD and the SMF: "On the basis of the general policy of second strike, the nuclear counterattack of the future will be implemented through a nuclear counterstrike campaign after the enemy's nuclear surprise attack. The first nuclear counterattack must strive to be immediate retaliation, that is, [we must] react quickly, and rapidly implement a nuclear counterattack after determining the enemy's missiles are coming, but before they have exploded."[55] Elsewhere the authors note, "second strike does not by any means imply passively suffering a beating. We must not wait until after the enemy's nuclear weapons explode, leaving confusion everywhere, before carrying out a nuclear counterattack."[56] One source calculated that with an early warning system that could give real-time intelligence of an enemy's launch, China could have as much as twenty minutes in which to launch its own missiles before enemy missiles hit.[57]

Other strategists appear to favor a more obviously preemptive operational doctrine. Recently, for instance, one analyst argued that ideally a state's "first strategic surprise attack" (*shou ci zhanlue tu ji*) should take place some time after the first two to three days of a crisis, and that a nuclear surprise attack within a general nuclear counterattack should take place in six or so hours. This counterattack should take place in three waves. The first would use ICBMs, SLBMs, and theater missiles and be aimed at enemy strategic missile forces and other targets deep in the enemy's rear areas. The second wave should use light bombers and nuclear strike aircraft to hit the enemy's shallow rear forces along with targets in the war theater. The final wave should use long-range nuclear bombers to attack the enemy's deep rear targets again. In a nuclear war, the first task of a strategic surprise attack is to "eradicate the

---

55. Academy of Military Sciences, *Junshi zhanlue*, pp. 115–116. Goldstein and Lin argue that China's launch doctrine might be "launch at any uncertain time"—days, weeks, even months, after an initial attack. This would induce sufficient uncertainty in the aggressor about the efficacy of its strike as to have a deterrent effect. See Goldstein, "Robust and Affordable Security"; and Lin, *China's Nuclear Strategy*. Similarly, Xue contends that the Chinese are uninterested in developing a launch-on-warning capability. See Xue, "Evolution of China's Nuclear Strategy," p. 180. However, the evidence here suggests that many strategists in the late 1980s and 1990s rejected these arguments on the grounds that the basis of deterrence is a real and communicated ability to fight and to inflict costly counterforce damage quickly in a nuclear conflict.
56. Academy of Military Sciences, *Junshi zhanlue*, p. 235. One analyst, referring to war in general, argued that China must flexibly apply the second-strike principle, with specific emphasis on "exploiting the first opportunity to defeat the enemy" (*xian ji zhi ren*). See Chen Huiban, "Guanyu xin shiqi zhanlue fangzhen he zhidao yuanze wenti" (Concerning questions relating to the guiding principles and strategic policies of the new period), in *Guofang daxue xuebao* (NDU Journal), in *Fuyin baokan ziliao—junshi*, No. 3 (1989), p. 28. Chinese strategists have noted that France's refusal to adopt NFU strengthens its deterrent by keeping enemies guessing as to its response to a conventional attack. See Lin, "Xiandai weishe zhanlue," pp. 56–57.
57. Liu and Meng, *Xiandai jundui zhihui*, p. 400.

enemy's nuclear surprise attack weapons and thus obtain nuclear superiority and strategic initiative. To this end the most important strategic objective becomes surprise-attacking the opponent's strategic missile bases, taking out its nuclear weapons aircraft and their bases, and nuclear submarines and related naval bases."[58] Still others argue disingenuously that a first strike on an enemy whose attack is imminent is still a retaliatory, second-strike act. One strategist noted, for instance, "As for the SMF's warfighting, in reality it is a counterstrike under nuclear conditions or *under nuclear threat*."[59]

Components of a Limited Deterrence Capability

In addition to articulating the general outlines of a limited flexible counterforce war-fighting doctrine, over the last few years Chinese strategists have explored in more detail some of the key requirements for this kind of deterrent, namely space technologies and weapons, ballistic missile defense, theater and tactical weapons, and civil defense.

SPACE

Some Chinese strategists contend that space will become a fourth leg in any nuclear capabilities. China will therefore need space-based early warning capabilities to speed up the reaction time of its limited deterrent: ASATs (both space-based and air-launched) to hit enemy military satellites, which are becoming increasingly important in directing nuclear and conventional campaigns; and space-based ballistic missile defense systems in order to increase the survivability of Chinese nuclear forces.[60] These strategists have already

58. Guan, *Gao jishu jubu zhanzheng*, pp. 112–113; emphasis added. The evidence indicates that some military strategists would prefer to avoid the NFU constraint. This suggests there is less consensus behind the value of NFU than Xue contends. Xue, "Evolution of China's Nuclear Strategy," p. 180.
59. Wang Xiancun, "Mao Zedong renmin zhanzheng sixiang zai zhanlue daodan budui zuozhan zhong de yunyong" (The application of Mao's thinking on peoples' war in the operations of the Strategic Missile Forces), in *Quan jun Mao Zedong junshi sixiang*, Vol. 1, p. 595, emphasis added. This argument is consistent with Chinese definitions of active defense in conventional conflicts. As one study of active defense noted, China's operations against Vietnam in 1979 were militarily offensive, but politically defensive. "[A] strategic counterattack carries the implications of a strategic offensive. From a political perspective, it makes more sense and is more advantageous not to call it 'attack' but to call it a 'counterattack'." See Zhang Jing and Yao Yanjin, *Jiji fangyu zhanlue qianshuo* (An introduction to the active defense strategy) (Beijing: Liberation Army Publishing House, 1985), p. 137. A recent analysis of limited war argued that the best time for a "counterattack" was when the enemy was preparing to launch an attack but before its planes and missiles had left the ground. Guan, *Gao jishu jubu zhanzheng*, pp. 141, 23–24.
60. One recent analysis obliquely remarked, "These kinds of weapons are not just in the hands of the superpowers; lots of middle-ranked states have research and development programs of considerable scale." Zhang Yinnan and Zhao Xu, "Gao jishu zhanzheng de tedian" (Special characteristics of high tech war), in NDU Research Department, ed., *Gao jishu ju bu zhanzheng*, p. 27.

begun to think in more detail about what a space capability should look like. One plan envisions the creation of a space warfare headquarters, with a space warfare political department, science and technology department, and logistics department. This command center would control a system of space stations and bases; a war-fighting capability consisting of satellites and weapons systems for fighting, command, reconnaisance, and early warning; training academies; and a fleet of aircraft and space-capable vessels for transportation, logistics, and war-fighting. The space leg would be designed to break the superpowers' monopoly on space weapons, protect China's space-based capabilities, support ground and naval operations, and maintain a capacity to intercept a portion of enemy ICBMs and reduce the destructiveness of any nuclear attack. This system would be assisted by ground-based BMD. While China would not be able to match the United States in these sorts of capabilities, it ought not to lag too far behind qualitatively, according to the author of this plan. China must strive for weapons of a comparable level of technology as those in the hands of the superpowers.[61]

Obviously there is a strong element of imagination in this conceptualization. Nonetheless, Chinese strategists are seriously concerned about the need to incorporate space satellites and weapons into China's nuclear and conventional operational doctrines. Indeed, space is now considered one of China's "strategic frontiers," along with land boundaries, territorial waters, and airspace.[62] This presents problems for China's present arms control position calling for banning ASATs and preventing the weaponization of space, established in the wake of the U.S. Strategic Defense Initiative (SDI). There may be some pressure from military strategists to rethink this. One Chinese expert on satellites and space weapons recently implied that China's position had become outdated because of the increasing importance of satellites in directing warfare. Military satellites are now legitimate targets in war, and thus ASATs are legitimate weapons.[63]

The Chinese space arms control position, however, does not exclude the development of ground-based BMD,[64] and strategists are increasingly

61. Bao Zhongxing, "Jianshe tian jun gouxiang" (The notion of building a space army), in NDU Research Department, Military Construction Research Institute, ed., *Jundui xiandaihua jianshe,* pp. 431–442; Zhang, "Dui xin shiqi zhanlue daodan budui," p. 417; and Hu and Xiao, *Yingxiang dao ershiyi shiji,* pp. 144–145.

62. Hu and Xiao, *Yingxiang dao ershiyi shiji,* p. 144.

63. Conversation with author, April 1994. See also Bao, "Jianshe tian jun," p. 426.

64. The Chinese list of destabilizing BMD systems that should be banned include space, land, or sea-based weapons designed to attack "spacecraft" (not re-entry vehicles or missiles), and space-

uninterested in defending China's official opposition to space-based BMD as well, since it is clear that BMD, in their view, would enhance the credibility of a limited deterrent.

BALLISTIC MISSILE DEFENSE

Due to Ronald Reagan's SDI program, and its reincarnation in the Theater High Altitude Area Defense (THAAD) program, ballistic missile defense has been closely studied by Chinese analysts. China was initially strongly opposed to SDI. The arguments tended to be similar to those of opponents in the United States and the Soviet Union: an effective U.S. defensive capability linked to a war-fighting offensive doctrine and capabilities would dramatically increase the U.S. ability to launch a disarming first strike, and thus increase the Soviet incentives to strike before the SDI system was complete. Indeed, the early arguments against SDI seemed to indicate that some Chinese analysts essentially endorsed the principles behind the Anti-Ballistic Missile (ABM) Treaty and the arguments of the assured destruction school.[65] Left less explicit were the arguments that China could not hope to compete in a U.S.-Soviet BMD race and that even moderately effective superpower BMD would degrade the credibility of China's small deterrent force.

In the mid-1980s, therefore, Chinese strategists began a more detailed analysis of China's options. Those who leaned towards assured-destruction thinking focused on ways of increasing the survivability and penetrability of Chinese warheads by using road, rail, or boat-mobile missiles; spinning or hardening missiles to neutralize beam weapons; or developing systems capable of baffling enemy BMD detection and tracking sensors.[66] Those who leaned towards counterforce–war-fighting options stressed the development of an offensive capability to destroy enemy capabilities, and defensive systems to use against a portion of enemy strategic forces. They were more sanguine about the possibility that adequate defense technologies could be developed; for every spear (*mao*) there was a shield (*dun*). This kind of response to BMD would entail

---

based systems designed to attack "objects" in the atmosphere, on land or at sea (presumably including RVs and missiles). Absent from this list are ground-based systems designed to attack "objects." See UN Conference on Disarmament Working Paper, CD/579, March 19, 1985, p. 1.

65. See, for instance, Zhuang Qubing, "Meiguo xinqiu da zhan jihua pouxi" (Analysis of the U.S. star wars plan), *Guoji wenti yanjiu*, (International studies), No. 4 (October 1984); He Qizhi, "Jiaqiang zhizhi waikong junbei jingai de falu cuoshi" (Strengthen the legal measures that prevent an arms race in space), *Guoji wenti yanjiu* (International studies), No. 4 (October 1984); and Wu, "Shilun zhanlue jingong wuqi."

66. Wu, "Shilun zhanlue jingong wuqi."

developing both space and ground-based terminal BMD, ASATs, defense suppression technologies, and more accurate offensive technologies.[67]

Judging from the consensus around the limited deterrence concept, it would seem the counterforce–war-fighting arguments are winning out. Since nuclear missiles are important war-fighting tools, they are also likely to be key targets of enemy attack. Because China is hobbled to some extent by its NFU pledge, this problem is especially pressing. Thus BMD is critical for preserving the war-fighting options provided by limited deterrence. "If a state has multi-level, multi-method nuclear attack power, and at the same time can basically protect itself from direct strike, then it has a wide range of strategic choices."[68] Proponents of limited deterrence make very little mention of the ABM Treaty, let alone demonstrate any concern for its principles.[69] The argument that an asymmetrical distribution of offensive and defensive capabilities can fundamentally destabilize deterrence is not challenged; it is simply ignored.

THEATER AND TACTICAL NUCLEAR WEAPONS (TNW)

Chinese strategists in the 1980s and 1990s have been relatively clear about their preference for TNW systems.[70] As one strategist at the NDU succinctly put it,

67. On Chinese responses to the SDI program, see John Garver, "China's Response to the Strategic Defense Initiative," *Asian Survey*, Vol. 26, No. 11 (November 1986), pp. 1220–1239; and Bonnie S. Glaser and Banning N. Garrett, "Chinese Perspectives on the Strategic Defense Initiative," *Problems of Communism*, Vol. 35, No. 2 (March/April 1986), pp. 28–44.

68. Hu "Weilai zhanzheng," p. 375. See also Liu and Yang, *Gao jishu zhanzheng*, pp. 179–180; Liu and Meng, *Xiandai jundui zhihui*, pp. 400, 415–416; Liu, Rong, and Chang, "Zhanlue daodan budui," pp. 329–330.

69. One of the fault lines in Chinese discussions of BMD may run between arms controllers and nuclear strategists in the military. The anti-BMD positions, most of which draw on the principles behind the ABM Treaty, have been espoused mainly by those with specific arms control expertise. Recent articulations of this position, for instance, have come from arms controllers in China's nuclear weapons lab and missile development systems. See Du Xiangwan and Li Bin, "Analysis and Discussion of Arms Control in Space," paper presented to ISODARCO Beijing Arms Control Seminar, May 1992; Li Bin, "The Effects of Ballistic Missile Defenses on Chinese Attitudes Towards Arms Control," *SSRC-MacArthur Newsletter*, No. 7 (May 1995), pp. 16–18; and Liu Erxun, "On the Subject of the Amendment of the ABM Treaty," unpublished paper, April 1995. However, the arms controllers may not have much influence on operational doctrine issues.

70. For earlier discussions of the advantages of TNW including nuclear artillery and mines, see Xu Baoshan, "We Must Prepare to Fight a Nuclear War in the First Stage of Any Future War," *Jiefangjun Bao*, September 16, 1979, translated in Joint Publications Research Service (JPRS), No. 88 (June 4, 1980); Wu Yigong, Zhang Shufa, and Zhong Weilun, *He Wuqi* (Nuclear weapons) (Beijing: Soldier Press, 1983); Zhou Shizong, "Kangji Sulian shou ci tu ji de ji ge wenti" (Several questions on resisting the first Soviet surprise attack), *Junshi xueshu* (Military Studies), No. 6 (1982), in *Junshi xueshu lun xuan* (Selected essays from Military Studies) (Beijing: Academy of Military Sciences Press, 1984), Vol. 2; and Li Baihong and Gao Guofeng, "Mogu zhuangyan yun xia de xin kangzheng" (The new resistance under the mushroom cloud), *Jiefangjun bao* (Liberation Army Daily), January 27, 1984. Li and Gao argued that the use of TNW involved "relatively small risks" and could advantageously speed the course of war. For a secondary analysis of China and TNW, see Malik, "Chinese Debate," pp. 18–19.

having TNW "greatly enriches" a state's nuclear stockpile. Their small size and limited yields mean that their use does not carry as great a risk as strategic nuclear retaliation. They help create a "nuclear ladder" and thus enhance deterrence.[71] Without this ladder, a state could not credibly react to, say, the seizure of a small portion of its territory.

France serves as an example. According to one Chinese analyst, in the 1970s French strategists realized that France's strategic nuclear capabilities could not deter all threats to its national interests and international obligations. As a result, more thought was given to the development of tactical nuclear weapons, and in the 1980s, some French strategists called TNW "pre-strategic nuclear weapons" and "front-line deterrence capabilities." TNW would be used to protect forward French interests (e.g., Germany's border with the Warsaw Pact), while its strategic forces would deter a direct attack on France.[72] The analogous argument for China might be that TNW could be useful for deterrence at the outer boundaries of China's "strategic frontiers" along its borders and territorial waters. Arguments for developing TNW are being pitched in the context of developing a capability to fight "high-tech limited wars" around China's periphery.

Initially in the late 1970s and early 1980s, Chinese materials on TNW tended to argue that these capabilities were essential to stop a Soviet armored blitzkrieg across the northern and western borders. In particular, Chinese military planners were worried that the People's Liberation Army (PLA) Air Force's strike aircraft were inadequate for battlefield delivery of nuclear weapons against Soviet tanks.[73] Nonetheless, by their own admission, research on the operational use of TNW was relatively underdeveloped among Chinese strategists. As one mid-1980s study argued, the "nuclear conception" was still comparatively weak in the PLA. There were restrictions on nuclear warhead tests useful for developing TNW, and a dearth of research on the actual effects of TNW explosions.[74] The PLA also lacked training under TNW conditions. Both

---

71. Hu, "Weilai zhanzheng," p. 376.
72. Wang Huaizhi, "Faguo de junshi zhanlue ji qi qishi" (French military strategy and its inspiration) in Academy of Military Sciences, Operations Analysis Research Department, ed., *Guoji xingshi yu guoji zhanlue*, pp. 128–129.
73. Lewis and Hua, "China's Ballistic Missile Programs," p. 6.
74. It is not clear whether the author referred to the Chinese government's announcement in early 1986 that it would eschew atmospheric tests, or simply to technical difficulties in testing miniaturized warheads. The moratorium on atmospheric testing presumably prevented the PLA from conducting above-ground tests for the effects of TNW on military equipment.

the United States and Russia were far ahead of China in thinking about and planning for limited nuclear war.[75]

Since the decline of the Soviet threat in the mid-1980s and the Chinese military's increasing interest in limited wars (occasioned originally by the Falklands War, and most dramatically by the Gulf War), research on limited war and TNW has picked up. Chinese strategists now believe the most likely future source of threat to be a limited conflict over resources and territory around China's periphery.[76] One Chinese study of limited war quantified the threat: 70 percent of China's 21,656 kilometer-long border and 66 percent of its over 3,000,000 square kilometers of territorial waters face some level of external threat.[77] Conflict over territory may or may not involve a clash with a nuclear power, but the nuclear strategists argue that China needs to have the ability to fight a limited nuclear war using TNW.[78] Even if the war were a conventional one, it should still be considered a war under nuclear conditions, since nuclear weapons would help deter both conventional and, if the opponent was a nuclear state, nuclear escalation.[79] Among the capabilities needed to fight limited border wars are theater and tactical missiles, including both cruise and ballistic missiles.[80] In this environment, ground forces will be relatively less important than naval, air, and strategic missile forces. Indeed, one author projects that by the year 2030, only 60 percent of the PLA will be ground forces, while the other branches will all increase to make up the remaining 40 percent.[81]

In a limited war, according to Chinese strategists, the premium will be on speed and overwhelming military superiority in order to defeat enemy forces early and decisively. It will require an ability to concentrate firepower on the enemy's own local air, naval, and missile forces. This is a mission for strike

75. The authors contended that most Chinese research on campaign theory neglected the nuclear viewpoint. Sang and Xiao, "Wo jun zhanyi lilun," pp. 811–812. One of the authors, Sang Zhonglin, with the GSD chemical defense department, is identified in Chinese sources as a strong proponent of nuclear war-fighting doctrines. See Hu and Xiao, *Yingxiang dao ershiyi shiji*, p. 143.
76. On local high-tech war in Chinese military doctrine, see Wang, Wang, and Huang, *Ju bu zhanzheng*, pp. 82–83; Guan, *Gao jishu zhanzheng*, pp. 23–24; Paul Godwin, "Chinese Military Strategy Revised: Local and Limited War," *Annals*, Vol. 519 (January 1992), pp. 191–201; and David Shambaugh, "The Insecurity of Security: The PLA's Evolving Doctrine and Threat Perceptions Towards 2000," *Journal of Northeast Asian Studies*, Vol. 13, No. 1 (Spring 1994), pp. 3–25.
77. Wang, Wang, and Huang, *Ju bu zhanzheng*, p. 82.
78. Hu, "Weilai zhanzheng," p. 372.
79. Song and Xiao, "Wo jun zhanyi lilun," pp. 804–805.
80. Su, "Shilun changgui liliang," p. 117; Guan, *Gao jishu zhanzheng*, pp. 12–13.
81. Guan, *Gao jishu zhanzheng*, pp. 12–13. The present proportion is about 75 percent ground forces. Calculated from the International Institute for Strategic Studies, *Military Balance, 1993–1994* (London: Brasseys, 1994).

aircraft, but also one for conventional and, if necessary, nuclear missiles. In the early stages of a limited war, then, it is best to choose "all types of effective methods of attack" to destroy the enemy's superiority in high technology weapons and air power before these come into play.[82] This means, for instance, using everything from computer viruses to disrupt enemy command, to missiles, aircraft, submarines, and elite special forces.[83]

For those targets that may be some distance away from the theater (e.g., aircraft carriers, air bases, naval bases, command headquarters, and strategic and theater missile bases), missile attacks would be especially useful in the early stages of the war.[84] Strategists are not explicit about whether these might be nuclear or conventionally armed missiles, but given the nature of some of the targets, and given that the adversary may well be a nuclear state, the dominant argument appears to be that the PLA should develop a limited nuclear deterrent based on the use of nuclear weapons in these theater roles.[85]

CIVIL DEFENSE

Proponents of nuclear war-fighting doctrines in the United States and Soviet Union believed that an important component of damage limitation was the protection of a good portion of the civilian population.[86] The literature on limited deterrence in China, however, has not paid special attention to civil defense, perhaps because civil defense was a prominent feature of Chinese military doctrine well before this literature emerged in the late 1980s. In the wake of Sino-Soviet border clashes in 1969, Mao launched a massive civil defense construction program known as the campaign to "dig tunnels deep and store grain everywhere." Throughout the 1970s, almost all work units in major cities across China built underground shelters that provided varying degrees of protection against blast, fire, and radiation. Underneath the center of Beijing, for instance, there is a vast underground city, originally designed for

82. Military strategists argue that China should plan to fight against a quantitatively and qualitatively superior adversary in local conflicts. This suggests that the United States, Japan, and Russia set the standards for the adversary against which the PLA should prepare. See Guan, *Gao jishu zhanzheng*, p. 11; and Liang and Zhao, "Shilun wo jun weilai hetong zhanyi zuozhan," p. 87.
83. Liang and Zhao, "Shilun wo jun weilai hetong zhanyi zuozhan," p. 80.
84. Ibid., p. 87; Guan, *Gao jishu zhanzheng*. pp. 110–111, 119.
85. Liu, Wang, and Huang, *Guofang fazhan zhanlue*, p. 154; Guan, *Gao jishu zhanzheng*; Wang, Wang, and Huang, *Ju bu zhanzheng;* Su, "Shilun changgui liliang"; Zhang and Zhao, "Gao jishu zhanzheng"; Liu, Rong, and Chang, "Zhanlue daodan budui."
86. Robert Scheer, *With Enough Shovels: Reagan, Bush and Nuclear War* (New York: Random House, 1982); Steven Kull, *Minds at War: Nuclear Reality and the Inner Conflicts of Defense Policymakers* (New York: Basic, 1988).

atomic, biological, and chemical (ABC) defense, and since the 1980s used as hospitals, stores, and hotels.[87]

But widespread testing of civil defense plans apparently took some time. In 1974 the Central Military Commission's (CMC) Construction Corps and the GSD organized the first all-China conference on civil defense engineering technology, and designated the Shenyang Military Region (MR), which faced the most likely route of a Soviet invasion through Manchuria, as a test point for civil defense activities. Changchun city civil defense authorities began a research program using computers to analyze the effects of nuclear strikes on cities and thus what the appopriate responses might be. Not until 1984, however, did the China Civil Defense Commission hold its first all-China Civil Defense meeting. Its circular ordered local authorities to step up ABC defense education. In 1987 and 1988 respectively, the cities of Taiyuan and Xian held civil defense exercises under simulated ABC conditions. In 1987 the Civil Defense Commission set a goal of formal education in ABC defense for 20 million students by the year 2000.[88]

The PLA's development of a literature on the protection of urban populations accompanied these exercises. The premise of these studies is that as centers of economic, industrial, and logistical power, cities are critical for ensuring that China retain sufficient "national strength" to maintain its war-fighting capability.[89] Thus, to minimize urban casualties, the GSD chemical defense department has examined proposals for building satellite cities to deconcentrate civilian populations and economic centers; proposals requiring that all new building meets civil defense specifications; and plans for underground transportation networks, production facilities, supply depots, etc. The GSD has recommended that 40–60 percent of the urban population should be dispersable. This requires plans for the organization, timing, method, and portion of populations targeted for dispersal, as well as evacuation routes, transportation means and logistics, and supplies to support the dispersed population.[90] Interestingly, however, the military strategists who write specifically on limited deterrence do not discuss in any detail the tasks of civil defense: the focus is almost entirely on the development of military and command technologies that will maximize the

87. Rosita Dellios, *Modern Chinese Defense Strategy: Present Developments, Future Directions* (London: Macmillan, 1989), p. 35.
88. General Staff Department, *Fanghua bing*, pp. 230–232.
89. Xiao Guangbo, *He zhanzheng yu ren fang* (Nuclear war and civil defense) (Beijing: Peoples Liberation Army Press, 1989), p. 37; Cui Zhangqi, *Xiandai fang kong* (Modern air defense) (Beijing: NDU Press, 1989), p. 379.
90. Xiao, *He zhanzheng*, pp. 253–301; Cui, *Xiandai fang kong*, pp. 382–401.

survivability and effectiveness of Chinese missiles, so it is not clear how central a role civil defense will play in limited deterrence concepts as these are refined.

The Doctrine-Capabilities Gap

Despite all this interest among Chinese strategists in a limited nuclear war-fighting capability, there is a large gap between these doctrinal arguments and China's present capabilities. Does this suggest that limited deterrence doctrine is or will be irrelevant for guiding the modernization of Chinese nuclear forces?

In mid-1995, just over half of China's ballistic missiles are liquid fueled with reaction times of two hours or more. For the most part, the land-based missiles are inaccurate enough to raise doubts about the ability to hit hardened, point counterforce targets. The circular error probability (CEP) of the DF3 and DF4, the mainstay of the land-based missile forces, for example, is worse than 1,000 meters.[91] With around 300 strategic warheads and bombs and only a handful of these on full-range ICBMs, Chinese decision-makers could not hope to hit nearly the range of counterforce and countervalue targets that limited deterrence theorists have outlined.[92] To this point there has been no obvious push for a rapid increase in the number of weapons deployed. Indeed, the numbers seem to have leveled off in the late 1980s as the second generation of missiles, DF21, came on line (see Figure 1).

Operationally, it is not likely that China's central command system in Beijing has the ability to acquire sufficient real-time intelligence about an adversary's military preparations and the possible changing status of potential targets to launch a rapid attack. Nor does the national command appear to have the capability to determine the size or effectiveness of a nuclear attack on China, intelligence that is crucial for gauging what kind of response is possible. The PLA did not begin to build a nuclear event detection and observation system until 1974. From 1974–80 it constructed a number of fixed observation posts around the country. In the early 1980s the GSD completed plans for the construction of reporting centers and a network linking all the military regions

91. Robert S. Norris, Andrew S. Burrows, and Richard W. Fieldhouse, *British, French and Chinese Nuclear Weapons* (Boulder, Colo.: Westview, 1994).

92. The number of nuclear weapons is one of China's most closely guarded secrets. The estimates from outsiders vary dramatically from around 200–300 strategic warheads (Sutter, "Chinese Nuclear Weapons"; IISS, *Military Balance*) to 500–650 (Malik, "Chinese Debate on Military Strategy"). One reason why the Chinese oppose participation in five-power strategic arms control may be to avoid transparency. Chinese strategists argue that transparency is not in the interests of weak states, who need to keep superior adversaries guessing about their capabilities. Author's interview, September 1994.

Figure 1. Growth of Chinese Nuclear Forces, 1964–93.

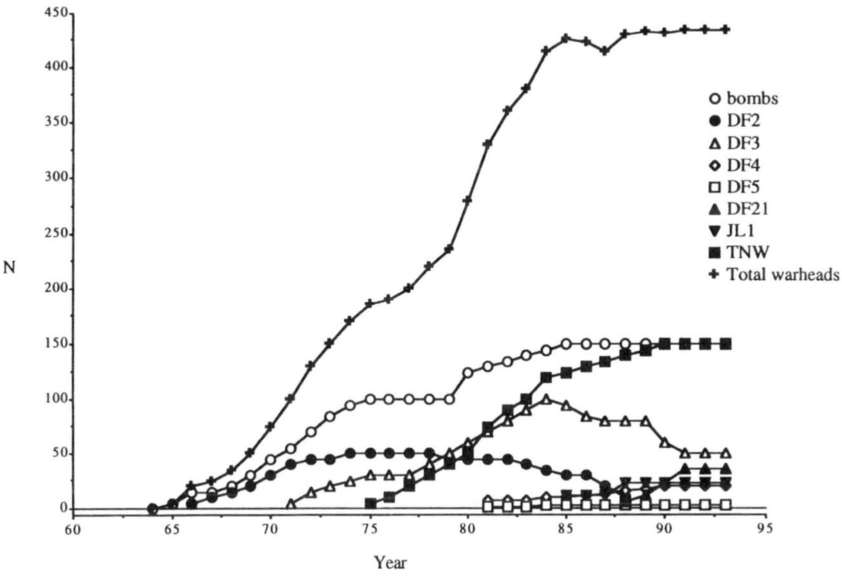

SOURCE: Robert S. Norris, Andrew S. Burrows, and Richard W. Fieldhouse, *Nuclear Weapons Databook,* Vol. 5, *British, French, and Chinese Nuclear Weapons* (Boulder, Colo.: Westview, 1994), Table 7.1, p. 359.

and service branches with the national command. The network was to determine the time, place, type, and yield of enemy nuclear explosions and to assess radiation and damage levels. A test point for this network was set up in the Lanzhou MR in 1984, but not completed until 1986. As of 1988 an all-China system had yet to be set up, though it is possible that since then it has been completed.[93]

The PLA is, of course, acutely aware of the shortcomings in the operational capabilities of its nuclear forces. In the mid-1980s, the PLA began exercises to train the SMF to launch under simulated nuclear war conditions.[94] Strategists are very explicit about the needs (and hence weaknesses) of the SMF command,

93. General Staff Department, *Fanghua bing,* pp. 226–228. This study was published in 1990. I have not come across any more recent sources on the nuclear detection system.
94. Ibid., pp. 216–217.

including clear intelligence about the nature of an enemy attack; up-to-date information about the position of enemy targets; "firepower plans" (*huoli jihua*) which specify targets, the types, deployment, survivability, sequencing, etc., of the missiles to be used in a counterattack; and confidence in the ability to issue effective launch orders at the most advantageous time.[95] No doubt there are concrete optional plans for the use of nuclear weapons, but recent Chinese writings suggest that these plans do not yet meet the standards required for limited deterrence.

The other components of limited deterrence also lag behind the requirements set by the concept. China has not deployed any ground-based BMD nor any space-based systems, though in 1993 it purchased 4 batteries (100 missiles) of S-300 air-defense missiles and related command technology from the Russians.[96] It has no ASAT capability at present either, and no satellite based early-warning (EW) capability (it relies on phased-array radars). As for China's civil defense program, it may in fact be more hollow than ever before. The tunnels and nuclear shelters built in the 1970s are either used for commercial purposes or have fallen into disrepair, and all along there were doubts about whether the shelters would protect against nuclear effects. There have been no large-scale evacuation or shelter exercises, and with a growing "floating population" in cities, it is likely that many people do not know where the closest operational shelter is and that no evacuation plans exist for millions of transient urban dwellers. Chinese civil defense programs may well be similar to the Potemkin-village nature of Soviet civil defense where, as the Soviet Interview Project showed, most citizens had no specific training in where they were supposed to go and what they were supposed to do in case of a nuclear attack.[97]

Training for conventional and nuclear operations during a nuclear war is the one area where the PLA has maintained a sustained effort. This training could be useful for limited nuclear wars or for conflicts in which TNW were used. According to one source, the PLA began training under simulated ABC conditions as early as 1955, but this was disrupted by the anti-Soviet movement in military affairs in China in the late 1950s.[98] In 1980, in reaction to the threat of

95. Liu and Meng, *Xiandai jundui zhihui*, pp. 404–407; Liu, Rong, and Chang, "Zhanlue daodan budui," p. 327; Zhang, "Dui xin shiqi zhanlue daodan budui," p. 419.
96. Kenneth Allen, Glenn Krumel, and Jonathan D. Pollack, *China's Airforce Enters the 21st Century*, MR-580-AF (Santa Monica, Calif.: RAND, 1995), p. 157.
97. See Stuart Kaufman, "Soviet Civil Defense: Hedging Against Armageddon," unpublished ms., University of Michigan, Ann Arbor, 1987.
98. Sang and Xiao, "Wo jun zhanyi lilun," p. 813. The 1955 ABC exercises took place in the Liaodong peninsula and involved field army–size forces. The objective was to resist a coastal

a Soviet blitzkrieg along the northern borders, the Central Military Commission decided that the PLA had to be able to fight a combined conventional and nuclear war, and ABC warfare began to receive greater attention. The CMC apparently ordered all units to set aside a specific time each year for ABC training. In the same year, the Shenyang MR organized field army–size exercises under ABC conditions. This was followed by ABC exercises at lower levels in most MRs, where units trained under different geographical and operational conditions through the 1980s (the exercises involved, e.g., motorized infantry units in 1983, coastal defense units and naval units in 1987 and 1988, and units along the Indian border in 1988). In some of these exercises the PLA simulated the use of its own TNW. The SMF also held strategic launch exercises under simulated nuclear attack beginning in the mid-1980s.[99] There is a growing research literature in the PLA on how to concentrate and disperse troops, develop survivable command structures, restore communications, close nuclear corridors, assist attacked areas, etc., under nuclear conditions.[100] It was not until June 1988, however, that an entire group army (*jituan jun*) underwent a complete test of its ability to avoid or reduce damage from ABC weapons.[101]

There is considerable debate in the West over the status of China's TNW. Most would agree that doctrinally, at least, the PLA has been investigating the operational role of TNW since the 1950s.[102] More controversial, however, is the evidence that the Chinese have actually developed TNW. Chong-pin Lin claimed in the late 1980s that the Chinese had tested very low yield warheads, suitable for TNW. There were reports that the PLA had deployed atomic demolition munitions in the early 1980s and had tested a neutron bomb in 1988.[103] Possibly as a result of a directive from the Ministry of Space Industry in 1984 to put more focus on the development of tactical missiles, the Chinese have developed short-range ballistic missiles (DF15), which could be used for TNW delivery.[104]

Estimates of China's TNW stockpile vary wildly across sources. In 1984 the U.S. Defense Intelligence Agency said there that were none. A recent study by

landing. This is three years earlier than what Lin reports as the first evidence that the PLA was training under ABC conditions. See Lin, *China's Nuclear Strategy*, p. 77.

99. Lin, *China's Nuclear Strategy*, pp. 90, 93; General Staff Department, *Fanghua bing*, pp. 215–217. There appears to have been a steady increase in the frequency of SMF launch exercises. From 1966 to 1974 it averaged 4.5 launches per year; in the mid to late 1970s, 6 per year; the mid to late 1980s, 7.7 per year. Sha Li and Min Li, *Jianguo hou Zhongguo guonei 10 ci junshi da xingdong* (Ten major military actions within China since the establishment of the state) (Chengdu: Sichuan Science and Technology Press, 1992), p. 257.

100. Sang and Xiao, "Wo jun zhanyi lilun."

101. General Staff Department, *Fanghua bing*, p. 184.

102. Lin, *China's Nuclear Strategy*, pp. 78–79.

103. Ibid., pp. 90–91.

104. Lewis and Hua, "China's Ballistic Missile Programs," p. 27.

the Natural Resources Defense Council claims that there were around 100 weapons in 1984, and that by the early 1990s a total of 150.[105] However, one authoritative Chinese source states plainly that as of the late 1980s, China did not have any theater or tactical nuclear weapons, but did have limited nuclear war options: "At present, although we have not yet equipped ourselves with theater and tactical nuclear weapons, this is not the same as saying in the future we will not arm ourselves. Moreover, our air force's nuclear bombs and the Second Artillery's nuclear missiles can also be used against the rear of the enemy's theater."[106]

The evidence suggests, then, that there is, with some exceptions, a considerable gap between what Chinese nuclear strategists are saying China's nuclear forces should be able to do and what these forces are in fact capable of doing. There are three possible reasons for this conclusion. The first possibility is that my analysis of the doctrinal discussions is wrong: China's limited deterrence may be much closer in kind to minimum deterrence, and there may be greater consistency between doctrine and capabilities than I have assumed. However, this is contradicted by evidence that, as the contours of limited deterrence thinking took shape, a number of Chinese strategists explicitly differentiated between minimum deterrence and limited deterrence and ascribed to the latter clear war-fighting, victory-denying functions.

A second possibility is that I have looked at the wrong sources. In the United States, for example, there has always been a disjuncture between the nuclear discourse in academia and government on the one hand, and the war plans devised by the Strategic Air Command on the other. Focusing too much on the former led to misconceptions about the latter. The policy intellectuals stressed everything from massive retaliation to assured destruction to flexible response to countervailing to war-winning, while the war planners tended to adhere more consistently to war-fighting, war-winning, even preemptive plans.[107] In

105. Norris, Burrows, and Fieldhouse, *British, French and Chinese Nuclear Weapons*, p. 371. A recent report by a respected analyst with the Congressional Research Service does not mention anything about a TNW stockpile. Sutter, "Chinese Nuclear Weapons."

106. Sang and Xiao, "Wo jun zhanyi lilun," pp. 806, 811. Sang and Xiao were with the GSD chemical defense department, which is in charge of ABC activities. The paper was presented at a 1987 conference on campaign theory organized by the GSD. The conference proceedings were not published until October 1989 and were not for public circulation. Their statement about China and TNW, therefore, may be accurate up to that date. This suggests that the data on the growth of the Chinese stockpile presented in Norris, Burrows, and Fieldhouse may need revision: their Table 7.1 lists 1976 as the first year in which tactical warheads appeared in the Chinese arsenal. Norris, Burrows, and Fieldhouse, *British, French and Chinese Nuclear Weapons*, p. 359.

107. Scott Sagan, "SIOP-62: The Nuclear War Plan Briefing to President Kennedy," *International Security*, Vol. 12, No. 1 (Summer 1987), pp. 22–51; Greg Herken, *Counsels of War* (New York: Knopf,

this study, however, many of the sources have been written by strategists in military units charged specifically with developing doctrine.

A final possibility is that the evolving limited-deterrence thinking has indeed established guidelines for operational plans, technology acquisition, and deployment in the mid-1990s and beyond. On average, it took eleven years for China's first generation of ballistic missiles (DF2 through DF5) to move from research and development (R&D) stages to deployment. The second-generation weapons (JL1/DF21 and DF41) have taken about as long.[108] Thus any R&D choices made on the basis of the requirements for limited deterrence will not come to fruition until the late 1990s and the first decade of the next century: if so, one should expect the size, mobility, diversity, and flexibility of Chinese forces to increase over the next decade or so. One should also expect to see efforts to develop ground-based and possibly some space-based BMD systems, ASATs, TNW, and improved early-warning capabilities (including satellite technologies). This does not mean that China will necessarily engage in a crash program to catch up to U.S. and Russian levels; limited deterrence does not require identical capabilities to those of the superpowers, only enough to damage enough enemy war-fighting capabilities at any level of violence such that the adversary is denied victory, even though China may suffer greater damage in the process. But it does suggest that Chinese military strategists are not as confident at the moment as some were in the past that China has a credible deterrent: if a limited war-fighting capability is what deters and China does not possess such a capability, the logical conclusion is that the deterrent is frail and that more concerted efforts are needed to shore it up.[109] This will especially be the case if the United States deploys Theater Missile Defense (TMD) systems with an inherent capability of intercepting strategic warheads, as the Clinton administration apparently intends to do.[110] China has sufficient fissile material to expand its warhead stockpile two to three times its present size,[111]

1985); Peter Pringle and William Arkin, *SIOP: The Secret U.S. Plan for Nuclear War* (New York: Norton, 1983).

108. Lewis and Hua, "China's Ballistic Missile Program," Table 1.

109. Such concerns about the present lack of a credible deterrent were communicated to Goldstein, and were also evident in some of my conversations with analysts connected with the nuclear weapons program. See Goldstein, "Robust and Affordable Security," p. 502.

110. See Lisbeth Gronlund, George Lewis, Theodore Postol, and David Wright, "Highly Capable Theater Missile Defense and the ABM Treaty," *Arms Control Today*, Vol. 24, No. 3 (April 1994), pp. 3–8.

111. The Natural Resource Defense Council (NRDC) estimates that China may have enough fissile material to expand its current forces 2 or 3 times (from 300 up to 600–900) warheads. Interview with NRDC analyst, July 1995. The Union of Concerned Scientists' lower-bound estimate is that China has stockpiled enough highly enriched uranium (HEU) and separated plutonium (PU) for about 200 more warheads. Lisbeth Gronlund, David Wright, and Yong Liu, "Chinese Participation

and Chinese officials and nuclear specialists have suggested through a number of avenues that U.S. TMD would probably speed up China's nuclear modernization efforts and reduce China's incentive to see an early Comprehensive Test Ban Treaty (CTBT) or fissile material production ban put in place.

These efforts to increase China's relative nuclear strength need not be unilateral, however. Much of the catching up will be done *for* China. As, or if, Strategic Arms Reduction Talks (START) II levels are reached early in the next century, the size of China's nuclear capabilities relative to the United States and Russia will increase dramatically. The Chinese have also made it clear that they would like to see a START III treaty that would bring U.S.-Russian forces down even lower, to 1,000 or even a "few hundreds" each. Apparently some Chinese strategists hope to see rough parity among the three states. Such a preference is clearly more consistent with a limited deterrent doctrine than with an undifferentiated second-strike or minimum deterrent doctrine.[112] Limited deterrent thinking is also consistent with China's adamant opposition to five-power strategic nuclear arms control and with its very lukewarm approach to an early CTBT.[113]

---

in a Fissile Material Production Cutoff Convention," unpublished paper, Union of Concerned Scientists, Cambridge, Mass., June 1995, p. 5. David Albright puts the stockpile of HEU at around 20 tons (± 25 percent) and PU at 3.5 tons (± 50 percent) or enough for 700 more warheads (± 50 percent). Interview, July 1995.

112. The idea of rough parity was first proposed by a Chinese strategist in 1988, around the time the PLA was paying closer attention to the war-fighting features of limited deterrence, although there may be no causal link. See Hua Di, "Nuclear Strategy and Arms Control from a Chinese Point of View," paper presented to the American Association for the Advancement of Science annual conference, February 1988, p. 13. The "1000 or less" condition is now standard in comments by the Chinese in discussions with the National Academy of Science, the Natural Resource Defense Council, and at the ISODARCO arms control seminars. Wu Zhan, a strategist with the Chinese Academy of Social Science, has used the term "comparability" to describe the desired levels, and suggested this would entail reductions of 95 percent in U.S. and Russian stockpiles. See Wu Zhan, "Prospects of Nuclear Disarmament," paper presented to the ISODARCO Beijing Arms Control Seminar, Beijing, October 1992, p. 12; Wu Zhan, "Some Thoughts on Nuclear Arms Control," paper presented to Workshop on Possible Interlinked South Asia and Worldwide Nuclear Arms Control and Disarmament Initiatives, sponsored by the Federation of American Scientists, Shanghai, February 1994, p. 10. As far as I can tell, these figures have not been articulated in official policy statements.

113. In the West, little is known about the arms control and national security policy process in China, so it is quite possible that this confluence of arms control positions and nuclear doctrine preference reflects independent decisions in these two policy spheres, rather than a coordinated policy. Nonetheless, the limited deterrence doctrine and China's arms control positions generally reinforce each other. The only arms control positions that would require dramatic revision to accommodate doctrinal preferences would be China's stance on banning anti-satellite weapons (ASATs) and its NFU pledge. The former may be modified or quietly dropped to accommodate the development of Chinese ASAT capabilities, while the latter may simply not be credible, hence costless to maintain. For a fuller discussion of China's approach to strategic arms control, see Alastair Iain Johnston, "Is There Learning in Chinese Arms Control Policy?" *China Journal*, forthcoming 1996; and Banning N. Garrett and Bonnie S. Glaser, "Chinese Perspectives on Nuclear Arms Control," *International Security*, Vol. 20, No. 3 (Winter 1995/96), pp. 43–78.

POLICY IMPLICATIONS: THE CONSTRAINTS ON LIMITED DETERRENCE

China's development of a limited nuclear war-fighting capability is not inevitable, despite the pressures to build one. There are obvious constraints on meeting the software and hardware requirements of limited deterrence. In a sense, limited deterrence presents a wish-list of capabilities from which the Chinese, constrained by money and the slippery slope of arms control, must choose.

The money constraint is hard to estimate, given the rapid growth in the Chinese economy. Real Chinese military expenditures are exceedingly hard to determine but are probably in the $30 billion range. The changing portion of funds allocated to the R&D and acquisition of nuclear weapons is unknown, with one estimate putting the figure at 3–5 percent of military expenditures.[114] The critical costs will not be the development of warheads, but of delivery systems and the command and control technologies needed for flexible response. Nonetheless, the Chinese themselves readily admit that what mainly constrains the size and quality of China's forces is the country's economic and technological backwardness.[115] Doctrine (e.g., the allegedly "defensive" nature of Chinese forces) is rarely mentioned as a specific constraint. Thus, even though for outside analysts the specific cost constraints are difficult to measure, one can make a general projection that if marginal costs decline, barring a change in doctrine, the Chinese will step up their efforts to develop a force structure more compatible with limited deterrence.[116]

The second constraint is arms control. China's approach to multilateral arms control issues since the early 1980s has essentially been characterized by defection and free-riding: China has rationally avoided to the extent possible any substantial commitments that would impose specific constraints on its military capabilities, while enjoying the benefits of the security public goods provided by others' arms control processes (e.g., the Intermediate-range Nuclear Force agreement, START). But in the course of free-riding, China has become

---

114. Richard Bitzinger and Chong-pin Lin, "Off the Books: Analyzing and Understanding Chinese Defense Spending," paper presented to fifth Annual Staunton Hill Conference on the People's Liberation Army, June 1994, p. 6. This is roughly consistent with CIA estimates for 1965–79. See CIA, "Chinese Defense Spending," p. 5.

115. Zhang, "Dui xin shiqi zhanlue daodan budui," p. 418.

116. Of course economic constraints are also political in nature, because ultimately China's top political and military leaders will decide how much to allocate to the nuclear weapons program. To be effective, any budgetary or doctrinal decisions that might constrain the nuclear program will probably have to be made before Deng passes away, because it is not clear that the post-Deng leadership will have the legitimacy in the eyes of the PLA to rule against military interests.

entrapped in processes that it would prefer to avoid. For example, despite China's public pledge to sign the CTBT by the end of 1996, Chinese nuclear weapons designers and the Chinese military have made it clear that they would prefer not to see an early treaty because in their view it would freeze qualitative asymmetries in nuclear capabilities among the United States, Russia, and China. Yet China is involved in CTBT negotiations in the UN Conference on Disarmament (CD) in Geneva, having been incrementally drawn into test ban issues in the CD because the agenda is essentially set by others. In the 1980s, China resisted any detailed discussions of nuclear test bans in the CD; this was relatively easy to do since there were no formal negotiations on a CTBT. But in the fall of 1993, the CD was given the mandate to begin negotiations toward a treaty, after the United States and Russia put the issue on the agenda. The Chinese had little choice but to participate, given the image costs that would be incurred from opposing a CTBT and undermining an important future pillar of the nonproliferation regime. So, barring a collapse of the negotiations, China may well have to sign on in 1996.

A CTBT would restrict China's ability to develop a wider range of warhead designs, though not new delivery systems. Thus a test ban will certainly not cripple the development of a limited deterrent. But the case illustrates a broader point: the Chinese can be pulled into arms control commitments that, even though costly to make and thus inconsistent with China's free-riding decision rule, are even more costly or difficult to avoid. A much more dramatic constraint on China's limited deterrent would be a fissile material control regime that limited or reduced existing stockpiles, not just future production, and multilateral agreements that placed restrictions on ballistic missile testing and deployment and on all forms of BMD and ASAT systems. These could be negotiated in a forum that would make it difficult for China to remain outside the process. The Conference on Disarmament is an obvious place: the five nuclear powers are conducting quiet negotiations on the CTBT there, and so the precedent for multilateral nuclear negotiations among the five has been set. Another possibility would be a separate nuclear weapon states forum in which issues high on China's agenda (such as NFU and some space arms control issues) could be discussed, along with ballistic missile and BMD restrictions. The former agenda issues would help to ensure that China would be formally committed to the forum, thus increasing the image costs of avoiding the latter issues.

Apart from money and arms control, there is a third possible constraint, namely, a shift in Chinese doctrine toward a more articulated minimum deterrence thinking. In the past, the agenda in discussions among Chinese strategists has been influenced by the U.S. and Soviet discourses on nuclear doctrine. Chinese analysts followed very closely the U.S. discussions of countervailing strategies that surrounded Presidential Directive 59 in 1979; the arguments for the deployment of theater nuclear weapons in Europe in the late 1970s and 1980s to counter Soviet Intermediate-Range Nuclear Force (INF) deployments; and the war-fighting–war-winning discourse in Caspar Weinberger's Department of Defense in the 1980s.[117] To the extent, then, that future discussions in the United States on nuclear doctrine in the post–Cold War focus on minimum deterrence, one should expect that Chinese strategists will take a closer look at the arguments.

The process might be assisted by encouraging intergovernmental and non-governmental linkages with Chinese strategists to open up multiple dialogues on nuclear doctrine, strategic stability, crisis bargaining, the nature of deterrence and related questions. Other constituencies that are generally outside of discussions on operational nuclear strategy might also be engaged through such dialogues; such constituencies might include arms control specialists in the nuclear weapons and missile labs, institutions such as the Foreign Ministry, influential think tanks such as the China Institute of Contemporary International Relations, and even academic centers such as the Arms Control and Regional Security Program at Fudan University. The objective would be to help pluralize discussions of nuclear strategy so as to break the near-monopoly held by PLA strategists.[118] Recent research on the origins of Soviet "new thinking," for instance, points to the crucial role of scientists and public policy science institutions in Europe and the United States (e.g., Pugwash, the National Academy of Sciences, the Natural Resources Defense Council) in disseminating the principles of the ABM Treaty and assured destruction ideas of strategic stability among scientists and civilian foreign policy specialists, and from there into the arms control and strategy debates inside the Kremlin.[119] The question is whether these effects can be reproduced in the China case.

---

117. See, for example, Hu, *Weilai zhanzheng*, p. 374, for a discussion of Weinberger's war-fighting thinking.

118. Most of these institutions do research on arms control related subjects, and from time to time will discuss nuclear doctrine issues in very general terms. But the compartmentalization of the Chinese security policy process and the general deference to the PLA on questions of operational strategy are major barriers to demilitarizing the discussions.

119. Emanuel Adler, "The Emergence of Cooperation: National Epistemic Communities and the International Evolution of the Idea of Nuclear Arms Control," *International Organization*, Vol. 46, No. 1 (Winter 1992), pp. 101–145; and Matthew Evangelista, "The Paradox of State Strength:

Conclusion

In the last five to ten years, Chinese military strategists have developed a concept of limited deterrence that is now used to describe what China's nuclear forces ought to be able to do. Limited deterrence rests on a limited war-fighting capability aimed at communicating China's ability to inflict costly damage on the adversary at every rung on the escalation ladder and thus denying the adversary victory in a nuclear war. It is this capability, Chinese strategists argue, that will deter such a war in the first place. Limited deterrence therefore requires the development of a greater number of tactical, theater, and strategic nuclear weapons that are accurate enough to hit counterforce targets, are mobile, can be used in the earliest stages of a nuclear crisis, and in a world of THAAD are capable of penetrating ballistic missile defense systems. These forces would thus require effective space-based early warning, and some configuration of BMD capabilities. Given that China does not now have such capabilities, the straight-line prediction would be that over the next decade or so, we should expect to see a discernible effort to shift the forces away from a minimum strike-back assured destruction posture, which China now has, toward limited war-fighting. This may or may not entail a dramatic short-run increase in the absolute numbers of warheads and delivery systems: the pace will depend in part on whether the United States proceeds with TMD deployment. The speed of change in China's nuclear capabilities will also depend in part on whether the implementation of START II leads to a steep relative increase in the size of the Chinese arsenal and reduces the relative number of counterforce targets. The primary constraints on any such efforts are exogenous, namely, budgetary and arms control constraints. It is an open question whether endogenous constraints—a shift in doctrine toward minimum deterrence—might be encouraged, though the case of Soviet new thinking suggests some interesting possibilities.

The argument here has largely been doctrine driven, where the impact of doctrinal change on force posture is mediated by economic and arms control constraints. There are, of course, alternative models for the development of Chinese nuclear forces in the future. Three in particular stand out—a technological inertia model, an organizational interest model, and an idiosyncratic leadership model. Not all of these are inconsistent with the doctrine-driven

Transnational Relations, Domestic Structures, and Security Policy in Russia and the Soviet Union," *International Organization*, Vol. 49, No. 1 (Winter 1995) pp. 1–38.

argument, and indeed, some may have interactive effects. Yet none of these offers completely convincing explanations for past nuclear policies, let alone reliable predictions for future behavior.[120] Testing all four models, however, requires far more information about China's nuclear weapons policy process, in particular about the relationship between those who think about doctrine and those who think about force posture, and about the integration of force posture decisions with budgetary, arms control, and broader foreign policy decisions. My analysis of the nature and implications of limited deterrence thinking requires additional testing through the careful study of any additional new materials that may surface, and the engagement of Chinese strategists in sustained discussions on nuclear deterrence and crisis stability.

But one thing is certain: PLA strategists have been struggling to figure out how to link conventional and nuclear weapons with the operational requirements of potential high-tech local wars over resources and territory around China's periphery. They are interested in how to integrate high technology weapons with "long-distance striking power" so as to deter and, if necessary, deny an adversary victory in any conceivable conventional and nuclear military conflict. PLA strategists have not been content with an undifferentiated, primitive, countervalue second-strike deterrent status quo. Indeed they appear to have their doubts about the credibility of this kind of deterrent, doubts that have probably been strengthened by the prospects of U.S. TMD development. Regrettably, in an era where much international effort is being put into delegitimizing the utility of nuclear weapons, Chinese military strategists have apparently been moving in the opposite direction.

120. Briefly, the technological inertia model appears to have applied in the past, in part because there were few specialists in nuclear strategy. But with the growth of a relatively sophisticated community of nuclear strategists in the 1980s and 1990s, their ideas may begin to guide R&D and acquisition. Even if doctrine plays a minor role in the future, this model would suggest that the structure of Chinese nuclear forces may evolve in limited war-fighting directions as economic and technological constraints diminish. As for an organizational interest model, there is little reason to believe that the nuclear forces will not remain a privileged component of the PLA. Nor is there as yet specific evidence of crippling debates over which leg of the strategic triad should be getting what share of resources. Finally, there is an idiosyncratic explanation whereby the key determinant of Chinese nuclear doctrine and posture is the preeminent leader's preferences. Individual leaders like Mao and Deng have, however, provided only general guidelines. Deng, for instance, has been a supporter of land-based mobile ICBMs and the SLBM program. His voice was also probably crucial in the allocation of resources to major weapons systems, and on arms control commitments that might constrain nuclear options. It is unlikely, however, than a weak post-Deng collective leadership will try to reverse the Maoist and Dengist legacies on nuclear force questions. Thus all four models might collectively or individually push the development of Chinese nuclear forces along limited deterrence lines.

Chinese Perspectives on Nuclear Arms Control

Banning N. Garrett & Bonnie S. Glaser

China's nuclear weapons and Beijing's arms control policies have become increasingly important factors in the post–Cold War era of U.S.-Russian strategic arms reductions and growing concern about proliferation of weapons of mass destruction. Unlike Russia and the United States, China is not constrained by any international arms control regime from modernizing and expanding its nuclear forces. In addition, the Chinese nuclear arsenal, the quality of which is likely to be significantly enhanced over the coming decade, will be an increasingly important strategic factor in regional and global security as China's nuclear weapons more closely match the capabilities of U.S. and Russian nuclear forces. Concern about Beijing's nuclear capability has also been heightened by China's rapid emergence as a major power with a huge economy, able to underwrite an extensive nuclear arms buildup in the next century should Chinese leaders choose to do so.

Uncertainty about China's nuclear weapons capabilities, its strategic intentions, and the long-run goals of its nuclear modernization program is exacerbated by China's lack of transparency in the military sphere. Beijing could be striving to become a full-service nuclear power on a qualitative par with the United States and Russia, which would provide Chinese leaders with a wide range of strategic options in a crisis or wartime; or, instead, the Chinese may have the more modest objective of enhancing the credibility of a minimal deterrent force.

China has an increasingly significant impact not only on the strategic nuclear balance but also on nuclear arms control efforts. Beijing can block or advance many key arms control processes. It could be a spoiler in the Comprehensive Test Ban Treaty (CTBT) negotiations under way at the United Nations Committee on Disarmament in Geneva. Without China's agreement, a CTBT is not likely to be completed and would be largely meaningless in any case if it were signed only by the other nuclear powers. Similarly, the Nuclear Non-Proliferation Treaty (NPT) would be substantially weakened if China as a nuclear-

Banning Garrett and Bonnie Glaser are Washington-based consultants on Asian affairs. They have visited China annually since 1983 to discuss strategic issues with Chinese analysts and officials.

The authors would like to thank Alastair Iain Johnston and Paul H.B. Godwin for their insightful comments on an earlier draft of this article.

International Security, Vol. 20, No. 3 (Winter 1995/96), pp. 43–78

weapon state capable of exporting nuclear weapons technology were not a signatory. In the long run, Beijing could block future efforts to reach agreement among the five declared nuclear powers to drastically reduce their strategic nuclear weapons.

China's involvement in multilateral arms control has been largely a reluctant response to international political pressure. Nevertheless, there is increasing support in Beijing for the view that China obtains security benefits from participation in international arms control regimes. Whether backing for this view will continue to grow is unclear, however, especially in light of China's growing mistrust of the United States in the aftermath of the Clinton administration's decision in May 1995 to permit Taiwan's president, Lee Teng-hui, to make a "private" visit to his alma mater, Cornell University. In formulating their arms control and nuclear modernization policies, the Chinese react to China's perceived "threat environment," which includes Beijing's assessment of U.S. strategic intentions toward China. Chinese leaders have become increasingly suspicious that the United States is pursuing a new containment strategy against China and may conclude that the potential military threat posed to China by the United States and other powers requires strengthening China's nuclear weapons capability.

Over the long run, if mutual trust and confidence cannot be restored in U.S.-Chinese relations, the Chinese are likely to be less cooperative with the United States on international arms control issues, especially efforts to halt proliferation of weapons of mass destruction and to eschew participation in nuclear arms control regimes that place limitations on Chinese forces. This could even include Chinese unwillingness to agree to a comprehensive nuclear test ban, particularly if the United States proceeds with deployment of theater missile defense systems in Asia that Beijing views as threatening the viability of China's nuclear deterrent.

Western writings on China and arms control have been sparse and have focused primarily on China's positions, interests, and behavior rather than on the range of thinking in China about arms control.[1] This is due in large part to

1. Recent articles include Gerald Segal, "China and Arms Control," *World Today*, August–September 1985; Alastair I. Johnston, *China and Arms Control: Emerging Issues and Interests in the 1980s*, Aurora Papers No. 3, Canadian Centre for Arms Control and Disarmament, 1986; Alastair I. Johnston, "China Enters the Arms Control Arena," *Arms Control Today*, July/August 1987; Gerald Segal, "Arms Control and Sino-Soviet Relations," in Gerald Segal, ed., *Arms Control in Asia* (London: Macmillan, 1987), pp. 43–65; Bonnie S. Glaser, "Soviet, Chinese and U.S. Perspectives on Arms Control in North-East Asia," in Andrew Mack and Paul Keal, eds., *Security and Arms Control in the North Pacific* (London: Allen and Unwin, 1988); Shirley Kan and Zachary Davis, "China," in

the limitations of Chinese public sources beyond official statements. Most articles published by analysts from Chinese foreign affairs institutes assess U.S. and Russian arms control processes or are descriptive, factual accounts of international arms control regimes; they do not address China's role, interests, or policies in detail.[2] Only a few writings by Chinese experts have departed from official formulations and cautiously discussed China's nuclear weapons program and interests in arms control.[3]

This article aims at providing insight into the thinking and debates behind China's official positions on nuclear arms control issues that are not discernible in public statements and documents.[4] It is based largely on interviews in Beijing and Shanghai with Chinese military and civilian analysts and officials.[5] These experts are part of a small but growing arms control community composed of officials, analysts from foreign policy and defense research institutes, and scientists involved in China's nuclear weapons and ballistic missile pro-

---

Mitchell Reiss and Robert S. Litwak, eds., *Nuclear Proliferation after the Cold War* (Washington, D.C.: Woodrow Wilson Center Press, 1994); Alastair Iain Johnston, "Learning Versus Adaptation: Analyzing Change in Chinese Arms Control Policy," paper prepared for the American Political Science Association Annual Conference, New York, September 1994; Paul H.B. Godwin and John J. Shulz, "China and Arms Control: Transition in East Asia," *Arms Control Today,* November 1994; and Zachary S. Davis, "China's Nonproliferation and Export Control Policies: Boom or Bust for the NPT Regime?" *Asian Survey,* Vol. 35, No. 6 (June 1995), pp. 587–603.

2. See, for example, Hu Yumin, "New Situation in International Arms Control and Disarmament and Their Prospects," *International Strategic Studies,* No. 1 (March 1995), pp. 34–38, published by the China Institute for International Strategic Studies (under the General Staff Department of the People's Liberation Army); and Tan Han, "The Prospects for the Treaty on the Non-Proliferation of Nuclear Weapons," *International Studies,* No. 2 (April 1995), pp. 14–17, published (in Chinese) by the China Institute for International Studies (under the Ministry of Foreign Affairs).

3. Exceptions to the general rule that writings by Chinese experts avoid discussion of Beijing's interests and policies are articles by Shen Dingli, co-director of the arms control program at Fudan University, including Shen, "Toward a Nuclear-Weapon-free World: A Chinese Perspective," *Bulletin of the Atomic Scientists,* March/April 1994; and Shen, "Toward Early Cessation of Nuclear Weapons Testing," *Pacific Research,* November 1994.

4. Chinese analysts and officials held a similarly wide range of views on the issue of ballistic missile defense and the Reagan administration's Strategic Defense Initiative (SDI) in 1985. See Bonnie S. Glaser and Banning N. Garrett, "Chinese Perspectives on the Strategic Defense Initiative," *Problems of Communism,* Vol. 35, No. 2 (March/April 1986), pp. 28–42.

5. Most of the discussions were held in Beijing and Shanghai, October 18–November 1, 1994, with scientists and engineers from organizations involved in testing nuclear weapons and developing ballistic missile delivery vehicles; arms control experts and foreign policy analysts from the People's Liberation Army (PLA) as well as from military-industrial and civilian research institutes; and Chinese officials involved in the Geneva CTBT negotiations and responsible for arms control in the Ministry of Foreign Affairs. The experts held candid discussions with us on the understanding that they would not be quoted by name. In the discussion below, therefore, we have presented as much information as seems necessary to the reader's assessment of the comments while being consistent with constraints on identification or more detailed citation of our sources.

gram who have increasing influence on China's arms control policymaking process.[6]

There has been a proliferation of Chinese arms control specialists in the last decade, largely as a result of the shift in Beijing from viewing arms control as a process that did not involve China but rather was largely an adjunct of the East-West struggle, to a recognition that China would have to participate directly in international arms control regimes and thus needed to develop expertise on the technical and security issues involved. As the Chinese leadership began to face questions such as whether to join the NPT, scientists and military analysts were encouraged to go abroad to study arms control and to create new organizations to research technical arms control matters. Many small arms control groups were established in scientific and military organizations as well as in foreign policy research institutes at the behest of the Chinese leadership, whose interest in arms control issues has been piqued in the last few years by a new awareness of the impact of arms control on Chinese economic, diplomatic, and security interests.

This article first explores Chinese thinking about the role of arms control in China's national security policy, and addresses whether Beijing is moving toward a more interdependent view of security. China's appreciation for the security implications of the NPT is then analyzed, followed by an assessment of Beijing's ambivalence toward the CTBT. The background of Beijing's decision to press for exclusion from the CTBT of peaceful nuclear explosions (PNEs), which can be used for oil and gas exploration as well as other purposes, provides insight into the arms control policymaking process in China. Often to the puzzlement of Western analysts and policymakers, the Chinese have placed a strong emphasis on obtaining pledges of no-first-use (NFU) of nuclear weapons by the five declared nuclear powers. Exploration of this issue offers a window into Chinese perspectives on arms control priorities. Next, the article presents Chinese views on the conditions under which Beijing should participate in future five-power nuclear arms reductions talks, and then examines the potential impact of possible deployment of ballistic missile defense (BMD) or theater missile defense (TMD) systems in Japan or the United States. Finally, we review the conditions that would encourage China to adopt security policies based on interdependence rather than self-help.

6. According to Chinese arms controllers, the number of arms control experts in China has reached approximately 100 people, although most are part-time participants in arms control research.

"Self-Help" and "Security Interdependence"

Chinese views of nuclear arms control have evolved significantly over the last three decades and are still in flux. In the 1970s, Beijing condemned the U.S.-Soviet Strategic Arms Limitation Talks (SALT) as "sham disarmament" providing a cover for continuation of the U.S.-Soviet arms race.[7] The Chinese were especially concerned that the superpowers might collaborate against China, including possible joint strikes on Chinese nuclear weapons facilities, or that the United States might accommodate the rising power of the Soviet Union, leaving it free to increase military pressure on China. In the 1980s, the Chinese came to see advantages for Beijing in "free-riding" on arms control agreements that placed restrictions on other powers to China's benefit, including the various accords between Moscow and Washington on reductions of strategic nuclear forces, elimination of intermediate-range nuclear forces, and limitations on anti–ballistic missile systems.

In the last decade, the Chinese have increasingly seen political and security benefits from participation in multilateral nuclear arms control negotiations and agreements. China pledged in 1986 to abide by the Limited Test Ban Treaty prohibiting atmospheric nuclear tests, and it joined the NPT in 1992. In 1993 Beijing committed itself to sign the CTBT no later than 1996. In the fall of 1994 the Chinese government agreed to participate in fissile material production cutoff talks under the UN Committee on Disarmament in Geneva. Beijing has also introduced its own proposals on nuclear arms control at the United Nations. The Chinese have proposed a convention on the complete elimination of all nuclear weapons, similar in form to the Chemical Weapons Convention which has been signed but not ratified by China, the United States, Russia, and most other powers. China has also called for a no-first-use (NFU) of nuclear weapons treaty among the five declared nuclear powers, and negative security assurances (NSA) by the nuclear-weapon states that they will not use nuclear weapons against non-nuclear-weapon states.

Participation in international arms control regimes and negotiations has not deterred Beijing from modernizing its nuclear forces and seeking to minimize restrictions on development and deployment of Chinese nuclear weapons. China continues to conduct nuclear warhead tests at a time when the other

---

7. For an analysis of Chinese views of the U.S.-Soviet strategic arms negotiations in the early 1970s, see Michael Pillsbury, *Salt on the Dragon: Chinese Views of the Soviet-American Strategic Balance*, P-5374 (Santa Monica, Calif.: RAND Corporation, February 1975).

nuclear powers—with the exception of France—are observing a nuclear test moratorium in anticipation of a CTBT. While the United States and Russia are reducing their arsenals, Beijing's testing program is aimed at modernizing its nuclear forces as well as enhancing warhead safety and reliability. China firmly opposes engaging in nuclear arms reductions talks among the five declared nuclear powers until the United States and Russia have drastically reduced their nuclear arsenals below the levels currently set by the Strategic Arms Reduction Talks (START) II treaty, a prospect seen by the Chinese as years away. In the meantime, China will have an opportunity to qualitatively improve—if not quantitatively expand—its nuclear forces, thus narrowing the gap with Russia and the United States.

Chinese leaders, officials, and foreign policy institute analysts still view the world in largely balance-of-power, *realpolitik* terms, including "self-help" in security. This orientation underlies China's foreign policy and military strategy in general and its nuclear weapons program in particular. The Chinese have "learned" from the United States and the Soviet Union that nuclear weapons enhance national prestige and bargaining leverage, deter pressure and threats, and can influence the outcome of crises and diplomatic confrontations. They have also drawn the lesson from the history of U.S.-Soviet arms control negotiations in the 1970s and 1980s that continued arms competition and further qualitative enhancement of nuclear forces go hand-in-hand with arms control agreements. Finally, there is widespread support in China for the view that development of strong military capability, including substantial nuclear forces, will enhance China's comprehensive national strength, thus enabling Beijing to assume its rightful place as a great power.

China's emphasis on self-help in security is reinforced by growing suspicion that Western powers, especially the United States, are seeking to thwart China's economic development and the concomitant growth of its political and military power. This suspicion provides one of the "lenses" through which many international negotiations, including arms control, are viewed by the Chinese. Underlying Beijing's constant refrain that China must be treated in all arms control fora on the basis of equality is a widely shared resentment of past "unequal treaties" and the "century of humiliation" at the hands of foreigners, from the first Opium War (1839–42) to the founding of the People's Republic of China (PRC) in 1949.[8] Chinese mistrust of the United States has been

8. See Godwin and Shulz, "China and Arms Control," p. 7.

heightened in the last few years by discussion in Washington of a potential military threat from China.

No Chinese arms control experts or officials responsible for arms control policy would advocate abandoning self-help measures in China's approach to national security. Nevertheless, there is growing support in China for the view that multilateral agreements to reduce mutual threats can provide meaningful complements to self-help measures to enhance Chinese security as well as be politically useful in deflecting criticism of China's nuclear weapons policies.[9] This nascent "security interdependence" perspective has been influenced in part by the exposure of Chinese nuclear scientists, military strategists, and civilian analysts to Western concepts of arms control through education in the United States and interaction with U.S. scientists and arms control experts.[10] China's increasing interdependence with the world economy and its involvement in international economic and political institutions have also led to greater appreciation of the potential for addressing some of China's security concerns through international arms control measures.

Chinese officials and foreign policy institute analysts continue to differ over the extent to which limited security interdependence approaches should guide Chinese policy. The tension between engaging in limited security interdependence arrangements and relying solely on self-help measures thus lies at the

9. Occasional published statements reflect a security interdependence view, although none that the authors could find pertain to nuclear weapons. A proponent of security cooperation in the Asia-Pacific region, Yan Xuetong, deputy director of the Center for China's Foreign Policy Studies, China Institute of Contemporary International Relations, argues forcefully for the security interdependence approach: "To speak figuratively, to join regional security cooperation by a country is like to carry a collective health insurance by an individual, which can help the individual to overcome his difficulties by collective efforts. Regional security cooperation in Asia-Pacific is evidently helpful to diminishing possible occurrences of any military conflicts between China and other countries because it can make use of multilateral cooperative forces to deter the aggressive behavior of any individual country. It is for this reason that China supports the development of regional security cooperation." Yan, "China's Post-Cold War Security Strategy," *Contemporary International Relations*, Vol. 5, No. 5 (May 1995), published by the China Institute of Contemporary International Relations, Beijing, p. 14. A more cautious and representative position on Asia-Pacific security cooperation was taken by Guo Zhenyuan, an analyst at the China Center for International Studies. Guo rejects the creation of a security system for the region like the Conference on Security and Cooperation in Europe (CSCE), insisting that "any suspicions between different countries should be cleared up through dialogue and other forms of exchange, rather than a compulsory and interventionist mechanism." Guo, "Prospects for Security Cooperation in the Asia-Pacific Region," *Beijing Review*, Vol. 37, No. 28 (July 11–17, 1994), p. 22.

10. For an extensive discussion of China's nascent arms control community and the growing contacts between Chinese arms control experts and Western arms controllers and scientists, see Johnston, "Learning Versus Adaptation," pp. 23–35.

heart of Chinese thinking about, and debates over, nuclear arms control regimes and initiatives.

The Chinese have not begun considering a more far-reaching notion of security interdependence that would be based on appreciation of the "security dilemma" between nations. Such a view would entail recognition that other nations can perceive Chinese military capabilities and activities as threatening to their security and take measures to counter this perceived threat. Acceptance of this action-reaction process could lead to consideration by Beijing of forgoing military programs or options with the aim of enhancing the security of other states and thus strengthening mutual security.

The Essential Role of the NPT

China threw its support behind the NPT in 1991, after more than two decades of condemning the Treaty for discrimination against non-nuclear countries and failure to curb the nuclear arms expansion of the superpowers sufficiently. Chinese Premier Li Peng announced during a visit of Japanese Prime Minister Toshiki Kaifu to Beijing in August 1991 that China would participate in the NPT regime,[11] and Beijing officially acceded to the Treaty in March 1992. The reversal of China's position was the result of many factors, including the June 1991 decision to join the NPT by France, the only other declared nuclear power that had not been an NPT member; Beijing's post-Tiananmen desire to improve its image with Western countries and to obtain economic assistance from Japan; the end of the Cold War and the U.S.-Soviet nuclear arms race; and growing appreciation in China of the value of arms control in enhancing Chinese security. In the fall of 1991, Chinese analysts remained critical of the NPT for its failure to prevent the United States and Russia from engaging in vertical proliferation of their nuclear arsenals while seeking to restrict horizontal proliferation to the developing world, and for its discrimination against non-nuclear countries seeking to develop nuclear power. They said that on balance, however, joining the Treaty would be more advantageous to China than remaining outside the NPT regime.

The Chinese increasingly view nuclear proliferation as a threat to Chinese and international security, and consider the NPT an essential tool in efforts to

11. Xinhua (China's official news agency), August 10, 1991, cited in "Beijing Agrees to Participate in Nonproliferation Treaty," FBIS (Foreign Broadcast Information Service)—Trends, FB TM 91-033, August 14, 1991, p. 23.

halt the spread of nuclear weapons.[12] An arms control expert at the China Institute of Contemporary International Relations under the State Council, which provides analysis and policy recommendations to the Chinese leadership, termed the NPT "the core treaty among all arms control treaties." An appreciation of the security benefits of the NPT, Chinese experts say, represents a major change in thinking among scientists, analysts, and officials in China that has taken place over the last four to five years. "We now see the NPT as enhancing China's security" as well as global security, asserted a nuclear physicist and leading arms controller. He maintained that while the likelihood of the nuclear-weapon states using nuclear arms is "very low," the probability of nuclear weapons use will substantially increase if more countries acquire atomic weapons. The most likely prospect of actual use of nuclear weapons, according to most Chinese analysts, is in a conflict between India and Pakistan.

Chinese scientists and arms control experts say they are especially concerned about the threat posed to Chinese security by proliferation in Northeast Asia. They view North Korean possession of nuclear weapons as posing a potential direct threat to Chinese security as well as a major stimulus to regional proliferation. "If North Korea acquires nuclear weapons," a Chinese ballistic missile designer asserted, "it will influence Japan and Taiwan to go nuclear." China is relatively confident that Japan will not develop nuclear weapons in the near term if the U.S.-Japan security relationship remains intact and the security situation in the Asia-Pacific region remains stable. They are concerned, however, that changes in Japan's security environment could trigger a decision by Tokyo to "go nuclear," and that the Japanese could build nuclear weapons and delivery systems in a short period of time, given Japan's high-technology base and its plutonium stockpile. For example, a scientist from China's Academy of Launch Vehicle Technology expressed concern about Japan's development of the H-2 rocket, which he maintained "could be used as an ICBM." The Chinese are also suspicious that Taiwan is secretly trying to develop nuclear weapons, although they maintain that Taipei has not yet achieved the ability to produce warheads.

The Chinese ultimately supported unconditional and indefinite extension of the NPT at the NPT Review and Extension Conference in the spring of 1995,

---

12. "After the [NPT] treaty came into effect, in such fields as the prevention of nuclear proliferation, the promotion of nuclear disarmament and the peaceful use of nuclear energy, it has played a key role. To maintain this treaty is of great importance to the enhancement of the international non-proliferation mechanism." Bu Ran, "The International Nuclear Non-Proliferation Mechanism," *Beijing Review*, Vol. 37, No. 51 (December 19–25, 1994), p. 20.

although they indicated that they would have backed extension by multiple periods of no less than twenty-five years each if that had been the majority position at the conference.[13] As was repeatedly indicated by Chinese officials prior to the opening of the conference, Beijing's foremost interest was in a "smooth" extension of the treaty. Failure of the parties to the NPT to agree on the terms of renewal would have been viewed as damaging to China's security interests and a setback to global efforts to contain nuclear proliferation.[14] The Chinese shared the U.S. objective of achieving extension of the NPT by consensus and worried that if extension were put to a vote, the Treaty's authoritativeness could be undermined and the global regime to stem nuclear proliferation could unravel.[15]

Prior to the opening of the NPT review conference, Chinese officials and institute researchers expressed support for revising the NPT to make it more equitable and thus, they maintained, more effective. Chinese Foreign Ministry officials and institute arms controllers indicated that Beijing favored making the Treaty less discriminatory against the non-nuclear states and providing those states with security assurances from the nuclear-weapon states that they will not face a nuclear attack. China also supported correcting the "imbalance" in responsibilities between the nuclear and non-nuclear parties to the NPT. "The non-nuclear states must commit themselves to not acquire nuclear weapons," noted one Chinese arms control expert, "but there is no provision in the Treaty preventing the nuclear-weapon states from further developing their nuclear weapons." Thus, Beijing backed the demands of the non-nuclear states to strengthen the nuclear-weapon states' commitment to Article VI of the Treaty, which commits them to the goal of total elimination of nuclear weapons. In addition, Chinese officials and analysts stressed the importance of strengthening and implementing the commitments in the NPT for the nuclear powers

---

13. Xinhua, April 18, 1995, FBIS-CHI-95-075, April 19, 1995, p. 1.

14. According to Du Gengqi, a researcher with the Chinese People's Association for Peace and Disarmament, "if the Treaty is renewed uneventfully, then not only will the existing mechanism for non-proliferation be maintained and strengthened, but the nuclear states, particularly the United States and Russia, will be spurred to further reduce their nuclear stockpiles. Otherwise, the 25-year-old NPT will collapse and the world will be thrown into a nightmare of nuclear proliferation." "NPT Treaty at a Crossroads," *Beijing Review*, Vol. 38, No. 17 (April 24–30, 1995), p. 19.

15. Chinese Disarmament Ambassador Sha Zukang said in an interview with Xinhua on May 1, 1995, that "the best method" to extend the NPT "is to have all signatory states reach a consensus through broad consultations; otherwise, it will be necessary to put the issue to a vote and have it voted through by simple majority. However, the vote's outcome will affect the authoritativeness of the 'treaty' regardless of the number of such a majority vote." Li Jianxiong, "Strictly Prevent Nuclear Proliferation and Peacefully Make Use of Nuclear Energy—an Exclusive Interview with Chinese Disarmament Ambassador Sha Zukang," Xinhua, May 2, FBIS-CHI-95-086, May 4, 1995, p. 5.

to share technology for the peaceful use of nuclear energy with the non-nuclear-weapon states.[16]

Such revisions of the NPT, Chinese arms controllers and officials maintained, would make it more likely that nuclear have-nots tempted to acquire nuclear arms would join the NPT—if they are not yet members—and that all members would comply with its terms. Effective implementation of the Treaty, Chinese analysts said, depends on the non-nuclear states perceiving its terms as reasonable. "If a country thinks that the treaty is unfair and that it adversely affects its security," said a civilian arms control expert, "it will find a way around it."

Preparing for a Comprehensive Test Ban Treaty

Agreeing to a comprehensive and permanent nuclear test ban is a more complicated decision for Beijing than joining the NPT. A CTBT would involve restrictions on China's freedom of action in a core area of national security, the viability of the Chinese nuclear deterrent. Signing and implementing a CTBT would be the first substantial decision by Beijing regarding nuclear arms control that reflected limited security interdependence, not just free-riding. A CTBT would crimp Chinese nuclear warhead modernization efforts, although China might calculate that after successful completion of its current series of tests it will have sufficiently narrowed the qualitative gap with the United States and Russia in warhead design to warrant agreeing to a universal halt to testing without weakening China's deterrent. The NPT, in contrast, does not require Beijing to pay a cost in opportunities forgone in China's self-help efforts to enhance security, although it does restrict Chinese exports of nuclear weapons technology.

China only reluctantly became a partner in the CTBT negotiations, which were convened in winter 1994 in the Nuclear Test Ban Ad Hoc Committee of the UN Committee on Disarmament.[17] Beijing agreed to participate in CTBT

16. China's ambassador to the UN Conference on Disarmament in Geneva, Hou Zhitong, said in October 1994 that "China firmly supports the just demand of the non-nuclear-weapons states of the Third World for enhancing international cooperation in peaceful uses of nuclear energy, which should be considered by the 1995 NPT conference as an important agenda item." Hou Zhitong speaking before the first committee of the United Nations General Assembly, October 21, 1994. Xinhua, October 22, 1994, FBIS-CHI-94-205, October 24, 1994, p. 1.

17. China's opening position on a comprehensive test ban was presented by Ambassador Hou Zhitong, head of the Chinese delegation to the UN Conference on Disarmament, March 24, 1994. The full text of the statement was released by the permanent mission of the People's Republic of China at Geneva.

talks partially in response to international criticism of its continued nuclear testing at a time when the other nuclear-weapon states had declared a test moratorium. China's recalcitrance on the test ban issue was primarily a function of Beijing's desire to continue nuclear testing for safety, reliability, and modernization of China's nuclear arsenal. The lack of enthusiasm in China for a CTBT was also due to a widely held view that halting nuclear testing has less significance than other measures aimed at curbing the spread and preventing the use of nuclear weapons. Chinese analysts and officials maintain, for example, that although a CTBT will contribute to international security, it will play a less significant role than a five-power pledge of no-first-use (NFU) and negative security assurances (NSA), or extension of the NPT. Most Chinese arms controllers would agree with Foreign Minister Qian Qichen's 1993 statement that "granted that a nuclear test ban is necessary, to undertake not to use nuclear weapons at all is far more crucial, because this will not only make their testing, development, production or deployment devoid of any meaning, but will give a great impetus to nuclear disarmament, which will contribute tremendously to world peace and security."[18] Nevertheless, most Chinese arms control experts and officials assert that on balance, the signing and implementation of a CTBT will be in China's security as well as political interest.

China first indicated its willingness to participate in CTBT negotiations in the fall of 1993.[19] On September 29, Foreign Minister Qian stated at a meeting of the UN General Assembly that China supported "an early start of negotiations for a comprehensive nuclear test ban treaty."[20] In a statement a week later defending a nuclear test, Beijing clarified its position by dropping its long-standing insistence that a test ban treaty could only be concluded within the "framework of the complete prohibition and thorough destruction of nuclear weapons."[21]

In the Geneva negotiations aimed at concluding a CTBT, China has pressed for inclusion of three controversial provisions: the right of declared nuclear-

18. *Beijing Review*, Vol. 36, No. 41 (October 11–17, 1993), p. 10.

19. On the eve of China's shift in policy on the CTBT and just before another Chinese nuclear test, Shih Chun-yu, a columnist for the pro-Beijing Hong Kong paper *Ta Kung Pao*, defended the Chinese nuclear testing program, saying that China has no choice but to develop its national defense capability because in this "hegemonist world" a country "without a defense capability" will be "bullied and humiliated." *Ta Kung Pao*, September 20, 1993, cited in "China-U.S.: Beijing Sees Need for Scheduled Nuclear Test," FBIS—Trends, FB TM 93-038, September 22, 1993, p. 26.

20. *Beijing Review*, Vol. 36, No. 41 (October 11–17, 1993), p. 10.

21. PRC Government Statement, October 5, 1993, Xinhua, October 5, 1993, cited in "Beijing Defends Nuclear Test, Calls for Test Ban Treaty," FBIS—Trends, FB TM 93-040, October 6, 1993, p. 44.

weapon states to conduct peaceful nuclear explosions (PNEs); NFU and NSA commitments by the nuclear-weapon states; and the primacy of the international monitoring system (IMS) over the use of national technical means (NTM) of individual states for verification. Chinese officials and institute arms control experts deny that Beijing is seeking to use ancillary issues to block agreement on a CTBT, insisting that China's proposals are based on genuine concerns. They predict, however, that Beijing will eventually give up these demands during the negotiations if they are not supported by other powers.

An early conclusion of a draft test ban treaty would not be in China's interest, since it would preclude conclusion of Beijing's current series of nuclear warhead tests, which are aimed at significantly narrowing the technology gap with the United States and Russia in warhead design and capability.[22] Some Chinese arms control experts openly acknowledge this and say that some of China's proposals for the CTBT may have the effect, if not the intention, of prolonging the negotiations. An arms control expert and professor at one of China's leading universities commented that in his view, China does not need to conduct peaceful nuclear explosions, and criticized the position as contrary to Beijing's objective in garnering Third World support. The expert suggested, however, that Chinese negotiators are raising the PNE issue in the Comprehensive Test Ban talks as part of "a strategy to delay the signing of a CTB." This was also China's objective in presenting a position paper that proposed a number of alternative verification regimes, according to the professor, "so that people would explore and discuss all of them and not reach an accord by 1996." Other Chinese arms controllers point out that China is not alone in opposing an early CTBT signing. One expert noted, for example, that France "has put forward some demands to delay the talks."

CHINA'S NUCLEAR TESTING GOALS

Although Chinese officials insist that Beijing is continuing to conduct nuclear tests solely to improve nuclear warhead safety and reliability, China's testing program is also aimed at developing a smaller, more powerful warhead. A higher yield-to-weight warhead is slated to provide the nuclear punch for a

---

22. For a Chinese negotiator's assessment of the prospects for reaching a CTBT, see Zou Yunhua, "Comprehensive Nuclear Test Ban Inevitable in the Developing Circumstances—Written on the Eve of Talks on a 'Comprehensive Nuclear Test Ban Treaty'," *Guoji Wenti Yanjiu*, No. 51 (January 13, 1994), in Joint Publications Research Service (JPRS), JPRS-CAR-94-030, May 12, 1994, pp. 1–4. Zou Yunhua is a PLA official from the Commission of Science, Technology and Industry for National Defense (COSTIND) and is a representative to the CTB negotiations in Geneva.

new generation of solid-fuel, land- and sea-based ballistic missiles currently under development. Solid-fuel missiles will enable Beijing to improve the response time of Chinese nuclear forces as well as their survivability by deploying a small, single-warhead mobile missile and improving China's submarine-launched ballistic missile (SLBM) forces.[23] The Chinese are also working to improve the accuracy of their nuclear weapon systems to increase Beijing's targeting options in a nuclear conflict. In addition, smaller warheads will enable the Chinese to develop and deploy multiple independently targeted re-entry vehicles (MIRVs) should Beijing perceive, for example, a need for a significant increase in the number of deployed warheads to overwhelm a ballistic missile defense system.

Some Chinese scientists and arms control experts acknowledge that China is seeking to modernize its nuclear warheads before a CTBT is finalized. The end of the Cold War and the U.S.-Soviet nuclear arms competition, these experts say, has provided an opportunity to significantly narrow the qualitative gap in warhead design. A former ballistic missile engineer with close ties to China's nuclear weapons development community maintained that "there is no more room for perfection of nuclear weapons by the United States and Russia" except for development of new types of weapons such as ground-penetrating warheads. For China, however, there is still a need to modernize its warheads, according to the engineer, who is now a senior researcher in the Chinese Academy of Social Sciences. He acknowledged that China "wants to lower the weight/yield ratio for MIRVs . . . or other purposes," noting that "Chinese warheads are much heavier" than those of the United States and Russia, which "are at the limit of specific megatonnage."

Chinese scientists and arms controllers as well as Western analysts maintain that Beijing plans its program for development of a high yield-to-weight warhead to be completed before the end of 1996. Once China has confidence in its warhead design, a halt to nuclear testing will not prevent development of advanced nuclear weapon systems to enhance survivability, accuracy, targeting flexibility, and response time. In addition, warhead design may be further refined through computer modeling, hydronuclear testing, and perhaps peaceful nuclear explosions in the unlikely event they are permitted under a CTBT.

23. China tested a solid-fuel ballistic missile, the Dongfang or DF-31, from a mobile launcher on May 29, 1995. The missile was tested over Chinese territory at a range of 2,000 km, but reportedly has a maximum range of 8,000 km. The DF-31 reportedly could be available as an SLBM early in the next century. See Nigel Holloway, "A Chill Wind: Stealthier Nuclear Missile Raises U.S. Fears," *Far Eastern Economic Review*, June 15, 1995, pp. 15–16.

CTBT SIGNING AND IMPLEMENTATION

Beijing's desire to complete its current series of nuclear tests has led to official ambiguity about when China expects to sign and implement a CTBT. China's official government position backs conclusion of a "comprehensive, effective and universal nuclear test ban treaty as early as possible and no later than 1996."[24] Beijing has been intentionally unclear about when in 1996 it is prepared to sign a CTBT, according to Chinese arms controllers, many of whom predict that an agreement will not be signed until the end of that year. Beijing's official position is that China will end nuclear testing once a CTBT enters into force.[25] Chinese officials and researchers admit, however, that whether Beijing should continue to test after a CTBT is reached, but before it enters into effect, is a subject of unresolved controversy in China.

Some Chinese officials assert that it would be legal but politically difficult for China to continue testing after a CTBT is concluded. A senior Foreign Ministry official in charge of arms control matters rejected the contention that the Vienna Treaty on Treaties—which prohibits a country from taking steps prior to a treaty entering into force that would violate the spirit of the treaty—would disallow China from conducting nuclear tests after an agreement was signed but before it was implemented. He acknowledged, however, that "once you sign a treaty, to do something that would undermine it is not good" and added that he "would not recommend it." An official from the Commission of Science, Technology, and Industry for the National Defense (COSTIND) under the State Council and the Central Military Commission said that although the

---

24. Statement by Ambassador Hou Zhitong to the first committee of the UN General Assembly, October 21, 1994. Xinhua, October 22, 1994, FBIS-CHI-94-205, October 24, 1994, p. 1.

25. A Chinese Foreign Ministry spokesman said on October 7, 1994, that "China will put an end to its nuclear tests once the [CTB] treaty comes into effect." Xinhua, October 7, 1994, FBIS-CHI-94-195, October 7, 1994, p. 21. The Chinese have proposed a lengthy procedure leading to entry into effect of the Treaty. On June 20, 1994, the Chinese delegation to the CTBT negotiations in the Ad Hoc Committee on a Nuclear Test Ban of the UN Conference on Disarmament offered the following formulation for the "entry into force" article of the CTBT: "1. This Treaty shall enter into force one year after the following requirements have been met: a) One year shall have elapsed since ratification by all States that were members of the Conference on Disarmament at the time when the Treaty was opened for signature and by all States known by the International Atomic Energy Agency to possess nuclear capabilities (i.e., to possess nuclear power stations or nuclear reactors); b) The Treaty shall have been open for signature for a minimum of two years. 2. The Treaty shall enter into force in respect of States that deposit their instruments of ratification or accession after its entry into force upon the date of deposit of such instruments of ratification or accession." Meeting these terms could take at least three years following the signing of the treaty. In any case, such language is unlikely to be accepted by the other states engaged in the CTBT negotiations. "China—Working Paper, Entry Into Force of the CTBT," CD/NTB/WP.123, June 20, 1994, original in Chinese.

Chinese government had not yet formulated a position on the issue, "any country that wants to conduct nuclear tests after the CTBT is signed will meet with great difficulties."

While the Foreign Ministry may urge cessation of testing once a treaty is signed, the People's Liberation Army (PLA) may press for more tests if China's nuclear testing objectives have not yet been attained. Chinese leaders thus may have to weigh the costs and benefits of continuing to conduct at most a few more tests before the treaty enters into force. A wild card that could affect Beijing's decision to halt testing could be Chinese leaders' concern that the deployment of ballistic missile defense (BMD) systems in the United States and Russia or theater missile defense (TMD) systems in Japan will degrade China's nuclear deterrent.

Discussions with Chinese officials and arms control experts indicate that China's cost/benefit calculus of the security and political implications of a test ban treaty is likely to lead Beijing to sign, ratify, and eventually implement a CTBT, although when China will halt testing remains uncertain. If necessary, Beijing may use debate over its controversial proposals for the CTBT to delay the signing of a treaty until late 1996, while the current series of Chinese nuclear tests is being completed.

CONTROVERSY OVER CTBT COSTS AND BENEFITS TO CHINA

Chinese officials and arms control experts acknowledge that Beijing faces strong political pressure to halt nuclear testing. Beijing provoked an unprecedented wave of international protest, especially from Asian states, when it conducted a nuclear test on May 15, 1995, just three days after the conclusion of the NPT Review and Extension Conference. Similar criticism followed China's forty-third nuclear test on August 17. China is especially sensitive to pressure from non-nuclear developing countries, many of which had demanded that the nuclear-weapon states sign a comprehensive nuclear test ban as a prerequisite for extension of the NPT. Neighboring Kazakhstan has expressed concerns about the medical, biological, and environmental impact of Chinese nuclear tests, in addition to charging China with undermining the NPT.[26] Beijing is expected to conduct several more nuclear tests before the end of 1996.

26. Following China's atomic explosion on October 7, 1994, the Foreign Ministry of Kazakhstan released a statement condemning the nuclear tests at Lop Nor as "undermining the Nuclear Nonproliferation Treaty regime against the background of present realities in the world nuclear policy." It also said: "The nuclear tests on the Lop Nor proving ground located in close proximity to the Kazakh-Chinese border are fraught with serious damage to the medical and biological and

Besides the political necessity of joining a CTBT regime, some Chinese arms control experts maintain that there are military-strategic benefits of a nuclear test ban for China, which include freezing the gap between China and other countries in development of nuclear weapons. They argue that halting nuclear testing would help maintain China's lead over India in nuclear weapons and prevent the gap between China and the other nuclear-weapon states, especially the United States and Russia, from growing even wider. Chinese arms controllers also contend that a CTBT would have broader benefits for Beijing in enhancing prospects of maintaining a peaceful and stable environment for China's economic development by discouraging nuclear proliferation. A missile engineer at the Academy of Launch Vehicle Technology, for example, asserted that "if a CTBT is reached by all states, many countries will not be able to develop nuclear weapons that might otherwise do so." An arms control expert from COSTIND, however, cautioned that at least some states, including Japan and Germany, "could make nuclear weapons without any tests."

Chinese civilian and military arms control specialists say that many people in the PLA are skeptical of the benefits to China of banning nuclear tests and only reluctantly support Beijing's decision to back negotiations to conclude a CTBT. A scientist from the Beijing Institute of Systems Engineering maintained that "some military people hope there will be more testing," although they accept that "this decision [to participate in a CTBT] has been made at the highest level." According to the scientist, "the military thinks that our nuclear forces are not developed enough" because "there is a gap between China and Russia, and between China and the United States," and "there is even a gap between China and France." The former ballistic missile engineer similarly noted that "the military would like to further improve nuclear weapons, but for political reasons, China has to sign the agreement."

Not all military personnel object to a CTBT, however. According to an arms control expert from the PLA, there is a "difference of opinion" on this issue; "more and more people in the military support finally ending nuclear testing." The main support for conducting more tests, according to the researcher, comes from "people in the nuclear weapons program." He also asserted that there is a debate in China similar to that in the United States over the relative importance of conventional and nuclear weapons. Proponents of a CTBT argue that with the end of the Cold War "there is no need to improve nuclear weapons because the importance of nuclear weapons has been reduced," he said.

---

technogene [sic] environment in the region." ITAR-TASS, October 7, 1994, FBIS-SOV-94-196, October 11, 1994, p. 62.

PEACEFUL NUCLEAR EXPLOSIONS

Chinese representatives at the CTBT negotiations have proposed language in the draft treaty protecting the right of nuclear-weapon states to conduct peaceful nuclear explosions. We review this issue in detail because it illustrates how arms control policies are made, affected, and modified. While tabling the PNE proposal serves China's interest in delaying conclusion of a treaty, Chinese officials and scientists are apparently sincere in their insistence that PNEs are potentially valuable and should not be banned in perpetuity. They realize, however, that non-nuclear states view PNEs as inherently discriminatory and that the United States abandoned PNEs as unviable. Chinese officials and analysts indicate that China will not use the PNE issue to prevent conclusion of a CTBT and hint that Beijing will eventually withdraw its proposal.

SCIENTISTS' SUPPORT FOR PNES. The main impetus for seeking to preserve PNEs in the CTBT has come from Chinese scientists who have argued that since a CTBT is a long-term treaty and the development of science cannot be foreseen, PNEs should not be permanently banned. The argument that PNEs may be proven useful or necessary at some time in the future is echoed by Ministry of Foreign Affairs (MFA) officials. A senior MFA official asserted, for example, that "PNEs haven't been used much for reasons of cost effectiveness, but since the CTBT will be indefinite, we should not rule them out." Some Chinese scientists favor a fall-back position of including compromise language in the treaty that would proscribe PNEs for a specified time period. A leading Chinese scientist who is a member of the Scientists Group on Arms Control under the Chinese People's Association for Peace and Disarmament (CPAPD)[27] suggested that PNEs "could be banned for a period of time—even for a long time—and then reevaluated."

Chinese scientists have been heavily influenced on the PNE issue by their Russian colleagues. Despite the Russian government's opposition to preserving the right to conduct PNEs—which were discontinued by Moscow in 1988—Russian scientists remain interested in pursuing the technology and want to cooperate with China on PNE research. A Chinese nuclear physicist and member of the CPAPD Scientists Group on Arms Control said that Russian reports on PNEs, including a recently published book, have been read by many Chinese nuclear scientists and that this was fueling enthusiasm in China for

27. Members of the Scientists Group on Arms Control have since 1991 held bilateral, annual conferences between the Chinese People's Association for Peace and Disarmament and the Committee on International Security and Arms Control of the U.S. National Academy of Science.

pursuing PNE research. Noting that Russia has used 200 PNEs at fifteen different sites, the nuclear physicist maintained that Russian scientists have demonstrated that PNEs are "a very successful, technologically feasible and profitable approach" for oil and gas exploitation. Another Chinese scientist indicated that China is already working with Russian scientists on PNEs but maintained that this cooperation is limited to discussions in conferences at the level of basic science.

China has never used PNEs and Beijing currently has no plan to do so, according to Chinese officials and scientists. China's failure so far to conduct PNEs may be primarily due to budgetary constraints. A COSTIND official asserted that "a few years ago" some people in the Chinese People's Political Consultative Conference "advocated use of PNEs to increase oil exploitation," and "scientists in the department of nuclear design asked for money to do a feasibility study." The petroleum ministry also wanted to study the problem, the official said, but no money was allocated "so nothing was done." According to one Chinese nuclear physicist, a segment of China's petroleum industry still wants to use PNEs to increase oil production, although there is no agreement on this. Another scientist–arms controller asserted that "there are many proposals to experiment with PNEs in China, but due to the priorities of economic construction" the experiments cannot be conducted.

Many Chinese nuclear scientists are confident that PNEs would be technically feasible and economically cost-effective for exploiting oil reserves. Using a sketch of a nuclear device exploding in the middle of a series of oil deposits, one Chinese nuclear physicist explained that "because of the high level of viscosity of Chinese oil, it is necessary to heat the oil to extract it."[28] Other Chinese scientists maintain that research in China shows that PNEs would also be useful for constructing large reservoirs and even for making diamonds.

The PNE issue is apparently controversial in China on technical as well as political grounds. A key concern of Chinese critics is possible contamination. A COSTIND arms controller asserted that preventing PNEs from being "very dirty" requires more advanced technology than is necessary just to build a nuclear bomb. A leading nuclear physicist, however, denied there was a serious contamination problem with extracting highly viscous oil, noting that "the oil fields are very deep" and "radiation never touches the oil." The scientist

28. According to a Chinese nuclear physicist, a 1994 paper presented by He Zuoxia, a researcher from the Institute of Theoretical Physics, advocated use of underground nuclear explosions to exploit China's oil deposits. The physicist noted that the paper was quite compelling and warmly received.

acknowledged, however, that "the explosions must be very carefully planned for placement of the device relative to the oil deposits," which, he said, would require large-scale computer simulations.

Other opponents to Beijing's efforts to preserve PNEs under the CTBT question the political wisdom of tabling a discriminatory proposal that permits only the declared nuclear states to conduct PNEs. Experts who hold this view contend that taking such a position is contrary to China's political interests in relations with the developing world and the non-declared nuclear states.

PNE VERIFICATION. China's serious interest in preserving the right to conduct peaceful nuclear explosions is evidenced by Beijing's extensive proposals for approval and verification of PNEs. A COSTIND official maintained, for example, that it is "technically impossible" to detect the difference between explosions for peaceful and for military uses. For this reason, the official claimed, the Chinese delegation to the UN Committee on Disarmament has proposed that a country be required to apply to the CTBT organization before conducting a PNE. China's proposal sets out a detailed process for approving PNEs that would have several stages and would require a country to explain the purpose of the proposed PNE as well as obtain approval from the CTBT member organization.

Some Chinese scientists also call for technical verification measures to ensure that a PNE is not used for weapons development purposes. One nuclear physicist noted that "to use an explosion for the purpose of developing nuclear weapons, it is necessary to take diagnostic measurements" to get parameters. This need for diagnostic information from the nuclear blast, the scientist contended, provides an opportunity for "verification steps to prevent measurements." He acknowledged that it would be "difficult to reach a consensus among world scientists on this issue."

ROLE OF NATIONAL TECHNICAL MEANS IN VERIFICATION OF CTBT COMPLIANCE

Chinese negotiators at the CTB talks have proposed treaty language that would not allow the national technical means of member states to be used as the primary source of evidence to justify on-site investigation of a suspicious event that could be in violation of a CTBT. The Chinese want the International Monitoring System (IMS) that is to be created under the test ban regime to have primary responsibility for detecting violations. They insist that data acquired by NTM should be used only as supplementary information and not to initiate an investigation.

Chinese officials and arms control experts are concerned that NTM could be used by countries with more advanced capabilities—the United States and Russia—to call for an investigation of China or other countries for political reasons, or to suppress evidence to hide their own activities in violation of the treaty. A member of the CPAPD Scientists Group on Arms Control asserted that "it would be easy to misuse this NTM advantage from a political standpoint." The country with NTM, the scientist said, could decide whether or not it was in its political interest to provide evidence of a treaty violation. "In practical terms," according to a Foreign Ministry arms control official, "countries like the United States will raise challenges against others because the United States has NTM and others don't." Chinese experts say they worry that such NTM-derived challenges could be used for intelligence-gathering purposes.

Chinese arms controllers object that reliance on NTM would be inherently unequal. A COSTIND official noted that while countries with advanced NTM could hide a suspicious event, "less advanced countries could not." Moreover, Chinese arms control experts say, countries with backward technology could not be certain whether other countries were observing the treaty, while those countries with strong NTM would be confident they could ascertain whether the treaty was being violated.

Chinese officials insist that concern about the IMS is part of Beijing's commitment to the principle that a CTBT must be balanced and equal. A senior MFA official maintained that China "can't allow a politically discriminatory treaty" because it has to "speak for the developing countries." He contended that "there is a political imbalance inherent in NTM," which is why China "won't accept NTM as the sole means of verification." Verification by an international secretariat would provide for "fairness and equality," the MFA official asserted, although information from NTM could used to "complement" the IMS. Chinese negotiators have proposed several schemes for a strong international monitoring system as an alternative to reliance on NTM. They call for the IMS to have the capability to detect, measure, and locate suspicious events. Chinese experts maintain that a satellite-based detection system is necessary to complement seismic monitoring, and thus propose that a global satellite network be made available for verification.

Although the Chinese see their interests best served by the creation of an independent IMS for verification of a CTBT, they do not expect the United States and Russia to agree to provide real-time sharing of data from their NTM nor to agree to the building of an expensive and elaborate satellite monitoring system under the International Secretariat of the CTBT Organization. Beijing nevertheless sees political advantages in its relations with developing states in pressing for equality in the verification provisions. The Chinese also realize that they can slow down the negotiations by forcing debate over their verification proposals. As with the issues of preserving the right to conduct PNEs, China is likely to drop its demand on NTM rather than use this issue to block conclusion of a treaty.

Priority on No-First-Use Pledges and Negative Security Assurances

For three decades, China has urged the other four nuclear-weapon powers—the United States, Russia, France, and Great Britain—to follow China's lead and commit themselves to not be the first to use nuclear weapons against any other nuclear weapons state (NFU); and to not use nuclear weapons or the threat of nuclear weapons against any non-nuclear country or nuclear-free zone at any time or under any circumstances (NSA).[29] The Chinese continue to place a high priority on obtaining NFU and NSA commitments from the other nuclear powers and have sought to include such pledges in the CTBT and the NPT.[30] They have also called for a separate five-power agreement on NFU and NSA. Chinese Foreign Minister Qian Qichen, speaking before the UN General Assembly on September 19, 1993, proposed that the nuclear-weapon states conclude an "international convention on unconditional nonfirst-use of nuclear weapons and the nonuse and nonthreat-of-use of nuclear weapons against nonnuclear states and nuclear-free zones." In December 1993, the Chinese

---

29. Prior to the opening of the NPT Review and Extension Conference, the Chinese government issued a statement on security assurances in which they qualified their long-standing position on NSA, saying, "this commitment is, of course, applicable to non-nuclear countries which are signatories of the Nuclear Nonproliferation Treaty or non-nuclear countries which have made a similar internationally binding pledge on the nonproduction and nonprocurement of nuclear devices." Xinhua, April 5, 1995, FBIS-CHI-95-066, April 6, 1995, p. 1. The Chinese statement was apparently aimed at India, which does not meet these revised conditions.

30. Beijing criticized as "not unequivocal" and "very much conditional" the statements on providing security assurances for non-nuclear states issued by representatives of the United States, Russia, France, and Britain on April 6, 1995, at the Conference on Disarmament in Geneva. According to Xinhua, the four nuclear powers made a commitment "to provide security assurances to only the nonnuclear-weapon states which are signatories to the NPT, and these nonnuclear-weapon states must not enter into associations or alliances with any nuclear-weapon states which may attack them or any other country with which they have signed a security agreement." Xinhua charged that these security assurances "serve as a warning to nonnuclear-weapon states—don't take any hostile actions against us, or we will use our nuclear weapons." Yang Qing and Ban Wei, "What Security Assurances Do Nonnuclear States Need?" Xinhua, April 8, 1995, FBIS-CHI-95-069, April 10, 1995, p. 1.

government called for formal five-power NFU negotiations to conclude an NFU Treaty, and three months later officially invited the other four nuclear-weapon states to hold NFU talks in Beijing.

MILITARY AND POLITICAL SIGNIFICANCE OF NFU AND NSA

Many Western analysts dismiss NFU pledges as political statements with little significance or credibility in a crisis. In contrast, Chinese analysts and officials insist that such commitments by the nuclear powers would enhance international security.[31] Most Chinese arms control experts agree with the Chinese government's claim that the benefits of an NFU treaty would include reduced risk of war, enhanced security of the five nuclear-weapon states, greater mutual trust, reduced likelihood of nuclear proliferation, and advancement toward the goal of complete nuclear disarmament. Some analysts also suggest that NFU pledges would reduce reliance on nuclear weapons for security and would mitigate the possibility that a nation such as China would face nuclear blackmail by another nuclear power. A leading Chinese nuclear physicist and arms control expert maintained, for example, that an NFU pledge has "strategic significance" and thus should not be viewed as "only a political statement" with little military consequence. Chinese arms controllers contend that NFU commitments by all the declared nuclear-weapon states would provide a greater deterrent to war than a CTBT or nuclear arms reductions agreements.

NFU pledges are especially important to Beijing, since Chinese assessments of the threat posed by another state begin with an analysis of its intentions. Thus, Chinese officials and analysts view a country's willingness or unwillingness to make an NFU pledge as a key indicator of its political and strategic intentions. They maintain that the nuclear powers, especially those with smaller arsenals such as China, would feel more secure with NFU pledges from the other nuclear powers and would therefore be better able to establish stable relationships among themselves.

Some Chinese researchers even suggest that an NFU agreement could move the world closer to complete elimination of nuclear weapons. A CPAPD researcher asserted that based on the assumption that the only reasonable function of nuclear weapons is to deter the use of nuclear weapons, a pledge by

---

31. An unnamed Chinese arms controller was quoted by Agence France Presse (AFP) in February 1995 as contending that obtaining commitments to NFU and NSA from all of the nuclear-weapon states was the "crux" of the nuclear issue in the post–Cold War period. AFP, February 17, 1995, FBIS-CHI-95-033, February 17, 1995.

the five nuclear powers not to be the first to use nuclear weapons against each other would obviate the need for nuclear weapons for this deterrent function. Thus, the researcher maintained that once this step has been taken, "in the not too distant future, nuclear weapons can be eliminated." Other Chinese analysts do not foresee an NFU treaty leading to eventual elimination of nuclear weapons, however. A scientist in China's Academy of Launch Vehicle Technology, asserted, for example, that although an NFU agreement would lead to "a safer world," nuclear weapons would continue to exist for "deterrence purposes."

In addition to an NFU pledge among the nuclear-weapon states, negative security assurances by the nuclear powers to the non-nuclear countries are considered necessary by Beijing to reduce the risk of nuclear war and halt the spread of nuclear weapons. Many Chinese arms control experts maintain that NSA commitments by all the nuclear-weapon states would make a more significant contribution to preventing proliferation of nuclear weapons than banning nuclear weapons tests. Noting that Western countries view the CTBT as aimed at preventing the threshold countries from developing nuclear weapons, a COSTIND official claimed that "a CTBT only has limited significance in promoting non-proliferation," because "the basic design of an atomic bomb is not sophisticated and a workable bomb can be built without testing." The official played down the local and regional factors spurring nuclear proliferation, contending that assurances from the nuclear-weapon states would more effectively address the security concerns that lead developing countries to seek to acquire nuclear weapons. "With a combined NFU and NSA," the COSTIND official insisted, "many non-nuclear-weapon states won't try to develop nuclear weapons."

Chinese analysts have recently expressed concern that further efforts to prevent the proliferation of nuclear weapons could be stymied by the deployment of advanced high-technology weapons systems. In their view, development of nuclear and chemical weapons may be perceived by Third World states as a relatively affordable means of deterring the high-tech weapons of the developed countries, especially the United States.[32]

China's advocacy of NFU and NSA is also intended to achieve Beijing's political objectives. One Chinese arms controller noted, for example, that "China's role in leading the Third World has been less prominent recently" and

---

32. This point was made by Chinese researchers to U.S. scholar Roxane Sismanidis in March 1995. See her "Chinese Security as Asia Evolves," prepared for presentation at the 1995 Annual Meeting of the Association for Asian Studies, Washington, D.C., April 7, 1995, p. 20.

asserted that by actively backing NSA for non-nuclear states China can "demonstrate a leadership role."

CHINA'S DESIRE FOR U.S. NFU PLEDGE

Chinese officials and analysts maintain that among the five nuclear states, China has greater need for an NFU treaty than the other nuclear powers and that Beijing is primarily concerned about an NFU commitment by the United States. Chinese arms control experts contend that China's requirement for reassurances from the United States is rooted in its historical experience with the United States. "China was threatened with nuclear weapons by the United States in the 1950s three times—the Korean War, Dien Bien Phu and Quemoy-Matsu," and "for this reason it developed nuclear weapons" sooner than it would have otherwise, declared one university professor. As a consequence, he said, China wants moral assurance that it "won't become a victim." A senior Foreign Ministry official placed the need for an NFU pledge from the United States in the context of the end of the Cold War and the demise of the Soviet Union, which he said had fundamentally changed the nuclear calculus. The official portrayed China as in a vulnerable, isolated position because the United States, France, and Britain are militarily allied, and the United States and Russia are now partners that would not use nuclear weapons against each other. "So it is four against one," he said. The official insisted that although the United States and China "don't see each other as security threats," United States participation in a five-power NFU treaty would nevertheless "have a strong psychological impact" on China.

Beijing needs an NFU pledge from the United States not just for psychological reasons, some Chinese analysts maintain, but also to reduce the risk that the United States will threaten to use nuclear weapons against China in the event of a confrontation over Taiwan. Although these experts say that the United States and China are not enemies, they nevertheless do not rule out the possibility that the United States might threaten to use nuclear weapons against China to prevent Beijing from seizing control of Taiwan by force.

There is also growing interest in China in obtaining an NFU pledge from Washington based on a more general concern about the United States posing a nuclear threat to China. A PLA analyst noted that "in China now there are many scholars who think the United States targets nuclear weapons at China" and therefore are suspicious of U.S. intentions.[33] The military expert asserted

---

33. Chinese suspicions of U.S. intentions are likely to have been exacerbated by a report in May 1995 that the Pentagon rejected a proposal to cut U.S. strategic forces levels further below the

that although he did not personally foresee circumstances under which the United States would use nuclear weapons against China, "when a person aims a gun at you, you are nervous." He contended, however, that a bilateral U.S.-China agreement to refrain from targeting their nuclear weapons at each other would provide inadequate assurance, insisting that a "no-targeting" accord should be combined with a bilateral NFU pledge, such as the agreement that China signed with Russia.[34]

Chinese arms control experts say that a U.S. NFU pledge—bilateral or multilateral—would enable Beijing to take concrete steps toward nuclear disarmament. Some researchers suggest that an NFU commitment from the United States would make it easier for China to accept a freeze in the development of its nuclear arsenal relative to the arsenals of the United States and Russia. One military analyst asserted that a U.S. NFU pledge to China would facilitate Beijing's participation in five-power nuclear arms reductions talks by reducing the nuclear threat to China.[35]

Some Chinese arms control specialists appreciate that U.S. security commitments will make it difficult for the United States to change its policy and sign

---

agreed-upon levels in the U.S.-Russian START II agreement, on the grounds of need for a hedge against the possible emergence of China as a new strategic threat. Backing the Pentagon, President Clinton reportedly rejected the proposal of some of his advisers that the United States agree to promise an eventual reduction of strategic nuclear forces under START II from the 3,500 allowed the United States to the 3,000 level specified in the accord for Russian strategic nuclear forces. "Defense officials have expressed particular concern that further reductions would require eliminating some costly nuclear-equipped submarines and bombers, forcing a complex retargeting of the residual U.S. nuclear arms. They have also argued that Washington must maintain the extra weapons as a hedge against a reversal of Russian political and military reforms and the possible emergence of China as a new strategic threat." Michael Dobbs and R. Jeffrey Smith, "U.S. Offers Assurances on NATO," *Washington Post*, May 7, 1995, p. 1.

34. On September 3, 1994, during Chinese President Jiang Zemin's visit to Moscow, a joint communiqué was issued in which China and Russia pledged not to use nuclear weapons against each other and not to aim nuclear weapons at each other. *Renmin Ribao*, September 5, 1994, FBIS-CHI-94-177, September 13, 1994, pp. 11–12.

35. Chinese hopes of securing a bilateral NFU pledge from the United States were raised in bilateral discussions with a senior U.S. official in the fall of 1994. These hopes were dashed, however, when the proposal was strongly rejected in Washington by officials in the State Department, Department of Defense, and the National Security Council. Subsequently, the United States offered to sign an agreement with China to refrain from targeting each other with nuclear weapons, but the Chinese refused, opting to hold out for both a bilateral NFU pledge and a no-targeting agreement, as they did with Russia. The Clinton administration's Nuclear Posture Review, the results of which were announced by Defense Secretary William J. Perry on September 22, 1994, concluded that the United States must retain the option of "last resort" use of nuclear weapons in response to a non-nuclear attack on U.S. forces, indicating that it is unlikely the U.S. government will change its policy and adopt a bilateral or universal NFU pledge any time soon. See R. Jeffrey Smith, "Clinton Decides to Retain Bush Nuclear Arms Policy," *Washington Post*, September 22, 1994, p. 1.

an NFU treaty or make a bilateral NFU pledge to China. A COSTIND arms controller noted, for example, that "adopting NFU would require the United States to abandon extended nuclear deterrence." Other Chinese analysts contend that the United States no longer needs nuclear weapons to assure its security and should revise its nuclear strategy. A PLA expert maintained that "it is a very different international environment than the Cold War when the Soviet Union had stronger conventional forces in Europe," and the United States needed nuclear weapons for deterrence. "Now there is no conventional threat to the United States," he said, "so it is a good time for the United States to make a no-first-use pledge."

The Chinese have more to gain from NFU pledges by the nuclear powers than does the United States. A bilateral U.S.-Chinese NFU pledge or a five-power NFU agreement would enhance Chinese security as well as advance Beijing's political interests. China is unlikely to be in a position in which first use of nuclear weapons would be advantageous, except perhaps on its own territory. Beijing has no security commitments requiring extended deterrence, while the other nuclear powers that it could potentially face, the United States and Russia, have far stronger nuclear forces that they could be inhibited from using or threatening to use by an NFU pledge. Thus, China's NFU commitment requires it to give up very little, while an NFU pledge by the United States could put at risk the credibility of U.S. security commitments to other powers as well as potential leverage in a crisis. A bilateral NFU pledge to China would benefit the United States, however, by easing Chinese suspicions of U.S. intentions and fostering forward movement in nuclear arms control, including eventual five-power nuclear arms reductions.

VERIFIABILITY OF NFU COMMITMENTS

Most Chinese officials and analysts maintain that as a statement primarily of intentions, an NFU treaty would not require a verification regime. This view was expressed by a senior Foreign Ministry official who insisted that the political decision to adopt an NFU commitment is significant in itself and that verification is unnecessary because the use of nuclear weapons would be "obvious." A COSTIND official also asserted that since an NFU treaty "would only be a political commitment, it would not need to be verified." Many Chinese arms controllers argue that an NFU commitment is not verifiable because even after signing an NFU pledge, a country can change its policy in a crisis. One expert commented that "we don't read your war plans so we don't know if you plan to attack us first." Chinese analysts insist, however, that a nation would pay a high political cost for abandoning its NFU commitment and that this would deter countries from initiating nuclear weapons use. "At this time in international society," a PLA researcher asserted, "if you make a pledge, all members of the international community will know it and will condemn you if you violate it."

Some Chinese arms control specialists maintain that in the long run, it would be possible and desirable to take steps to make an NFU agreement verifiable. An analyst in COSTIND's arms control program asserted that while at first, "just making the pledge would be an important confidence-building measure," later "an agreement could be reached to keep warheads and delivery systems separate." Several arms control experts also proposed that the nuclear-weapon states revise their nuclear doctrines to reflect a no-first-use policy, and that they reach no-targeting agreements with the other nuclear powers. A nuclear physicist from the Chinese Academy of Engineering Physics and a member of the CPAPD Scientists Group on Arms Control advocated taking nuclear forces off alert as well as separating warheads from delivery vehicles. By restricting the "use and scope of nuclear weapons," he said, the role of nuclear weapons in military doctrine could be de-emphasized, which would relegate nuclear arms solely to a retaliatory mission.

The Chinese government is unlikely to adopt Chinese arms controllers' ideas for NFU verification, however. Measures such as separating warheads and delivery systems would probably require on-site inspection procedures that China, as well as the United States and Russia, might reject as excessively intrusive. Taking nuclear forces off alert might be an easier step but it would not be especially significant, particularly for the United States, which has long had its forces on a low-alert status. Ultimately, changes in U.S. and Russian nuclear doctrines could be more significant, but are not likely in the near future.

Prerequisites for Five-Party Nuclear Arms Reductions

A major step that will signal China's desire to engage in security interdependence measures in the nuclear sphere will be Beijing's willingness to engage in talks on strategic nuclear arms reductions. China officially holds the position that Beijing will eventually join in nuclear arms reductions talks with the other declared nuclear powers.[36] Chinese officials deny that Beijing plans to avoid

36. The Chinese have waffled since 1981 in their official position on terms for participation in strategic nuclear arms reductions talks with the other four declared nuclear powers. See Johnston, "Learning Versus Adaptation," pp. 42–43 and note 33.

joining five-power talks for as long as possible. "China must participate in the nuclear arms reductions process," asserted a senior Foreign Ministry official, since "China has all along stood for the complete prohibition of nuclear weapons." The official quickly added, however, that "there is the question of when China should participate and the answer is certainly not now."

The Chinese have intentionally left vague their position on the necessary preconditions for Chinese participation in five-power nuclear arms reductions talks. "China doesn't want to say what numbers the United States and Russia have to reduce to before it will participate," explained a PLA researcher. Beijing provided a general guidepost in January 1992 when a Chinese foreign ministry spokesman indicated that Beijing's requirement for joining five-power nuclear arms reductions talks was an undefined "parity" of nuclear forces. "China will naturally take part in the process of nuclear disarmament and join efforts for the complete destruction of nuclear weapons once the United States and Russia reduce their nuclear capacity to a level matching that of China," the MFA spokesman said.[37]

The precise level of nuclear forces to which the United States and Russia must reduce before Beijing will participate in five-power nuclear arms reductions talks has been a subject of study and debate in China in the last few years. Several Chinese scientists indicated that although China would prefer that Washington and Moscow reduce to a number equal to China's, Beijing would be willing to participate when the U.S. and Russian strategic nuclear arsenals are below 1,000 warheads each. At this level, the nuclear arsenals of China, France, Britain, the United States, and Russia would be "the same order of magnitude—in the hundreds—so that the five powers could talk together," said a member of the CPAPD Scientists Group on Arms Control. An even lower number was cited by a COSTIND arms control expert, who said that a computer-modeled study conducted in China in 1990 concluded that for China to consider engaging in five-power arms reductions talks, the superpowers should come down to about 600 warheads each compared with about 300 warheads each for the other three nuclear powers.

Although officially China favors the complete elimination of nuclear weapons, many Chinese arms controllers question whether a ban on nuclear weapons would be in China's interests. These experts share the concerns of many

37. Zhongguo Xinwen She, January 30, 1992, cited in "China-U.S.-CIS: Beijing Defines Nuclear Disarmament Conditions," FBIS—Trends, FB TM 92-005, February 5, 1992, p. 46. In June 1994, Australian Deputy Prime Minister Brian Howe said he was told by Chinese officials in Beijing that the ball was in the court of the other nuclear powers to reduce their stocks to achieve "a situation of parity." AFP, June 13, 1994, FBIS-CHI-94-114, June 14, 1994, p. 15.

U.S. strategists about potential strategic instability at extremely low force levels. One Chinese scientist maintained that "maybe 100 weapons would be enough for countries to maintain deterrence and still have stability." Another scientist similarly cautioned that force levels should not be reduced below between 100 and 200 per country because the nuclear balance could be rendered unstable. Such low levels of nuclear weapons "would require good verification measures," he maintained, "otherwise it could be quite dangerous."

Despite skepticism in some circles in Beijing about the possibility of safely reducing to zero nuclear weapons, the Chinese government nevertheless sees political value in reiterating its proposal for an international convention banning nuclear weapons, under which the nuclear-weapon states would undertake to destroy all their nuclear weapons. The proposal, which Chinese officials and analysts do not view as likely to be accepted in the foreseeable future, allows China to take the political high ground while Beijing continues its nuclear testing program in the face of a test moratorium honored by three of the other four nuclear-weapon states.

The Chinese are likely to continue to resist participation in five-party nuclear arms reductions talks until the United States and Russia cut their strategic force levels far below those stipulated in the START II Treaty, which in 2003 will leave the two sides with 3,500 and 3,000 warheads respectively. However, if the United States and Russia resume the nuclear arms reductions process and aim at substantially decreasing their force levels below those agreed to in START II, China may be compelled by international pressure to engage in informal talks about strategic arms reductions bilaterally, trilaterally, or multilaterally. At first, such talks might only discuss the conditions under which China would join in five-power negotiations as well as the principles that would guide the negotiating process. China would be unlikely to engage in formal negotiations until the United States and Russia had reduced—or agreed to reduce—their nuclear arsenals to 1,000 strategic warheads or less.

Missile Defense Threats to China's Nuclear Deterrent

China may be less willing to sign a CTBT, join five-power nuclear arms reductions talks, or participate in any other "security interdependence" regimes that restrict its nuclear weapons programs if Beijing fears that the viability of its nuclear deterrent may be placed in jeopardy by the deployment of a theater missile defense system in Japan or homeland ballistic missile defense systems deployed in the United States and Russia. Chinese concern is exacerbated by suspicion that TMD deployment in Japan would be part of a U.S.-Japan collaborative effort to contain China militarily and politically.

Fear that China's nuclear forces could be neutralized by U.S. deployment in Asia of an advanced TMD system was voiced publicly by a Chinese official in February 1995.[38] "If a country with nuclear weapons has a spear and then gets a shield, you can imagine what would happen," he said. The official, who refused to be identified, also repeated Beijing's position, first put forward in the mid-1980s, that deployment of advanced BMD would "trigger an arms race in outer space" and "increase the danger of nuclear war."[39]

China opposes revision of the Anti-Ballistic Missile (ABM) Treaty to allow for expanded U.S. and Russian BMD systems or TMD in Asia, which, Chinese scientists maintain, would violate the Treaty. The scientists contend that the technology for BMD and that for TMD systems are nearly identical, and indicated concern that the THAAD (theater high-altitude area defense) system under development by the United States could be upgradeable to defense against strategic ballistic missiles, and thus could pose a threat to the viability of China's deterrent. One missile designer asserted that the THAAD system will be able to "intercept both tactical and strategic missiles in outer space at an altitude of more than 100 km."[40] Another Chinese scientist noted that the ABM Treaty permits intercept of missiles at no more than 1 km/sec, the speed of tactical missiles, since "any faster interceptor speed is strategic according to the treaty." He claimed that the United States is seeking a 5 km/sec capability for THAAD, which, he said, is close to the 7 km/sec speed of intercontinental ballistic missile (ICBM) reentry vehicles (RVs). While some Chinese scientists

---

38. Comments made by an unnamed senior Foreign Ministry official in an interview with Patrick Tyler of the *New York Times*, "China Warns Against 'Star Wars' Shield for U.S. Forces in Asia," February 18, 1995.

39. See Garrett and Glaser, "Chinese Perspectives on Reagan's Strategic Defense Initiative," for an account of the wide range of views on SDI held by Chinese analysts in 1985.

40. In an unpublished April 1995 paper assessing the implications of amending the ABM Treaty, an arms control expert from a scientific research institute involved in China's nuclear weapons program calculated that 80 percent of Chinese land-based "strategic" missiles would fall into the category of "theater" missiles and would be vulnerable to U.S. and Russian TMD systems aiming at countering missiles with ranges up to 3,000 km. The analyst further contended that a TMD system capable of destroying warheads entering the atmosphere at 5 km/sec would have significant capabilities against China's longer-range strategic missiles. The analyst maintained that if the United States deployed such a "strategic-capable" TMD system, China would be reluctant to sign a CTBT since it would need to make qualitative improvements to its nuclear weapons systems. In addition, the Chinese researcher asserted that an agreement by the United States and Russia to modify the ABM Treaty so that it no longer placed meaningful constraints on BMD would lead China to doubt U.S. and Russian commitments to other arms control agreements and to be far more cautious about future participation in arms control negotiations and regimes.

and arms controllers stress their concern about deployment of a TMD system in Japan, others insist that China is more worried about the possibility of wide-area BMD systems being deployed in the United States and Russia.

Chinese scientists warn that if the United States proceeds with BMD or TMD deployments, this would alter Beijing's strategic calculus and make it unlikely that China would join in future five-power talks on the reduction of strategic nuclear forces. "As a precondition for further reductions involving all five powers," maintained a member of the CPAPD Scientists Group on Arms Control, "the ABM Treaty should be adhered to" and "no additional ABM systems should be allowed beyond the Treaty."

Deployment of BMD or TMD systems might also prompt China to upgrade and expand its nuclear arsenal, according to Chinese scientists. They warn that if faced with new ABM systems, China will take military countermeasures to try to preserve the viability of its deterrent. One scientist asserted, for example, that "military sectors" in China will be concerned about the effectiveness of Chinese nuclear weapons if BMD systems are built and "will ask experts to develop methods to defeat it or increase the number of warheads." There are many steps China can take to strengthen the credibility of its deterrent in the face of enhanced BMD or TMD, asserted a Chinese missile engineer, such as deployment of MIRVs to overwhelm the system, or MARVs (maneuverable re-entry vehicles) which zigzag to avoid being intercepted. "If THAAD is deployed," he predicted, "many countries will develop missiles to penetrate it."

Prospects for Security Interdependence in Chinese Policy

China has not abandoned its traditional balance-of-power, self-help, and free-riding approach to national security and arms control. Beijing continues to pursue self-help measures to enhance Chinese security unilaterally even as it engages in limited security interdependence arrangements. This is demonstrated by its apparent determination to delay a CTBT until it can complete its current nuclear testing program. If successful, the tests will enable China to narrow the gap between the capabilities of Chinese nuclear forces and those of the United States and Russia. Beijing also continues to obtain the benefits of free-riding on the ABM and START treaties and other arms control agreements to which it is not a party, and which therefore place no restrictions on Chinese military activities.

The Chinese view their country as an emerging great power and measure their military capabilities against those of the United States and Russia, not those of lesser powers. Most Chinese intellectuals as well as officials and leaders harbor a deeply held ambition that China will acquire the military as well as economic and political attributes and leverage of a great power, including sophisticated, high-tech conventional weapons as well as advanced nuclear arms.[41]

As they seek to enhance China's military capabilities, including its nuclear forces, the Chinese have so far shown little willingness to consider the possibility that their self-help efforts to enhance China's security may exacerbate the sense of insecurity of other states in East Asia. They claim that declarations of China's benign intentions and opposition to hegemony are sufficient to assuage other states' concerns about China's intentions. Only a small minority of Chinese analysts and officials accepts the mutual security notion that one's own security is assured only when other states also feel secure. Rather, most still seem to believe that China is more secure if other states are weaker and thus less secure. Since the Chinese do not acknowledge that their nuclear weapons could be perceived as posing a threat to other countries' security, they reject the view that steps by Beijing toward nuclear disarmament are necessary to enhance the security of countries that face a potential nuclear threat from China.

Chinese leaders, officials, and most analysts thus dismiss concerns voiced in Asia about China's military modernization program as unjustified exaggeration of a "China threat" with the aim of keeping China weak or sowing discord between China and its neighbors. Under pressure from the United States, Japan, and other Asia-Pacific states, Beijing may respond positively in the next year or two to calls for greater transparency in its military affairs, including publication of a defense "white paper," similar to that produced annually by Japan, outlining defense programs and military strategy. This should not necessarily be interpreted as movement by China toward adoption of a mutual security perspective on the impact of its defense programs on other states, however, but rather that Beijing concluded that it was politically necessary to be more open about its military activities.

---

41. President Jiang Zemin, who is also chairman of the Central Military Commission, was quoted as having stated in early 1995 that "to further consolidate national defense and safeguard national security, we must improve our military forces and have some of our own 'sophisticated' arms. With them, our words will carry different weight." Cited by Leng Mou, "Supreme Commander Jiang Plans for High-Intelligence Defense System—China's Army Building Strategy for the New Period," *Kuang Chiao Ching*, No. 270 (March 16, 1995), FBIS-CHI-95-086, May 4, 1995, p. 39.

So far Chinese participation in international nuclear arms control regimes and negotiations has been driven largely by political concern that China not be isolated on these issues. Beijing's decisions in 1992 to become a signatory to the NPT and in 1993 to agree to join negotiations aimed at concluding a CTBT were made primarily in response to international political pressure. The Chinese see political costs should China fail to sign a CTBT, as well as potential political gains from backing inclusion of specific additional security measures in the CTBT that are favored by some Third World states.

Limited security interdependence is nevertheless playing an increasingly important role in Beijing's national security and foreign policies as the Chinese realize that a self-help approach alone is inadequate—as well as politically untenable—for ensuring a peaceful and stable international environment in which they can pursue their top national priority of economic development and modernization. Since a CTBT would place restraints on China's military programs, signing, ratifying, and implementing a CTBT would constitute an unmistakable signal of Chinese acceptance, however limited, of security interdependence.

Although the basis of Beijing's decision to participate in the CTBT negotiations is difficult to ascertain and may be largely or even entirely political, there is growing appreciation among scientists, arms controllers, and officials in China that a nuclear test ban can advance some of China's security interests. These experts are increasingly mindful of the potential security benefits to China of participating in international nuclear arms control regimes, including the NPT and a nuclear test ban. They recognize, for example, that while self-help measures can only deter or defend against a nation such as Japan that might obtain nuclear weapons and pose a potential threat to China,[42] the NPT can reduce the likelihood that China's neighbors will acquire nuclear weapons with which to threaten China. The scientists and arms controllers see security gains for China in a test ban that further discourages nuclear proliferation, freezes the gap in nuclear weapons development between China and India, and prevents the gap between China and the United States and Russia from widening.[43]

42. China's concern that Japan might acquire nuclear weapons is apparently growing. An internal Chinese government report acquired by Kyodo news service in Japan concluded that "in the future, Japan cannot completely depend on the U.S. nuclear umbrella and as a [on the] pretext to protect itself from nuclear attack, it may begin to develop its own nuclear force." July 1, 1995, Kyodo, FBIS-CHI-95-127, July 3, 1995, p. 11.

43. China's commitment in principle to negotiating and signing an international fissile material production cutoff treaty also reflects a willingness to place restraints on China's nuclear weapon program, although Chinese scientists say that Beijing has ample stockpiles of fissile material.

Beijing's enthusiasm for involvement in international arms control regimes and negotiations could be dampened by a worsening of U.S.-Chinese relations and increasing Chinese suspicion that the United States is pursuing a containment policy toward China. The Chinese might be especially reluctant to accept restrictions on their nuclear force modernization program or to engage in nuclear arms reductions talks if they concluded that the United States was deploying an extensive homeland BMD system or a TMD system in Japan that posed a challenge to the credibility of China's nuclear deterrent and represented anti-China cooperation between Tokyo and Washington. China might then take steps to hedge against this threat, including development and deployment of large numbers of MIRVed warheads or even MARVs to overwhelm or circumvent ballistic missile defense systems. A U.S.-Chinese security dialogue on BMD/TMD might assuage Chinese concerns on this issue, head off a potential new source of tension in U.S.-Chinese relations, and remove a potential obstacle to further international nuclear arms control efforts.

Conversely, China's willingness to move farther down the road of relying on security interdependence and forgoing self-help measures such as modernization of Chinese nuclear forces would be enhanced by developments such as the adoption of a no-first-use policy by the United States, or a U.S.-Russian agreement to make substantially deeper cuts in strategic forces than called for by the START II accord. Even without such steps—which are unlikely in the near term—Beijing would be more likely to respond positively to security interdependence measures in a more favorable international security environment, especially better U.S.-Chinese relations and reduced suspicions of U.S. strategic intentions toward China.

The size and influence of China's arms control community are likely to continue to grow in the next few years in response to new demands from Chinese leaders for information and advice on arms control and security issues. The United States can influence the development of this loose grouping of arms control experts and bolster the nascent tendency in China to view global and regional security in interdependence terms through increased official and unofficial U.S.-Chinese dialogue and exchanges on arms control issues. This could include more official discussions between the two militaries, as well as by U.S. arms control experts from the Arms Control and Disarmament Agency and State Department with disarmament officials from China's Foreign Ministry.

Chinese officials and arms controllers maintain that the proposed treaty would modestly enhance China's security by contributing to further curtailment of nuclear arms development, especially by the United States, Russia, and India. They also assert that a fissile material production cutoff treaty is not a high priority and predict that it will not be concluded in the near future.

In addition, unofficial contacts between scientists, arms control experts, and foreign policy institute researchers can be encouraged. The concrete impact on Chinese thinking of past arms control discussions between Chinese and Americans is evidenced by Beijing's decision to join the NPT and by Beijing's support for permanent extension of the NPT. The United States could further promote the trend toward security interdependence by supporting opportunities for Chinese to study arms control in the United States, as well as more bilateral meetings between Chinese and U.S. non-governmental experts. The strengthening of a Western-influenced arms control community in China could affect thinking in Beijing on a broad range of international arms control issues, from non-proliferation to confidence-building measures and greater military transparency in Asia, and foster movement in China toward taking more responsibility for maintaining international peace and stability.

Part III:
The Future of Japan's Security Role

Japan's National Security

Structures, Norms, and Policies

Peter J. Katzenstein and Nobuo Okawara

Japan's national security policy has two distinctive aspects that deserve analysis. First, Japan's definition of national security goes far beyond traditional military notions. National security is viewed in comprehensive terms that also include economic and political dimensions. The second feature of Japan's security policy worth explanation is a distinctive mixture of flexibility and rigidity in the process of policy adaptation to change: flexibility on issues of economic security, rigidity on issues of military security, and flexibility combined with rigidity on issues of political security.[1] With the end of the Cold War and changes in the structure of the international system, it is only natural that we ask whether and how Japan's national security policy will change as well. Optimists insist that the Asian balance of power and the U.S.-Japan relationship will make Japan aspire to be a competitive, noninterventionist trading state that heeds the universal interest of peace and profit rather than narrow aspirations for national power.[2] Pessimists warn us instead that the new international system will finally confirm Herman Kahn's prediction of 1970: Japan will quickly change to the status of a nuclear superpower, spurred perhaps by what some see as a dangerous rise of Japanese militarism in the 1970s and 1980s.[3]

Peter J. Katzenstein is the Walter S. Carpenter, Jr. Professor of International Studies at Cornell University. Nobuo Okawara is Associate Professor of Political Science at Kyushu University.

This article summarizes some of the findings of our monograph *Japan's National Security: Structures, Norms and Policy Responses in a Changing World* (Ithaca, N.Y.: Cornell University, East Asia Program, Cornell East Asia Series, 1993). For their helpful comments on an earlier version of this paper the authors are grateful to James Goldgeier, David Laitin and Robert Smith, as well as five anonymous reviewers of this journal. Peter J. Katzenstein received partial financial support for research and writing from a grant awarded by the German Marshall Fund of the United States (No. 3-53597).

---

1. The comprehensive character of Japan's security policy has been noted by most scholars and policy analysts. The characterization of policy adaptation in terms of its flexibility and rigidity has emerged from our research. In contrast to common usage in Japanese politics, our use of the terms flexibility and rigidity do not reflect any particular policy orientation.
2. Davis B. Bobrow, "Playing for Safety," *Japan Quarterly*, Vol. 31, No. 1 (January–March, 1984), pp. 33–43; Kenneth B. Pyle, *The Japanese Question: Power and Purpose in a New Era* (Washington, D.C.: AEI Press, 1992).
3. Edwin P. Hoyt, *The Militarists: The Rise of Japanese Militarism since WWII* (New York: Fine,

---

International Security, Vol. 17, No. 4 (Spring 1993)

Both optimists and pessimists, we argue, are mistaken. The notion that Japan is destined to be the first example in history of a state wielding huge economic and technological power without corresponding military might is as implausible as the case for the inevitability of a nuclear-armed Japan. Both notions are profoundly ahistorical. Optimists overlook a long historical record that makes their strong claim problematic. Pessimists subscribe to a notion of disembodied structure without historical content. As variants of realist political thought, both seek causal primacy in the structure of the international state system and the putative effects of that structure on rational state actors seeking to maximize their relative gains in the international system. Since they arrive at opposite conclusions, each places in question the claim of the other. Taken together, both underline the fact that international structures do not determine Japan's foreign policy choices.

This article seeks to explain these choices by turning instead to two different areas of scholarship. First, we draw on insights from the field of foreign economic policy which point to the domestic structure of the state as a major determinant of policy choice.[4] Secondly, we rely on a growing literature in international political economy and comparative politics dealing with the role of norms and ideas in politics.[5] For an analysis of foreign policy choice, rather

---

1985); Herman Kahn, *The Emerging Japanese Superstate: Challenge and Response* (Englewood Cliffs, N.J.: Prentice-Hall, 1970).

4. G. John Ikenberry, David A. Lake, and Michael Mastanduno, eds., *The State and American Foreign Economic Policy* (Ithaca, N.Y.: Cornell University Press, 1988); Peter J. Katzenstein, *Small States in World Markets* (Ithaca: Cornell University Press, 1985); Peter J. Katzenstein, ed., *Between Power and Plenty: Foreign Economic Policies of Advanced Industrial States* (Madison: University of Wisconsin Press, 1978). See also Jack Snyder, *Myths of Empire: Domestic Politics and International Ambition* (Ithaca, N.Y.: Cornell University Press, 1991); Matthew Evangelista, "Issue-Area and Foreign Policy Revisited," *International Organization*, Vol. 43, No. 1 (Winter 1989), pp. 147–171; Matthew Evangelista, *Innovation and the Arms Race: How the United States and the Soviet Union Develop their New Military Technologies* (Ithaca, N.Y.: Cornell University Press, 1988); Athanassios Platias, "High Politics in Small Countries," Ph.D. dissertation, Cornell University, 1986.

5. Friedrich Kratochwil, *Rules, Norms, and Decisions* (Cambridge: Cambridge University Press, 1988); Friedrich Kratochwil and John G. Ruggie, "International Organization: A State of the Art, an Art of the State," *International Organization*, Vol. 40, No. 4 (Fall 1986), pp. 753–775; Alexander Wendt, "Anarchy is What States Make of It: The Social Construction of Power Politics," *International Organization*, Vol. 46, No. 2 (Spring 1992), pp. 391–425; Ann Swidler, "Culture in Action: Symbols and Strategies," *American Sociological Review*, Vol. 51, No. 2 (1986), pp. 273–286; George M. Thomas, John W. Meyer, Francisco O. Ramirez, and John Boli, *Institutional Structure: Constituting State, Society, and the Individual* (Beverly Hills: SAGE Publications, 1987); Walter W. Powell and Paul J. DiMaggio, eds., *The New Institutionalism in Organizational Analysis* (Chicago: University of Chicago Press, 1991); Stephan Haggard and Beth A. Simmons, "Theories of International Regimes," *International Organization*, Vol. 41, No. 3 (Summer 1987), pp. 491–517; Ernst B. Haas, *When Knowledge is Power: Three Models of Change in International Organizations* (Berkeley: University of California Press, 1990); Emanuel Adler, "Cognitive Revolution," in Adler and Beverly Craw-

than systemic outcomes, what matters are not international but domestic structures. Yet domestic structures do not alone determine the conception of interests that inform actors. These conceptions are shaped also by the normative context that defines standards of appropriate behavior. Analyzing how such standards gradually change makes it possible to unravel the process by which the interests that inform foreign policy are formulated in the first place. Because domestic structures and norms are shaped by history, so, indirectly, is the process of foreign policy choice.

In short, Japan's security policy, we argue here, is influenced both by the structure of the state broadly conceived and the incentives it provides for policy on the one hand, and on the other by the context of social and legal norms that help define policy interests and the standards of appropriateness for specific policy choices. The structure of the Japanese state has made it virtually impossible, short of a domestic political revolution, for an autonomous and powerful military establishment to emerge in Japan. Inside the government, the military is fenced in by a number of institutional procedures that severely circumscribe the access of military professionals to the centers of political power. The civilians' control over the military is firmly entrenched in Japan. The structure of state-society relations in Japan isolates the military from a public which musters at best no more than passive tolerance for the armed forces. This effect is countered, however, by the trans-national relations between the Japanese and the American militaries that have grown increasingly close during the 1980s and have thus enhanced the professional standing of the Japanese military.[6]

The second main determinant of Japan's security policy is the normative context, both social and legal, in which the government develops its security

---

ford, eds., *Progress in Postwar International Relations* (New York: Columbia University Press, 1991), pp. 43–88; Judith Goldstein and Robert O. Keohane, eds., *Ideas and Foreign Policy: Beliefs, Institutions and Political Change* (Ithaca, N.Y.: Cornell University Press, forthcoming); Judith Goldstein, *Ideas, Interests and American Trade Policy* (Ithaca, N.Y.: Cornell University Press, 1993); Henry R. Nau, *The Myth of America's Decline: Leading the World Economy into the 1990s* (New York: Oxford University Press, 1990); Kathryn A. Sikkink, *Ideas and Institutions: Developmentalism in Brazil and Argentina* (Ithaca, N.Y.: Cornell University Press, 1991); Peter A. Hall, ed., *The Political Power of Economic Ideas: Keynesianism Across Nations* (Princeton: Princeton University Press, 1989); Emanuel Adler, *The Power of Ideology: The Quest for Technological Autonomy in Argentina and Brazil* (Berkeley: University of California Press, 1987).

6. We address only one of the three dimensions of state structure, the effect of the organization of the government on Japan's security policy; for reasons of space, we do not take up the other two, state-society relations and transnational relations. For a more complete analysis of all three, see Peter J. Katzenstein and Nobuo Okawara, *Japan's National Security: Structures, Norms and Policy Responses in a Changing World* (Ithaca: Cornell University, East Asia Program, 1993).

policies. There is a far-reaching consensus on economic security issues: to most Japanese it is self-evident that, where possible, the country's very substantial economic vulnerability, as shown by its reliance on the import of raw materials, should be reduced. Similarly uncontroversial is the idea that Japan should strive for technological autonomy, both for its intrinsic merits and as a useful mechanism for reducing Japan's dependence on raw materials. This consensus on issues of Japan's economic security contrasts starkly with the continued contest over the norms that should inform Japan's military security policy. An anti-militarist public climate continues to mark debates on military issues, reinforced by the provisions of Japan's Peace Constitution. At the same time it is also true that Japan's public has gradually come to accept the necessity of a small national defense and has quietly assented in the 1980s to a substantial build-up of the Self-Defense Forces (SDF) and an increasingly close defense cooperation with the United States. Finally, issues which touch on Japan's political security—most prominently Japan's relation with the United States in all of its economic, military and diplomatic dimensions—fall between these two extremes. They show neither full consensus nor deep contestation, but rather political disagreements and debate.

The structure of the Japanese state and the interaction between legal and social norms, we argue, explain the comprehensiveness of Japan's national security policy as well as its mixture of policy flexibility and rigidity in the face of change. The structure of the Japanese state creates incentives for a broad definition of security favoring economic and political dimensions over strictly military ones. On questions of economic security, prevailing norms facilitate flexibility, for example in Japan's energy and technology policies, while on military issues, such as the deployment of the SDF overseas, they encourage policy rigidity. Political issues of security show a variable pattern mixing elements of flexibility on questions of military cooperation with the United States and rigidity in the area of transferring militarily relevant technologies to the United States.[7] The article surveys existing explanations of

7. The distinctiveness of Japan's security policy along two dimensions of comprehensiveness and flexibility/rigidity is particularly striking when compared to Germany's. Since 1949 Germany's definition of national security has focused almost exclusively on political and military issues. Between the early 1950s and the mid-1960s, for example, West Germany used its foreign policy of rearmament as a lever to reestablish its place in the Western alliance. And since the mid-1960s West Germany's Eastern policy sought to combine political détente with military deterrence. In contrast to Japan, the notion of economic security did not figure prominently in either period. In the face of change German security policy has, like Japan's, been flexible at some times and rigid at others. But the difference between flexibility and rigidity has been much

Japan's security policy, and proceeds to analyze the governmental structures, the normative context, and Japan's policy choices. Finally, we conclude that what matters most for how Japanese foreign policy adjusts to changes in U.S.-Japan relations is the normative context, rather than the economic or military subject matter of particular foreign policy issues.

Existing Explanations

Analytical perspectives that focus attention exclusively or predominantly at the level of the international system suffer from serious weaknesses if we wish to understand Japan's security policy. We are reminded of these limitations by the fact that different authors, relying on different variants of systemic explanations, arrive at fundamentally different predictions about Japan's security policy. Systemic analyses that focus on Asia's regional balance of power suggest that the international system creates few incentives for change in policy; some authors who analyze the U.S.-Japan relationship suggest that there will be dramatic change in policy; and those examining the swing from a pacifist Japanese foreign policy in the 1920s to a militarist one in the 1930s suggest that Japan's security policy will be incoherent. Therefore, we turn our attention to the effects of Japan's domestic structures and norms. They may help us in circumventing these difficulties.

CONVENTIONAL WISDOM

The conventional wisdom among both American and Japanese foreign policy experts focuses on the effect the international system has on Japan's security policy. The consequences of the end of the Cold War, according to this line of argument, are much less evident in Asia than in Europe. While the Cold War in Europe defined the balance of power along clear lines of division between East and West, in Asia this split was only one among many. The

---

less marked. The reason for this difference between Japanese and German security policy lies in different state structures and different legal and social norms. Germany's armed forces are not isolated domestically but internationalized fully under NATO command. And Germany's constitution and public opinion have been less firmly opposed to the threat or use of military force than have Japan's. There exist then significant differences between these two trading states that, after the end of the Cold War, have emerged as major powers. Recent comparative studies include Jeffrey T. Bergner, *The New Superpowers: Germany, Japan, the U.S. and the New World Order* (New York: St., Martin's, 1991); Jeffrey E. Garten, *A Cold Peace: America, Japan, Germany, and the Struggle for Supremacy* (New York: Times Books, 1992); and Hanns W. Maull, "Germany and Japan: The New Civilian Powers," *Foreign Affairs*, Vol. 69, No. 5 (Winter 1990/91), pp. 91–106.

collapse of Communism and the disintegration of the Soviet Union have created much less compelling incentives for a change in Japan's security policy than is true for European states such as Germany. Therefore, in focusing on the regional balance of power, the conventional explanation seeks to account for the conservative and incremental responses of Japan's security policy to the international changes that have occurred since the late 1980s.[8]

HOBBESIAN VISION

A second explanation also focuses on the effects of international structure but emphasizes a different aspect of the balance of power in U.S.-Japan relations. It comes to dramatically different conclusions. George Friedman's and Meredith Lebard's recent book argues that war between the United States and Japan is inevitable. "The struggle between Japan and the United States, punctuated by truces, friendships, and brutality, will shape the Pacific for generations. It will be the endless game about which the philosophers have written, the game of nations—the war of all against all."[9] For Friedman and Lebard, geography is destiny.[10] Both the United States and Japan are naval powers. The United States needs to control the sealanes because of its expansive notion of self-defense. Japan needs to control the sealanes because of its dependence on the import of virtually all important raw materials. Japanese vulnerability and American assertiveness will make a break between the two countries inevitable. A showdown is unavoidable since Japan cannot

---

8. This argument appears in a number of recent writings, among others, in Fred C. Iklé and Terumasa Nakanishi, "Japan's Grand Strategy," *Foreign Affairs*, Vol. 69, No. 3 (Summer 1990), pp. 81–95; Richard Holbrooke, "Japan and the United States: Ending the Unequal Partnership," *Foreign Affairs*, Vol. 70, No. 5 (Winter 1991–92), pp. 41–57; Yoichi Funabashi, "Japan and the New World Order," *Foreign Affairs*, Vol. 70, No. 5 (Winter 1991–92), pp. 58–74; Howard H. Baker, Jr., and Ellen Frost, "Rescuing the U.S.-Japan Alliance," *Foreign Affairs*, Vol. 71, No. 2 (Spring 1992), pp. 97–113. See also Takashi Inoguchi, "Japan's Global Responsibilities and Its Role in the New World Order," paper presented at the JIIA-IISS Joint Symposium on Japan's Strategic Priorities in the 1990s, Keidanren Guest House, November 18–20, 1991; David P. Rapkin, "Japan and World Leadership?" in David P. Rapkin, ed., *World Leadership and Hegemony* (Boulder: Lynne Rienner, 1990), pp. 191–212; Masataka Kosaka, *Japan's Choices: New Globalism and Cultural Orientations in an Industrial State* (London: Pinter, 1989); Mike M. Mochizuki, "Japan after the Cold War," *SAIS Review*, Vol. 10 (Summer–Fall, 1990), pp. 121–137; Mochizuki, "U.S.-Japan Security Relations in a New Era," in Chae-Jin Lee, ed., *U.S.-Japan Relations in the Post–Cold War Era* (in press); Mochizuki, "Japanese Security Policy beyond the Cold War: Domestic Politics and International Change," in Miles Kahler, ed., *Beyond the Cold War in the Pacific* (La Jolla: University of California, Institute on Global Conflict and Cooperation [IGCC], Studies in Conflict and Cooperation, Volume 2, 1991), pp. 57–70.

9. George Friedman and Meredith LeBard, *The Coming War with Japan* (New York: St. Martin's, 1991), p. 403.

10. Ibid., p. 259.

permanently subordinate itself to America's political demands and since America, trapped by its empire, is unable to revitalize its competitiveness and thus cannot forgo naval supremacy as its most important military asset.[11] From this perspective, therefore, dramatic changes in Japanese security policy are in the offing.

INTERNATIONAL REGIMES

Better than the first two structural perspectives, an analysis that includes the effects of different international regimes can explain the difference between the unforgiving power politics that characterized Western imperialism before 1945 and the beneficial effects of American hegemony after 1945.[12] International regimes are shaped not only by the distribution of international capabilities but also by international institutions, international processes, and trans-national politics, which help define the normative basis of international order. Such an analysis suggests a variety of alternate futures for Japan's security policy, depending on the international regimes that will prevail: a reassertion of American leadership based on the existing system of multilateral institutions; a new *Pax Nipponica* that might link First and Third World institutions; Japan's continued playing of its familiar role of supporter state in the U.S.-Japan relationship; and a new "bi-gemony" uniting the United States and Japan in the exercise of joint leadership of an emerging Pacific Community, in institutions such as ASEAN.[13] In stressing the importance of international institutions, this perspective offers Japan the prospect of assuming gradually a position of leadership on particular issues, thus smoothing the period of transition in global politics.

But applied to the foreign policy of states this modified realism suffers from a potentially serious flaw. A focus on international institutions and processes is often insufficient for explaining foreign policy choices unless the domestic structures and norms that help establish and support international orders are included explicitly in the analysis. Japanese security policy, for example, was relatively peaceful in the 1920s. And it was militarist in the

---

11. Ibid.
12. Akira Iriye, "Japan's Defense Strategy," in Solomon B. Levine and Koji Taira, eds., "Japan's External Economic Relations: Japanese Perspectives," *The Annals of the American Academy of Political and Social Science*, Vol. 513 (January 1991), pp. 38–47.
13. ASEAN is the Association of South-East Asian Nations. See Takashi Inoguchi, "Japan's Images and Options: Not a Challenger but a Supporter," *Journal of Japanese Studies*, Vol. 12, No. 1 (Winter 1986), pp. 95–119; Inoguchi, *Japan's International Relations* (London: Pinter, 1991), pp. 155–177.

1930s and 1940s. These dramatically different security policies occurred, however, in the same international order, marked by the preeminence of Western imperialism in a multipolar international system. Applied to the analysis of Japan's contemporary national security policy, a focus on international institutions must therefore pay close attention to the domestic structures and normative contexts that shape Japan's foreign policy choices.

DOMESTIC FACTORS

Hisahiko Okazaki draws our attention to some of these domestic factors in his sobering historical analogy between the Japan-U.S. relationship today and the naval rivalry between the Netherlands and England in the seventeenth century.[14] At the root of that conflict was England's jealousy of Dutch prosperity. "England may not have had the economic and technical prowess needed to out-trade the Dutch, but it could use its geographical and strategic advantages to control their trade routes and fishing grounds and so cut them off from the source of their wealth and power."[15] A pacifist trading nation, Holland believed that a common enemy (Spain), a shared ideology (Protestantism), and similar political institutions (republicanism), would make war between the two countries impossible. It was wrong. With the vanishing of the Spanish threat England, and in particular Parliament, increasingly came to view Dutch economic power as England's most serious threat. English protectionism in form of the Navigation Act of 1651 was so ruinous to foreign competition that the Dutch were drawn reluctantly into a war which, without friends, they could not win. Based on this analogy, Okazaki argues that Japan's interests are best served not by confrontation with the Americans or a turn to Asia but by strong links to the Anglo-American world. "Was there some way," he asks, "for the Netherlands to avoid conflict with England even while preserving its own security and maintaining its status as a major economic power? If so, where did the Dutch go wrong?"[16] These are important current questions. They direct our attention to a more detailed examination of the state structures and normative context that are shaping Japan's security policy in recent years, within the broad options and constraints provided by the international system.

---

14. Hisahiko Okazaki, *Hanei to Suitai to: Oranda-shi ni Nihon ga Mieru* (Prosperity and decline: Japan in the light of Dutch historical experience) (Tokyo: Bungei Shunju, 1991); Okazaki, "The Anglo-Dutch Conflict: A Lesson for Japan," *Japan Echo*, Vol. 17, No. 1 (Spring 1990), pp. 13–16.
15. Okazaki, "The Anglo-Dutch Conflict," p.14.
16. Okazaki, "The Anglo-Dutch Conflict," p.16.

The Structure of Government

Japan's security policy is formulated within institutional structures that bias policy strongly against a forceful articulation of military security objectives and accord pride of place instead to a comprehensive definition of security that centers on economic and political dimensions of national security. Existing mechanisms of policy coordination do not encourage the articulation of military objectives by either Japan's Defense Agency (JDA) or the Prime Minister. And the structure of government creates a set of controls which constrain sharply the institutional autonomy of the JDA, thus further weakening the political articulation of military objectives.

MECHANISMS OF COORDINATION

Japanese security policy is formulated and implemented largely by the Ministries of Foreign Affairs (MOFA), Finance (MOF), and International Trade and Industry (MITI), as well as the JDA. These ministries and government agencies operate along two different dimensions. On questions of economic security MITI, the MOF and the MOFA constitute the core in which Japanese policy is articulated. On questions of military security the central bureaucratic organizations are the MOF, MOFA, and the JDA. Because of the prominence of legal issues in the postwar defense debate, the Cabinet Legislation Bureau, an elite unit that oversees all legal aspects of government policy, has also played an important role.[17] For example, the Bureau has been primarily responsible for the government's interpretation of Article 9 of the Constitution.[18]

Typically the two dimensions and two sets of issues—economic and military—are separated. This separation rests on the premise that the use or threat of military force to ensure Japan's economic security is simply not a viable political option. While an informal process of interministerial coordination routinely takes place on the various issues of security policy, distinctive institutional arrangements affecting issues of military security assure that political and economic perspectives retain paramount importance in Japan's national security policymaking. First, major defense decisions (involving, for

---

17. B.C. Koch, *Japan's Administrative Elite* (Berkeley: University of California Press, 1989), pp. 197–198.
18. Hiromitsu Kataoka, *Naikaku no Kino to Hosakiko—Daitoryosei to Giin Naikakusei no Hikaku Kenkyu* (The cabinet's functions and staff system: A comparative study of presidential and parliamentary systems) (Tokyo: Seibundo, 1982), p. 257.

example, weapon systems, defense build-up plans, and annual budgets) which require the approval of the Cabinet need to be cleared first by the Security Council. While limited to ratifying decisions that are made elsewhere, the Council is an institutional expression of the notion that any important defense policy proposal must go through an especially cautious consensus-building process in which virtually all relevant ministries participate. When the Security Council was created in 1986, the Cabinet Secretariat was also reorganized and a Security Office was set up to replace the Secretariat of the National Defense Council. It serves as the staff for the Council and coordinates government policy on all security matters. The Office has been headed by JDA officials with prior service at the bureau director level.[19] Officials from various ministries are delegated on temporary assignments to the Security Office.

Generally speaking the different offices in the Cabinet Secretariat have failed to transcend the interests of individual ministries.[20] The Security Office has been no exception to this tendency. It is simply one arena for interministerial coordination, which involves the JDA as one participant among several.[21]

The prime minister has little control over the Cabinet Secretariat. The different offices in the Cabinet Secretariat tend to be arenas for interministerial coordination that impede the exercise of strong prime-ministerial leadership. In fact the institutional infrastructure for leadership by the prime minister is simply inadequate for transcending the interests of strong ministries such as the MOF or MITI. A prime minister's inner circle is penetrated by the major ministries. In each of the major ministries there are only two posts that can be filled by political appointees, the minister and the parlia-

---

19. Paul S. Kim, *Japan's Civil Service System: Its Structure, Personnel, and Politics* (New York: Greenwood Press, 1988), p. 104.
20. Hiromitsu Kataoka, "Naikaku to Gyosei: 'Koshiki Seifu' to 'Hikoshiki Seifu' no Yakuwari" (Cabinet and administration: Roles of 'formal government' and 'informal government'), in Nihon Gyosei Gakkai, ed., *Naikaku Seido no Kenkyu* (A study of the cabinet system), *Nempo Gyosei Kenkyu*, Vol. 21 (Tokyo: Gyosei, 1987), p. 15; Hiromitsu Kataoka, "Naikaku Kanbo" (Cabinet secretariat), *Gyosei Kanri Kenkyu*, No. 51 (September, 1990), pp. 3–16; Seizaburo Sato and Tetsuhisa Matsuzaki, *Jiminto Seiken* (LDP government) (Tokyo: Chuo Koron-sha, 1986), pp. 159–160; Akio Watanabe, "Nihon no Taigai Seisaku Keisei no Kiko to Katei" (Structures and Processes in Japanese Foreign Policymaking), in Chihiro Hosoya and Joji Watanuki, eds., *Taigai Seisaku Kettei Katei no Nichibei Hikaku* (A comparison of Japanese and U.S. foreign policy decision processes) (Tokyo: Tokyo Daigaku Shuppankai, 1977), p. 46.
21. Katsuya Hirose, *Kanryo to Gunjin: Bunmin Tosei no Genkai* (Bureaucrats and soldiers: The limits of civilian control) (Tokyo: Iwanami Shoten, 1989), p. 56.

mentary vice-minister. And since the latter post has not been important in policymaking, it has been nicknamed "appendix."[22] Because of intra-party dynamics, appointing loyal supporters to ministerial positions and keeping them in these positions is an exceedingly difficult task for any prime minister.

Prime ministers have also suffered from the fact that they do not have the option of relying either on groups inside the Liberal Democratic Party (LDP), such as the "defense tribe," or on the factions they lead. The "defense tribe" is a group of LDP Diet members routinely involved in the JDA's decision making. However, like other groups in the LDP, it cannot afford to be associated too closely with a prime minister, who is usually a faction leader. Tribes act across factional boundaries, and the maintenance of their cohesion necessitates distancing themselves from factional politics.[23] To a certain degree LDP factions are loyal to their leaders. However, party factions are not policy-oriented groups.[24] "Factions as such do not take positions on policy issues, nor do they exhibit any ideological coherence."[25]

In the absence of a secure foundation of political leadership either in government or in the LDP, prime ministers have resorted to making use of ad hoc groups. In negotiating the normalization of Japan's relations with the Soviet Union in 1955–56, Ichiro Hatoyama formed a core decision-making group which was composed of LDP influentials and former MOFA officials. Current MOFA officials were excluded.[26] Takeo Miki relied on his personal advisors in handling foreign policy, much to the chagrin of the MOFA.[27] Yasuhiro Nakasone created an advisory commission on security policy, the "Peace Issue Study Group," which recommended in 1984 the dismantling of the one percent ceiling on defense spending.[28]

On occasion prime ministers have been able to lead, even to the point of overriding the interests of important ministries. But the institutional infra-

---

22. Tetsuhisa Matsuzaki, *Nihongata Demokurashii no Gyakusetsu—Nisei Giin wa Naze Umarerunoka* (The paradox of Japanese democracy: Why are second-generation Diet members born?) (Tokyo: Toju-sha, 1991), p. 71.
23. Sato and Matsuzaki, *Jiminto Seiken* (LDP government), p. 93.
24. Sato and Matsuzaki, *Jiminto Seiken* (LDP government), pp. 54–55, 79.
25. Gerald L. Curtis, *The Japanese Way of Politics* (New York: Columbia University Press, 1988), p. 88.
26. Watanabe, "Nihon no Taigai Seisaku Keisei no Kiko to Katei" (Structures and processes in Japanese foreign policymaking), pp. 34–35.
27. Ibid., pp. 52–53.
28. Robert C. Angel, "Prime Ministerial Leadership in Japan: Recent Changes in Personal Style and Administrative Organization," *Pacific Affairs*, Vol. 61, No. 4 (Winter 1988–89), p. 595; Reinhard Drifte, *Japan's Foreign Policy* (London: Routledge, 1990), p. 17.

structure for supporting them remains underdeveloped. In brief, what has been institutionalized are arenas of interministerial coordination such as the Offices in the Cabinet Secretariat. They constrict prime ministerial leadership, and they shape the policy process dealing with security affairs.

MECHANISMS OF CONTROL

The embedding of the JDA in interministerial coordination processes is complemented by its lack of institutional autonomy. Important ministries such as MOF, MITI and MOFA have placed their officials inside the JDA, thus "colonizing" the process of defense policy making at its inner core. Officials on temporary assignment from these ministries constitute a significant part of the agency's personnel.

The JDA has eleven top bureaucratic posts: the administrative vice-minister, chief of the secretariat, five bureau chiefs, and four councillors. Of these eleven positions, at least four are always reserved for officials from other ministries. One bureau chief position (Equipment) is always held by a MITI official, another one (Finance) is almost always occupied by an official from the MOF. Two councillor posts (one in charge of international relations, the other in charge of health) are reserved for the Ministries of Foreign Affairs and of Health and Welfare. In such cases officials typically have had no prior working experience in the JDA. This makes it virtually impossible for them to be inculcated with the perspectives of the professional military.[29]

In the lower echelons of the JDA, this pattern of outside penetration recurs. Additional positions are also staffed by officials from other ministries who serve in the JDA for the first time in their careers. There exists a great asymmetry in the flow of personnel between the JDA and the major ministries. JDA officials are usually dispatched to other ministries for educational purposes, that is, to experience work in non-military areas and to widen their horizons. They are expected neither to participate in important decisions nor to utilize their military expertise in their host ministries or agencies.[30]

Inside the JDA the uniformed officers of the SDF are subordinate to a layer of civilian personnel. The administrative hierarchy for military operation is under the control of the civilian administration, which in turn answers to the director of the JDA, who has consistently been an elected official with

---

29. Hirose, *Kanryo to Gunjin* (Bureaucrats and soldiers), pp. 85–89, Appendix 1, 2.
30. Authors' interviews, Nos. 3, 15, Tokyo, June 11, 17, 1991.

cabinet rank.[31] The Occupation introduced a system of strict supervision of the professional military by a civilian bureaucracy that lacks all military ethos and perspective. This arrangement has been endorsed wholeheartedly by Japan's postwar political and economic elite which, on the basis of its prewar experience, retains a profound distrust of the professional military.[32]

Military professionals have chafed under this system of civilian control, without being able to dislodge or seriously undermine it. In the eyes of the professional military the principle of "civilian control" implies that it should be the exclusive responsibility of the professional military to advise the political leadership on matters requiring professional military expertise.[33] Indeed, Article 9 of the Self-Defense Forces Law stipulates that the chiefs of the three services are the highest professional advisors to the JDA director on all matters concerning Japan's ground, air, and sea forces. The article implies that there are two parallel hierarchies, one civilian and the other military, serving under the director.[34] In the late 1970s the chairman of the Joint Staff Council, General Kurisu, argued in his stormy and brief tenure that the highest ranking uniformed officer under the law establishing the JDA was equal in rank to an administrative vice-minister and should, under the correct interpretation of the true meaning of the concept of "civilian control," take his orders from the director but not from civilian bureaucrats.[35] In the eyes of the SDF, the time-consuming chain of command from various civilian bodies to the military might nullify Japan's capacity to repel a surprise attack.[36] Kurisu was in fact advocating a reorganization of the JDA along the lines of the U.S. Department of Defense, where two hierarchies, made up of armed services and civilian administrators, come together in the office of the Secretary of Defense.[37]

The uniformed officers' possession of military expertise and the principle of consensual decision-making suggest that it would be a mistake to under-

---

31. Hirose, *Kanryo to Gunjin* (Bureaucrats and soldiers), pp. 60–72; Tetsuya Kataoka and Ramon H. Myers, *Defending an Economic Superpower: Reassessing the U.S.-Japan Security Alliance* (Boulder: Westview Press, 1989), p. 72.
32. Hideo Otake, *Nihon no Boei to Kokunai Seiji: Detanto kara Gunkaku e* (Japan's defense and domestic politics: From détente to military buildup) (Tokyo: Sanichi Shobo, 1983), p. 192.
33. Hirose, *Kanryo to Gunjin* (Bureaucrats and soldiers), p. 5.
34. Hirose, *Kanryo to Gunjin* (Bureaucrats and soldiers), p. 63.
35. Otake, *Nihon no Boei to Kokunai Seiji* (Japan's defense and domestic politics), p. 185.
36. Taketsugu Tsurutani, "Japan's Security, Defense Responsibilities, and Capabilities," *Orbis*, Vol. 25, No. 1 (Spring 1981), p. 100.
37. Kataoka and Myers, *Defending an Economic Superpower*, pp. 72, 74.

estimate all military influence in policymaking.[38] Uniformed officers can also provide inputs to the policy process on security issues through their links with the U.S. military. These links can influence communications between the two governments and thus help shape the policy process.[39]

But inherent in the civilian-military arrangements inside the JDA is a strong bias against any military interpretation of Japan's national security requirements. It has frequently been pointed out that the JDA's civilian bureaucracy lacks cohesion because it draws its members from various ministries. The heterogeneity of the civilian bureaucracy, however, is closely linked to the prominence of a political and economic definition of security. This bias has been reinforced by embedding the JDA in a variety of interministerial arrangements. Such arrangements are deeply entrenched. One observer pointed out in 1975 that Japan's military defense lacked a mobilization plan, a military court system, emergency legislation, and a civil defense system.[40] It still lacks all of these elements today. Even after a decade of rising military tension in the Far East, with the exception of the Air Self-Defense Forces (ASDF), the SDF lacks rules for engaging the enemy.[41] It is thus particularly noteworthy that the Second Cold War in the early 1980s did not affect measurably the political arrangements either within the JDA or within the government; neither did the end of the Cold War in the late 1980s and early 1990s.

Normative Context

National security policy is deeply affected by the social and legal norms that help shape the interests which inform Japanese security policy. These norms are, on questions of economic security, largely consensual, and on questions of military security deeply contested; issues of Japan's political security, and in particular its relation to the United States, fall between the two extremes.

---

38. Daniel I. Okimoto, "Ideas, Intellectuals, and Institutions: National Security and the Question of Nuclear Armament in Japan," Ph.d. dissertation, The University of Michigan, 1978, p. 396.
39. Hirose, *Kanryo to Gunjin* (Bureaucrats and soldiers), pp. 227–229; Ichiro Miyake, Yasushi Yamaguchi, Michio Muramatsu, and Eiichi Shindo, *Nihon Seiji no Zahyo: Sengo 40 Nen no Ayumi* (The coordinates of Japanese politics: The course of forty postwar years) (Tokyo: Yuhikaku, 1985), pp.48–49; Otake, *Nihon no Boei to Kokunai Seiji* (Japan's defense and domestic politics), p. 194.
40. Gaston J. Sigur, "Power, Politics and Defense," in James H. Buck, ed., *The Modern Japanese Military System* (Beverly Hills: SAGE, 1975), p. 193.
41. Interview No. 3, Tokyo, December 9, 1991; Masashi Nishihara, "Expanding Japan's Credible Defense Role," *International Security*, Vol. 8, No. 3 (Winter 1983/84), p. 200.

UNCONTESTED NORMS OF ECONOMIC SECURITY

For over 100 years economic security has been a powerful idea that has galvanized the Japanese people to collective action. The purpose of action was to "catch up and surpass the West" (*oitsuki, oikose*). Military industries designed to enhance national security directly were the spearhead of Japan's industrialization after the Meiji Restoration. Eventually the normative consensus on the imperative of economic security led a militarist regime down the path to imperialism and war. Since 1945, however, the ideology of economic security has focused largely on the development of technology as the most plausible way for reducing Japan's dependence on the import of critical raw materials, such as oil, and as a potent force for gaining growing shares in the markets for commercial products.

The lack of debate about the desirability of reducing Japan's economic vulnerability is not surprising. Japanese policy makers welcomed the free trade of the *Pax Americana* as the only way to reduce their economic vulnerability, after the failure of military expansion to control foreign markets. "Although the concept of free trade requires globalism, the immediate concern of Japanese economic planners was whether Japan would be allowed access to markets and raw materials in Asia."[42] Karel Van Wolferen puts the point more sharply when he writes that the Japanese have a strong "fear of being victimized by circumstances they cannot control. A common Japanese term, *higaisha ishiki* (victimhood consciousness), reflects a diffuse but fairly strong sense that the world cannot be trusted and that Japan will always be a potential victim of capricious external forces."[43] Susan Pharr agrees when she writes that Japan's foreign policy choices "emerged out of debate, discussion, and the collective mood among successive generations of policymakers faced by pressures inside and outside Japan who shared a perception that the world was a dangerous place."[44] Japan's extreme dependence on foreign sources of energy and other raw materials is one illustration for virtually all Japanese. Indeed the idea of Japan as a small and isolated island nation, easily held hostage in a hostile international environment, still retains

42. Akio Watanabe, "Southeast Asia in U.S.-Japanese Relations," in Akira Iriye and Warren I. Cohen, eds., *The United States and Japan in the Postwar World* (Lexington: University of Kentucky Press, 1989), p. 86.
43. Karel Van Wolferen, "No Brakes, No Compass," *The National Interest*, Vol. 26 (Fall 1991), p. 26.
44. Susan Pharr, "Japan's Defensive Foreign Policy and the Politics of Burden Sharing," in Gerald L. Curtis, ed., *Japanese Foreign Policy* (forthcoming).

a very powerful hold over Japanese thinking. This is not to say that Japanese elites do not, at times, mobilize this idea to achieve particular political objectives by appealing to the need for the Japanese to counter international vulnerability through collective effort and hard work. Japan's economic vulnerability, it is agreed by all, requires defense, and characteristically the means are relatively uncontested.

Japan's commitment to increasing its technological autonomy is similarly uncontroversial. Technology is desirable because it opens up the prospect for sustained, long-term growth. It may also help to reduce Japan's economic vulnerability by leading to sustained economic growth that is less dependent on importing raw materials. As Friedman and Samuels have recently shown, the norm of enhancing Japan's technological autonomy prescribes gaining access to foreign technologies which can then be appropriated and diffused throughout society and economy. The distinction between military and civilian technology is not essential in the enhancing of such autonomy. What matters instead is that acquired know-how is "diffused aggressively throughout the Japanese economy as a matter of security ideology, national policy and private practice. In the process, defense technology is valued as much for its ability to elevate the fundamental capacities of the economy than as [sic] a means for actually producing military hardware . . . Indigenization, diffusion and nurturing combine the belief that Japan is more secure when it achieves independent scientific and technological capabilities to design, manufacture and innovate. Each is derived from a pervasive sense that Japan must compensate for its special vulnerabilities in a Hobbesian world."[45] Friedman and Samuels argue that this normative consensus about the value of technological autonomy leads to a view of industry totally different from that which can be found in the United States. Industries are valued for the knowledge they generate as much as the products they produce. This national consensus is now so basic that it is virtually unquestioned.[46]

Ideological unanimity on the desirability of defending Japan's economic security through a reduction of its dependence on raw materials and the enhancement of indigenous technology has not permeated the military security debate. The closely related concern with macro-economic manage-

45. David Friedman and Richard J. Samuels, *How to Succeed without Really Flying: The Japanese Aircraft Industry and Japan's Technology Ideology* (Cambridge: Japan Program, Center for International Affairs, Massachusetts Institute of Technology, 1992), pp. 4–5.
46. Friedman and Samuels, *How to Succeed without Really Flying*, p. 55.

ment, however, is to some extent reflected in the economic language in which security issues are at times discussed in Japan. Furthermore, the concept of comprehensive security that informs that discussion is very attuned to economic and political considerations. Talking about national security only in military terms is simply not legitimate for the mainstream of Japanese politics; the conceptual base of public discourse thus does not rest on a narrow notion of military strategy.

DEEPLY CONTESTED NORMS OF MILITARY SECURITY

Public attitudes reflect the depth of social learning which came with the disastrous loss of World War II and the American occupation. Many, although by no means all, studies of Japanese foreign policy credit public opinion with a substantial impact on national security policy. In the 1950s and 1960s this impact resulted from the combined weight of popular and Diet opposition to any policy that suggested a return to Japan's militarist past; the vehement criticism which most of the mass media reserved for any attempt to enhance the status of the military and to develop a more active defense policy; and the possibility of popular demonstrations in the street. The conservatives who held power in the 1950s, in particular Prime Minister Kishi, chose to advance their political agenda by seeking to contest the pacifist social norms that the Constitution embodied by advocating constitutional reform and, in a broader sense, a return to the substance of prewar politics.[47] In the 1970s and 1980s, however, the fronts have been reversed. Increasingly the government has sought both to exploit and to mold the gradual change in a public opinion that has come to accept grudgingly the existence of the SDF and the necessity of a modest national defense. Without relinquishing its efforts, particularly in the media, to counter the government's policy, the opposition has relied, among other instruments, on a strategy of litigation so as to contest the normative context in which Japan's national security policy is formulated. It did so even when legal redress did not promise a reversal in policy. Litigation itself was a powerful political signal to the public that government policy lacked full legitimacy and thus should not and could not be pursued vigorously.

---

47. Hideo Otake, "Defense Controversies and One-Party Dominance: The Opposition in Japan and West Germany," in T.J. Pempel, ed., *Uncommon Democracies: The One-Party Dominant Regimes* (Ithaca: Cornell University Press, 1990), pp. 128–61.

The preoccupation of the political elite with public opinion has resulted in literally dozens of public opinion polls. The results of these polls have been unambiguous over the years. In a recent article David Bobrow has taken stock of a voluminous literature about Japanese public opinion on international affairs.[48] His conclusions support established assumptions about the views of the Japanese public on security policy. Public attitudes favor a passive over an active stance, alignment with the United States over a policy of equidistance between the United States and the Soviet Union, political dependence over autonomy, and minimal over extensive military spending. Furthermore, generational effects have been relatively small in the last two decades. The overwhelming majority of Japanese have been skeptical about any dramatic departure from the status quo throughout the 1980s.[49] The public favors economic strength, peaceful diplomacy, and a low-key consensus approach; it does not feel seriously threatened by the Soviet Union or Russia; it does not think very highly of the Self-Defense Forces; and it overwhelmingly supports Article 9 of the Constitution. The military is viewed as marginal, and the public shows a marked lack of willingness to resort to armed defense even if Japan were to be attacked. "Fewer than one in five respondents would resort to force to resist invasion."[50] The evidence available suggests that to date the end of the Cold War has not led to great changes in this profile.

The evolution in the social norms affecting Japan's military security policy is not simply a spontaneous social process. Public opinion has been the target of deliberate policies, by both the SDF and the civilian government. Public officials have tried to stem the powerful influence that the media have had on maintaining or reinforcing public skepticism about all issues dealing with Japan's military security. The SDF have worked very hard trying to win public acceptance. Disaster relief in particular provided a natural way for winning public confidence. "In the minds of many Japanese, the SDF became not a force created to defend the country but an organization devoted to relief and welfare."[51] Throughout the 1960s and 1970s, about three-quarters

48. Davis B. Bobrow, "Japan in the World: Opinion from Defeat to Success," *Journal of Conflict Resolution*, Vol. 33, No. 4 (December 1989), p. 597.
49. Thomas Risse-Kappen, "Public Opinion, Domestic Structure, and Foreign Policy in Liberal Democracies," *World Politics*, Vol. 43, No. 4 (July 1991), p. 495.
50. Davis B. Bobrow, "Japan in the World," p. 597.
51. John K. Emmerson, *Arms, Yen and Power: The Japanese Dilemma* (New York: Dunellen, 1971), p. 117.

of the poll respondents indicated that emergency relief in fact was the major function of the SDF, with an increasing share of the public also recognizing the defense functions of the SDF in the 1970s.[52] In the public image that the SDF is trying to project, the fight against nature has replaced in many ways the fight against other states. In the late 1970s, according to one public opinion poll, less than 40 percent of the respondents thought that in the future the primary mission of the SDF would be related to national security.

Over time the outright hostility of the Japanese public has moderated to an abiding skepticism toward the SDF. The proportion of the Japanese public that supports a minimal defense posture has increased considerably, in line with the government's reinterpretation of the meaning of Article 9. In the mid-1950s only half of the Japanese public supported such a posture; two decades later that proportion had risen to 80 percent.[53] But despite these shifts, in 1987 the public ranked questions of national security at the very bottom of its list of priorities, in contrast to questions of law and order which it ranked at the very top.[54]

Deliberate political attempts to shape the public climate, as well as the fading of historical memories and the waxing and waning of international tensions, have left their mark on Japan's slowly changing defense consensus. Proponents of unarmed neutrality and autonomous defense define the two ends of a spectrum; but the consensus on defense policy has been altered because "the weight of the conservative mainstream has shifted."[55] With the end of the Cold War the debate is shifting away from the traditional issue of the legitimacy of Japanese rearmament toward a concern over the role of the

---

52. Douglas H. Mendel, Jr., "Public Views of the Japanese Defense System," in James H. Buck, ed., *The Modern Japanese Military System* (Beverly Hills: SAGE, 1975), p. 163; Jim Marshall, "Japanese Public Opinion on Defense and Security Issues," unpublished paper, Washington, D.C., U.S. International Communications Agency, Office of Research, Charts 7 and 8.
53. Mendel, "Public Views of the Japanese Defense System," p. 161. John E. Endicott, "The Defense Policy of Japan," in Douglas J. Murray and Paul R. Viotti, eds., *The Defense Policies of Nations: A Comparative Study* (Baltimore: The Johns Hopkins University Press, 1982), pp. 447–448; Thomas U. Berger, "America's Reluctant Allies: The Genesis of the Political-Military Cultures of Japan and West Germany," Ph.d. dissertation, Massachusetts Institute of Technology, 1992, pp. 364–367, 503–508.
54. Takashi Inoguchi, *Japan's International Relations*, pp. 158–160. See also Peter J. Katzenstein and Yutaka Tsujinaka, *Defending the Japanese State: Structures, Norms, and the Political Response to Terrorism and Violent Social Protest in the 1970s and 1980s* (Ithaca, N.Y.: Cornell University Press, Cornell East Asia Series, 1991).
55. Steven K. Vogel, *Japanese High Technology, Politics, and Power* (Berkeley Roundtable on the International Economy, Research Paper No. 2, University of California, Berkeley, March 1989), p. 66.

SDF in relation to Japan's growing international responsibilities in areas such as regional security, international peace-keeping, and disaster relief.[56]

The social norms expressed in Japan's changing public opinion interact with the legal norms that help define Japan's military security policy. Japan's "linkage between internal constitutionalism and foreign policy is admittedly unique among the world's democracies."[57] And it is equally unique that the opponents to Japan's rearmament have since 1955 frequently challenged the constitutionality of Japan's armed forces in the courts.[58] The courts have given indirect support to the government's defense policy. But what matters politically is not only the result of litigation but the fact that legal disputes remain unresolved. This signals to all that the normative basis of Japan's security policy remains contested.

Japan's Constitution renounces war as an instrument of national security policy. The core of this distinctive aspect of Japan's policy is the famous Article 9 of the Constitution, which imposes severe restraints on the conduct of Japan's security policy. In it, Japan renounces war as a sovereign right of the nation; repudiates the use of force as means for settling international disputes; and does not recognize the right of belligerency of the state.[59] "Article IX is to the Japanese constitution what the right to life, liberty, and the pursuit of happiness is to the American constitution: more than mere written words on a piece of document, it has become the very essence of the Japanese regime or polity."[60] As Chalmers Johnson notes, "Most Japanese equate Article 9 of the Constitution with democracy itself; to alter one is to alter the other."[61] Attempts to revise the Constitution in line with a gradually changing government policy failed. With the hope of rewording Article 9, Prime Minister Kishi set up in 1957 the Investigation Committee for the Constitution. But a commission report finally issued in 1967 failed to settle

---

56. Interview Nos. 19, 20 and 21, Tokyo, June 18 and 19, 1991.
57. Lawrence W. Beer, "Law and Liberty," in Takeshi Ishida and Ellis Krauss, eds., *Democracy in Japan* (Pittsburgh: University of Pittsburgh Press, 1989), p. 69.
58. Isao Sato, "Debate on Constitutional Amendment: Origins and Status," *Law in Japan,* Vol. 12 (1979), pp. 1–22; Tomosuke Kasuya, "Constitutional Transformation and the Ninth Article of the Japanese Constitution," *Law in Japan,* Vol. 18 (1985), pp. 1–26; Osamu Nishi, *The Constitution and the National Defense Law System in Japan* (Tokyo: Seibundo, 1987).
59. Kyoko Inoue, *MacArthur's Japanese Constitution: A Linguistic and Cultural Study of Its Making* (Chicago: University of Chicago Press, 1991).
60. Tetsuya Kataoka, *Waiting for a "Pearl Harbor": Japan Debates Defense* (Stanford: Hoover Institution Press, 1980) p. 5.
61. Chalmers Johnson, *Japan in Search of a "Normal" Role,* Institute on Global Conflict and Cooperation, University of California, Policy Paper No. 3 (July 1992), p. 24.

the controversial issue of revision. Over the years, support for a possible revision to legalize full-scale rearmament has decreased. Since the early 1960s the opponents of constitutional revision have outnumbered supporters by a margin varying between two- and three-to-one.[62]

The prolonged process of litigation that the opposition has waged in order to keep a firm policy consensus around Japan's enlarged defense role from emerging has given the government its share of victories. Some legal cases, such as the Mito District Court ruling in the *Hyakuri* case of February 1977, have strengthened the position of the SDF. These decisions indicate in essence that Article 9 forbids only armed forces that have the capacity for making war. At what point the strength of the SDF would exceed the capacity for self-defense "is a matter for political decision."[63] In fact over the years court interpretations have backed the view of successive Japanese cabinets that "legal arguments have . . . reached a point at which the right of self-defense and the existence of the SDF are accepted as constitutional."[64]

The normative consensus that embraces Japanese security policy is shaped by the historical lessons of World War II and the reemergence of Japan as a peaceful and prosperous actor in world politics since 1945. Characteristic of Japan's political culture is the fact that a pacifism deeply ingrained in a substantial segment of the Japanese public has a very complex relation to the constitutional mandate imposed by Article 9. The Constitution has been reinterpreted over time to fit an evolving public consensus on what were judged to be the requirements of Japanese security policy in a changing world. This accounts perhaps for the fact that the overwhelming majority of the Japanese public now has come to accept the SDF while at the same time refusing adamantly to amend Article 9.[65] This process of reinterpretation is grounded in a deep public resentment and fear of any experimentation with a policy that might rely on the threat or use of military force. The normative constraints have made it impossible to revise Article 9 of the Constitution; to build nuclear weapons or to agree to their deployment on Japanese soil; to dispatch Japanese troops abroad in combatant roles even as part of an

---

62. Bobrow, "Japan in the World," pp. 598–599.
63. Isao Sato, "Debate on Constitutional Amendment: Origins and Status," *Law in Japan*, Vol. 12 (1979), p. 17.
64. Hisahiko Okazaki, "The Political Framework of Japan's Defense," in Murray and Viotti, eds., *The Defense Policies of Nations*, p. 470.
65. Shinkichi Eto, "Japanese Perceptions of National Threats," in Charles E. Morrison, ed., *Threats to Security in East Asia–Pacific: National and Regional Perspectives* (Lexington, Mass.: D.C. Heath, 1983), pp. 56–57.

international peacekeeping force; to sell weapons abroad; or to raise the JDA to ministerial status. Any or all of these measures connote the strengthening of the military, and thus raise fears of a return to political conditions and practices that prevailed before 1945.

That the complex interplay between social and legal norms that helps define Japan's national security policy is likely to persist is indicated by the striking difference between public opinion and legal opinion on the issue of military security. A 1981 poll, for example, indicated that 61 percent of the public favored the SDF at its present level of strength and 22 percent wanted to see the SDF grow stronger. At the same time a survey of legal scholars showed that 45 percent wanted to see the SDF abolished and another 15 percent wanted it weakened. "83 percent of the public favored preserving or increasing the SDF while 60 percent of legal experts favored abolition or reduction of the forces. . . . while 17 percent of the public felt the SDF were unconstitutional 47 percent felt that they were not unconstitutional. By contrast, 71 percent of the legal experts believed that the forces were unconstitutional and only 27 percent found they were not unconstitutional."[66]

Japan's Security Policy

How do the structures and norms described in the two preceding sections affect Japan's security policy? Japan's national security policy has two distinguishing features. It is comprehensive: besides military issues it also includes economic and political security concerns. And it is characterized by a variable mix of policy flexibility and rigidity. The comprehensiveness of policy is shaped by the structures of Japanese politics. The organizational structure of the Japanese state strengthens the economic and political dimensions of security policy. The normative context in which Japan's security policy is defined helps explain the mix of flexibility and rigidity in policy change. On economic issues uncontested norms of security facilitate policy flexibility. On military issues deeply contested security norms lead to policy rigidity. Finally, on political security issues the normative context has at some times favored policy adjustment and at others worked against it. In short, the interaction of structures and norms explain the comprehensive definition of security as well as the pattern of policy adjustment.

66. Theodore McNelly, "Disarmament and Civilian Control in Japan: A Constitutional Dilemma," *Bulletin of Peace Proposals*, Vol. 13, No. 4 (December 1982), p. 357.

REDUCING ECONOMIC VULNERABILITY

The history of Japan's policy of economic security shows that structures and norms have favored flexible adjustment to changing international conditions. The oil crisis of 1973 was a dramatic event for most industrial countries. Their responses revealed starkly different visions of how to manage their affairs in a world of high-priced energy. The United States, for example, responded to the energy crisis of 1973 with "Project Independence" and the creation of a military Rapid Deployment Force for times of crisis. The instinctive reaction of American policymakers and the American public was to restore a situation of energy independence and self-reliance. This was not the reaction of Japan. Central to the conception informing the energy policy of the Japanese government was the notion that Japan's dependence on foreign energy supplies was inescapable.[67] If nuclear energy generated by imported uranium is included, Japan's dependence on foreign energy resources was still an astounding 91 percent in 1985.[68] Vulnerability is a fact of life that Japan had no choice but to accept. Within that general context, "the policies that have been selected have followed a coherent line and have been more or less responsive to the country's need . . . Japan succeeded in implementing its plans to a degree that other governments found difficult to achieve."[69]

Japan has attempted to ameliorate its vulnerability through diplomatic initiatives of the government. But diplomacy was coupled with the technological innovativeness of Japanese industry responding to the cues of market prices. An adaptable private sector response has led to greater national security. What could be ameliorated through the government's policy was not international vulnerability but an excessive dependence on Mideast oil

---

67. Nobutoshi Akao, ed., *Japan's Economic Security* (New York: St. Martin's, 1983); J.W.M. Chapman, Reinhard Drifte, and I.T.M. Gow, *Japan's Quest for Comprehensive Security* (New York: St. Martin's, 1982); Makoto Momoi, "Basic Trends in Japanese Security Policies," in Robert A. Scalapino, *The Foreign Policy of Modern Japan* (Berkeley: University of California Press, 1977), pp. 341–364; Shoko Tanaka, *Post-War Japanese Resource Policies and Strategies: The Case of Southeast Asia* (Ithaca, N.Y.: Cornell University China-Japan Program, East Asian Papers Series No. 43); Richard J. Samuels, *The Business of the Japanese State: Energy Markets in Comparative and Historical Perspective* (Ithaca: Cornell University Press, 1987); Davis B. Bobrow and Robert T. Kudrle, "How Middle Powers Can Manage Resource Weakness: Japan and Energy," *World Politics*, Vol. 39, No. 4 (July 1987), pp. 536–565.

68. Hiroaki Fukami, *Shigen Enerugi Korekara Konaru* (Predicting the future of natural resources and energy) (Tokyo: PHP Kenkyujo, 1988), p. 157.

69. Raymond Vernon, *Two Hungry Giants: The United States and Japan in the Quest for Oil and Ores* (Cambridge, Mass.: Harvard University Press, 1983), pp. 82, 97.

as the primary source of energy. Put differently, the government's role did not eliminate dependence but sought to provide more stable energy supplies in an unstable world. On the other hand in lowering its dependence on foreign sources of energy, private business enhanced Japan's national security over time through the application of energy-efficient technologies.

After 1973 Japan's raw materials policy became tightly integrated with a general economic policy that had recognized the rise of high-technology industries as the most promising avenue for reducing Japan's dependence on resource-intensive industries in the long term.[70] The government adopted a two-pronged policy of reducing dependence on oil and increasing the efforts of private industry to develop new energy-saving technologies. Japan's policy did not change after the second energy crisis of 1979. The government trusted the country's general economic strength and flexibility to cope with adjustments and to maintain or forge additional links with oil-producing countries in the Third World. The Japanese government made the point explicitly when it released, soon after the second oil shock, a MITI report which showed that in the 1970s Japan had been more flexible in adjusting to energy constraints than had been its industrial competitors, in part through greater gains in labor productivity and overall economic growth.[71] Market trends thus were as important in changing Japan's energy policy as was direct government intervention in energy markets.[72] This is an element of Japan's search for "comprehensive security" that is frequently overlooked. The government expected that the private sector, heeding market signals, would realize gains in rationalizing its energy costs and thus remain, at a minimum, on par with Japan's major competitors.

RESISTING MILITARY ENTANGLEMENTS

The deeply contested and therefore rigid nature of Japan's military security policy is illustrated well by the longstanding controversy over Japan's participation in collective security measures which has, in the eyes of its advocates, immobilized Japan's security policy. Policy rigidity has been very noticeable in Japan's steadfast refusal to send members of the SDF abroad in combat roles, even as members of UN peacekeeping operations. The dispatch of SDF

---

70. Laura Hein, *Fueling Growth: The Energy Revolution and Economic Policy in Postwar Japan* (Cambridge, Mass.: Harvard Council on East Asian Studies and Harvard University Press, 1990).
71. *Far Eastern Economic Review*, December 14, 1979, pp. 47–48.
72. Ronald A. Morse, "Japanese Energy Policy," in Wilfred Kohl, ed., *After the Second Oil Crisis* (Lexington, Mass.: Lexington Books, 1982), p. 255.

engineers to Cambodia in the fall of 1992 did not break with Japan's longstanding policy of avoiding any potential for entanglement in any armed conflict. This is the result of a deliberate policy of caution and restraint rooted in the traumatic experience of losing a disastrous war.

SENDING MINESWEEPERS TO THE GULF. In response to the crisis following Iraq's invasion of Kuwait, the United States suggested in August 1990 that Japan send minesweepers and tankers to the Gulf.[73] The Japanese government refused on the grounds that minesweepers might get drawn into hostilities. SDF ships were finally sent to the Gulf in April 1991, after the end of the war. The Maritime Self-Defense Forces (MSDF) had carefully prepared for this eventuality since August 1990. And after the end of the war MOFA's Security Division also had begun serious consideration of this policy option. Various factors favored deployment. Germany's decision to send minesweepers prodded the MOFA into stronger advocacy for Japan to take a similar stance. MITI recognized the need for sending minesweepers so that the Japanese-owned Arabian Oil Company could again begin exporting oil from Saudi Arabian ports. Yet MITI apparently refrained from taking a public stance, preferring instead that business organizations press for the dispatch of SDF ships. Public opinion supported this move. According to one poll conducted in March 1991, 63 percent of the respondents backed the deployment while 29 percent were opposed. Some of the opposition parties were not strongly opposed either. Komeito did not formally approve the dispatch of the minesweepers. But the government's decision enjoyed the support of a substantial number of Komeito's Diet members.[74] This episode indicated that the categorical opposition to the overseas deployment of the SDF had lost some of its persuasiveness in Japanese domestic politics.[75]

---

73. Courtney Purrington and A.K., "Tokyo's Policy Responses during the Gulf Crisis," *Asian Survey*, Vol. 31, No. 4 (April 1991), pp. 307–323; Manfred Pöhl, "Die japanischen Streitkräfte in die Golfregion? Diskussion um den 'japanischen Ernstfall'," in Heinz Eberhard Maul, ed., *Militärmacht Japan? Sicherheitspolitik und Streitkräfte* (Munich: Iudicium, 1991), pp. 338–362; Ian Buruma, "The Pax Axis," *New York Review of Books*, Vol. 38, No. 8 (April 25, 1991), pp. 25–28, 38–39; Takashi Inoguchi, "Japan's Response to the Gulf Crisis: An Analytic Overview," *Journal of Japanese Studies*, Vol. 17, No. 2 (1991), pp. 257–273; Eiichi Katahara, *Japan's Changing Political and Security Role* (Singapore: Institute of Southeast Asian Studies, 1991); Ministry of Foreign Affairs, *Japan's Post Gulf International Initiatives* (Tokyo: Ministry of Foreign Affairs); Masaru Tamamoto, "Trial of an Ideal: Japan's Debate over the Gulf Crisis," *World Policy Journal*, Vol. 8, No. 1 (Winter 1990–91), pp. 89–106; *Japan Echo*, Vol. 19, No. 1 (Spring 1992).

74. *Asahi Shimbun*, May 4, 6, 9, 10 ,15, 16, and 18, 1991, 13th ed.

75. Interview Nos. 1, 4, 5 and 18, Tokyo, June 11, 12 and 18, 1991; Sadako Ogata, "Japan's United Nations Policy in the 1980s," *Asian Survey*, Vol. 27, No. 9 (September 1987), pp. 957–972.

THE FIRST PKO BILL. The United Nations Peace Cooperation Bill that Prime Minister Kaifu introduced in the Diet in October 1990 revealed the political constraints under which the government was operating. The UN Peace Cooperation Corps that the government was proposing to form for participation in UN peacekeeping operations (PKO) was to be composed of volunteers on loan from government agencies including the SDF and the Maritime Safety Agency (part of the Ministry of Transportation). Its task was to include a variety of noncombatant functions including the monitoring of a truce, administrative consultations with governments after the cessation of hostilities, the monitoring of elections, the provision of medical, transportation and communication services, and the rendering of assistance to refugees and reconstruction activities. Under no circumstances was the Corps to be allowed to engage in the "use of force" or the "threat of the use of force." Like a police force, members of the Corps would only carry small arms to be used exclusively for self-protection. But according to the bill the Corps would be permitted to cooperate with nations acting to put UN resolutions into effect. Diet deliberations made clear that the government intended to have the SDF operate in the area of logistics and support for multi-national forces deployed in the Gulf at the time. Critics contended that cooperation with the multinational forces, even if restricted to logistics and support, would constitute a use of force. Thus only 20 to 30 percent of the public backed the bill.[76] All opposition parties were against it, and even inside the LDP less than half of the Lower House members supported the bill.[77] The bill died in November 1990 in the Diet without having been put to a vote.

THE SECOND PKO BILL. In September 1991, the government submitted the United Nations Peacekeeping Operations Cooperation Bill to the Diet. The writing of the new bill evidently took into account the low level of support the 1990 version had generated. The bill restricts itself to authorizing the SDF's participation in UN peacekeeping operations and humanitarian international rescue operations. The 1980 Cabinet decision that interpreted Article 9 of the Constitution to prohibit sending the SDF overseas with any mission involving the use of force remained a major obstacle for the government in preparing the 1991 bill. Whether the use of arms by the dispatched SDF personnel in the face of organized attack constitutes legitimate self-defense

---

76. Akihiko Tanaka, "Japan's Security Policy in the 1990s," paper prepared for delivery at the Eighth Shimoda Conference, November 16–17, 1990, p. 19.
77. *Asahi Shimbun*, November 9, 10, 1990, 13th ed.

or instead is a use of force banned by the constitution was a major issue debated inside the government.[78] The final version of the government bill reflects an apparent decision in favor of the latter interpretation. It made overseas deployment of the SDF as part of a peacekeeping operation conditional on the opposing sides' agreement to a ceasefire, their acceptance of the deployment of the peacekeeping force, and the neutrality of that force.[79] Furthermore, in order to prevent the use of force by Japanese personnel abroad, the government claimed that the SDF would not be placed under the operational command of the United Nations. SDF personnel would be permitted to use arms only for individual self-defense, not as part of any organized military action.[80] This attenuated version of the original legislation passed the Lower House in 1991 and was sent to the Upper House.

The government's interpretation of Article 9 appears to have made compliance with Japan's Constitution incompatible with United Nations norms on peacekeeping operations. Whether it would be feasible to maintain a national command over SDF personnel deployed abroad on peacekeeping operations was one of the major points of contention in the Diet debates.[81] Placement of SDF personnel under UN command would require a major change in the government's interpretation of Article 9. Thus the government faced a difficult dilemma. The bill, amended in the Upper House, passed both Houses in June 1992. The final version of the bill did not resolve the dilemma. But it prohibited, until authorization by a future law, SDF participation in peacekeeping operations that might involve a combat role. Furthermore, the three-party coalition supporting the final bill informally agreed not to implement SDF participation in logistical operations such as the transporting of weapons.[82] SDF units sent abroad under the new law will "stay far from the sound of gunfire."[83] The final compromise is consistent with the public's response to the bill. In a public opinion poll taken in November 1991, 33 percent of the respondents were in favor of and 58 percent were

---

78. Interview No. 19, Tokyo, June 18, 1991.
79. *Asahi Shimbun*, September 19, 1991, 11th ed.
80. Tadashi Tanaka, "Kokuren Heiwa Iji Katsudo to Nihon no Sanka-Kyoryoku" (UN peacekeeping operations and Japan's participation and cooperation), *Hogaku Seminar*, No. 443 (November 1991), pp. 40–41.
81. Yoshitaka Sasaki, "Abunai Garasu Zaiku" (Dangerous glass artifact), *Sekai* (November 1991), p. 201.
82. *Asahi Shimbun*, June 16, 1992, 13th ed.
83. David E. Sanger, "Japan's Troops May Sail, and the Fear is Mutual," *New York Times*, June 21, 1992, p. E4.

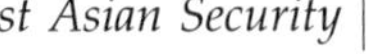

against SDF participation in lightly armed peacekeeping forces whose mission it was to separate combatants.[84] These figures are consistent also with the result of an opinion poll taken in September 1992, when, under the new law, the dispatch of the SDF had begun. Fifty-two percent favored, and 36 percent opposed, the SDF's Cambodia mission. In the same poll 71 percent supported, and 20 percent were against, limiting Japan's "international contribution" to the area of nonmilitary affairs.[85]

The issue of sending military personnel abroad illustrates with great clarity the rigidity of Japan's security policy even though the pressure from the United States and rapidly changing conditions in the international system made policy flexibility appear advantageous to many. But the constraints of Japan's domestic structures and the normative context in which its security policy was defined appeared to prevent major changes in Japan's security policy in the early 1990s. In its organizational structure the Japanese government is severely hampered in pursuing policies aiming at collective defense measures in bilateral or regional alliances. And as long as Japan has not been the target of direct aggression, public opinion appears to support the domestic laws that make it unconstitutional for Japan to come to the assistance of an allied country that has been attacked by a hostile third country.[86] Because of Japan's disastrous defeat in World War II, that is, for essentially historical reasons, the domestic norms that circumscribe Japan's security policy make formal collective defense arrangements a highly implausible policy option for Japan's political leaders.

POLITICAL SECURITY AND THE U.S.-JAPAN RELATIONSHIP

The security relationship between Japan and the United States which has been central to Japan's security policy since World War II subordinates politically both military and economic dimensions. Despite the restraints imposed on the overseas deployment of the SDF, Japan has served at times *de facto* as a forward base of the U.S. military in Asia.[87] At no time was this clearer than during the Vietnam War. Logistically Okinawa handled about three-quarters of the 400,000 tons of goods that the American forces consumed in Vietnam each month. The Kadena air base on Okinawa averaged

84. *Asahi Shimbun,* May 1, 1992, 13th ed.
85. *Asahi Shimbun,* September 28, 1992, 13th ed.
86. Okazaki, "The Political Framework of Japan's Defense," p. 471.
87. Emmerson, *Arms, Yen and Power,* pp. 89–97.

a takeoff or landing every three minutes around the clock, for a total of more than a million flights between 1965 and 1973.[88] Tokyo's civilian airport at Haneda processed almost 100,000 American service personnel during the first year of major troop commitments as well as over 2,000 military charter flights in 1967.[89] A 1966 report for the Military Preparedness Subcommittee of the U.S. Senate noted that "it would be difficult to fight the war in Southeast Asia without Yokosuka and Sasebo."[90] The government took the position that the U.S. forces stationed in Japan could, under Article 6 of the Security Treaty, operate in Vietnam, which is not a part of the Far East. Indeed, the Foreign Minister acknowledged that Japan was not neutral in the Vietnam War.[91]

The broad interpretation of Article 6 was also quite evident in the aftermath of the Gulf War. Japan did not object to the fact that U.S. troops stationed in Japan were sent off to military engagements outside of Asia. The meaning of the concept of "Far East," defense of which justifies the stationing of U.S. troops in Japan, was never a central point of discussion. The regional security aspects which were controversial during the Vietnam war have now been redefined, as the Security Treaty apparently has acquired a global function. In the government's view, legally speaking U.S. troops are free to leave Japan without consent of the Japanese government, since they are starting their military "operations" only when approaching the area of engagement, in this case the Mideast. This avoids the necessity of reaching explicit agreements between the U.S. and Japanese governments on the objectives of particular troop movements, and thus sidesteps the controversial issue of "prior consultations" under the provisions of the Security Treaty, arguably the umbrella under which all of Japan's security policy is conducted.[92]

Accompanying the broad interpretation of the Security Treaty has been a stretching of the concept of individual self-defense. Japan's *de facto* support for the U.S. military role in Asia was extended in the 1970s and 1980s. The 1978 "Guidelines for Defense Cooperation" stipulated greater cooperation on military matters, including the sharing of information and joint planning of military exercises.[93] This set the stage for more far-reaching agreements that

---

88. Thomas R.H. Havens, *Fire Across the Sea: The Vietnam War and Japan, 1965–1975* (Princeton: Princeton University Press, 1987), pp. 87–88.
89. Havens, *Fire Across the Sea*, p. 159.
90. Havens, *Fire Across the Sea*, p. 87.
91. Emmerson, *Arms, Yen and Power*, p. 84.
92. Interview Nos. 15 and 22, Tokyo, December 14 and 18, 1991.
93. James R. Van de Velde, "Japan's Emergence into Western Security Doctrine: U.S.-Japan

were reached in the 1980s. The established constitutional interpretation of Article 9 permitting individual self-defense thus has gradually been relaxed. Successive conservative governments have broadened the concept of "individual self-defense." Prime Minister Nakasone, for example, argued after he took office that it would be constitutional for Japanese naval forces to help protect U.S. naval forces outside of Japan's territorial waters in wartime, if those forces were on their way to defend Japan. This new interpretation widens the permitted scope of joint operations between American and Japanese naval forces and moves Japan closer to the role of a typical military ally of the United States.[94] An additional example of how the government has reinterpreted prior practice to meet new demands occurred in June 1991, when the JDA approved for the first time the refueling of U.S. ships by Japanese ships in the Gulf. Refueling of U.S. ships by the SDF had previously been permitted only in joint exercises.[95]

The notions of individual and collective self-defense have shifted over time, thus permitting incremental policy change. Instead of being confined to a narrowly conceived definition of the Japanese home territories, the SDF have extended their mission to defend the sea and air spaces surrounding Japan, as articulated in the joint communiqué signed after a meeting of Prime Minister Suzuki and President Reagan in May 1981.[96] The original, narrow conception of defending only the Japanese home territories thus has been replaced without any explicit change in constitutional interpretation, by a politically restrained defense posture which aims at both a strengthening of the U.S.-Japan "alliance" and a "stabilization" of Asian affairs.[97] In the words of Masashi Nishihara, a well-known defense analyst who welcomes such a change, "the concept of self-defense is basically stretchable. Japan can be a regional power" by coordinating its individual self-defense measures with security measures of other countries.[98]

In contrast, Japan's tight control over the export of military technologies has been loosened explicitly for the benefit of the United States in the 1980s

---

Defense Cooperation 1976–1986," Ph.d. dissertation, Fletcher School of Law and Diplomacy, Tufts University, 1988, pp. 177–82.

94. Masashi Nishihara, "The Security of East Asia: Part I," in Robert O'Neill, ed., *East Asia, The West and International Security: Prospects for Peace,* Adelphi Paper No. 218 (London: International Institute for Strategic Studies, 1987), p. 8.

95. *Asahi Shimbun,* June 21, 1991, 13th ed.

96. Nishihara, "Expanding Japan's Credible Defense Role," p. 183.

97. Interview No. 21, Tokyo, June 19, 1991.

98. Daniel Sneider, "In the Name of 'Self-Defence'," *The Daily Yomiuri,* July 13, 1986, p. 5.

without producing any significant reverse flow of technology. This issue remains a source of considerable friction between the two countries. Policy adjustment has been difficult and slow. Efforts to increase the flow of technology from Japan to the United States failed for a variety of reasons. As a result the United States applied for only three technology transfers in the 1980s. Japan transferred technology related to surface-to-air missiles, the construction of naval vessels, and the modification of U.S. naval vessels.[99] This is a paltry figure considering the 40,000 separate contracts that Japanese firms signed between 1951 and 1984 to acquire foreign technology, the more than 100 military co-production agreements in which Japanese manufacturers were using U.S. technologies in the 1980s, and the 10:1 ratio in the flow of Japanese researchers sent to the United States as contrasted with American researchers sent to Japan in the second half of the 1980s.[100]

When President Reagan invited Japan to join Britain, West Germany, and France to participate in searching for what he described as an alternative to the system of nuclear deterrence, Prime Minister Nakasone took considerable time before signing in 1987 an agreement laying out the conditions of Japan's participation in the Strategic Defense Initiative (SDI).[101] The delay was due not only to slow decisionmaking in Tokyo but also to some serious political hesitations about the ambiguity of the technological and strategic implications of the SDI program.[102] Furthermore, the economic incentives that Japanese business initially saw in participating in the development of potentially revolutionary military technologies with direct implications for commercial products was soon tempered. For it became quickly apparent that West German businessmen failed to gain substantial research funding from the SDI program. In addition Japanese businessmen worried increasingly over a drain

99. Interview No. 14, Tokyo, June 17, 1991; U.S. Congress, Office of Technology Assessment, *Arming our Allies: Cooperation and Competition in Defense Technology*, OTA-ISC-449 (Washington D.C.: U.S. Government Printing Office, May 1990), p. 69.
100. Interview No. 11, Tokyo, June 14, 1991; Ellen Frost, "Realizing U.S.-Japan Defense Cooperation," *Asian Wall Street Journal*, September 1, 1985; Jacob M. Schlesinger and Andy Pasztor, "U.S., Japan Neglect Defence-Trade Issue," *Asian Wall Street Journal*, August 7, 1990; Richard J. Samuels, "Reinventing Security: Japan since Meiji," *Daedalus*, Vol. 120, No. 4 (Fall 1991), p. 54.
101. Peggy L. Falkenheim, *Japan and Arms Control: Tokyo's Response to SDI and INF*, Aurora Papers No. 6 (Ottawa: The Canadian Centre for Arms Control and Disarmament, 1988); Glenn D. Hook, "The Erosion of Anti-Militaristic Principles in Contemporary Japan," *Journal of Peace Research*, Vol. 25, No. 4 (December 1988), p. 388; Vogel, *Japanese High Technology*, pp. 37–39.
102. Wayne Decker, "Japanese Decision Criteria on the Strategic Defense Initiative," in Richard B. Finn, ed., *U.S.-Japan Relations: A Surprising Relationship* (New Brunswick, N.J.: Transaction Books, 1987), pp. 163–73.

of Japanese technology to the United States.[103] In the end the Japanese decision was made not on military or economic but on political grounds. On this issue, as on many others, Japan simply had to play the role of loyal ally.

Recognizing persisting problems in the field of technology transfer from Japan to the United States, Secretary of Defense Cheney's visit to Tokyo in February 1990 became the occasion for singling out six technology areas of particular interest for the U.S. military.[104] U.S.-Japanese working groups have been set up since September 1990 to lay the groundwork for a broadening flow of dual-use technology from Japan to the United States.[105] With technology flow-back quickly becoming "a buzz word for the 1990s,"[106] other organizations of the United States government, such as the Defense Advanced Research Projects Agency (DARPA) and the Strategic Defense Initiative Organization (SDIO), regularly send delegations to Tokyo on fact-finding missions. Japanese governmental units such as TRDI (Technical Research and Development Institute) and MITI help establish the necessary contacts with Japanese firms.[107] It is too early to judge the effectiveness of these recent attempts at creating new links in the vital area of technological cooperation between Japan's firms and government agencies and their American counterparts.

Conclusion

Since the Meiji Restoration a wealthy nation and a strong military have been the traditional objectives of Japanese security policy. With the end of the Pacific War this maxim has been modified rather than abandoned. Since 1945 military security has been embedded in a broader definition of national security. Both state structure and social and legal norms explain why Japan's security policy has eschewed the traditional trappings of military status and power. Only a small fringe of Japanese society currently views the possession of nuclear weapons as a symbol of international stature that Japan should aspire to. Economic factors reinforce the strong political preferences against building up a powerful military. A rough estimate of the costs Japan would

103. Decker, "Japanese Decision Criteria," p. 169.
104. Udai Fujishima, *Gunji-ka suru Nichibei Gijutsu Kyoryoku* (Militarization technology cooperation between Japan and the United States) (Tokyo: Mirai-sha, 1992), p. 144.
105. Interview No. 3, Tokyo, June 11, 1991.
106. Interview No. 20, Tokyo, December 18, 1991.
107. Interview No. 20, Tokyo, December 18, 1991.

incur if it were to build a conventional military force commensurate with its economic strength and the size of its population suggests annual expenditures of 150 to 200 billion dollars for a decade—considerably more, that is, than current estimates of the economic costs of German unification in the 1990s.[108] These are very large sums even for an economy of Japan's size. Most Japanese are convinced that nuclear weapons and a strong military would generate neither wealth nor strength but, at great economic cost, immense political and military risks instead.

What are the political and theoretical implications of this argument? One of the core tenets of the realist study of international relations holds that rational state actors seek to maximize relative gains in the international system and in doing so adjust their behavior to the dictates of a changing international situation. Since the mid-1970s Japan has experienced great changes in the international system which affect its security. The weakening of the American position in East Asia and the growth of a Soviet military presence in the late 1970s, the second Cold War in Europe in the early 1980s, dramatic changes in Soviet defense and foreign policy since the mid-1980s, and the breakup of the Soviet Union in 1991 have, however, elicited no sharp changes in Japan's security policy. There exists then no close relation between the transformations that have affected the international system during the past two decades and the gradual evolution of Japan's security policy along economic, military and political dimensions.

Rather than following the logic of realist doctrine, Japanese policy makers have responded instead to the incentives provided by the structure of the Japanese state and the normative context in which security policy is formulated and implemented. Domestic structures account for the comprehensive character of Japan's security policy, which embeds military security concerns in broader economic and political notions. The organization of power in Japanese politics, especially within the government's bureaucracy as well as the party system, and more broadly in state-society relations, tends to suppress military concerns and interests. Because the interests that we can derive from structures are plastic and can be conceived in different ways, depending on the normative context, both social and legal, in which they are placed, the normative context helps us understand how and where the adaptation of Japan's security policy to a changing world will be flexible or rigid. When

108. Richard Halloran, *Chrysanthemum and Sword Revisited: Is Japanese Militarism Resurgent?* (Honolulu, Hawaii: The East-West Center, 1991), pp. 18–19.

international structures change as rapidly as they have in the late 1980s, Japanese policymakers have defined the objectives and modalities of their political strategies partly in response to the cues that domestic structures provide and in part to accord with the standards of appropriateness that the normative context of thought and action suggests to them. An understanding of the politics by which norms are, and are not, contested is thus particularly important.

Domestic structure and normative context do not closely track the rapid changes in the international system. It is possible that dramatic future change in the structure of the international system might pose security threats much greater for Japan than it has experienced since 1945. And such upheaval might fundamentally alter Japan's state structure and norms and thus transform its security policy. But we should not forget that a number of basic changes have had a profound effect on Japan's international position since the end of the Pacific War, without leading to fundamental changes in its security policy. For example, Japan has risen to the rank of the second most important industrial power in the world, while America's economic influence has diminished, especially in Asia. And Japan has witnessed the breakup of the Soviet Union.[109] Discontinuities in the international system thus make it possible that Japan will choose to change its security policy in dramatic fashion. But the record of the last forty years makes such change highly improbable, for Japan's security policy is shaped largely by domestic rather than international determinants.

Japan's social and legal norms account for the flexibility and rigidity with which its security policy adapts to a changing world. We have distinguished three dimensions of Japan's security policy: economic, military and political. Normative agreement makes for flexible policy adjustment (such as that of reducing economic vulnerability) while contested norms create rigid policies (such as that of resisting military entanglement). The political dimensions of Japan's security policy reveal a variable pattern of flexible and rigid policy adjustment. Military aspects like the changing role of the SDF in the growing defense cooperation with the United States have not been deeply contested and have been handled relatively flexibly. By contrast, economic issues like the transfer of militarily relevant technology from Japan to the United States have been quite controversial and thus have proven to be very difficult to

109. Gilbert Rozman, *Japan's Response to the Gorbachev Era, 1985–1991: A Rising Superpower Views a Declining One* (Princeton, N.J.: Princeton University Press, 1992).

manage politically. From this we can conclude that in U.S.-Japan relations it is the normative context rather than the military or economic content of policy that is decisive for shaping Japan's pattern of policy adjustment.

We have argued here that recent changes in world politics will not translate into sharp breaks in Japan's security policy. The comprehensive definition of Japan's security interests is unlikely to change quickly in the foreseeable future. And in its gradual change Japan's security policy will exhibit a mixture of flexibility and rigidity that will be shaped by the degree of consensus over the normative basis for policy. American foreign policy makers should be mindful of the fact that in the past it was domestic structures and norms, rather than the external balance of power, that has shaped Japan's security policy. There is little reason to believe that this fact has been altered by the end of the Cold War. The domestic structures and norms that shape Japan's security policy suggest at the end of the Cold War a simultaneous choice of a growing economic involvement with Asia on the one hand and a continued, close, if altered security relationship with the United States on the other. The future role of Japan in the international system is likely to be shaped by the intersection of these two spheres of policy and politics.

From Sword to Chrysanthemum

Japan's Culture of Anti-militarism

Thomas U. Berger

The end of the Cold War and the phenomenal increase in Japan's economic and technological power put Japan today in the position to become, if it chooses, a military as well as economic superpower. The diminution of the Soviet threat and the increasing U.S. preoccupation with domestic problems give Japan a latitude for independent action it has not had since the end of World War II. At the same time the U.S.-Japanese security alliance, which has enabled Japan to adopt a minimalist approach to defense and national security, is being weakened by ideologically charged trade and other economic frictions and a growing American perception of Japan as a threat to its interests.[1] Moreover, in the long run Japan faces the prospect of having to deal with other rising regional powers, most notably the People's Republic of China. This changing international security environment thus raises question whether Japan, having become an economic rival of the United States, may not in the future become a military competitor as well; whether, after having adopted a pacifist stance for half a century, Japan may choose to unsheathe its sword once again.[2]

Thomas U. Berger is a Fellow at the Harvard Academy for International and Area Studies. He wrote this article while a fellow at the Olin Institute, Harvard University.

The author would like to express his appreciation to Masashi Nishihara, Seizaburo Sato, and Yoshihide Soeya, as well as to three anonymous readers at *International Security*, for their helpful comments and suggestions.

1. Among those who see Japan as a threat is the so-called revisionist school of Japan experts, including Chalmers Johnson, "Their Behavior, Our Policy," *The National Interest*, No. 17 (Fall 1989); Clyde Prestowitz, *Trading Places* (New York: Basic Books, 1989); James Fallows, "Containing Japan," *Atlantic*, Vol. 263, No. 5 (May 1989); Karel Van Wolferen, *The Enigma of Japanese Power: People and Politics in a Stateless Nation* (New York: Knopf, 1990); and Pat Choate, *Agents of Influence* (New York: Knopf, 1990). American public opinion is also moving towards a more negative view of Japan; according to a February 1992 *Times/Mirror* poll, 31 percent of those surveyed now view Japan as the country that presents the greatest danger to the United States. See William Watts, "Japan Focus of America's Worst Fears," *The Japan Times*, July 15, 1992, p. 21, for a review of recent surveys.
2. See George Friedman and Meredith Lebard, *The Coming War with Japan* (New York: St. Martin's Press, 1991). See also Simon Winchester, *Pacific Nightmare: A Third World War in the Far East* (London: Sidgwick and Harrison, 1992). Such concerns can be seen in the recently leaked Pentagon report which emphasized that the United States must remain actively engaged in

International Security, Vol. 17, No. 4 (Spring 1993)

In this article I argue that such fears are largely misplaced and that in the short to medium term it is unlikely that Japan will seek to become a major military power. The primary reason for Japan's reluctance to do so is not to be found in any structural factor, such as a high degree of dependence on trade or the absence of any potential security threats, but rather is attributable to Japan's postwar culture of anti-militarism. This anti-militarism is one of the most striking features of contemporary Japanese politics and has its roots in collective Japanese memories of the militarist takeover in the 1930s and the subsequent disastrous decision to go to war with America.

The chief lesson Japan has drawn from these experiences is that the military is a dangerous institution that must be constantly restrained and monitored lest it threaten Japan's postwar democratic order and undermine the peace and prosperity that the nation has enjoyed since 1945. This particular view of the military has become institutionalized in the Japanese political system and not only is supported by Japanese public opinion, but to a surprising degree is shared by large segments of Japan's political and economic elites as well.

Japan's culture of anti-militarism originally developed under the aegis of a benevolent U.S. hegemon during the 1950s and 1960s. Since then it has taken root and is no longer a hothouse plant that would wither and die the moment American commitment to East Asia security affairs weakens. Nonetheless, Japan's anti-militarism in its present form could not survive both a weakening of its alliance with the United States and the emergence of a new regional security threat. In such a scenario Japan's political system would undergo a profound crisis and a new coalition of political actors might come to power, possibly with a far more aggressive approach to national security. Indeed, rather than a resurgence of militarism, I will argue that the main danger Japan faces today is precisely the opposite; because of its unwillingness to make a greater military contribution to regional and international security, Japan threatens to damage its alliance with the United States, the key element that enables Japan to maintain a relatively low posture on defense. Thus, paradoxically, Japan's extreme anti-militarism increases the likelihood of a shift in the opposite direction.

After first briefly examining and evaluating both the arguments that predict that Japan will adopt a more activist military posture and those that do not,

---

maintaining regional security in order to prevent Japan and Germany from feeling compelled to build up their military forces. See Patrick Tyler, "U.S. Strategy Plan Calls for Insuring No Rivals Develop," *New York Times*, March 8, 1992, p. 1 and 14.

I trace the evolution of Japan's postwar culture of antimilitarism and examine its impact on defense policy formation. I conclude that it is in the interest of the United States to help Japan manage a slow and orderly evolution of this peculiar culture toward a more realistic stance with regard to security affairs, one that is prepared to meet potential military threats actively and could survive a reduction in America's regional military presence. In particular, I argue that Japan should be encouraged to play a larger role in the post–Cold War security order, especially in the area of regional security. With the assistance of the United States, Japan should seek to create a diverse network of institutional security ties centering on, but not relying exclusively on, the present Mutual Security Treaty with the United States.[3] Such a development would not only help lighten the U.S. military burden and contribute to peace and stability in the Far East, but would also help the Japanese preserve the most admirable features of their new political-military culture, namely their determination not to pursue a destructive course of military expansionism and nationalist self-assertion.

Arguments Predicting an Increased Japanese Military Role

Two sets of very different though potentially complementary arguments predict that Japan will begin to develop military capabilities commensurate with its enormous economic and technological ones in the not too distant future. The first set of arguments is based on purely international systemic factors, focusing on regional instability in East Asia and on the changing distribution of power between Japan and the United States. The second set of arguments stresses domestic political variables, pointing to rising Japanese nationalism and growing irritation with the United States over trade and other issues.

PRESSURES FROM THE STRUCTURE OF THE INTERNATIONAL SYSTEM

Many realist theorists have argued that there is a historical tendency for powerful nations to try to establish themselves as hegemonic powers who

3. The Mutual Security Treaty is the cornerstone of the U.S.- Japanese security relationship and commits the United States to help defend Japan militarily in return for Japanese cooperation on security issues. For an overview of the origins of the Mutual Security Treaty system, see Martin E. Weinstein, *Japan's Postwar Defense Policy, 1947–1968* (New York: Columbia University Press, 1971).

define the rules of interstate relations.[4] In the modern age the two leading international hegemons have been Britain in the nineteenth to early twentieth centuries and the United States in the post–World War II era. Because of disparate rates of economic growth, concentrations of power in the international system are fluid and inevitably discrepancies develop between the international hegemonic structure and the distribution of real power. With time hegemons tend to become increasingly weak relative to other, non-hegemonic states who enjoy a higher rate of economic growth. When such disequilibria occur the old dominant power is displaced by a more vital rising nation. The new power then takes on the hegemonic role, or else the international system lapses into a state of anarchy. Historically such periods of transition have been marked by military conflict as rival states have sought to assume the mantle of international leadership.[5]

From this perspective it seems inevitable that Japan, with its combination of demographic weight and economic and technological prowess, will seek to play a greater military role than it has in the past. Some have voiced the hope that Japan will expand its partnership with the United States and help promote not only its own but regional security as well.[6] Other analysts, most prominently George Friedman and Meredith Lebard, have predicted that Japan will begin to behave like other historical rising powers, converting some of its enormous economic strength into commensurate military capabilities and eventually seeking to replace the United States as the new hegemonic power.[7]

A second strain of realism, sometimes called defensive realism, does not share the classical realist assumption that nations always seek to maximize their power. Instead, defensive realists subscribe to the rather more modest proposition that most nations are inclined to expand their military capabilities only insofar as needed to achieve security from perceived external threats.[8]

---

4. Classical statements of this point of view include Hans Morgenthau, *Politics Among Nations* (New York: Free Press, 1954); and Martin Wight, *The System of States* (Atlantic Heights, N.J.: Humanities Press, 1977).
5. See Robert Gilpin, *War and Change in World Politics* (London: Cambridge University Press, 1981).
6. See, for example, James E. Auer, "May the U.S.-Japan Defense Alliance Continue Going from Strength to Strength," *The Japan Times*, February 26, 1989; and Jimmy Carter and Yasuhiro Nakasone, "Ensuring Alliance in an Uncertain World: The Strengthening of U.S.-Japan Partnership in the 1990s," *The Washington Quarterly*, Vol. 15, No. 1 (Winter 1992), pp. 43–56.
7. Friedman and Lebard, *The Coming War with Japan*.
8. This is one of the key distinctions between classical realist theorists such as Morgenthau, Wight, and Gilpin, and the so-called structural-realist or defensive realist school represented by

Yet from this perspective as well, there is reason to expect that Japan will want to rearm. The end of the Cold War has witnessed the emergence of a host of regional disputes which had been suppressed by the U.S.-Soviet rivalry since World War II. Though so far such conflicts have been confined to Eastern Europe and the territory of the former Soviet Union, Asia too has many potential conflicts. The situation on the Korean peninsula remains tense, and though dialogue between the sides continues, the North may still acquire nuclear weapons.[9] In Southeast Asia, regional powers are rapidly acquiring new and more advanced weapons systems. One potential hot spot is the territorial dispute by China, Vietnam, Malaysia, and Brunei over the Spratley Islands, which are thought to have valuable oil resources and are located on the strategic sea lanes running through the South China Sea.[10] The Russian military presence in Northeast Asia remains considerable. Finally, there looms the long-term problem of a rapidly industrializing but politically repressive People's Republic of China.[11]

All of these risks may prove acceptable to Japan, as long as it enjoys the firm support of the United States. The United States, however, appears exhausted by its long struggle with the Soviet Union and is plagued by serious domestic economic and social problems.[12] With the external Soviet threat gone, these internal problems seem likely to command increasing attention from American leaders and lead to a reduction in U.S. commitments abroad. The U.S. withdrawal from the Philippines and planned troop reductions in Korea can be interpreted as the first steps in this direction.[13] Some Japanese even worry that the United States will come to see Japan rather than the Soviet Union as its chief international adversary.[14]

Stephen Van Evera, "The Cult of the Offensive and the Origins of the First World War," *International Security*, Vol. 9, No. 1 (Summer 1984), pp. 58–108; Barry R. Posen, *The Sources of Military Doctrine: France, Britain and Germany between the World Wars* (Ithaca, N.Y.: Cornell University Press, 1984); and Stephen M. Walt, *The Origins of Alliances* (Ithaca: Cornell University Press, 1987).

9. On Japanese fears concerning a potential North Korean nuclear threat, see *The Japan Economic Journal*, May 18, 1991.

10. See Mark Mihovjec, "The Spratley and Paracel Islands Conflict," *Survival*, Vol. 31, No. 1 (January/February 1989), pp. 70–78.

11. The author is grateful to comments made on this point by Professor Masashi Nishihara.

12. Paul Kennedy, *The Rise and Fall of Great Powers: Economic Change and Military Conflict from 1500 to 2000* (New York: Random House, 1987).

13. On Asian fears that the U.S. military commitment to East Asia is weakening, see *The International Herald Tribune*, January 31, 1991.

14. See for example Hisahiko Okazaki, *Hanei to Sutai to Orandashi ni Nihon ga Mieru* (Tokyo: Bungeishunju, 1991). Okazaki, a career diplomat who has served as ambassador to Saudi Arabia

Given the potentially volatile security situation in East Asia and Japanese doubts concerning the U.S. commitment to Asian security, Japan may come to feel compelled to provide for its own defense. Japan would then be forced to confront the potential for conflict in its own backyard and would need to ensure that nearby crises would not threaten vital Japanese interests. In such a scenario Japan would find itself trying to fill the East Asian and Southeast Asian power vacuum with some version of *Pax Nipponica*. Whether other nations would accept Japan in such a role, however, is an open question.[15]

DOMESTIC PROPENSITIES TOWARD REMILITARIZATION

Parallel to arguments that predict Japanese rearmament on the basis of international systemic factors are those that concentrate on domestic, primarily political-cultural, factors. Three aspects of Japanese society could contribute to a remilitarization of its defense policies: its strong sense of ethnocentric nationalism, its peculiar combination of strong group loyalty with a lack of centralized decision making, and the relative absence of a sense of war guilt.

Many analysts have argued that Japan's national identity is based on a widespread belief in its uniqueness. This belief takes many different forms and shapes, all of which share the premise that the Japanese are so fundamentally different from other peoples that there is an almost impenetrable barrier to mutual understanding and interaction.[16] These beliefs are linked to a widely shared conviction that Japan possesses a unique cultural advantage in its ability to produce quality goods and maintain an orderly society, and is reinforced by the popular view that ethnic homogeneity is central feature of its culture. Conversely, many Japanese feel that ethnic diversity is at the root of the relative decline of Western society in general, and American society in particular.[17] In recent years a number of far right-wing figures,

---

and Thailand, compares Japan with sixteenth-century Holland, which he describes as a trading nation that fell victim to the envy of France and Britain once the unifying threat of the Spanish Empire had receded. See also Yukio Matsuyama, "Kokusai Rashimban," *Asahi*, November 8, 1991, p. 1. For an overview of Japanese reactions to the end of the Cold War, see *International Herald Tribune*, June 21, 1990.

15. See John Mearsheimer, "Back to the Future: Instability in Europe after the Cold War," *International Security*, Vol. 15, No. 1 (Summer 1990), pp. 5–56, for a similar argument about Germany and Europe.

16. For a good overview, see Peter N. Dale, *The Myth of Japanese Uniqueness* (New York: St. Martin's Press, 1986); and Kosaku Yoshino, *Cultural Nationalism in Contemporary Japan* (New York: Routledge, 1992).

17. See, for example, Bill Powell and Bradley Martin, "What Japan Thinks of America," *Newsweek*, April 2, 1990, pp. 16–22, which notes public opinion data showing that 57 percent of all Japanese believe that ethnic diversity is a factor in America's decline.

such as Shintaro Ishihara and Jun Eto, have tried to use trade and economic disputes with the United States to rouse nationalist sentiments[18]; at the same time the Japanese government, especially under Prime Minister Nakasone, has been more active in trying to promote a sense of national pride.[19] It is not difficult to imagine that such sentiments could be provoked to rally popular support for a massive military buildup of society.

A second reputed feature of Japanese society that makes it susceptible to remilitarization is its combination of extraordinary group loyalty and lack of central control.[20] From kindergarten to the corporate boardroom, the Japanese have demonstrated a remarkable capacity to create highly efficient organizations to which individuals develop a degree of loyalty and of attachment that, in other societies, is usually reserved for the family or religion. At the same time, there is no tradition of strong central decision making in Japan as there is in the West, and policy is made on the basis of mutual accommodations between the leading institutions that command individual loyalties. Once a consensus has formed, such as one in favor of remilitarization, it becomes very hard for the national leadership to steer the decision-making process rationally because of the number of different and competing groups involved.[21] This combination of ethnocentric nationalism and a political culture prone to inertia might provide fertile grounds for an ultranationalist explosion, possibly triggered by rising resentment over a Japanese perception of unfair U.S. demands on trade and other foreign policy issues.

Such apprehensions are further heightened by Japan's apparent unwillingness to confront the grim historical legacy of atrocities committed by its forces

---

18. See Shintaro Ishihara and Akio Morita, *No to ieru Nihon e* (Tokyo: Kobunsha, 1989), translated into English, minus Morita's contributions, as *The Japan That Can Say "No": The New U.S.-Japan Relations Card* (New York: Simon and Schuster, 1991); and Jun Eto, *Nichibei Senso wa owatte inai* ("The Japanese-American war is not over") (Tokyo: Nesco, 1987).

19. Among other measures taken to raise Japanese national consciousness during the Nakasone period, there was the reintroduction into school textbooks of military figures as role models for Japanese children; *Japan Times*, Febrary 11, 1989; the creation of a national center for the study of Japanese culture; *Asahi*, February 29, 1988; and making compulsory the singing of the national anthem and flying of the national flag at school events; *Asahi*, March 28, 1989, p. 1.

20. This view of Japanese society has been much popularized in recent years by Van Wolferen, *The Enigma of Japanese Power*.

21. See Karel Van Wolferen, "No Brakes, No Compass," *The National Interest*, No. 25 (Fall 1991). This point of view is shared by many Japanese concerned with the danger of Japanese rearmament. One of the earliest formulations of this point of view can be found in Masao Maruyama's discussion of the social basis of pre-war Japanese militarism, "The Ideology and Dynamics of Japanese Fascism," in Masao Maruyama, *Thought and Behaviour in Modern Japanese Politics* (London: Oxford University Press, 1969), edited by Ivan Morris.

during World War II. Many outside observers contrast Japan with West Germany, where after an initial period of hesitation, the Germans have been remarkably forthright in trying to come to grips with the Holocaust and other dark corners of their history.[22] It is argued that Japan's failure to do the same indicates that the Japanese, unlike the Germans, have failed to draw any lessons from the war and thus are more inclined to revert to their pre-war patterns of behavior.[23]

WEAKNESSES IN ARGUMENTS PREDICTING JAPANESE MILITARY EXPANSION

The chief problem with arguments predicting a more militarily assertive Japan is that little evidence suggests that Japan is preparing to embark on a major armaments program. Three recent developments are typically identified as signs of movement towards a more expansive defense policy: increased Japanese defense expenditures, the growth of the Japanese defense industry, and the rise of Japanese nationalism. Upon closer examination, however, all three reveal themselves to be considerably less significant than they might first appear.

Japanese defense expenditures have risen at the rate of 6.5 percent a year since 1978, and in dollar terms Japan now has the world's third largest defense budget after the United States and Russia (over 30 billion dollars).[24] Nonetheless, there is considerable debate over the cost-effectiveness of Jap-

---

22. See Charles Maier, *The Unmasterable Past: History, Holocaust and German National Identity* (Cambridge, Mass.: Harvard University Press, 1988). While the Japanese did not carry out a program of systematic mass murder on the same scale or in the same cold-blooded fashion as did the Nazis, it is important not to overlook the extent of Japanese atrocities in East Asia, of which the Nanjing massacre is only the most infamous example. For more on Japanese war crimes, see Saburo Ienaga, *The Pacific War 1931–1945* (New York: Pantheon Books, 1978); Ienaga, *Senso Sekinin* (Tokyo: Iwanami Shoten, 1985); Meirion and Susie Harries, *Soldiers of the Sun: The Rise and Fall of the Imperial Japanese Army* (New York: Random House, 1991). Since the death of Emperor Hirohito in 1989 there has been slow but considerable progress towards open recognition by the government of Japanese wartime atrocities, in part motivated by a desire to improve relations with Japan's Asian neighbors. For example, the Japanese government has decided to officially investigate the cases of an estimated 200,000 women, mostly Korean, who were forced to serve as prostitutes for the Japanese Imperial Army. *Asahi,* July 7, 1992. Japanese textbooks have also been revised recently to include more explicit recognition of the aggressive nature of the Japanese drive for conquest in East and South-East Asia; *Asahi,* July 1, 1992, p. 1.

23. See, for example, Steven R. Weisman, "Pearl Harbor in the Mind of Japan," *New York Times Magazine,* November 3, 1991, p. 32.

24. Currently Japanese defense expenditures stand at over 30 billion dollars, or approximately 1 percent of its Gross National Product (GNP). The actual figure is even higher, since Japanese figures do not include military pensions and benefits. If the Japanese defense budget were calculated using the common method employed by NATO countries, the actual level of defense spending is closer to 1.7 percent of GNP.

anese defense spending. The cost of both military manpower and equipment is, like virtually everything else in Japan, extraordinarily high.[25] Moreover, the increase in defense expenditures came as part of a deliberate strategy adopted in the early 1970s to strengthen the military relationship with the United States rather than to try to pursue an even more expensive (and dangerous) program of developing more autonomous Japanese military capabilities.[26] Japan's military buildup during the late 1970s and 1980s took place in close consultation with the United States. Consequently the Japanese force structure is designed to complement that of U.S. forces in the region, with a heavy emphasis on defensive weaponry, and little independent capacity for power projection.

In addition, in good measure the increase in defense spending during the 1980s was presented to the Japanese public as a means of appeasing U.S. demands to do more; without external pressure from the United States, it is doubtful that the Japanese would have supported an extension of their military establishment to the extent they have. With the end of the Cold War the rate of increase has begun to decline, despite the fact that many East Asian countries are continuing to invest heavily in their armed forces,[27] and for 1993 the growth in Japan's defense expenditures is expected to be around 3 percent.[28]

Some argue that because of Japan's tremendous economic and technological strength, it will inevitably seek to develop an independent military-industrial base.[29] To date, however, Japanese industry has continued to be reluctant to commit itself to arms manufacturing. No major Japanese weapons manufacturer is dependent on arms contracts for more than 10 percent of its sales. Though the traditional Japanese arms lobby has been campaigning for decades for looser restrictions on the export of weapons, the govern-

---

25. See, for example, Ikuhiko Hata, "Jietai wa Tatakaeru no Ka," *Gendai*, February 1987, pp. 212–236.
26. The best available sources on this subject are Hideo Ohtake, *Nihon no Boei to Kokunai Seiji* (Tokyo: Sanichi Shobo, 1983); and Katsuya Hirose, *Kanryo to Gunjin: Bunmin Tosei no Genkai* (Tokyo: Iwanami Shoten, 1989).
27. For example Chinese defense expenditures, the third largest in the region after the Soviet Union's and Japan's, have increased 12.5 percent in 1990, 15.3 percent in 1991, and an estimated 13.9 percent in 1992. See David Shambaugh, "China's Security in the Post–Cold War Era," *Survival*, Vol. 34, No. 2 (Summer 1991), p. 103.
28. See *Nikkei*, June 5, 1992, concerning the current negotiations over the defense budget; and *Nikkei*, June 22, 1992, on the rapid increase in defense expenditures in South East Asia.
29. See Jeffrey T. Bergner, *The New Superpowers: Germany, Japan, the U.S. and the New World Order* (New York: St. Martin's, 1991), pp. 175–181.

ment and mainstream business leadership has refused to comply for fear of triggering a popular and diplomatic backlash, and in order to avoid creating an overly powerful arms lobby.[30] With the exception of the aircraft industry, most leading Japanese high technology companies, especially those specializing in electronics and new materials, are reluctant to expand their weapons production, and even the aeronautics industry is primarily interested in using military contracts as a means of promoting the civil aeronautics industry.[31] Japanese business leaders are aware of the danger of creating a "military-industrial complex," and they view the distorting impact of arms research and production on America's economic and technological competitiveness as an instructive negative example. They feel that Japan's industry has been successful precisely because it has concentrated on producing quality goods for the demanding civilian market, and they believe that increased defense production would more likely weaken rather than strengthen the nation's technological base.[32]

Perhaps the most convincing evidence for the view that Japan may soon adopt a more aggressive military posture is the widely publicized upsurge in Japanese nationalism, accompanied by an increasingly negative, even hostile, view of the United States. Yet, while this upsurge in nationalism bodes ill for relations between the two countries, especially in the areas of trade and economics, there is little indication that it is translating into support for a stronger Japanese military or a more assertive Japanese stance on international security issues. Rather, efforts since 1945 to revive the old pre-war nexus between the state, the nation, and the armed forces have been consistently rejected by Japanese public opinion and the majority of the

---

30. See Richard J. Samuels, "'Rich Nation, Strong Army' and Japanese Technology," in Ethan Kapstein and Raymond Vernon, eds., *National Security and the Global Economy* (forthcoming). On the debate around 1980, see Shoichi Oikawa, *Jietai no Himitsu: Tozai Gunji Baransu no Henka no Naka de* (Tokyo: Ushiobunsha, 1981), pp. 171–176. See also the comments of Japanese business leaders in *Nikkei*, April 9, 1980. This reluctance to export weapons, however, does not extend to so-called "dual-use" technology having both civil and military applications. See Marie Söderberg, *Japan's Military Export Policy* (Stockholm: University of Stockholm, 1987).

31. See Richard J. Samuels and Benjamin C. Whipple, "Defense Production and Industrial Development: The Case of Japanese Aircraft," in Chalmers Johnson, Laura Tyson, and John Zysman, eds., *Politics and Productivity: How Governments Create Advantage in World Markets* (Cambridge, Mass.: Ballinger Books, 1988).

32. Interviews in spring 1988 with Ken Moroi, President of Chichibu Cement, and Genya Chiba, Director of the Research Development Corporation of Japan. For more on the historical development of these views in the 1950s, see Hideo Ohtake, "Nihon ni Okeru 'Gunsankanfukugotai' no Keisei no Zasetsu," in Ohtake, ed., *Nihonseiji ni Okeru no Sooten* (Tokyo: Sanichishobo, 1984).

Japanese political elite.[33] While Japanese leaders often make use of nationalist rhetoric, the use of nationalist symbols in connection with military issues remain highly controversial and the target of fierce criticism in the national media.[34]

Indeed, not only is it difficult to find any evidence that Japan is preparing to expand its military role in response to the changed international environment, but precisely the opposite seems to be true. Japan's reluctance to contemplate any expansion of its military role in the world, despite external pressures to do so, was illustrated by its recent behavior in the Gulf Crisis. Just when the world was expecting Japan, together with the newly united Germany, to begin to take over from the United States the mantle of leadership in their respective regions, both countries were plunged into virtual policy paralysis by Saddam Hussein's invasion of Kuwait.[35] Instead of revealing a new assertiveness, Japan had great difficulty responding to the crisis, dispatching a token mine-sweeping flotilla only after hostilities had ceased, and only grudgingly offering financial support after much internal bickering.

The Japanese public appeared totally unimpressed with arguments stressing the importance of meeting aggression or defending the principle of national sovereignty. There seemed relatively little appreciation of the need to prevent the Gulf's vital oil resources from falling under the control of a leader like Saddam Hussein. Instead of raising international ethical or political issues, the domestic debate focused almost entirely on the need to appease the Americans versus adherence to Japan's position as a peace nation, as embodied in Article 9 of the constitution, and guarding against a rekindling of militarism. Although most Japanese condemned the Iraqi invasion of Kuwait, many Japanese preferred to see the United States as a bully, overeager to resort to armed force in the Gulf in order to reaffirm its global hegemonic role.[36]

---

33. See Thomas U. Berger, *America's Reluctant Allies: The Genesis of the Political Military Cultures of Japan and West Germany* (Ph.D. Dissertation, Massachussetts Institute of Technology, 1991).
34. A good example was provided by the negative domestic response to Prime Minister Nakasone's 1988 visit to the Yasukuni Shrine dedicated to the spirit's of Japan's war dead. See *The Japan Times,* August 16, 1988, p. 2; and *Asahi,* August 16, 1988, p. 1.
35. See Courtney Purrington and A.K., "Tokyo's Policy Responses During the Gulf Crisis," *Asian Survey,* Vol. 31, No. 4 (April 1991), pp. 307–323.
36. The most comprehensive summary to date of Japan's reaction to the Gulf war is Asahi Shimbun Wangankiki Shuzaihan, *Wangan Senso to Nihon* (Tokyo: Asahi Shimbunsha, 1991). See also Courtney Purrington, "Tokyo's Responses during the Gulf War and the Impact of the 'Iraq

Japan is now capable of developing a formidable military-industrial base independent of the United States, and as a result of its economic and other achievements, there has also emerged an increased sense of patriotic pride in Japan. Yet, to an extent that is baffling from a traditional realist point of view, the Japanese apparently remain content to rely on the United States for their military security, and there is little indication that contemporary Japanese nationalism is translating into greater support for the armed forces. What is the source of this reluctance on the part of Japan to increase its military capabilities? Is it likely to change in the near future?

Arguments that Japan will not Increase its Armed Forces

Three arguments have been offered by various analysts of international relations to explain the absence of conflict among the advanced industrial nations of the West: the peaceful nature of of liberal democracies[37], the moderating influence of international institutions such as the Conference on Security and Cooperation in Europe (CSCE)[38], and the growing importance of economic relative to military sources of power in a world marked by increased and complex economic interdependence.[39] All three of these arguments, however, appear to have only limited applicability to East Asia. While democracies have historically proven reluctant to wage wars on one another, they suffer from no such inhibitions *vis-à-vis* non-democratic regimes, and aside from Japan and South Korea, there are no democratic regimes in East Asia. Likewise there are no international institutions in the region that could defuse potential crises and reassure member states about their neighbors' intentions. Finally, while undoubtedly the most vibrant economies in the region depend largely on foreign trade, the trade they conduct with one another (i.e., with their most likely adversaries) is still small compared to their trade with the United States and Europe. Moreover, the largest

---

Shock' on Japan," *Pacific Affairs*, Vol. 65, No. 2 (Summer 1992), pp. 161–181; and Purrington and A.K., "Tokyo's Policy Responses during the Gulf Crisis."

37. Michael N. Doyle, "Liberalism and World Politics," *American Political Science Review*, Vol. 80 No. 4 (December 1986); and Jack Snyder, *Myths of Empire: Domestic Politics and International Ambition* (Ithaca, N.Y.: Cornell University Press, 1991), pp. 49–52.

38. See, for example, Jeffery Anderson and John Goodman, *Mars or Minerva? A United Germany in a Post–Cold War Europe* (Cambridge, Mass.: Harvard University, Center for International Affairs [CFIA] Working Paper No. 91-8, 1991), pp. 1–3.

39. The now classic formulation of this thesis is Robert O. Keohane and Joseph S. Nye, *Power and Interdependence: World Politics in Transition* (Boston: Little, Brown, 1977), especially pp. 27–29. See also Richard Rosecrance, *The Rise of the Trading State* (New York: Basic Books, 1986).

military powers in the region—Russia, the PRC, and India—have far less external commerce than do Japan and the other East Asian trading states. Consequently, the economic costs of military conflict between East Asian countries may count far less than they might in Western Europe, and the political and social ties that commercial relations bring are also correspondingly weaker.

The one external factor that seems to provide an adequate explanation for Japan's anti-militarism is its extreme dependence on the United States to provide for its external security. Yet, even from this point of view, the depth of Japan's aversion to using military instruments is difficult to explain. Indeed, Japan's lack of willingness to share in the risk of military actions in the Gulf threatened to damage its relations with the United States. If Japan were determined to preserve its free ride on the security order created by the United States, it should have sent at least some forces to support the international effort against Iraq, if not on the same scale as the efforts of Britain and France, then at least on a scale comparable to those of Italy and Belgium.[40] To explain the phenomenon of Japanese anti-militarism, it is therefore useful to look beyond structural factors and to take Japanese domestic politics, and in particular its new anti-military culture, into consideration.

Japan's Culture of Anti-Militarism

The experience of defeat, and how that experience came to be interpreted and institutionalized in the Japanese political system and in Japanese defense policy, continue to shape Japan's willingness to make use of the military today. In this context it may be useful to compare Japan with West Germany, for while both nations' experiences were similar in many respects[41], the differences between them led them to draw very different lessons from their experiences of the war and to develop correspondingly very different forms of pacifism.

Japan's defeat in World War II was devastating. Over two and a half million Japanese had lost their lives in the course of the struggle; its cities were

40. Conversations with Motoo Shiina, Spring 1991, and Professor Seizaburo Sato, Summer 1992.
41. Both Japan and Germany were late-industrializing, rising non–status quo powers with illiberal, even anti-democratic traditions. After brief experiences with more democratic forms of government in the 1920s, in both Japan and Germany there emerged authoritarian states bent on territorial expansion. Both were then defeated by the United States and its allies, were occupied, and in both new liberal democratic institutions were introduced.

ruined; it was the target of atomic bombing; and for the first time in its recorded history it was conquered by a foreign power. As in Germany, the defeat had delegitimated Japan's prewar regime and its expansionist ideology. By the end of 1945 the dream of building a Greater East Asian Coprosperity Sphere under Japanese control had turned to ashes, and the average Japanese citizen was completely absorbed in the task of merely staying alive.

Three important differences between Japan and Germany at the end of the war were to lead to different interpretations of these broadly similar experiences. First, the nature of Japanese militarism differed from that of German Nazism. The Nazis were a mass-based movement centered on a political party. Although the Nazis were aided and abetted by segments of the traditional German political and economic elites, the Nazi leadership was separate from these groups, drew much of its support from the lower middle class, and ultimately proved inimical to many of the same elites who had originally tried to use Nazism as a weapon against the Communists.

The Japanese militarists, on the other hand, were far more organic to the old elite. Though they were heavily concentrated in the military, they were also represented in the media, segments of the business world, the bureaucracy, and the political parties.[42] And whereas the Nazis were voted into power, and thus could claim broader political legitimacy, the Japanese militarists took over through a far more insidious and protracted process of political assassinations, attempted *coups d'état*, and engineered military emergencies abroad.[43] The independent position of the army under the Meiji constitution allowed it to evade civilian control and stage military incidents abroad to expand Japanese control over North China. This isolated Japan internationally and weakened more moderate Japanese political forces. At the same time radical young officers and fanatical members of various ultranationalist organizations killed or intimidated whoever opposed the precipitous expansion of the empire.[44] While the military as an institution enjoyed

---

42. This point is made by Masao Maruyama in "Patterns of Politics in Present-day Japan," in Maruyama, *Thought and Behaviour,* pp. 456–461.
43. It might be pointed out that the Nazis were originally elected by only a plurality in 1933. Subsequently, however, Hitler was able to augment his popular support greatly. See Karl Dieter Bracher, *The German Dictatorship* (New York: Praeger, 1970).
44. For more on how the militarists took control of Japan in the 1930s, see James B. Crowley, *Japan's Quest for Autonomy: National Security and Foreign Policy, 1930–1938* (Princeton: Princeton University Press, 1966); Richard Storey, *The Double Patriots* (Boston: Houghton Mifflin, 1957); Dorothy Borg and Shumpei Okamoto, eds., *Pearl Harbor as History: Japanese-American Relations,*

broad popular support, especially in rural areas, no one ever freely voted for a militarist government or for a single charismatic leader like Hitler or Mussolini. Instead, policy emerged out of struggles among elite groups. It was therefore far easier for individual Japanese than for most Germans to feel, in the war's devastating aftermath, that they had been the victims of political forces beyond their control.

A second crucial difference between Japan and Germany was that far more of the old Japanese elite were able to survive the war, and in many cases to hold or return to their old positions of power. In part this was because the Allied Occupation in Japan ruled indirectly, relying on the existing Japanese bureaucracy to administer American policies. And in part this was because it was even more difficult in Japan to identify who had been an active supporter of the regime. Unlike Germany, there had been no real, effective opposition to the war-time government, and aside from the relatively few Japanese communists and union leaders who had been jailed by the secret police, and who were to become increasingly suspect as the Cold War progressed, there were no leaders with clean records on whom the Allies could count to take over in the new Japan.

One reflection of this was that as early as 1958 Kishi Nobusuke, who had been arrested for war crimes and was a signatory of the declaration of war on the United States, became prime minister of Japan. Even though many old Nazis not only survived but even prospered in postwar West Germany, none could have hoped to achieve this kind of rehabilitation.

Third and finally, the conditions under which the war broke out in Asia were qualitatively different from those in Europe. Although Hitler claimed he was standing up to foreign powers determined to cripple Germany through the Treaty of Versailles, the initial victims of German aggression, Czechoslovakia and Poland, were innocent bystanders. The Japanese, on the other hand, found themselves in a world made up of western empires, led by nations which exhibited a racist ideology.[45] The ideal of self-determination of peoples was ignored outside of Europe by the same European powers—France, Britain and Holland—that condemned Japanese aggression in Asia. When the Japanese expanded into Korea and China, Asia was already being

---

1931–1941 (New York: Columbia University Press, 1973); and Masaki Miyake, ed., *Gumbushihai no kaimaku* (Tokyo: Daiichi Hoki Shuppangaisha, 1983).

45. Even the United States, it should be recalled, had closed its doors to Asian immigrants for explicitly racist reasons.

carved up by the Western powers. Japan's professed mission was to liberate and unite all of Asia in order to protect Japan and the rest of Asia from outside aggression. This message ultimately was not accepted by most other Asian peoples, for in fact it turned out the Japanese were merely replacing the yoke of the white Westerners with an even more brutal and equally racist yoke of their own.[46] Nonetheless, at least within Japan this bestowed on Japanese expansionism a degree of legitimacy even among many on the left who were opposed to the militarists for other reasons.[47]

These differing conditions in Japan and Germany led their citizens to interpret their experiences in very different ways, and to draw very different, almost inverse, lessons from them. In the German case, the unbridled passions of pre-war German nationalism were identified as the primary cause of the *deutsche Katastrophe* (as Friedrich Meinecke called it). Nationalism was associated with virulent racism and blind national ambition, which were blamed for all the dark episodes of modern German history, from the expansionism of Kaiser Wilhelm II to Hitler and the Holocaust. The military establishment, while hardly viewed in a favorable light in postwar West Germany, was seen as a secondary evil which had served as a tool of nationalism, but not the primary cause of the rise of nationalism and the *Katastrophe*.

In Japan, on the other hand, it was the military institution itself which became the primary target of criticism after the war. Nationalism, while viewed as a destructive force, especially by the political left, was seen more as an instrument of militarist control than as the root cause of the demise of Japan's brief pre-war democracy and its catastrophic entry into World War II. This point of view was greatly encouraged by the non-military elites, who were all too happy to make the military into a scapegoat in order to direct blame away from their own shoulders.[48]

---

46. Mark Peattie's biography of Kanji Ishiwara, *Ishiwara Kanji and Japan's Confrontation with the West* (Princeton, N.J.: Princeton University Press, 1975) provides a fascinating and insightful look at one of the chief ideologists of Japan's military expansion in the 1930s.
47. For more on the role of racist thinking in the Pacific war, see John W. Dower, *War without Mercy: Race and Power in the Pacific War* (New York: Pantheon Books, 1986). For one Japanese intellectual's effort to detail the crimes committed by Japanese forces, see Ienaga, *Pacific War.* See also Harries, *Sheathing the Sword*, especially pp. 97–183, for a good summary of the Japanese view of responsibility for the war. The author is also grateful for the insights offered by Professors Masamichi Inoki and Seizaburo Sato on Japanese views of the war.
48. See Hans Baerwald, *The Purge of Japanese Leaders under the Occupation* (Westport, Conn.: Greenwood Press, 1977). It should be noted that even before the end of the war many Japanese leaders were convinced that the military was a hotbed of (ironically, potentially communist) subversion and therefore had to be restrained. See John Dower, *Empire and Aftermath: Yoshida*

The popular perception that the war in Asia was a response to Western imperialism, the lack of popular involvement in the militarist takeover of the government, and efforts by the ruling elites to pin the blame of the war exclusiviely on the Imperial Army, all worked together to make most Japanese citizens feel less recrimination over Japan's role in starting World War II, and over the atrocities that Japanese forces had committed throughout Asia, than Germans did over their country's misdeeds in Europe. Instead of feeling remorse over Pearl Harbor, most Japanese felt victimized, a sentiment strongly reinforced by the atomic bombings of Nagasaki and Hiroshima.[49]

This again may be taken as a reflection of the continued influence of the old party, economic, and political elites who had led the country into the war in the first place and who still believed in the justice of their cause. While the Occupation purges had been intended to remove these people from power, in practice these purges were very difficult to implement because guilt was often difficult to determine, and because the skills and knowledge of the old elite were desperately needed to rebuild the country, a goal which received growing priority with the start of Cold War. In addition, since the militarists had far more successfully coopted the old political elite, there were far fewer domestic victims of the wartime regime who could bear witness against their oppressors than was the case in Germany. There never has been a Japanese head of state ready to publicly atone for the war crimes of his nation, as German Chancellor Willy Brandt did in 1970 by publicly falling to his knees before the memorial for the victims of the Warsaw Uprising.

This general lack of self-recrimination does not mean that the Japanese did not draw any lessons from the war, but the lessons that they drew were different from those the Allies had hoped they would draw.[50] The Japanese felt doubly victimized. First they felt victimized by the West, which they felt had cynically refused to respect Japan's right to defend its legitimate interests in Manchuria, and had threatened it with a crippling oil embargo.[51] At the

---

Shigeru and the Japanese Experience, 1878–1954 (Cambridge, Mass.: Council on East Asian Studies, Harvard University Press, 1979), chapter 7.

49. See, for example, the relative lack of attention to the Pearl Harbor issue in Ienaga, *The Pacific War.* The author is grateful for points made in this regard in conversations with Professors Mark Peattie, Carol Gluck, Masamichi Inoki, and Seizaburo Sato.

50. For more on the Western failure to get the Japanese to recognize their guilt, see Harries, *Sheathing the Sword,* part 3.

51. Beginning in 1937 the United States had imposed progressively sharper economic sanctions on Japan to protest its policies in North China and to create incentives for a more moderate Japanese foreign policy. These sanctions culminated in a complete oil embargo in 1941. The Japanese military planners perceived the embargo as an effort to cripple their economy and

same time, the majority of Japanese also felt victimized by their own military for having dragged them into a war that rationally could only end in tragedy, and for conducting that war without regard for the suffering that was inflicted on the Japanese people. Consequently the military was seen as innately inclined to take matters into its own hands, and hostile towards human rights and democracy. The profound Japanese distrust of its own military has consistently been reflected in the Japanese debate over defense and national security throughout the postwar era. For example, the Japanese have been extraordinarily reluctant to allow their armed forces to engage in military planning for fear that, as in the 1930s, the military might try to engineer an international incident that could drag Japan into a war in Asia.[52]

After World War II, West German conservatives and centrists both sought to contain the forces of nationalism through integration with the West. But in Japan there was no such drive to integrate the nation in transnational structures (other than the United Nations), both because the extreme economic and political disparities between Japan and its neighbors did not favor any but the most superficial form of integration, and because Japanese people on both the left and the right were more ambivalent than were the Germans about their relationship with the United States. Domestically, many of the conservatives who were strong defenders of the security relationship with the United States were also critical of many of the American reforms of the Occupation period.[53] And in terms of foreign policy, Japanese leaders beginning in the 1950s were highly averse to becoming involved in U.S. strategy in the Far East.[54]

---

reacted by speeding up their plans for war with the United States. See Michael Barnhart, *Japan Prepares for Total War: The Search for Economic Security, 1919–1941* (Ithaca, N.Y.: Cornell University Press, 1987), especially pp. 120–135 and 215–241.

52. See Ohtake, *Nihon no Boei*; and Georg Mammitzch, *Die Entwicklung der Selbstverteidigungs-Streitkräfte* (Ph.D. dissertation, Friedrichs-Wilhems-Universität, Bonn, 1985). Japanese suspicions regarding the military also reemerge whenever there is an incident involving the armed forces. For example, after a 1988 collision between a Maritime Self Defense Forces' submarine and a private yacht, the press and media were filled with accusations that the Self Defense Forces had the same lack of regard for human life and the rights of civilians that the old Imperial Army had. See public opinion data in *Asahi*, November 6, 1988, p. 11; and media reaction in *Shukan Bunshun*, August 4, 1988, pp. 30–36; *Shukan Yomiuri*, August 14, 1988, pp. 20–27; and *Sandeii Mainichi*, August 14, 1988, pp. 20–24.

53. For example, they were critical of U.S. efforts to strengthen the unions, reform school curriculum, and decentralize the police. See Dower, *Empire and Aftermath*; and Ohtake, *Boei to Kokunai Seiji*.

54. The United States wanted Japan to play a more active role in regional security, entering into an alliance structure similar to that of NATO in West Europe and becoming an arms supplier to U.S. regional allies. See John Welfield, *An Empire in Eclipse: Japan in the Post-War Alliance*

This negative view of the military is shared all along the political spectrum in postwar Japan, and was held not only by the far left, but by many conservatives and even far right-wing figures as well.[55] Where these groups differ, however, is in how they propose to prevent the military from becoming a danger again.

JAPAN'S POLITICAL-MILITARY CULTURE

In postwar Japan there emerged an ideological constellation of contending political groups, each with very different interpretations of Japan's past and each holding very different visions for Japan's future. It is possible to identify three main groups: the left idealists, the centrists, and the right idealists. The left idealists were associated largely with the Japanese Socialist Party (JSP), the Japanese Communist Party (JCP), and the Buddhist Clean Government Party (CGP). The centrists were to be found in the Democratic Socialist Party (DSP) and in parts of the ruling Liberal Democratic Party (LDP). The right idealists were for the most part found in the LDP.[56]

For each of these groups, but especially for the idealists of the right and left, the military issue was not merely a technical problem of how to secure the nation from the threat of external attack, but a reflection of a much deeper debate about the shape of the Japanese domestic order and Japan's proper place in international society. This inward-looking tendency of the Japanese defense debate was strengthened by the fact that, except for the period immediately following the outbreak of the Korean War, the threat of attack from abroad did not seem very credible to either the Japanese public or much of the political elite.

The right idealists held the most favorable view of Japan's past, and were determined to preserve as much of its cultural core as possible.[57] The right

---

System (London: Athlone Press, 1988); Dower, *Empire and Aftermath;* Thomas R. Havens, *The Fire across the Sea: Japan and the Vietnam War 1965–1975* (Princeton, N.J.: Princeton University Press, 1977); and Frank Kowalski, *Nihon no Saigumbi* (Tokyo: Simul Press, 1969), pp. 72–73.

55. See Dower, *Empire and Aftermath;* Ikuhiko Hata, *Shiroku Nihon no Saigumbi* (Tokyo: Bungeishunju, 1976); and Hideo Ohtake, *Nationarizumu to Saigumbi* (Tokyo: Chukoshinsho, 1988).

56. This section draws heavily on Mike Mochizuki, "Japan's Search for Strategy," *International Security*, Vol. 8, No. 3 (Winter 1983/1984), pp. 152–189; Tetsuya Umemoto, *Arms and Alliance in Japanese Public Opinion* (Ph.D. dissertation, Princeton University, 1985); and Kiyofuku Chuma, *Saigumbi no Seijigaku* (Tokyo: Chishikisha, 1985), pp. 177–180.

57. The exact content of this core is difficult to define even for the conservatives themselves, but generally speaking it includes respect for the Emperor, a spirit of self-sacrifice for the common weal, and pride in Japan's past and its traditional values and customs. See Umemoto, *Arms and Alliance.*

idealists were highly critical of many of the Occupation's reforms, such as the decentralization of the police forces and the strict separation of church and state, which they saw as debilitating to the Japanese nation. Chief among the reforms they objected to was the constitution, which had been written and imposed upon the Japanese by General Douglas MacArthur and the Occupation authorities. In particular they objected to Article 9, renouncing Japan's right as a sovereign nation to use force for the settlement of international disputes. The right idealists wished to revise Article 9 in part because they believed that a strong and independent military is an essential component of any sovereign nation, but also because they wished to use the military issue to spark a broader debate about the postwar reforms, from the use of patriotic symbols in the schools to the legal status of the emperor. They hoped to rekindle a sense of national pride, which they believed must include pride in the nation's armed forces.

For the most part, the right idealists were critical of the pre-war militarists, who they felt had foolishly led the country into an unwinnable war, and they certainly did not wish a return to the 1930s. They were also not overtly anti-American, believing that alliance with the United States was necessary to counter the far more dangerous threat of communism. Rather they wanted to move back closer to the type of social and political system that had existed toward the end of the Meiji period (before World War I), with greater centralization of authority and a stronger sense of national pride and purpose than existed in postwar Japan, but backed by a modern economy.[58]

The left idealists, on the other hand, were the most critical of Japan's past and its traditions, which they saw as feudalistic and exploitative.[59] Part and parcel of this past were Japan's martial traditions, and in particular the Imperial Japanese army. Like the right idealists, however, the left idealists were interested in defense issues not only within the context of national security, but also because they too hoped to use the military issue as a means of sparking a larger debate on contemporary Japanese society. They argued that many of the same groups in the conservative parties and business world

58. See Umemoto, *Arms and Alliance.*

59. The mainstream in the left-idealist camp centered on the Japanese Socialist Party and included the majority of Japanese intellectuals. The Japanese Communist Party represented a sizable minority in the left-idealist camp and advocated the creation of a large, independent people's militia. Since 1958 the communists and the socialists have between them received approximately 26–35 percent of the vote and enjoy considerable support from the Japanese intelligentsia, media, and trade labor movement.

who were responsible for the rise of militarism were still in control of Japanese politics. The only way, from their standpoint, to attack the root causes of militarism was to reform the Japanese social, economic, and political systems along more socialist lines. For this reason they opposed the alliance with the capitalist West, which they feared solidified the control of reactionary forces. In place of the Mutual Security Treaty relationship with the United States, the mainstream within the left favored the adoption of a stance of strict unarmed neutrality.

The popular image that the left idealists promoted was of Japan as a "peace nation." As the only country to have suffered atomic bombings, they argued, Japan alone among the world's nations fully appreciated the horrors of modern warfare. Through its idealistic renunciation of force, embodied in Article 9 of the constitution, Japan should serve as an example to the rest of the world of the futility and immorality of war. In this way the left idealists took the war guilt issue and stood it on its head by allowing the Japanese to seize the moral high ground from the Americans who had defeated them.[60]

The centrists were the most pragmatic of the three groups. While they were more favorably disposed towards Japan's traditional culture and values than the left idealists were, they saw far greater need for fundamental reform than did the right idealists. At the same time, they took their models for reform not from the socialist East, as did the left, but from the capitalist West. The centrists were eager to adopt as much as possible of the American way of doing things in order to create a more prosperous and modern Japan. They were relatively uninterested in defense matters, except insofar as the United States forced them to be. Their primary policy objective was economic reconstruction and expansion, while keeping as low a profile on defense and foreign policy issues as possible.

This ideological cleavage between right idealists, centrists, and left idealists continues to run through Japanese politics today. The stances that the different groups take on issues have shifted somewhat, and on balance their positions have become less polarized. Few right idealists would still look to Meiji Japan for their ideals, and most left idealists now look to the social democratic and green parties of Europe for inspiration, rather than to Marxism-Leninism. Nonetheless, to a surprising extent the basic preferences of

---

60. This idea was first advanced by Japanese intellectuals soon after the war ended. See Tatsuo Morito, "Heiwakokka no Kensetsu," *Kaiso*, January 1946.

these three groups on defense and related domestic political issues remain unchanged.

THE EVOLUTION OF JAPAN'S ANTI-MILITARISM

Over the course of the 1950s the centrist position basically won out in the Japanese policymaking process. The urgent task of rebuilding the economy, the need to end the U.S. occupation as soon as possible, and the necessity of U.S. cooperation to achieve these goals allowed no other course of action but alignment with the West in the intensifying atmosphere of the Cold War. At the same time, widespread fears of a militarist revival, anxiety that over-involvement in the U.S. alliance might drag Japan into a land war in Asia, and unwillingness to divert resources from economic reconstruction compelled the Japanese political leadership to keep its military commitments to a minimum.

The centrist position was associated with the Yoshida doctrine, named after centrist Prime Minister Shigeru Yoshida who had led the country in the early 1950s. While the Yoshida Doctrine was never clearly defined, its main elements included close alignment with the United States (even at the cost of Japan's traditional ties to mainland Asia), a focusing of national energies on economic pursuits, and the maintenance of a minimal military establishment for the purposes of maintaining domestic security and satisfying U.S. demands for burden sharing.[61] This doctrine, in somewhat more clearly articulated and developed form, continues as the basis for Japan's defense policies today.

Despite the evident rationality of the Yoshida doctrine in light of the international environment, in the beginning its basis of domestic support was narrow. The centrists were seriously challenged by both the left idealists, who dominated the opposition parties and had strong mass appeal, and by the right idealists, who were particularly strong within the conservative parties. After the creation of the conservative Liberal Democratic Party (LDP) in 1955, the centrists temporarily lost control of government. Under Prime Ministers Hatoyama and Kishi, the right idealists tried to lay the groundwork for a major expansion of the armed forces, a reversal of some of the more

61. For more on the intense pressure that the United States, and especially John Foster Dulles, placed on Japan to do more militarily, see Dower, *Empire and Aftermath*, chapter 10; Hata, *Shiroku Nihon no Saigumbi*, pp. 131–135, 179–190; and Michael Schaller, *The Origins of the Cold War in Asia* (New York: Oxford University Press, 1985).

liberal reforms of the American Occupation (beginning with the anti-war clause in the constitution), and a fostering of national pride.

In 1960, however, the Kishi government's efforts to revise the Mutual Security Treaty triggered popular opposition that began on the left but ultimately came to be supported by the political center as well. For weeks the Diet Building was besieged by protestors, and as the demonstrations became increasingly violent, public opinion, the media, and even Japanese business leaders became increasingly critical of the Kishi government's handling of the situation. Many of Kishi's fellow conservatives within the LDP, out of both ideological conviction and political opportunism, deserted him and in effect joined the left-wing opposition. While ultimately the Treaty was reformed, the Kishi government fell and further efforts to change Japan's domestic system through a transformation of its international role were, at least for the time being, abandoned.[62]

The pattern established in 1960 has repeated itself several times over the course of the postwar era. The ruling LDP is essentially an alliance of centrists and right idealists, united by a common interest in the survival of the present economic system and the alliance with the United States. Whenever it has appeared, however, that a radical departure from the centrist Yoshida line was imminent, or that right idealists might succeed in linking nationalism with military issues, the political center has defected and supported opposition forces in blocking the new defense initiative.

One of the best recent examples of this pattern was Prime Minister Nakasone's effort in 1986 to exceed the limit on defense spending of 1 percent of GNP, which he linked to what he called the final resolution of postwar Japanese politics and, through his official visit to the Yasukuni shrine, to a revival of pride in Japan's armed forces. Although in principle there was broad consensus that the 1 percent limit would have to be abolished at some point, there was near-universal opposition to Nakasone's tactics and to his right-idealist political agenda. In the end, Nakasone was forced to abandon the project, which was then realized in a low-key fashion less than a year later.[63]

---

62. The definitive English-language study of the Mutual Security Treaty riots is George Packard, *Protest in Tokyo: The Security Treaty Crisis of 1960* (Westport, Conn.: Greenwood Press, 1966). Perhaps the best scholarly Japanese work on the subject, outstanding for its coverage of the debate within the LDP and the Foreign Ministry, is Yoshihisa Hara, *Sengonihon to Kokusaiseiji: Ampokaitei no Seijirikigaku* (Tokyo: Chuokoronsha, 1988).

63. See Akio Kamanishi, *GNP 1% Waku: Boeiseisaku no Kensho* (Tokyo: Kakugawa, 1986); and Taro Akasaka, "1% Waku de tsumazuita Nakasone Shuho," *Bungeishunju*, November 1985.

Because of the inhibitions imposed by the ideological divisions among Japan's political elites, defense policy has been forced to develop almost surreptitiously, through a process of what is called *kiseijijitsu no tsumiage*, or the accumulation of *faits-accomplis*. Whenever there is a consensus between the right idealists and the centrists that something must be done to improve national security, changes in policy are made quietly and with a minimum of public debate. Simultaneously, with every new defense initiative, new safeguards have been placed upon the armed forces (commonly referred to as *hadome*, or breaks). The Japanese defense system does change in response to international pressures, but it changes incrementally, at a deliberate pace subject to the constraints of the domestic political situation. As the recent Gulf crisis shows, an urgent need which was nonetheless short of a direct invasion can throw the system into crisis and lead to policy paralysis.

A good example of the way in which Japanese defense policy evolves when there is an internal consensus is offered by the 1978 Guidelines for U.S.-Japanese Defense Cooperation, a set of administrative regulations negotiated by the Foreign Ministry and the Defense Agency that revolutionized the relationship between U.S. forces in the Pacific and Japan's Self Defense Forces (SDF). The Guidelines were created without any serious debate in the Diet, on the grounds that they did not represent a legally binding treaty and thus did not need to be ratified by the legislature. While supported by pro-defense right idealists, they were also backed by moderate centrists, who believed that growing tensions between the two superpowers necessitated an improvement in Japan's national defenses, but who also wanted to make sure that any such agreement would remain under close supervision by civilians and would contain the Japanese Self Defense Forces by integrating them into the U.S. force structure. With the Guidelines in place, Japan was then able to embark upon an expansion of its defense budget during which defense expenditures grew at a rate of approximately 6.5 percent a year.[64]

The 1992 International Peace Cooperation Law, which for the first time permits Japanese Self Defense Forces to participate in overseas peace-keeping

---

64. See the chart in the 1987 edition of the *Boei Handobukku* (Tokyo: Asagumo Shimbunsha, 1987), pp. 224–225. While the rate of expansion actually declined after 1978, this should be balanced against the fact that following the second oil shock, Japanese economic growth declined as well. The budget deficit ballooned and a zero ceiling had been imposed on increases in virtually all areas of government expenditures other than defense, foreign aid, and social security, reflecting the high priority that these areas were given. Thus the share of defense expenditures as a percentage of GNP rose from .88 percent in 1977 to over 1 percent in 1987; ibid., pp. 222–223.

operations, also fits this basic pattern. Although the bill was fiercely attacked by the left, the LDP was careful to avoid any hint of nationalist rhetoric in connection with the overseas dispatch of forces, and placed sufficient safeguards in the bill to reassure the political center both within the LDP and in the small centrist Clean Government and Democratic Socialist parties. The new law limits the number of personnel dispatched overseas to 2000, requires Diet approval before any mission, prohibits the use of weapons except for self-defense, and restricts the dispatch of Japanese personnel to situations where there is already a cease-fire in place. Even certain non-military missions, such as supervising the collection and disposal of weapons, have been suspended for the time being.[65]

In this way the Yoshida doctrine has been able to evolve and adapt to the changing pressures of the Cold War. At the same time, beginning in the early 1960s, the domestic basis of support for the Centrist position grew steadily. As Japan began to enjoy enormous economic success and standards of living began to improve markedly, the Japanese people became reluctant to tamper with the basic institutions of the postwar order, including its national security arrangements. This growing support was reflected in public opinion data, which revealed steady growth in public approval of both the armed forces and the Mutual Security Treaty, from less than 50 percent in

---

65. For the main points of the new legislation see *The Japan Times*, June 17, 1992, p. 1; *Nikkei*, June 16, 1992, p. 1; and *Asahi*, June 16, 1992, p.1. For the full text, see *Asahi*, June 2, 1992, p. 14. The decision to suspend certain missions is not written into the law, but is an added limitation that the government has officially chosen to adhere to for the time being in order to minimize the chance that Japanese personnel might come into combat. The new law was almost immediately put into effect, as Japan for the first time sent Self Defense Forces on a UN peacekeeping mission, to Cambodia. See Philip Shenon, "Japanese Sun Again Rises Overseas," *New York Times*, September 27, 1992, p. 10.

Soon after the bill was passed, the Ministry of Education released a revised version of grammar-school textbooks that stresses Japan's right to self defense under international law while admitting that Japanese forces were guilty of atrocities in East Asia during World War II. See *Asahi*, July 1, 1992, p. 1; and *The Japan Times*, July 1, 1992, p. 3. The linkage of the textbook and defense issues has been a recurring feature of the postwar Japanese defense debate and it is interesting to note that the Japanese government continues to view indoctrination as a integral component of national security policy. The recent revisions indicate that the government is determined to avoid projecting a reactionary image, and in effect has chosen to harden its stance by stressing Japan's right to self defense while giving in to the left by acknowledging the dark corners of Japanese history. Thus the latest revision of the textbooks can be seen as a victory for the pragmatic Japanese political center, rather than of either left or right idealism. For more on the textbook debate in Japan, see Teruhisa Hori, *Educational Thought and Ideology in Modern Japan: State Authority and Intellectual Freedom* (Tokyo: University of Tokyo Press, 1988), pp. 106–212.

the late 1950s to well over 70 percent by the mid-1970s.[66] Equally important, there was a gradual shift towards the center by political actors of both the left and the right. So, for example, in 1970 the LDP party leadership rejected the proposals of Nakasone and other hawks to establish a more independent defense policy. Meanwhile in 1976, the opposition parties at least tacitly accepted the National Defense Policy Outline, the first time that a statement of the goals and missions of the Self Defense Forces was approved by the Japanese diet.[67]

There also emerged a new, widely shared redefinition of the place of the military within national security and of its place in Japanese history. National security became increasingly defined not merely in terms of defending against military threats, but more broadly to embrace a range of goals, including U.S.-Japanese relations, diplomatic relations with the Soviet Union and the PRC, energy security, guaranteeing Japan's food supplies, and contributing to global progress through overseas development assistance. All of these goals were increasingly perceived as vital to overall national security, and as requiring tradeoffs against one another. One of the first official formulations of this was the concept of "comprehensive security" developed in 1980 under the Ohira administration.[68]

At the same time there emerged a new view of Japanese history consistent with the preferred centrist image of Japan. Increasingly, Japanese of all political stripes, not only on the left, but on the right and center as well, came to believe that not only is Japan today not a martial culture, but that in fact it never was one. This belief is rooted in the so-called *Nihonjinron* (or the "theory of Japaneseness") debate of the 1960s and 1970s, on what features distinguish Japan from the rest of the world.[69] One common theme in the vast and disparate literature arising from this debate is that, unlike the European nations and mainland Asia, Japan is a racially homogeneous nation that has never been subjected to successive invasions by different ethnic groups, and that consequently the nature of armed conflict has been far more

66. See *Handobukku*, pp. 496–498; Umemoto, *Arms and Alliance*, pp. 79–85. See also *Asahi*, November 6, 1988, pp. 1 and 12.
67. The best English-language overview of these developments is Welfield, *An Empire in Eclipse*. See also Ohtake, *Nihon no Boei*.
68. See the report of the Comprehensive Security Research Group, *Sogoanzenhosho kenkyuu gruupu hokokusho*, delivered to the Prime Minister on July 2, 1980, pp. 7–13. See also Endo, *Sogoanzenhosho*, on the evolution of the concept of comprehensive security.
69. For more on the Nihonjinron debate see Dale, *The Myth of Japanese Uniqueness*; and Yoshino, *Cultural Nationalism*.

circumscribed in Japan than in other countries. It is this aspect of Japanese culture which is said to make the Japanese so inept at the game of Machiavellian power politics as it is played elsewhere in the world. Variations of this theory are sometimes even offered as an explanation for why Japan was "dragged into" the Second World War and why it lost.[70] What makes this new view of Japanese history all the more remarkable is that until 1945 Japan saw itself as the land of *bushido,* the samurai or warrior spirit. Japanese thinkers of the 1920s and 1930s argued that it was this spirit that distinguished Japan from the spiritually weak and morally corrupt West. Yet, even many members of the older generation, despite direct experience with Japan's prewar military ethos, seem ready to perceive that militarism in Japan was of a defensive nature, an ultimately inadequate reaction to the more deeply rooted aggressive nature of the West.

Of course these new redefinitions are more than a bit self-serving. Naturally the Japanese seek to capitalize on their comparative strengths as a nation, which now lie primarily in the non-military area.[71] Likewise, the reinterpretation of Japanese history can be viewed as an effort to legitimate this new definition of security. Conveniently, at the moment when the international environment seems to favor economic over political-military strength, the Japanese like to believe that their prowess in this area is innate and deeply rooted in their history. A larger role in world affairs thus seems almost predestined.

Nonetheless, it is important to recognize that to a very large extent those espousing these new views of national security and Japanese history seem to believe in them. These redefinitions are at least as much wishful thinking as cynical manipulations. Japanese hope that the world has changed in a way that makes their particular approach to military security not only logical, but even compelling. And rather than face up to the reality of their sometimes brutal past, as the Germans have, they have reinterpreted that reality to lend legitimacy and historical roots to the patterns of behavior that they prefer today. The broad acceptance of these points of view by the public[72] and,

70. A sophisticated version of this argument can be found in Hisahiko Okazaki, *Senryakuteki Kangaekata to wa Nani ka* (Tokyo: Chukoshinsho, 1983), pp. 9–13, 24–26.
71. There is an additional domestic political factor in that many Japanese bureaucratic actors wanted to take advantage of the increased interest in national security of the early 1980s and therefore advocated a broader definition of security that would include their institutional interests. That this was perceived as being legitimate, however, is again a reflection of Japan's postwar political culture.
72. One reflection of this is the extraordinary Japanese reluctance to approve the use of force

perhaps more importantly, by a broad spectrum of the political elite[73] is a very good indication that the new political-military culture, and the anti-militarist ideals that it supports, have now become embedded in the larger political culture of the society and have achieved a certain degree of stability.

The strength of Japan's culture of anti-militarism is reflected by a number of other indicators as well. Japanese public opinion, despite the end of the Cold War and growing trade frictions with the United States, continues to favor a gradualist approach to defense policy, and opposes any large increase in the Japanese defense budget.[74] Japanese elites as well, though deeply concerned by the erosion in relations with the United States, see no alternative to the Mutual Security Treaty system,[75] and are deeply worried by the implications for Japanese domestic politics of an independent defense posture.

Finally, Japanese defense policy making continues to reflect the deep suspicion with which much of the Japanese political system views the Self Defense Forces. At the time of the Gulf crisis, the Kaifu government deliberately excluded Defense Agency personnel from reporting directly to the cabinet for fear that, if they were allowed to do so, the influence of military thinking would distort government decision making.[76] Few nations in the world would exclude the advice of their own military experts from the councils of government at the time of a national security crisis. Likewise the new International Peace Cooperation Law, while allowing the Self Defense Forces to be dispatched abroad for the first time, has also placed a wide variety of restrictions on their use which are designed to maximize civilian

---

to resolve international disputes. According to a recent poll only 26 percent of those Japanese surveyed felt it appropriate to use military force to maintain international order and justice, while 70 percent felt it was not. In contrast, 72 percent of Americans surveyed felt the use of force was justified, and a mere 20 percent felt it was not. See *New York Times*, December 3, 1991.

73. In interviews in Tokyo during 1988–89, the author found these views widespread among a broad range of Japanese political elites, including pro-defense diplomats, hawkish members of the LDP, and even senior officers in the Self-Defense Forces. Groups vary, however, in how they believe Japan should cope with its supposedly anti-military nature. The left feels that this makes unarmed neutrality the only natural course of action for Japan, while the right idealists feel it is a handicap that has to be overcome in a sometimes hostile world through a program of promoting national and defense consciousness through the schools.

74. Large majorities prefer that defense expenditures be kept at their present level (55.6 percent in 1991) and only a small minority (8.1 percent) favor increasing spending on defense. *Handobukku*, p. 517. See also *Asahi*, November 6, 1988, pp. 1 and 12.

75. See for example Yasuhiro Nakasone, Seizaburo Sato, Yasusuke Murakami, and Susumu Nishi, *Kyodo Kenkyuu 'Reisenigo'* (Tokyo: Bungeishunju, 1992).

76. Interviews with Japanese Defense Agency and Foreign Ministry officials, Fall 1991.

control and prevent the armed forces from running out of control.[77] Although Japanese defense policy has changed, the basic pattern of policy making, and the underlying culture of anti-militarism that shapes its leadership's perceptions of the military as an institution and of the use of force, still reflect their postwar origins.

Conclusions

Although Japan today is perfectly capable of acquiring greater independent military capabilities, and the changing international security environment provides it with some opportunities and incentives to do so, I have argued that it is highly unlikely that the Japanese would set out to become a military superpower. Even if Japanese policy makers were to conclude that dramatic change was necessary, given the existing culture of anti-militarism they would encounter strong opposition from the general populace as well as from large sections of the elite. Japan's approach to defense will certainly continue to evolve as a result of changes in the international system. Yet change is likely to be incremental, and the direction in which it evolves will be influenced by the preferences that the Japanese people and their leaders have formed over the past forty-five years.

Popular fears that economic tensions between the United States and Japan will develop into a classic hegemonic political-military struggle need not be realized, and comparisons with either the pre-1941 situation in the Pacific or the pre-1914 situation in Europe are misleading. This does not mean that U.S. and Japanese policy makers should rest secure in the knowledge that all is well. Japan's current stance on defense is viable only as long as the U.S.-Japanese relationship is sound. That relationship is coming under increasing pressure both as a result of trade frictions[78] and tensions over security burden-sharing. Even if these strains develop to the point where they start to undermine the Mutual Security relationship or make the U.S. security guarantee less credible in Japanese eyes, this does not mean that Japan will rush to develop an independent defense capability. Rather the immediate result would be to make Japan more vulnerable to external shocks

---

77. See page 143 above for a list of such safeguards.
78. This friction is reflected dramatically by the controversy over the planned development of Japan's next generation of fighter aircraft, the FSX. Prestowitz, *Trading Places*; and Ryuichi Teshima, *Nippon FSX o Ute* (Tokyo: Shinchosha, 1991).

generated by the relatively unstable security environment of East Asia. If a serious threat to Japan's security arose without the insulation of the Mutual Security Treaty, Japanese political leaders would find themselves unable to respond. At first Japan would be likely to try to appease a potential aggressor, or to look to the United States for assistance, but if such policies seemed to lead to disaster (for example if Japan were threatened with nuclear attack or its oil supplies were cut off), the Japanese government would be compelled to consider a dramatic expansion of Japan's military capabilities, including the acquisition of nuclear weapons and of the means of defending its sea lines of communication.

In such an eventuality, given the persistence of Japanese suspicions towards their own military, Japan would then be plunged into the most serious political crisis of the postwar era, and the political culture would be likely to change. Cultures can and do change, but usually they do so in an evolutionary fashion. Dramatic change only occurs when the type of behavior that a culture produces no longer meets its basic needs.[79] Since 1945, Japan been enormously successful operating on the basis of its present culture of antimilitarism, and as long as that approach seems viable, change will be incremental, and core preferences for a small military and avoidance of the use of force will remain unchanged. If, however, this approach appears to have led to a disaster then, as at the end of World War II, the fundamental assumptions of the existing political culture would be thrown into doubt. It is hard to predict what kind of government would emerge under such circumstances, but there exists the potential that a very different political leadership could take control, one perhaps less opposed than the present elites to stoking the fires of ethnocentric nationalism in order to legitimate military expansion.

Two main steps could forestall such an eventuality. First, in the short to medium term it is vital that the United States remains involved in East Asian security and that the U.S. military alliance with Japan be preserved. Second, in the long run it is also important that the United States help Japan gradually adapt its political culture so that it can use its growing power to help sustain a stable regional and global security order. The best way of doing this is to strengthen the U.S.-Japan security relationship by broadening it. The Mutual Security Treaty system is but a single anchor for Japan's new culture of anti-

79. See Harry Eckstein, "A Culturalist Theory of Change," *American Political Science Review*, Vol. 82 (1988), pp. 789–804.

militarism, and is thus vulnerable to the strains produced by the tossing and turning of a sometimes stormy U.S.-Japanese relationship. In contrast to Germany, which is embedded in a network of transnational institutions for dealing with security issues, Japan is secured only by a single bilateral link, the Mutual Security Treaty with the United States. This link, and with it Japan's culture of anti-militarism, would be greatly stabilized if a network of lesser transnational anchors could be added, designed not to replace the relationship with the United States, but to strengthen it.

From an American point of view such a network of relationships would have the disadvantage of reducing the potential leverage of a U.S. threat to withdraw its security guarantee and thus increasing the likelihood that Japan would pursue a more independent foreign policy. At the same time, it would reduce the dangerous temptation for U.S. politicians to make use of this leverage in trade negotiations. More importantly, a security system with a multi-national dimension would enhance the legitimacy of Japan's security arrangements in the eyes of the Japanese people, who all too often tend to see Japan's defense and foreign policies as being dictated by U.S. interests. Given the present political-military culture, broader Japanese participation in any future military operations requires such a multi-national framework.

The passage of the 1992 International Peace Cooperation Law is an important first step in this direction, but it is not enough. In the long run Japan should be prepared to share the risk of any future Gulf-like confrontation, if only to forestall American isolationism fed by a perception that Japan is free-riding. As an intermediate step, Japanese forces could become active in a variety of non-combat missions, such as mine sweeping, intelligence gathering, logistics, and the like.[80]

While the UN is the most convenient vehicle for Japanese involvement in global security (and Japanese participation in the Security Council is desirable), Japan should also be supported in its efforts to establish and participate in regional security arrangements. Prime Minister Miyazawa has indicated that Japan is interested in pursuing such a two-track approach to Asian security, based on the alliance with the United States but also using regional consultative groupings, such as the Asian Pacific Economic Cooperation (APEC) forum, to discuss security issues.[81] Beyond this it might be possible

80. Some of these ideas are similar to recent proposals by former diplomat Hiroyuki Kishino, "Creating a Japan-U.S. Global Partnership," International Institute for Global Peace (IIGP) Policy Paper 68E, September 1991.
81. See *The Japan Times*, July 4, 1992; and *Asahi*, July 3, 1992.

to explore the creation of a "Conference on Security and Cooperation in East Asia and the Pacific," similar to the CSCE. Such an institution should be open to all nations in the region, including Japan, China, Russia, and the United States. (Korean and Taiwanese participation, though highly desirable, pose some thorny diplomatic problems.) It would seek to enhance cooperation between the major military actors and would focus on instituting confidence-building measures.

It might also be useful to establish an East Asian Security Fund, which could help foster the exchange of information on security-related developments, conduct research on defense problems in the region, and help defray the costs of basing and training exercises by member forces in the region. The Fund could also provide a venue for intensified consultations on security affairs between Japan and other U.S. regional allies. It would include all current U.S. friends and allies in the region; Japan, along with the United States, might play a pivotal role.[82]

The U.S. government has been suspicious of such initiatives for fear that they would hamper America's latitude for action in the region and possibly undermine existing U.S. bilateral security ties.[83] Nonetheless, the creation of such a network of regional institutions for dealing with security issues might not only serve a useful function in building trust and cooperation among the nations of East Asia, but more importantly would help Japan transcend its self-centered stance on military security and aid the further evolution of Japan's culture of anti-militarism so that it can continue to meet Japan's and Asia's security needs pragmatically. A policy that moors Japan's security in a broader internationalist framework is the best way of ensuring that the Japanese sword will remain sheathed.

---

82. Such a fund has been proposed by Masashi Nishihara, *Senryaku kenkyu no Shikaku* (Tokyo: Ningen no Kagakusha, 1988), pp. 274–275.
83. Interviews in April 1992 with senior and mid-level officials responsible for East Asian policy in the U.S. State Department and National Security Council.

The Glorification of War in Japanese Education

Saburo Ienaga

Our ultimate target is not so much children at school, as the adults which those children are to become. When we correct a schoolbook, we sow seeds which may bear fruit after a generation. But when we secure publicity for such correction, we contribute to this year's harvest.

—E.H. Dance, *History the Betrayer*[1]

The content of Japan's history textbooks has for several decades been an issue both in Japan's domestic debate and in its international relations.[2] *In the early 1980s, the ruling Liberal Democratic Party (LDP) undertook a campaign seeking revision of some 100 textbooks, with a "thrust toward greater respect, in effect, for State Shinto, big business, duties instead of rights, and the military instead of pacifism." The minister of education asked that high school textbook writers and publishers "soften their approach to Japan's excesses during World War II, the horrors of the atom bombs*

Saburo Ienaga was professor emeritus of education at Tokyo University of Education. Among his books are The Pacific War 1931–45, *trans. Frank Baldwin (New York: Pantheon, 1978) (published in Tokyo as* Taiheiyo Senso *by Iwanami Shoten, 1968); and* Senso sekinin *(War responsibility) (Tokyo: Iwanami Shoten, 1985).*

The editors of *International Security* thank Frank Baldwin and the Asia Foundation, Tokyo, for translating this article from Japanese. For help in providing additional notes to English-language sources, all of which were approved by the author, the editors thank Barton Bernstein, John Dower, Ted Hopf, Marc Trachtenberg, and Stephen Van Evera.

1. E.H. Dance, *History the Betrayer: A Study in Bias* (London: Hutchinson, 1960; Westport, Conn: Greenwood, repr. 1970), p. 146.
2. Nationalism and the glorification of war in school texts and university teaching has been an issue in many countries. See, for example, Frances Fitzgerald, *America Revised* (Boston: Atlantic, Little Brown, 1979; new ed. 1992); Katherine Bishop, "Bill on Internees Raises New Alarm; Descendants of Japanese Fear Proposal in California on World War II Teaching," *New York Times*, August 28, 1990, p. A19; Paul M. Kennedy, "The Decline of Nationalistic History in the West, 1900–1970," *Journal of Contemporary History*, Vol. 8, No. 1 (January 1973), pp. 77–100; and on Germany, Holger Herwig, "Clio Deceived: Patriotic Self-Censorship in Germany After the Great War," *International Security*, Vol. 12, No. 2 (Fall 1987), pp. 5–45; Richard J. Evans, *In Hitler's Shadow: West German Historians and the Attempt to Escape from the Nazi Past* (New York: Pantheon, 1989); Peter Baldwin, ed., *Reworking the Past: Hitler, the Holocaust, and the Historian's Debate* (Boston: Beacon Press, 1990); Judith Miller, *One, by One, by One: Facing the Holocaust* (New York: Simon and Schuster, 1990).

International Security, Vol. 18, No. 3 (Winter 1993/94), pp. 113–133

. . . and the pacifist requirements of the Constitution (Article 9). More stress was suggested on patriotism, [and] the constitutionality of the Self-Defense Forces."[3]

Japanese critics of these efforts were joined in July 1982 by protests, both public and diplomatic, from North and South Korea, China, Taiwan, and other countries. "Blistering attacks were leveled at Japan's leaders by [other] Asians for insensitivity to East Asian memories of Japan's arrogant and inhumane treatment of its neighbors before 1945 and for outright dishonesty in the textbook presentation of historical fact."[4]

The author of this article has played a pivotal role in Japan's debate over the presentation of its history in textbooks.[5] *Professor Ienaga has written numerous studies of the war and of modern Japan, and many school textbooks, including (as co-author) one of the first postwar history texts.*[6] *By the early 1960s, his history textbook for high-school students,* Shin Nihonshi *(A new history of Japan) was one of the three most used in Japan. When, in 1962, the third edition was submitted to*

---

3. "Every detail of the school curriculum . . . is decided centrally by the Ministry of Education. . . . Textbooks must be approved by the ministry. . . . One of the most reactionary and secretive bits of the bureaucracy, this ministry has systematically tried to prevent schools teaching the grisly details of Japan's modern history. Textbooks have referred to the 'advance' into Manchuria, not its invasion; sometimes no reference at all is made to Japan's brutal rule of Korea between 1910 and 1945." "Japan's Schools: Why Can't Little Taro Think?" *The Economist,* April 21, 1990, pp. 21–24. The process of MOE review and certification is described in detail by Lawrence Ward Beer, *Freedom of Expression in Japan: A Study in Comparative Law, Politics, and Society* (New York: Kodansha/ Harper & Row, 1984), pp. 260–262.

4. Beer, *Freedom of Expression in Japan,* pp. 270, 271, 272.

5. "In a 1980 [Ienaga] text, the ministry ordered 240 changes and still rejected it as 'inappropriate' on 70 other points once revisions were made. The word 'aggression,' for instance, could not be used, and Ienaga's lengthy description of Japanese atrocities in China in the 1930s would have to go, regardless of protests from Beijing and Seoul." Patrick L. Smith, "A Textbook Warrior in Japan," *International Herald Tribune,* November 1, 1989, p. 18. See also Ienaga, "Teaching War," in Haruko Taya Cook and Theodore F. Cook, *Japan at War: An Oral History* (New York: New Press, 1992), pp. 441–447; and David E. Sanger, "A Stickler for History, Even if It's Not Very Pretty," *New York Times,* May 27, 1993, p. A4.

6. Beer, *Freedom of Expression in Japan,* pp. 257, 258, notes that this textbook, "*Kuni no Ayami* (The progress of Japan) . . . propounded a new 'open world,' rationalist, social studies approach to Japan's past that has been influential ever since. Professor Ienaga, as one of the four authors, wrote the section on early Japanese history which 'defined the approached followed throughout the book and [was] later made explicit' in the Guiding Principles for Instruction (*Gakushu shido yoryo*) of the Ministry of Education. Though adopted under Occupation supervision of textbooks, 'the evidence shows that postwar values sprang not from American but Japanese sources.' There is poetic justice in the fact that, of all the politicians, scholars, teachers' union members, and social critics who have been alert to prevent educational drift back toward statism, Ienaga Saburo should be in the eye of the stormy trials over textbook review in during the 1960s and 1970s." On the role of the U.S. occupation in revising Japan's textbooks and its system of education, see Gordon Daniels, "The Re-education of Imperial Japan," chap. 9 in Nicholas Pronay and Keith Wilson, *The Political Education of Germany and her Allies after World War II* (Totowa, NJ: Barnes and Noble Books [London: Croom Helm], 1985).

the Japanese Ministry of Education (MOE) for the review that is mandatory for all textbooks used in Japan's schools, the MOE requested changes which, in many cases, sought to tone down Professor Ienaga's description of Japan's activities during the fifteen years of war that began with Japan's invasion of China in 1931.

In response, Professor Ienaga filed an unprecedented lawsuit against the MOE's textbook certification system, alleging violations of his constitutional freedom of expression and academic freedom.[7] *The lawsuit continued for nearly three decades, with final disposition in March 1993 from Japan's Supreme Court.*[8] *It has been called a "landmark" constitutional law case, and has served as a focal point for a continuing debate over Japan's role in the war, the conduct of its armed forces and political leaders during the war, and the willingness of its government and its people to examine that role and that conduct.*[9]

—The Editors

In the period before August 1945, Japan was a "warfare state."[10] Bristling with armaments and dominated by a professional military caste, the nation waged war against its neighbors—China twice (1894–95, 1931–45) and Tsarist Russia (1904–05), and turned the Korean Peninsula into a colony in 1910. Inculcated with militarism through the school system, the Japanese people believed that dying for the nation on the battlefield was the supreme virtue.

---

7. See Beer, *Freedom of Expression in Japan*, pp. 264–266, and "Ienaga textbook review case," *Encyclopedia of Japan* (Tokyo: Kodansha, 1983), Vol. 3, p. 261.
8. The court held against Professor Ienaga. See "Textbook screening upheld; historian's 28-year suit fails," *Japan Times*, March 19, 1993, p. 18. An editorial in the same paper described the lawsuit, one of a series brought by Professor Ienaga against the MOE, as having done "invaluable service in keeping before the public eye a government activity that many view as excessive interference, which has angered textbook authors and publishers over the years and has led to international criticism that this country was whitewashing its wartime actions. . . . The point that critics of the system make is that it too easily allows Japan to deny responsibility for its past and has led to objections at the highest levels from the governments of nearby countries. . . . There have been major revisions in the screening method in the last few years which make it quite different from the one in use when Mr. Ienaga's suit began. The changes were welcomed by many authors and publishers as making the entire system more transparent. . . . Japan's youth can best be prepared for their global responsibilities by not denying the nation's past." Editorial, "The challenge of the textbook ruling," *Japan Times*, March 19, 1993, p. 18. The decision in the third lawsuit, issued by the Tokyo High Court on October 20, 1993, awarded damages but dismissed the constitutional claims. Both sides may appeal. See "Text author wins damages; But constitutionality of state screening is upheld," *Japan Times*, October 21, 1993; and "Court awards 300,000 yen in censorship suit," *Mainichi Daily News*, October 21, 1993, pp. 1, 12.
9. "Many Japanese observers consider the two resulting 'Textbook Trials' (*Kyokasho saiban*) among the great constitutional cases of modern Japan." Beer, *Freedom of Expression in Japan*, pp. 254–255.
10. See Fred J. Cook, "The Warfare State," *The Nation*, October 28, 1961.

The media—newspapers, magazines, and books—were full of news and stories exalting martial values and romanticizing war. The steady diet of chauvinistic information encouraged jingoism.[11]

Of course, many Japanese realized that war was a great evil. Families grieved for husbands, sons, and brothers killed or wounded overseas; some men tried to evade the draft. From the turn of the century, Christian pacifism and European socialism had gained adherents in Japan who organized antiwar and peace movements. However, the state restricted freedom of speech by internal security laws, banning activities critical of the military. Thus, the great majority of the population, whose main sources of information promoted war, passionately supported the nation's conflicts; even in peacetime the soldier and the role of the military were glorified.

Defeat in World War II transformed Japan into a "peace state." The U.S. Occupation dismantled the Imperial Army and Navy, and under the 1946 Constitution, Article 9, Japan explicitly renounced war and the possession of war potential.[12] Educational policy also changed to promote these ideals. The curriculum was revamped to train students for "a peaceful state and society." In the early part of the postwar period, the United States sponsored sweeping reforms to demilitarize and democratize Japan.

However, popular consciousness was not totally restructured overnight, because neither the termination of hostilities nor the new Constitution had been accomplished through popular struggle. Nor was the 1946 charter drafted by the Japanese on their own initiative; it was instead enacted at the insistence of the Supreme Commander for the Allied Powers (SCAP), which was determined to prevent a revival of Japanese aggression. Thus how Article 9, the "peace clause" of the Constitution, was perceived and applied would inevitably be affected by changes in the political context.

As the Cold War intensified, the Occupation's priorities shifted, a shift known as the "reverse course." When the Korean War erupted on June 25, 1950, Washington moved swiftly to integrate Japan into an anti-communist

---

11. See Saburo Ienaga, *The Pacific War, 1931–1945: A Critical Perspective on Japan's Role in World War II,* trans. Frank Baldwin (New York: Pantheon, 1978; orig. publ. in Japanese 1968), esp. chap. 2, "Thought Control and Indoctrination."

12. Article 9 of Japan's Constitution states: "Aspiring sincerely to an international peace based on justice and order, the Japanese people forever renounce war as a sovereign right of the nation and the threat or use of force as a means of settling international disputes. . . . (2) In order to accomplish the aim of the preceding paragraph, land, sea, and air forces, as well as other war potential, will never be maintained. The right of belligerency of the state will not be recognized."

military bloc and directed Prime Minister Shigeru Yoshida to start rearming. The former ruling strata regained control. Ex-members of the Imperial Army and Navy by the thousands joined the new armed forces. (The National Police Reserve formed in 1950 was renamed the National Safety Forces in 1952 and became the Self-Defense Forces 1954.) The Occupation's new priorities were evident throughout Japanese society, including education. It even seemed for a while that the clock would be turned back to the militaristic norms taught in prewar Japan.

At the present time, however, the old guard have been unable to revise the Constitution and delete Article 9.[13] The wording of the preface has been staunchly defended: "Never again shall we be visited with the horrors of war through the action of government." Militarism of the prewar stripe will not be resurrected in Japan. Those committed to the letter and spirit of Article 9 are pitted against those trying to weaken it gradually.

For the past forty years, I have been involved in this debate as an educator and as a writer of school textbooks. Thus I have observed at first hand how the Ministry of Education (MOE) shapes what the youth of Japan learn about their country's behavior during the militarist period before 1945. I am not attributing the Pacific War (1931–45) to the influence of textbooks alone. However, there is no doubt that the emphasis on militarism in the curriculum, combined with the media's glorification of war and the government's suppression of pacifist and liberal views, was a major factor in socializing the great majority of Japanese to support aggression enthusiastically.[14] The generation who lived through the war need no scholarly proof of this; they know it from personal experience.[15] This *tanka* (a 31-syllable poem) by a housewife appeared in a national newspaper: "Millions of people / Were killed by the official textbooks, / Japanese and Asians alike."[16]

---

13. On the debate over changing Article 9, see, e.g., Peter J. Katzenstein and Nobuo Okawara, "Japan's National Security Policy: Structures, Norms, and Policies," *International Security*, Vol. 17, No. 4 (Spring 1993), pp. 101, 103–104, 110. *[Eds. note: on this and some subsequent notes, the editors provided assistance with English-language citations and related notes, all of which were approved by the author.]*
14. See also Ienaga, *The Pacific War*, chap. 6, "The War at Home: Democracy Destroyed."
15. A soldier who participated in Japan's bacteriological warfare experiments in China was asked whether he felt pity for the human subjects of the experiment. He replied, "Well. None at all. We were like that already . . . we were already implanted with a narrow racism . . . If we didn't have a feeling of racial superiority, we couldn't have done it. People with today's sensibilities don't grasp this. That's why I'm afraid of the power of education." Tamura, "Unit 731," Cook and Cook, *Japan at War*, p. 164.
16. The poet was Chika Mikihara, in *Asahi Shimbun*, July 26, 1981.

In this article, I present examples of how war, militaristic values, and episodes from Japan's past have been presented to Japan's schoolchildren in the 1920s, the period before and during World War II, the Occupation and the "reverse course" of the Cold War years, and from my own experiences since the early 1960s. Japan's textbooks have taught generations of its children that war is glorious, and have concealed many of the sad truths of war, with sometimes tragic results.

Prewar Education and Militarism

Before World War II, primary school textbooks were written and issued by the Ministry of Education (MOE); middle school textbooks were prepared by private publishers in accordance with the MOE's curriculum and had to be approved by the ministry. Since the use of official authorized texts in the nation's schools was mandatory, the government effectively decided the entire content of education for these grades. Classroom instruction closely followed the textbooks; all pupils were taught the same material and beliefs. Teachers instilled an identical consciousness in all the children under their sway. Given the prominence accorded militaristic ideas, the schools were a powerful instrument for maintaining the "warfare state."

The curriculum was loaded with militaristic notions even during the moderate period of Taisho democracy (1912–26) after World War I. But when the Japanese army seized Manchuria in 1931 and hostilities spread across China, and even more after Japan went to war against the United States and Great Britain in December 1941, pro-military sentiment became pervasive in the textbooks. The following examples are drawn from these two periods.[17]

THE 1920S

Even during the comparatively liberal and peaceful period during which I attended school (1920–31), when Japan was engaged in no conflicts abroad, all the textbooks we used were laced with accounts that glorified war and the military.

---

17. Reverence for the emperor and statism were the central values of prewar education and the spiritual underpinnings of militarism. However, space limitations preclude a full discussion of these issues; in this article I focus specifically on the glorification of war and the whitewash of history in the curriculum.

First, consider the coverage of Japanese history. Most of the section about the Meiji period (1868–1912) in *Elementary School Japanese History*, Vol. II, was filled with accounts of Japan's foreign wars.[18] Combat was described as a heroic undertaking in order to make a positive impression on young minds. The treatment of the bombardment of Port Arthur and the battle of the Tsushima Strait during the Russo-Japanese War (section six, chapter fifty-one) is typical: "Our brave, loyal officers and men, resolved to repay His Majesty's benevolence with their lives, launched assault after assault and finally seized Hill 203. From there they sank all the enemy warships that were still hiding in the harbor. . . . [Admiral Togo's] flagship *Mikasa* displayed this message: 'This battle will decide the fate of our empire. Be more courageous than ever before and do your best.'. . . . Amid fierce winds and raging waves, our navy fought tenaciously. . . . It was the greatest naval victory of all time."

Ethics textbooks, even from the lowest grades, included militaristic content. A first-grade lesson cited an example from the battlefield: "Kiguchi Kohei was hit by an enemy bullet and died, but the bugle was still at his lips."[19] Lesson 16 of the second-grade ethics text was entitled "Loyalty": "Commander Hirose Takeo set out on a dark night to block the harbor entrance at Port Arthur with a steamship. Braving enemy fire, he . . . was about to leave the ship [when he discovered that] Chief Warrant Officer Sugino was missing. The commander searched all over the boat three times. [As he] finally . . . left the larger ship . . . he was hit by enemy fire and died a glorious hero's death."[20]

Fourth-graders were taught about Yasukuni Shrine, the Shinto shrine dedicated to the nation's war dead:[21] "Yasukuni Shrine is on the Kudan Hill in Tokyo. Men who died for the emperor and country are enshrined there. An Imperial Messenger is present at the spring and autumn observances. Their Imperial Majesties the Emperor and Empress attend certain special events. The Emperor has ordained that those who have died for the sovereign and the country should be enshrined and rites carefully performed. Mindful of

---

18. *Elementary School Japanese History* (Tokyo: Ministry of Education, 1920).
19. *Elementary School Ethics*, Vol. I (Tokyo: Ministry of Education, 1918).
20. *Elementary School Ethics*, Vol. II (Tokyo: Ministry of Education, 1918).
21. The Yasukuni Shrine, founded in 1869 to enshrine war dead as *kami*, or living gods, has frequently been the focal point for heated debates over whether visits by state officials constitute a promotion of militaristic values inconsistent with Article 9 or the separation of church and state appropriate to a democracy. See Kiyama Terumichi, "Meeting at Yasukuni Shrine," Cook and Cook, *Japan at War*, pp. 447–453, and especially editors' introduction, pp. 47–48.

the Emperor's deep benevolence, we should emulate those who are interred here and do our utmost for the sovereign and country."[22]

Textbooks used to teach the Japanese language and singing sought to implant the military spirit through the emotions. Fourth-graders learned this song in their Japanese lesson: "The cannons roar, the shells scream/ Standing on the deck awash with waves/ The commander's call pierces the darkness:/ 'Sugino, where are you? Are you there?'/ He searches every corner of the boat three times;/ He calls but gets no answer, looks but finds no trace;/ The boat gradually sinks beneath the waves;/ Enemy shells fly thick and fast/ The commander moves to the small boat/ A flying shell, he is dead./ How tragic his death outside Port Arthur/ Heroic Hirose's fame lives on."[23]

In a fifth-grade music lesson entitled "Meeting at Suishiei," children learned about the surrender of Port Arthur in a song glorifying the victory, the emperor, and the meeting of the generals.[24] In the sixth grade students memorized a song about "The Battle of Tsushima Strait": "Enemy vessels are sighted/ and draw near/ 'This battle will decide / the fate of our empire./ Be more courageous than ever/ and do your best,'/ the flagship's ensign signals./ Clear skies but strong winds and/ high waves off Tsushima Island./ Dawn in the eastern sky./ As the fog lifts/ the morning sun rises/ brightly over the Japan Sea./ No way to escape!/ Russian ships are hit and sink;/ Some surrender./ The enemy fleet is completely vanquished./ Long live the empire! Long live the empire!"[25]

The textbooks for many subjects contained exciting accounts of great victories and soldiers' valor. Stories about Commander Hirose, the capture of Port Arthur, and the battle of Tsushima Strait were repeated in different contexts to pull the children' minds and hearts toward militarism.

THE 1930S TO THE EARLY 1940S

Pearl Harbor still lay ahead when the April 1941 edition of the sixth-grade history textbook was published, but Japan had been engaged in a full-scale war in China for more than three years. Much of the text was a justification of that expansion. Typical is the following passage:[26]

---

22. *Elementary School Ethics*, Vol. IV (Tokyo: Ministry of Education, 1920).
23. *Elementary School Ethics*, Vol. II (Tokyo: Ministry of Education, 1918).
24. *Elementary School Music*, Vol. V (Tokyo: Ministry of Education, 1925.
25. *Elementary School Music*, Vol. VI (Tokyo: Ministry of Education, 1932).
26. *Elementary School Japanese History*, Vol. VI (Tokyo: Ministry of Education, 1941).

China has repeatedly doubted our country's sincerity and many Japanese residing there have been injured or killed. Some of our special rights in Manchuria were even threatened. We frequently urged China to reflect on its actions, but day by day Chinese actions became more violent. Finally, in September 1931, Chinese troops blew up a section of the South Manchurian Railroad. Our country had no choice but to dispatch troops and drive Chinese forces out of Manchuria. These events are called the Manchurian Incident. . . . [27] When the Manchurian Incident was over, Japan concluded a truce with China and, through the mutual cooperation between the three countries—Japan, Manchukuo and China—strove to create eternal peace in the Orient. However, the Chinese government failed to comprehend our sincerity and in a provocative act sought help from Europe and the United States. Determined at all costs to expel the Japanese from the continent, the Chinese built up their military forces and even tried to hinder the development of Manchukuo. In July 1937, Chinese troops bombarded and attacked Japanese units training at the Marco Polo Bridge near Beijing.[28] Japanese residents, too, were violently attacked. To correct the mistaken views of the Chinese and establish eternal peace in the Orient, Japan sent its righteous forces into action. Our forces have continued their brilliant campaign on the land and sea and in the air, unstintingly supported on the homefront by the civilian populace. United in purpose, we shall persevere to accomplish this great mission. We are laying the foundation for eternal peace in East Asia.

Japanese language textbooks used from 1938 also contained militaristic content. First-graders had a lesson entitled: "Advance, advance! Soldiers advance!"[29] Lesson 11 in the third-year text was about "Army Flags," accompanied by a drawing of troops charging ahead, flags held high, and contained phrases in praise of "precious army flags . . . graciously granted by the Emperor . . . ripped by bullets, the mark of victory"; of "risking death for the empire"; and of "honored" and "revered" army flags.[30]

A third-grade language lesson was entitled "The Submarine": "Submerged, we draw close to approaching enemy warships and sink them with torpe-

---

27. The explosion was in fact caused by Japan's Kwantung Army, and served as a pretext to launch Japan's seizure of Manchuria. Fifteen years of death and destruction were sparked that night by army officers acting illegally. See Ienaga, *Pacific War*, pp. 38–38, and sources there cited.

28. Japanese control of Manchuria relied upon railway lines; the two that connected Peking with Nanking and Hankow converged at the Marco Polo Bridge. Japanese troops on maneuvers near the bridge on July 7, 1937, engaged Chinese troops in what became a pretext for widened hostilities; Tienstin and Peking were in Japanese hands by the end of the month, and most histories date the outbreak of Japan's war from this event.

29. *Elementary School Reader*, Vol. I (Tokyo: Ministry of Education, 1938).

30. *Elementary School Reader*, Vol. III (Tokyo: Ministry of Education, 1938).

does. Sometimes we steal into the enemy's port and suddenly attack his warships. When the enemy vessel is weak, we remain on the surface and sink him with our cannon or torpedoes."[31] Fifth-grade students read about Major Tachibana in the Russo-Japanese War, who ignored danger and led his troops under a "hail of enemy bullets," and who, "hit in the right hand . . . held his sword in his left" and led his unit to victory.[32]

In a sixth-grade Japanese-language class, pupils read a story about "The Mechanized Unit":

> The tank unit commander hoisted a signal flag high. . . . The squadron moved into combat formation and struck at the left flank of the enemy tanks. . . . Ignoring the enemy's cannon fire, which was exploding all around, our tanks closed the distance. . . . The squadron sought out and attacked enemy tanks, one after another. On the right side, one of our brave crews rammed into an enemy tank. It was a free-for-all battle with some tanks disabled and burning, others moving ahead. There was hand-to-hand fighting between our infantry and engineer troops and theirs. Our forces suffered considerable casualties but . . . the triumph brought great honor to the fighting men of Japan.[33]

The 1941 Japanese language textbook for third-grade students had a song entitled "Brave Soldiers," which glorified three soldiers, known as "the human bombs," who strapped explosive charges to themselves and charged into Chinese barbed wire on the Shanghai front, killing themselves but clearing the way for others.[34]

In the fourth grade, pupils learned a song about "The Young Tankers": "They've come!/ The young tankers/ In their steel chariots/ In their steel helmets/ Clang, clang, clang, clang/ Rumble, rumble!/ They've come!/ The young tankers/ Lips clenched / Looking ahead/ Clang, clang, clang, clang/ Rumble, rumble!/ They've come!/ The young tankers/ Rolling over the enemy trenches/ Clang, clang, clang, clang/ Rumble, rumble!"[35]

These examples show how prewar Japanese youth were indoctrinated.[36]

---

31. *Elementary School Reader,* Vol. III (Tokyo: Ministry of Education, 1935).
32. *Elementary School Reader,* Vol. V (Tokyo: Ministry of Education, 1937).
33. *Elementary School Reader,* Vol. VI (Tokyo: Ministry of Education, 1938). Although the fighting under way in China was not explicitly mentioned, the Ministry of Education probably had the spreading conflict in mind when it prepared this text. News from the battlefield was severely censored; nothing about atrocities was reported. Coverage was slanted to emphasize "friendship" betwen Japanese and Chinese with, for example, photographs of Imperial Army soldiers patting Chinese children on the head.
34. *Elementary School Music,* Vol. III (Tokyo: Ministry of Education, 1941).
35. *Elementary School Music,* Vol. IV (Tokyo: Ministry of Education, 1941).
36. *Elementary School Music,* Vol. IV (Tokyo: Ministry of Education, 1941). A Japanese historian

The Occupation and the "Reverse Course"

Such militaristic conditioning ended with Japan's defeat. In 1948 the Occupation abolished the system of official texts and refashioned education along American lines. Ultra-nationalistic material was banned from textbooks but otherwise enormous latitude was permitted. New textbooks still had to be certified, however, because SCAP feared the inclusion of objectionable, undemocratic passages. The Occupation wanted to end government authorization, and hoped that commercial publishers would bring out varied and distinctive texts. Initially the Occupation intended to allow local boards of education, which were then elected, to certify textbooks; the Ministry of Education was only supposed to approve texts until the paper shortage was over. However, the authority was never actually transferred to the boards of education; the Ministry retained the prerogative.

During the period that government-certified textbooks were still subject to Occupation censorship; especially in the immediate postwar years, the books and supplementary readers had strong, explicit statements about Japan's role in the Pacific War. For example, the Ministry of Education's 1947 publication *Atarashii kenpo no hanashi* (Our new constitution) contained this passage:

> Many of your fathers and older brothers went off to serve in the war. Have they come back safely? Or did they never come back? Many of you probably lost homes and family members in the air raids. The war is finally over. Don't you think that sad and terrifying experience should never be repeated? What did Japan gain from the war? Nothing. Was not the only result enormous grief and suffering? War destroys human life and culture. The countries that started World War II must bear a grave responsibility.

The 1949 Ministry of Education publication *Minshushugi* (Democracy) refers to "the folly of the Pacific War," and contains this passage:

> Citing the need to prepare for war, [the state] enormously expanded military expenditures and armaments, imposed tight controls on industry and restricted speech and thought. The military trumpeted grandiose strategies of

---

has said, "When I was a teenager, we had no other books than those with the 'Imperial-nation' view of history. . . . The goal of our education was only to create men who would fervently throw away their lives for the sake of the Emperor, men who were full of loyalty. We had no way of knowing anything other than what we knew. Therefore, we just did what we were told, and we did it believing in it. . . . We went out without even having a healthy fear of war and ended up being slaughtered." Ota Masahide, "A Quest for Meaning," Cook and Cook, *Japan at War*, p. 429.

kogi kokubo (comprehensive national security), seized political power, trampled on the rights of the people, and planned a reckless war.

As the Cold War raged, however, the Occupation modified its policy.

THE REVERSE COURSE

After Japan regained its sovereignty in 1952, certification standards and procedures increasingly reflected the ideology of the ruling conservative politicians, and the process itself became engulfed in controversy. Despite the abolition of censorship and constitutional guarantees of freedom of expression and scholarship and the right to an education, textbooks had to pass a prepublication screening. In the first few years, the reviewers were very lenient, rarely objecting to an author's work. From the mid-1950s, however, their scrutiny intensified. When the number of disapproved manuscripts and demands for revisions rose dramatically, writers, editors at publishing firms, school teachers, historians and others attacked the certification procedure.[37]

The "Textbook Case"

I have been writing high school Japanese history textbooks since 1952 and have detailed personal knowledge of how the system works. What follows are some of the more striking examples from my own experiences—the kind of intervention that makes me apprehensive about the revival of jingoistic values in Japan. I have not been pressured to include specific phrases that flagrantly glorify war or praise the military; rather, the government has sought to exclude as much as possible vivid depictions of the horrors of war, and of Japan's responsibility for war and war crimes. I consider this a conscious tilt toward militarism.

In 1952, 1955, and 1957, I submitted manuscripts for high school history textbooks to the MOE. Although examiners challenged my wording in places, the issues were resolved and the manuscripts were approved. In 1963, however, the MOE rejected my manuscript for the third edition of *Shin Nihonshi* (A new history of Japan, first published in 1953). The MOE objected to numerous passages whose deletion was thus mandatory before the book

---

37. In 1956 and again in 1957, several hundred issued statements protesting censorship.

could be approved and published.[38] For example, in this textbook I had written that: "World War II was glorified as a 'holy war' and most of the populace, ignorant of its true nature, had no choice but to support the reckless conflict." The MOE required that this passage be deleted. I included an illustration entitled "Bereaved family of a soldier killed in the Sino-Japanese War" with the caption "The price of victory"; it showed a wife, son, and crying daughter of a soldier killed in the war. The examiner commented: "This picture shows the wife's dignity under stress. The impression one receives from it is that the family was resolutely behind the nation in the Sino-Japanese War. However, the explanation does not convey that meaning. Delete." Only when the caption was removed was the manuscript approved.

Among the other reasons the MOE examiner gave for rejecting my proposed text were that it contained "grim photographs on p. 242 entitled 'Air raid on Japan proper' and 'Hiroshima destroyed by the atomic bomb'," even though the ministry's own books and supplementary readers had presented such topics during earlier years. The examiner also objected on the grounds that illustrations like "the photograph on p. 245 captioned 'The horrors of war' make the overall tone too negative."[39]

The examiner insisted that: "If atrocities by Japanese troops are described, similar actions by Soviet forces should also be included or the text will be biased. And what about the Americans?"

In the manuscript, I used the phrase "reckless war" about the Pacific conflict, a phrase that the MOE itself had used, before the "reverse course" of the Cold War, in its 1949 publication *Democracy.* Now, however, the examiner objected: "From a worldwide perspective, it is too harsh to affix blame on only Japan. For pedagogical reasons as well, the word 'reckless' should be deleted." To get the manuscript approved, I had to comply with this request.

Elsewhere I wrote: "Some wartime government and military leaders were arrested and executed as war criminals." The examiner countered: "Add that the trials [International Military Tribunal for the Far East] were a unilateral action by the victorious nations." In the approved text I managed to insert a

---

38. In the MOE textbook approval system, if an author resubmits a manuscript without revising the challenged portions, it is automatically rejected.

39. The picture showed maimed veterans begging for money; the caption was: "The war has ended but many soldiers lost their limbs. Their sad figures most eloquently express the meaning of the words in the Constitution's Preface: 'Resolved that never again shall we be visited with the horrors of war through the action of government'."

footnote: "In Germany, the Allied Forces conducted military trials. Subsequently, the Germans vigorously pursued the issue of war responsibility by bringing more Nazis to justice. In Japan, only trials by the Allied forces were held; Japanese conducted no war crimes proceedings." This was a rare instance where I was able to turn the tables on an examiner.

In 1981, I submitted another high school history text manuscript to the MOE for review. I wrote: "The Chinese . . . resisted Japanese aggression and desperately tried to regain their sovereignty." The examiner commented: "In writing about your own country, shouldn't you reconsider, from a pedagogical perspective, the use of value-laden words in a textbook?" Objecting to the word "invasion," the examiner said, "Regarding Japan, as well, you have used the expression 'military advance' at least twice. To standardize terminology, couldn't you repeat it again?" I refused to make the change and left the word "invasion" in the manuscript. In this case, it was approved. Although I could not read the examiner's mind, I believe that his acquiescence was related to a 1970 court decision that favored my position in my lawsuit against the the MOE, described below.

I had also written: "Immediately after the occupation of Nanjing, Japanese forces killed a large number of Chinese soldiers and civilians. This is known as the Nanjing atrocities." The examiner objected: "How can you tell it was 'immediately after'? Furthermore, this wording could be misinterpreted as indicating that the army officially sanctioned it. . . . One could say 'During the confusion of the occupation of Nanjing many Chinese soldiers and civilians were killed.' Although embarrassing to Japan, it is a fact. If you would write the sentence this way, it would be within the guidelines. Please reconsider your wording. The present construction, particularly the words 'Japanese forces,' suggests that [the killings] were systematically carried out by the Japanese army."[40]

The approved version reads as follows: "Japanese forces crushed the staunch Chinese defense and occupied Nanjing. Enraged by their heavy casualties, the troops killed a large number of Chinese soldiers and civilians.

---

40. Japanese soldiers murdered, raped, and brutalized Chinese civilians and prisoners in the weeks following the capture of Nanking on December 12, 1937. How many were killed is the subject of dispute, but estimates range as high as 200,000 to 300,000; Japanese sources generally give lower numbers. The rest of the world learned of the "Rape of Nanking" or "Nanking Incident" from the accounts of survivors and of foreign residents and visitors to Nanking, but little news of the atrocities reached Japan at the time. See Cook and Cook, *Japan at War,* p. 39 and sources there cited.

This is known as the Nanjing atrocities." Again, I attribute this concession to my lawsuit and the attendant publicity.

However, MOE reviewers were less lenient with another high school history textbook that I submitted in 1983.[41] There, I wrote of the fighting in China after 1937: "Japanese forces everywhere killed civilians, burned villages to the ground and raped women. The loss of life and property, and the number of Chinese women violated, were incalculable." The examiner noted that rape by soldiers was "a common occurrence in wartime" and to cite only such conduct by Japanese troops was inappropriate in a textbook. The words "rape" and "violated" should be removed, he said. I could not get the manuscript approved without complying.

I also wrote: "A biological warfare detachment, the 731 Unit, was set up in the suburbs of Harbin and for several years conducted experiments on foreign prisoners, including thousands of Chinese. These cruel experiments, which continued until the Soviet Union entered the war, were murder." According to the examiner, "No credible scholarly research—articles or books—have yet been published on this issue; it is premature to discuss it in a textbook." I deleted the paragraph in order to get the manuscript approved.[42]

In 1982, the year before I submitted this manuscript for review, the dispute over textbook censorship by Japan's Ministry of Education had escalated to an international incident. The People's Republic of China and the Republic of Korea had objected through diplomatic channels to whitewashed depictions in the new textbooks. Bowing to Chinese and Korean criticism, the Japanese government reluctantly promised to correct certain parts.[43] Thus in reviewing my book in 1983, the examiners refrained from comment about the word "invasion" or the atrocities in Nanjing; they did not deny facts or say a writer should not portray the actions of Japanese forces in a negative light. Instead, the examiners objected indirectly, with their suggestions that

---

41. Published as *Shin Nihonshi* (New Japanese history) (Tokyo: Sanseido, 1983).
42. On Unit 731, see "Germ War Exhibit Begins Japan Tour," *Boston Globe*, July 6, 1993, p. 40; Tamura Yoshio, "Unit 731," Cook and Cook, *Japan at War*, pp. 158–167; Peter Williams and David Wallace, *Unit 731: Japan's Secret Biological Warfare in World War II* (New York: Free Press, 1989); Robert Gomer, John W. Powell, Bert V.A. Röling, "Japan's Biological Weapons: 1930–1945," *Bulletin of the Atomic Scientists*, October 1981; Ienaga, *The Pacific War, 1931–1945*, pp. 188–189 and sources there cited (p. 288).
43. Tracy Dahlby, "Japan's Texts Revise WWII: 'Invasion' becomes 'Advance'; Asians become Irate," *Washington Post*, July 28, 1982, p. A1; the 1982 PRC and ROK protests are detailed in Beer, *Freedom of Expression in Japan*, pp. 271–273.

rape was "a common occurrence in wartime," or that discussion of Japan's germ warfare was "premature." Nevertheless, the ministry insisted on the deletions. Despite the government's pledges to the People's Republic of China and the Republic of Korea, there was no change in the long-standing policy of attempting to exclude embarrassing material about World War II.

Convinced that this kind of review process violates the Constitution and the Basic Law on Education, since 1965 I have filed three suits against the government.[44] The first court battle finally concluded after twenty-eight years, in March 1993, with a decision from the Supreme Court, and in October 1993 the Tokyo High Court issued a decision in the third lawsuit.[45] I lost the battle but it generated tremendous publicity about the MOE's policies and actions, and many people joined the fight against censorship of textbooks. For example, almost 30,000 people joined the organization to support the legal campaign, and countless others gave me moral support. I received thousands of postcards and letters of encouragement. Also, many legal scholars who had ignored the question of state interference with scholarship became interested in the problem and wrote about it.

Recent Events

In 1989, when the curriculum was completely revised, the Ministry of Education, in another move to undermine the pacifist spirit of the Constitution, suggested forty-two individuals who might be included in the textbooks as historical figures and explained by teachers. One was Admiral Heihachiro Togo, whose actions provoked the Sino-Japanese War.[46] The notion of elementary school pupils studying Togo drew fire even before the new curriculum was announced. A letter to the editor of the *Asahi Shimbun* went to the heart of the matter: "Togo was a professional soldier and is inappropriate for discussion in elementary schools where a major objective is [should be] to explain Japan's rejection of war and the importance of peace. . . . The

---

44. Saburo Ienaga, "The Historical Significance of the Japanese Textbook Lawsuit," *Bulletin of Concerned Asian Scholars*, Vol. 2, No. 4 (Fall 1970); Ronald P. Dore, "Textbook Censorship in Japan: The Ienaga Case, Notes and Comment," *Pacific Affairs*, Vol. 43, No. 4 (Winter 1970–71).
45. "Text author wins damages"; "Court awards 300,000 yen in censorship suit"; "Textbook screening upheld; historian's 28-year suit fails." For background, see Lawrence W. Beer, "Education, Politics and Freedom in Japan: The Ienaga Textbook Review Cases," *Law in Japan*, Vol. 8 (1975); Beer, *Freedom of Expression in Japan*, pp. 264–270.
46. Togo commanded the Japanese squadron that sank Chinese vessels on the open sea prior to an official declaration of war.

Asia, he spoke of Japan's "remorse for past history."[51] However, if the new textbooks devoid of reflection about World War II aggression are indicative, the nation's remorse is so insincere as to inspire distrust in the international community. I fervently wish that the textbooks would attest to our devotion to peace.[52]

The selections above show the dangerous extent of biased historiography imposed by the government through the review process. Even more alarming is a 1987 high-school textbook, apparently prepared in response to the government's policy of instilling patriotism in the younger generation but far more overtly jingoistic than the Ministry of Education was ready to be.[53] *Shinpen Nihonshi* (New edition: Japanese history) was written by a private group, the National Congress to Protect Japan, a nationalistic organization that advocates constitutional revision, including deletion of Article 9.

The original manuscript contained a preposterous repudiation of the Tokyo war crimes trial and denial of Japan's responsibility for the Pacific War:

This court [the International Military Tribunal for the Far East, IMFTE] in the name of "civilization" ruled that waging a war of aggression was a "crime against peace." But no law stipulated that warfare was a crime; the IMFTE's jurisdiction was dubious. The court rejected Justice Pal's opinion that Japan was innocent,[54] and branded Japanese as outlaws who had launched a war of aggression. War occurs among nations because of mutual misunderstanding; after the conflict both sides must reflect on their conduct and attain mutual understanding. For this reason, many people are calling for a reexamination of the IMFTE's unilateral condemnation of Japan as the guilty party.

This jingoistic tone is found throughout the book. For example, in the section on the Russo-Japanese War we find: "In May [1905] the Combined

51. During the same visit, "Akihito expressed 'deepest regret for the sufferings and pain' Japan inflicted on Korea during its colonial rule from 1910 to 1945. Japanese Prime Minister Toshiki Kaifu extended his 'sincere remorse and honest apologies.' Kaifu's apology was Japan's clearest statement of regret over its military past. . . . . Roh's visit [to Japan] sparked far bigger protests in South Korea. Before he left, radicals and human rights groups demonstrated almost daily, demanding that he cancel his visit. One man slashed his abdomen with a knife in protest in front of the Japanese embassy in Seoul." "Roh urges Koreans to forgive Japanese," *Boston Globe*, May 27, 1990, p. 15.
52. Yoshiaki Miyakawa (letter to the editor), "The Gods of War Return," *Asahi Shimbun*, June 7, 1991.
53. See "Text Glosses Over Japan's War Actions," *Washington Post*, May 29, 1986, p. A18.
54. On the opinion by Justice Radhabinod Pal of India (the sole dissenter from the Tribunal's opinion), see John W. Dower, *War without Mercy: Race and Power in the Pacific War* (New York: Pantheon, 1986), pp. 37–38. See also Ienaga, "Bias in the Guise of Objectivity," *The Japan Interpreter*, Vol. 11, No. 3 (Winter 1977), pp. 271–278.

Asia, he spoke of Japan's "remorse for past history."[51] However, if the new textbooks devoid of reflection about World War II aggression are indicative, the nation's remorse is so insincere as to inspire distrust in the international community. I fervently wish that the textbooks would attest to our devotion to peace.[52]

The selections above show the dangerous extent of biased historiography imposed by the government through the review process. Even more alarming is a 1987 high-school textbook, apparently prepared in response to the government's policy of instilling patriotism in the younger generation but far more overtly jingoistic than the Ministry of Education was ready to be.[53] *Shinpen Nihonshi* (New edition: Japanese history) was written by a private group, the National Congress to Protect Japan, a nationalistic organization that advocates constitutional revision, including deletion of Article 9.

The original manuscript contained a preposterous repudiation of the Tokyo war crimes trial and denial of Japan's responsibility for the Pacific War:

This court [the International Military Tribunal for the Far East, IMFTE] in the name of "civilization" ruled that waging a war of aggression was a "crime against peace." But no law stipulated that warfare was a crime; the IMFTE's jurisdiction was dubious. The court rejected Justice Pal's opinion that Japan was innocent,[54] and branded Japanese as outlaws who had launched a war of aggression. War occurs among nations because of mutual misunderstanding; after the conflict both sides must reflect on their conduct and attain mutual understanding. For this reason, many people are calling for a reexamination of the IMFTE's unilateral condemnation of Japan as the guilty party.

This jingoistic tone is found throughout the book. For example, in the section on the Russo-Japanese War we find: "In May [1905] the Combined

---

51. During the same visit, "Akihito expressed 'deepest regret for the sufferings and pain' Japan inflicted on Korea during its colonial rule from 1910 to 1945. Japanese Prime Minister Toshiki Kaifu extended his 'sincere remorse and honest apologies.' Kaifu's apology was Japan's clearest statement of regret over its military past. . . . . Roh's visit [to Japan] sparked far bigger protests in South Korea. Before he left, radicals and human rights groups demonstrated almost daily, demanding that he cancel his visit. One man slashed his abdomen with a knife in protest in front of the Japanese embassy in Seoul." "Roh urges Koreans to forgive Japanese," *Boston Globe*, May 27, 1990, p. 15.

52. Yoshiaki Miyakawa (letter to the editor), "The Gods of War Return," *Asahi Shimbun*, June 7, 1991.

53. See "Text Glosses Over Japan's War Actions," *Washington Post*, May 29, 1986, p. A18.

54. On the opinion by Justice Radhabinod Pal of India (the sole dissenter from the Tribunal's opinion), see John W. Dower, *War without Mercy: Race and Power in the Pacific War* (New York: Pantheon, 1986), pp. 37–38. See also Ienaga, "Bias in the Guise of Objectivity," *The Japan Interpreter*, Vol. 11, No. 3 (Winter 1977), pp. 271–278.

Although the regular review period had ended, the MOE "requested" that the authors make additional changes. The final published version was greatly toned down.[56]

Conclusion

Looking back over the past decade, I see scant possibility of a revival of the militarism that overwhelmed prewar Japan. Yet we must be mindful of the constant strengthening of the Self-Defense Forces to the point where they now rank among the major military organizations in the world and have been dispatched overseas (minesweeping operations in the Persian Gulf after the U.S.-led war against Iraq; peacekeeping operations in Cambodia). Public opinion has shifted; for example, the number of Japanese who believe the existence of the Self-Defense Forces is compatible with the Constitution is much greater than in the past. The Social Democratic Party of Japan, formerly the Japan Socialist Party, has softened its position against the Self-Defense Forces. The General Council of Trade Unions of Japan (*Sohyo*)—once a fierce opponent of the Self-Defense Forces and a staunch defender of Article 9—is now gone. This trend is even stronger since SDF units were dispatched to Cambodia in 1991 to participate in the UN operation there.

Furthermore, there is an increasing promilitary slant in education that I have documented above.[57] It is not surprising therefore that China and other Asian nations fear a resurgence of militarism in this country. Having paid the terrible price of imperialistic expansion in the past, many Japanese share those misgivings.

---

56. For this episode, see Ienaga testimony in the third textbook lawsuit, August 30, 1988, and September 27, 1988; *Kokumin shiso tosei no tame no kyokasho kentei* (Textbook certification: Thought control in action) (Tokyo: National Council to Support the Lawsuits against Textbook Certification, September 1988), pp. 95–97.

57. For more examples, see Colin Nickerson, "In Japan, war and forgetfulness," *Boston Globe*, August 15, 1988, p. 6; Urban C. Lehner, "Changed History: More Japanese Deny Nation Was Aggressor During World War II: Youths Learn Little of Era; Spread of Revisionist View Irks Many Other Asians: Was Nanking Really Raped," *Wall Street Journal*, September 8, 1988, pp. 1, 16; Susan Chira, "For Japanese, A Book Drops A War Lesson," *New York Times*, October 5, 1988, p. A5. The latter discusses right-wing pressure on the MOE to drop a previously approved English-language textbook that contained a lesson called "War." Cf. Michael Richardson, "From Japanese Schoolchildren, a Lesson for their Elders; Without awareness, Asian officials say, Japan will never be able to dispel lingering resentment throughout the region," *International Herald Tribune*, October 26–27, 1991.

Although this essay concerns trends toward militarism in education, military power is not the only problem at hand. Among the troubling developments of recent years are the rebirth of popular veneration for the emperor, seen during the ascension of Emperor Akihito, and an increase in authoritarianism, evidenced by the government forcing schools to display the Hinomaru (Sun Flag) and students to sing "Kimigayo" as the national anthem.[58] The rise of state Shinto—the erosion of the postwar legal principle of the separation of state and religion—in worship by cabinet ministers at Yasukuni Shrine and the public funding of Shinto rituals in Akihito's accession ceremonies cannot be ignored.

What I call portents of militarism must be seen in this context, as part of a historical matrix. Will these recidivist trends coalesce and lead to militarism and war, or can they be halted and reversed? International calls for an end to censorship have been very helpful. They have, for instance, ended the MOE's censorship of atrocities committed in World War II by Japanese troops. Ultimately, however, the answer depends on the willingness of all Japanese to defend the Constitution's ideals of peace and democracy.

---

58. Another example is described in David E. Sanger, "Mayor Who Faulted Hirohito Is Shot," *New York Times,* January 19, 1990, p. A6; David E. Sanger, "Elements of Japan's Far Right Praise Shooting of Mayor Motoshima," *New York Times,* January 26, 1990, p. A3.

International Security
Center for Science and International Affairs
John F. Kennedy School of Government
Harvard University

Articles in this reader were previously published in **International Security**, a quarterly journal sponsored and edited by the Center for Science and International Affairs at the John F. Kennedy School of Government at Harvard University, and published by MIT Press Journals. To receive subscription information about the journal or find out more about other readers in our series, please contact MIT Press Journals at 55 Hayward Street, Cambridge, MA, 02142.